32d Congress, 2d Session. | [SENATE.] | Ex. Doc. No. 52.

# REPORT

OF

# THE SECRETARY OF STATE,

COMMUNICATING

*Abstracts of the diplomatic and consular correspondence, in that department, respecting the commercial regulations of foreign nations.*

February 26, 1853.—Referred to the Committee on Foreign Relations, and ordered to be printed.

April 6, 1853.—*Ordered,* That 2,000 additional copies be printed for the use of the Senate.

Department of State,
*Washington, February,* 1853.

Sir: I have the honor herewith to transmit a report, in compliance with a resolution of the Senate of the United States of the 19th of July last:

"That the Secretary of State be requested to prepare and communicate to the Senate, at the next session of Congress, abstracts or selections of such portions of the diplomatic and consular correspondence in the department, within the last four years, as respect new commercial regulations adopted in the several nations with which we have intercourse; and such other information as may, in his opinion, promote the commercial interests of the United States."

I have the honor to be, sir, very respectfully, your obedient servant,

EDWARD EVERETT.

Hon. David R. Atchison,
*President of the Senate of the United States.*

---

*Report in compliance with a resolution of the Senate of the United States of the* 19*th of July*, 1852, *viz:*

"That the Secretary of State be requested to prepare and communicate to the Senate, at the next session of Congress, abstracts or selections of such portions of the diplomatic and consular correspondence in the department, within the last four years, as respect new commercial regulations adopted in the several nations with which we have intercourse; and such other information as may, in his opinion, promote the commercial interests of the United States."

[Compiled in the Department of State, and transmitted to the President of the Senate, February, 1853.]

*Names of countries, and their dependencies, in the order in which the following pages relate to changes in their commercial regulations, &c.*

England:

1. Extracts of statutes of the United Kingdom repealing, &c., certain commercial regulations.
2. Synopsis of general orders, &c., of the Board of Customs.
3. Extracts from treaties.
5. Tariffs, &c., of *colonies*, viz: Heligoland, Canada, Newfoundland, New Brunswick, Bahamas, Jamaica, St. Vincent, Trinidad, Dominica, Grenada, St. Lucia, Turk's and Caicos Islands, Tobago, Barbadoes, Antigua, St. Christopher's, Nevis, Virgin Islands, B. Guiana, Falkland Islands, Gibraltar, Malta, Ceylon, Bengal; colonial acts East Indies, Hong Kong, Labuan, Australia, *Western;* Australia, *Southern;* Australia, *N. South Wales;* Van Dieman's Land, Gambia, Natal, Sierra Leone, Cape of Good Hope, St. Helena, Mauritius, New Zealand.

France.—*Colonies:* Senegal, Gorée.
Russia.
Spain.
Portugal.
Netherlands.
Belgium.
Austria.
Prussia.
Denmark.—*Colony:* St. Croix.
Sweden.
Sweden and Norway.
Two Sicilies.
Sardinia.
Parma.
Turkey.
China.
Morocco.
Hayti.
Mexico.
San Juan de Nicaragua, or Grey Town.
Venezuela.
New Grenada.
Brazil.
Uruguay, or Cisplatine Republic.
Peru.
Chile.
Society Islands.
Sandwich Islands.

ENGLAND.

*Extracts of statutes of the United Kingdom, repealing, &c., certain commercial regulations.*

DUTIES UPON SPIRITS IMPORTED.

"An Act to alter the duties payable upon the importation of spirits or strong waters."—[*14th August*, 1848.]

[Extract.]

*Be it therefore enacted, &c.*, That the several duties on spirits and strong waters, imposed by the said recited act [10 and 11 Vict., c. 23] shall be and they are hereby repealed, and that from and after the passing of this act, in lieu thereof, there shall be raised, &c., the following duties: Spirits or strong waters—for every gallon of such spirits or strong waters, of any strength not exceeding the strength of proof by Sykes's hydrometer, and so in proportion for any greater or less strength than the strength of proof, and for any greater or less quantity than a gallon; that is to say, spirits or strong waters, the produce of any British possession in America, not being sweetened spirits, or spirits mixed with any article, so that the degree of strength thereof cannot be exactly ascertained by such hydrometer:

If imported into England, the gallon ........................ 8*s.* 2*d.*
If imported into Scotland, the gallon........................ 4*s.* 0*d.*
If imported into Ireland, the gallon......................... 3*s.* 0*d.*

Rum, the produce of any British possession within the limits of the East India Company's charter, not being sweetened spirits, or spirits so mixed as aforesaid, in regard to which the conditions of the act of the fourth year [Vict. c. 8] have or shall have been fulfilled:

If imported into England, the gallon ........................ 8*s.* 2*d.*
If imported into Scotland, the gallon ........................ 4*s.* 0*d.*
If imported into Ireland, the gallon......................... 3*s.* 0*d.*

Rum shrub, however sweetened, the produce of and imported from such possessions, in regard to which the conditions of act 4 Vict., c. 8, have or shall have been fulfilled, or the produce of and imported from any British possession in America:

If imported into England, the gallon ........................ 8*s.* 2*d.*
If imported into Scotland, the gallon........................ 4*s.* 2*d.*
If imported into Ireland, the gallon ......................... 3*s.* 0*d.*

—

"An Act to repeal the duties of customs upon the importation of sugar, and to impose new duties in lieu thereof."—[*4th September*, 1848.]

[Extract.]

Whereas, by an act passed in the session of Parliament holden in the ninth and tenth years of the reign of her present Majesty, intituled

"An act for granting certain duties on sugar and molasses," certain duties of customs were imposed upon the importation of sugar and molasses; and whereas it is expedient that the said duties should be repealed, and that other duties should be raised and levied in lieu thereof—

*Be it therefore enacted, &c.*, That the several duties on sugar and molasses imposed by the said recited act shall be, and they are hereby repealed; and that from and after the tenth day of July, one thousand eight hundred and forty-eight, in lieu thereof there shall be raised, levied, collected, and paid unto her Majesty, her heirs and successors, upon sugar or molasses, already or hereafter to be imported into the United Kingdom, the several duties of customs as the same are respectively inserted, described, and set forth in figures, and according to the respective dates and periods following—(that is to say)—

On sugar or molasses, the growth and produce of any British possession into which the importation of foreign sugar is prohibited, being imported from any such possession, the duties following—(that is to say)—

| | From and after July 10, 1848, to July 5, 1849, inclusive. | From and after July 5, 1849, to July 5, 1850, inclusive. | From and after July 5, 1850, to July 5, 1851, inclusive. | From and after July 5, 1851. |
|---|---|---|---|---|
| | £ s. d. | £ s. d. | £ s. d. | £ s. d. |
| Candy, (brown or white,) refined sugar, or sugar rendered by any process equal in quality thereto, for every cwt. | 17 4 | 16 0 | 14 8 | 13 4 |
| White clayed sugar, or sugar rendered by any process equal in quality to white clayed, not being refined or equal to refined, for every cwt...... | 15 2 | 14 0 | 12 10 | 11 8 |
| Muscovado, or any other sugar not being equal in quality to white clayed, for every cwt.................... | 13 0 | 12 0 | 11 0 | 10 0 |
| Molasses, for every cwt.............. | 4 10 | 4 6 | 4 2 | 3 9 |

And so in proportion for any greater or less quantity than a hundred weight.

And from and after the respective days next hereinafter mentioned—

On sugar and molasses the growth and produce of any other British possession, being imported from any such possession, the duties following—(that is to say)—

| | From and after July 10, 1848, to July 5, 1849, inclusive. | From and after July 5, 1849, to July 5, 1850, inclusive. | From and after July 5, 1850, to July 5, 1851, inclusive. | From and after July 5, 1851, to July 5, 1852, inclusive. | From and after July 5, 1852, to July 5, 1853, inclusive. | From and after July 5, 1853, to July 5, 1854, inclusive. | From and after July 5, 1854. |
|---|---|---|---|---|---|---|---|
| | £ s. d. | £ s. d. | £ s. d. | £ s. d. | £ s. d. | £ s. d. | £ s. d. |
| Candy, (brown or white,) refined sugar, or sugar rendered by any process equal in quality thereto, for every cwt.......... | 1 2 0 | 1 0 4 | 18 8 | 17 0 | 16 4 | 15 4 | 13 4 |
| White clayed sugar, or sugar rendered by any process equal in quality to white clayed, not being refined or equal to refined, for every cwt.... | 18 4 | 16 11 | 15 5 | 14 0 | 13 5 | 12 10 | 11 8 |
| Brown clayed sugar, or sugar rendered by any process equal in quality to brown clayed, and not equal to white clayed, for every cwt.......... | 17 0 | 15 8 | 14 4 | 13 0 | 12 5 | 11 10 | 10 0 |
| Muscovado, or any other sugar, not being equal in quality to brown clayed sugar, for every cwt.... | 15 9 | 14 6 | 13 3 | 12 0 | 11 6 | 11 0 | 10 0 |
| Molasses, for every cwt... | 5 10 | 5 5 | 4 11 | 4 6 | 4 4 | 4 2 | 3 9 |

And so in proportion for any greater or less quantity than a hundred weight.

On sugar or molasses, the growth and produce of any foreign country, and on all sugar or molasses not otherwise charged with duty, the duties following—(that is to say)—

| | From and after July 10, 1848, to July 5, 1849, inclusive. | From and after July 5, 1849, to July 5, 1850, inclusive. | From and after July 5, 1850, to July 5, 1851, inclusive. | From and after July 5, 1851, to July 5, 1852, inclusive. | From and after July 5, 1852, to July 5, 1853, inclusive. | From and after July 5, 1853, to July 5, 1854, inclusive. | From and after July 5, 1854. |
|---|---|---|---|---|---|---|---|
| | £ s. d. | £ s. d. | £ s. d. | £ s. d. | £ s. d. | £ s. d. | £ s. d. |
| Candy, (brown or white,) refined sugar, or sugar rendered by any process equal in quality thereto, for every cwt.......... | 1 6 8 | 1 4 8 | 1 2 8 | 1 0 8 | 19 4 | 17 4 | 13 4 |
| White clayed sugar, or sugar rendered by any process equal in quality to white clayed, not being refined or equal to refined, for every cwt.... | 1 1 7 | 19 10 | 18 1 | 16 4 | 15 2 | 14 0 | 11 8 |
| Brown clayed sugar, or sugar rendered by any process equal in quality to brown clayed, and not equal to white clayed, for every cwt.......... | 1 0 0 | 18 6 | 17 0 | 15 6 | 14 6 | 13 0 | 10 0 |
| Muscovado, or any other sugar not being equal in quality to brown clayed sugar, for every cwt.... | 18 6 | 17 0 | 15 6 | 14 0 | 13 0 | 12 0 | 10 0 |
| Molasses, for every cwt... | 6 11 | 6 4 | 5 9 | 5 3 | 4 10 | 4 6 | 3 9 |

And so in proportion for any greater or less quantity than a hundred weight.

Bounties, or drawbacks, upon the exportation from the United Kingdom of the several descriptions of refined sugar hereinafter mentioned:

| | From and after July 10, 1848, to July 5, 1849, inclusive. | From and after July 5, 1849, to July 5, 1850, inclusive. | From and after July 5, 1850, to July 5, 1851, inclusive. | From and after July 5, 1851. |
|---|---|---|---|---|
| | £ s. d. | £ s. d. | £ s. d. | £ s. d. |
| Upon refined sugar in loaf, complete and whole, or lumps duly refined, having been perfectly clarified and thoroughly dried in the stove, and being of a uniform whiteness throughout, or such sugar pounded, crushed, or broken, or sugar candy, the cwt............ | 16 4 | 15 0 | 13 9 | 12 6 |
| Upon bastard or refined sugar, broken in pieces, or being ground or powdered sugar, or such sugar pounded or crushed, or broken, for every cwt. | 13 0 | 12 0 | 11 0 | 10 0 |

And so in proportion for any greater or less quantity than a hundred weight.

II. *Provided always, and be it enacted,* That if at any time satisfactory proof shall have been laid before her Majesty in council, that, as respects any British possession, the importation of foreign sugar has been prohibited, it shall and may be lawful for her Majesty, and she is hereby empowered, from time to time, by any order or orders in council, to declare that sugar and molasses, the growth or produce of any such British possession, may be imported from thence into the United Kingdom, and entered at the lower rate of duties hereinbefore imposed on sugar and molasses the growth or produce of British possessions into which the importation of foreign sugar is prohibited; and from and after the publication of such order, whilst the same shall continue in force, the sugars and molasses therein mentioned may be so imported and entered accordingly.

III. *Provided always, and be it enacted,* That any sugars or molasses, the produce of any British possession within the limits of the East India Company's charter, in which the importation of foreign sugar is or shall be prohibited, which shall be entered for home use at the lower rates of duty hereinbefore imposed on sugar and molasses the produce of such possessions, shall be entered in the same and the like manner, and under the same or the like conditions, in and under which sugar the growth of the Presidency of Bengal might be entered for home use, under the provisions of an act passed in the session of Parliament holden in the sixth and seventh years of the reign of his late Majesty King William the Fourth, intituled "An act for the granting to his Majesty, until the fifth day of July, one thousand eight hundred and thirty-seven, certain duties on sugar imported into the United Kingdom, for the service of the year one thousand eight hundred and thirty-six, at the lower rate of duty therein mentioned."

* * * * * * * *

V. *And be it enacted,* That the commissioners of customs shall provide samples of white clayed sugar, and of sugar rendered by any process equal in quality to white clayed sugar, with reference to color, grain, and saccharine matter, which samples shall be deemed to be standard samples for the purpose of comparing therewith such white clayed sugar, or sugar rendered by any process equal in quality to white clayed sugar, as from and after the passing of this act may be entered for home consumption; and such standard samples shall from time to time be renewed whenever the said commissioners may deem it expedient; and no sugar shall, as regards the payment of duty, be deemed, or taken to be, white clayed sugar, or sugar rendered by any process equal in quality to white clayed, unless it shall, with reference to color, grain, and saccharine matter, equal the standard samples so respectively provided by the said commissioners.

VI. *And be it enacted,* That the commissioners of customs shall provide samples of brown clayed sugar, and of sugar rendered by any process equal in quality to brown clayed sugar, which samples shall be deemed to be standard samples for the purpose of comparing therewith such brown clayed sugar, or sugar rendered by any process equal in quality to brown clayed sugar, as from and after the passing of this act may be entered for home consumption; and such standard samples shall from time to time be renewed whenever the said commissioners may deem it expedient; and no sugar shall, as regards payment of duty, be deemed, or taken to be, brown clayed sugar, or sugar rendered by any process equal in quality to brown clayed sugar, unless it shall equal the standard samples so respectively provided by the said commissioners.

VII. *And be it enacted*, That all sugar or molasses imported, but not entered, or which shall have been warehoused, without payment of duty on the first importation thereof, and which shall be in port or warehouse at the respective periods at which the duties imposed by this act shall become chargeable, shall be deemed, and taken to be, liable to the duties so imposed by this act. And the rate or rates of duty chargeable by this act upon sugar or molasses, from the tenth day of July, one thousand eight hundred and forty-eight, to the fifth day of July, one thousand eight hundred and forty-nine, shall be deemed, and taken to be, applicable to sugar or molasses delivered for home consumption prior to the passing of this act and subsequently to the tenth day of July, one thousand eight hundred and forty-eight.

---

"An Act to reduce the duties on copper and lead."—[*5th September*, 1848.]

[Extract.]

Whereas it is expedient to reduce the duty now payable upon the importation of copper and lead into the United Kingdom:

*Be it therefore enacted by the Queen's most excellent Majesty, by and with the advice and consent of the Lords spiritual and temporal, and Commons, in this present Parliament assembled, and by the authority of the same*, That from and after the passing of this act, in lieu and instead of the duties of customs now payable upon the articles mentioned in the table to this act annexed, there shall be raised, levied, collected, and paid unto her Majesty, her heirs and successors, upon the said articles imported into the United Kingdom only, the several duties of customs, respectively, inserted, described, and set forth in figures in the table to this act annexed.

II. *And be it enacted*, That all such goods as are enumerated in the said table as shall have been warehoused without payment of duty upon the first importation thereof, and which shall be in the warehouse at the commencement of the duties imposed by this act, shall be deemed and taken to be liable to such duties.

*Table referred to in this act.*

| | £ | s. | d. |
|---|---|---|---|
| Copper, ore of, per ton | 0 | 1 | 0 |
| Copper, regulus of, per ton | | 1 | 0 |
| Copper, old, fit only to be manufactured, per ton | | 2 | 6 |
| Copper, unwrought, viz; in bricks or pigs, rose-copper, and all cast-copper, per ton | 2 | | |

| | £ | s. | d. |
|---|---|---|---|
| Copper, part wrought, viz: bars, rods, or ingots, hammered or raised, per ton | 0 | 2 | 6 |
| Copper in plates, and copper coin, per ton | | 2 | 6 |
| Lead, pig and sheet, per ton | | 2 | 6 |

—

"An Act to amend the laws in force for the encouragement of British shipping and navigation."—[26*th June*, 1849.]

[Extract.]

Whereas it is expedient to amend the laws now in force for the encouragement of *British* shipping and navigation:

*Be it enacted by the Queen's most excellent Majesty, by and with the advice and consent of the Lords spiritual and temporal, and Commons, in this present Parliament assembled, and by the authority of the same,* That from and after the first day of January, one thousand eight hundred and fifty, the following acts and parts of acts shall be repealed; (that is to say,) a certain act passed in the session of Parliament holden in the eighth and ninth years of the reign of her present Majesty, intituled "*An act for the encouragement of* British *shipping and navigation;*" and so much of a certain other act passed in the said session of Parliament, intituled "*An act for the registering of* British *vessels,*" as limits the privileges of vessels registered at *Malta, Gibraltar,* and *Heligoland;* and so much thereof as provides that no ship or vessel shall be registered, except such as are wholly of the build of some part of the British dominions; and so much as relates to the disqualification of ships repaired in a foreign country; and so much as prevents British ships, which have been captured by or sold to foreigners, from becoming entitled to be again registered as British in case the same again become the property of British subjects; and so much of a certain other act passed in the said session of Parliament, intituled "*An act to regulate the trade of* British *possessions abroad,*" as provides that no goods shall be imported into or exported from any of the British possessions in America by sea from or to any place other than the United Kingdom, or some other of such possessions, except into or from the several ports denominated free ports; and so much thereof as provides for the limitation of the privileges allowed to foreign ships by the law of navigation, in respect of importations into the British possessions in Asia, Africa, and America; and so much thereof as provides that no vessel or boat shall be admitted to be a British vessel or boat on any of the inland waters or lakes of America, except such as shall have been built at some place within the British dominions, and shall not have been repaired at any foreign place to a greater extent than in the said act is mentioned; and so much of a certain other act passed in the said session of Parliament, intituled "*An act for the general regulation of the customs,*" as prohibits the importation of train oil, blubber, spermaceti oil, head-matter, skins, bones, and fins, the produce of fish or creatures living in the sea, unless in vessels which shall have been cleared out regularly with such oil, blubber, or other produce on board, from some foreign port; and so much thereof as prohibits the importation of tea, unless from the Cape of Good Hope, or from places eastward of the same to the Straits of

Magellan; and so much of a certain act passed in the session of Parliament holden in the seventh and eighth years of the reign of her present Majesty, intituled "*An act to amend and consolidate the laws relating to merchant seamen, and for keeping a register of seamen,*" as provides that the master or owner of every ship belonging to any subject of her Majesty, and of the burden of eighty tons or upwards, (except pleasure yachts,) shall have on board at the time of her proceeding from any port of the United Kingdom, and at all times when absent from the United Kingdom, or navigating the seas, one apprentice, or more, in a certain proportion to the number of tons of his ship's admeasurement, and that if any such master or owner shall neglect to have on board his ship the number of apprentices thereby required, together with their respective registered indentures, assignments, and register tickets, he shall forfeit and pay the sum of ten pounds in respect of each apprentice, indenture, assignment, or register ticket, so wanting or deficient; also, an act passed in the thirty-seventh year of the reign of King *George* the Third, intituled "*An act for regulating the trade to be carried on with the* British *possessions in* India, *by the ships of nations in amity with his Majesty;*" and so much of a certain act passed in the session of Parliament holden in the fourth year of the reign of King *George* the Fourth, intituled "*An act to consolidate and amend the several laws now in force with respect to trade from and to places within the limits of the charter of the* East India *Company, and to make further provisions with respect to such trade, and to amend an act of the present session of Parliament for the registering of vessels, so far as it relates to vessels registered in* India," as enacts that no Asiatic sailors, Lascars, or natives of any of the territories, countries, islands, or places within the limits of the charter of the *East India* Company, shall, at any time, be deemed or taken to be British seamen within the intent and meaning of any act or acts of Parliament relating to the navigation of British ships by subjects of her Majesty; and also the following acts and parts of acts: so much of a certain act passed in the fourth year of the reign of King *George* the Fourth, intituled "*An act to authorize his Majesty, under certain circumstances, to regulate the duties and drawbacks on goods imported or exported in foreign vessels, and to exempt certain foreign vessels from pilotage,*" as relates to the regulation of duties and drawbacks; also, an act passed in the fifth year of the reign of King *George* the Fourth, intituled "*An act to indemnify all persons concerned in advising, issuing, or acting under a certain order in council for regulating the tonnage duties on certain foreign vessels, and to amend an act of the last session of Parliament for authorizing his Majesty, under certain circumstances, to regulate the duties and drawbacks on goods imported or exported in any foreign vessels;*" also, so much of an act passed in the session of Parliament holden in the eighth and ninth years of the reign of her present Majesty, intituled "*An act for granting duties of customs,*" as empowers her Majesty in council, in certain cases, to direct that additional duties shall be levied on articles the growth, produce, or manufacture of foreign countries, or upon goods imported in the ships of foreign countries, or to prohibit the importation of manufactured articles the produce of foreign countries; also, so much of an act passed in the session of Parliament holden in the fifth and sixth years of the reign of her present Majesty, intituled "*An act to amend the laws for the importation of corn,*" as enables her Majesty, under certain circumstances, to prohibit the importation of corn, grain, meal, or flour from the dominions of certain foreign powers; and the said several acts and parts of acts before mentioned are hereby accordingly repealed, except so far as the said acts or any of them repeal any former act or acts, or any part of such act or acts, and except so far as relates to any penalty or forfeiture which shall have been incurred under the said act or acts hereby repealed, or any of them, or to any offence which shall have been committed contrary to such act or acts, or any of them.

II. *And be it enacted,* That no goods or passengers shall be carried coastwise from one part of the United Kingdom to another, or from the United Kingdom to the *Isle of Man,* or from the *Isle of Man* to the United Kingdom, except in British ships.

III. *And be it enacted,* That no goods or passengers shall be imported into the United Kingdom from any of the islands of *Guernsey, Jersey, Alderney,* or *Sark,* nor shall any goods or passengers be exported from the United Kingdom to any of the said islands, nor shall any goods or passengers be carried from any of the islands of *Guernsey, Jersey, Alderney, Sark,* or *Man,* to any other of the said islands, nor from one part of any of the said islands to another part of the same island, except in British ships.

IV. *And be it enacted,* That no goods or passengers shall be carried from one part of any British possession in *Asia, Africa,* or *America,* to another part of the same possession, except in British ships.

V. *Provided always, and be it enacted,* That if the legislature or proper legislative authority of any such British possession shall present an address to her Majesty, praying her Majesty to authorize or permit the conveyance of goods or passengers from one part of such possession to another part thereof, in other than British ships; or if the legislatures of any two or more possessions, which, for the purposes of this act, her Majesty in council shall declare to be neighboring possessions, shall present addresses or a joint address to her Majesty, praying her Majesty to place the trade between them on the footing of a coasting trade, or of otherwise regulating the same, so far as relates to the vessels in which it is to be carried on, it shall thereupon be lawful for her Majesty, by order in council, so to authorize the conveyance of such goods or passengers, or so to regulate the trade between such neighboring possessions, as the case may be, in such terms and under such conditions, in either case, as to her Majesty may seem good.

VI. And with regard to the coasting trade of *India, Be it enacted,* That it shall be lawful for the Governor General of *India,* in council, to make any regulations authorizing or permitting the conveyance of goods or passengers from one part of the possessions of the *East India* Company to another part thereof in other than British ships, subject to such restrictions or regulations as he may think necessary; and such regulations shall be of equal force and effect with any laws and regulations which the said Governor General in council is now or may hereafter be authorized to make, and shall be subject to disallowance and repeal in like manner as any other laws or regulations made by the said Governor General in council, under the laws from time to time in force for the government of the British territories in *India,* and shall be transmitted to England, and be laid before both Houses of Parliament, in the same manner as any other laws or regulations which the Governor General in council is now, or may hereafter be, empowered to make.

VII. *And be it enacted,* That no ship shall be admitted to be a British ship unless duly registered and navigated as such; and that every British-registered ship (so long as the registry of such ship shall be in force, or the certificate of such registry retained for the use of such ship) shall be navigated during the whole of every voyage (whether with a cargo or in ballast) in every part of the world, by a master who is a British subject, and by a crew whereof three-fourths at least are British seamen; and if such ship be employed in a coasting voyage from one part of the United Kingdom to another, or in a voyage between the United Kingdom and the islands of *Guernsey*, *Jersey*, *Alderney*, *Sark*, or *Man*, or from one of the said islands to another of them, or from one part of either of them to another of the same, or be employed in fishing on the coasts of the United Kingdom, or of any of the said islands, then the whole of the crew shall be British seamen: *Provided, always,* That if a due proportion of British seamen cannot be procured in any foreign port, or in any place within the limits of the *East India* Company's charter, for the navigation of any British ship; or if such proportion be destroyed during the voyage by any unavoidable circumstance, and the master of such ship make proof of the truth of such facts to the satisfaction of the collector and controller of the customs at any British port, or of any person authorized in any other part of the world to inquire into the navigation of such ship, the same shall be deemed to be duly navigated: *Provided, also,* That every British ship (except such as are required to be wholly navigated by British seamen) which shall be navigated by one British seaman for every twenty tons of the burden of said ship, shall be deemed to be duly navigated, although the number of other seamen shall exceed one-fourth of the whole crew.

VIII. *And be it enacted,* That no person shall be deemed to be a British seaman, or to be duly qualified to be a master of a British vessel, except persons of one of the following classes: (that is to say,) natural-born subjects of her Majesty; persons naturalized by or under any act of Parliament, or by or under any act or ordinance of the legislature or proper legislative authority of one of the British possessions, or made denizens by letters of denization; persons who have become British subjects by virtue of the conquest or cession of some newly acquired country, and who have taken the oath of allegiance to her Majesty, or the oath of fidelity required by the treaty or capitulation by which such newly acquired country came into her Majesty's possession; Asiatic sailors or Lascars, being natives of any of the territories, countries, islands, or places within the limits of the charter of the East India Company, and under the government of her Majesty or of the said company; and persons who have served on board any of her Majesty's ships-of-war, in time of war, for the space of three years.

IX. *And be it enacted,* That if her Majesty shall at any time, by her royal proclamation, declare that the proportion of British seamen necessary to the due navigation of British ships shall be less than the proportion required by this act, every British ship navigated with the proportion of British seamen required by such proclamation shall be deemed to be duly navigated, so long as such proclamation shall remain in force.

X. *And be it enacted,* That, in case it shall be made to appear to her Majesty that British vessels are subject in any foreign country to any prohibitions or restrictions as to the voyages in which they may engage, or as to the articles which they may import into or export from such country, it shall be lawful for her Majesty, (if she think fit,) by order in council, to impose such prohibitions or restrictions upon the ships of such foreign country, either as to the voyages in which they may engage, or as to the articles which they may import into or export from any part of the United Kingdom, or of any British possession in any part of the world, as her Majesty may think fit, so as to place the ships of such country on as nearly as possible the same footing in British ports as that on which British ships are placed in the ports of such country.

XI. *And be it enacted,* That in case it shall be made to appear to her Majesty that *British* ships are, either directly or indirectly, subject in any foreign country to any duties or charges of any sort or kind whatsoever from which the national vessels of such country are exempt, or that any duties are imposed upon articles imported or exported in *British* ships which are not equally imposed upon the like articles imported or exported in national vessels, or that any preference whatsoever is shown, either directly or indirectly, to national vessels over British vessels, or to articles imported or exported in national vessels over the like articles imported or exported in British vessels, or that British trade and navigation is not placed by such country upon as advantageous a footing as the trade and navigation of the most favored nation; then, and in any such case, it shall be lawful for her Majesty, (if she think fit,) by order in council, to impose such duty or duties of tonnage upon the ships of such nation entering into or departing from the ports of the United Kingdom, or of any British possession in any part of the world, or such duty or duties on all goods, or on any specified classes of goods, imported or exported in the ships of such nation, as may appear to her Majesty justly to countervail the disadvantages to which British trade or navigation is so subjected as aforesaid.

XII. *And be it enacted,* That in every such order her Majesty may, if she so think fit, specify what ships are to be considered as ships of the country or countries to which such order applies, and all ships answering the description contained in such order shall be considered to be ships of such country or countries for the purposes of such order.

XIII. *And be it enacted,* That it shall be lawful for her Majesty, from time to time, to revoke any order or orders in council made under the authority of this act.

XIV. *And be it enacted,* That every such order in council as aforesaid, shall, within fourteen days after the issuing thereof, be twice published in the *London Gazette,* and that a copy thereof shall be laid before both houses of Parliament within six weeks after the issuing the same, if Parliament be then sitting; and if not, then within six weeks after the commencement of the then next session of Parliament.

XV. *And be it enacted,* That if any goods be imported, exported, or carried coastwise, contrary to this act, all such goods shall be forfeited, and the master of the ship in which the same are so imported, exported, or carried coastwise, shall forfeit the sum of one hundred pounds, except where any other penalty is hereby specially imposed.

XVI. *And be it enacted,* That all penalties and forfeitures incurred under this act shall be sued for, prosecuted, recovered, and disposed of, or shall be mitigated or restored, in like manner and by the same authority as any penalty or forfeiture can be sued for, prosecuted, recovered and disposed of, or may be mitigated or restored, under an act passed in the said session of Parliament holden in the eighth and ninth years of her present Majesty, intituled "*An act for the prevention of smuggling;*" and that the costs of all proceedings under this act shall be defrayed out of the consolidated duties of customs.

XVII. *And be it enacted,* That all natural-born subjects of her Majesty, and all persons made denizens by letters of denization, and all persons naturalized by or under any act of Parliament, or by or under any act or ordinance of the legislature or proper legislative authority of any of the British possessions in *Asia*, *Africa*, or *America*, and all persons authorized by or under any such act or ordinance to hold shares in British shipping, shall, on taking the oath of allegiance to her Majesty, her heirs and successors, be deemed to be duly qualified to be owners or part owners of British-registered vessels, anything in the said recited act for the registering of British shipping to the contrary, in anywise, notwithstanding.

XVIII. *And be it enacted,* That the following form of certificate shall be substituted for the form of certificate prescribed by the said act for the registering of British shipping:

"This is to certify, that [*here insert the names, occupations, and residence of the subscribing owners*] having made and subscribed the declaration required by law, and having declared that [he *or* they,] together with [*names, occupations, and residence of non-subscribing owners,*] is [*or* are] sole owner [*or* owners] in the proportions specified on the back hereof of the ship or vessel called the [*ship's name*] of [*place to which the vessel belongs,*] which is of the burden of [*number of tons*] and whereof [*master's name*] is master, and that the said ship or vessel was [*when and where built or condemned as prize, referring to builder's certificate, judge's certificate, or certificate of last registry, then delivered up to be cancelled, or (if the vessel was foreign-built, and the time and place of building not known)* was foreign, and that he *or* they did not know the time or place of building,] and [*name and employment of surveying officer*] having certified to us that the said ship or vessel has [*number*] decks and [*number*] masts, that her length from the inner part of the main stem to the fore part of the stern-post aloft is [ feet tenths,] her breadth in midships is [ feet tenths,] her depth in hold at midships is feet tenths,] that she is [*how rigged*] rigged with a [standing *or* running] bowsprit, is [*description of stern*] sterned, [carvel *or* clincher] built, has [*whether any or not*] gallery, and [*kind of head, if any*] head, that the frame-work and planking [*or* plating] is [*state whether of wood or iron,*] and that she is [*state whether a sailing vessel or a steamer, and if a steamer, state whether propelled by paddle-wheels or screw-propellers;*] and the said subscribing owners having consented and agreed to the above description, as having caused sufficient security to be given as required by law, the said ship or vessel called the [*name*] has been duly registered at the port of [*name of port.*] Certified under our hands at the custom-house in the said port of [*name of port,*] this [*date*] day of [*name of month*] in the year [*words at length.*]

"(Signed) ——— ———, *Collector.*
"(Signed) ——— ———, *Comptroller.*"

And on the back of such certificate of registry there shall be an account of the parts or shares held by each of the owners mentioned and described in such certificate, in the form and manner following:

| Names of the several owners within mentioned. | Number of sixty-fourth shares held by each owner. |
|---|---|
| [Name] ........................... | Thirty-two. |
| [Name] ........................... | Sixteen. |
| [Name] ........................... | Eight. |
| [Name] ........................... | Eight. |

(Signed) ——— ———, *Comptroller.*
(Signed) ——— ———, *Collector.*

XIX. *And be it enacted,* That the following declaration shall be substituted for the declaration, by the said act, directed to be made by the owner or owners of any vessel previous to the registry thereof:

"I, A. B., of [*place of residence, and occupation,*] do truly declare: That the ship or vessel [*name,*] of [*port or place,*] whereof [*master's name*] is at present master, being [*kind of build, burden, etc., as described in the certificate of the surveying officer,*] was [*when and where built, or, if prize or forfeited, capture and condemnation as such; or, (if the vessel be foreign-built, and the owner does not know when and where she was built,)* that the said vessel **is** foreign-built, and that I do not know the time and place of her **building,**] and that I, the said A. B., [*and the other owners' names and occupations, if any, and where they respectively reside,*] am [*or are*] sole owner [*or owners*] of the said vessel, and that no other person or persons whatever hath or have any right, title, interest, share, or property therein, or thereto; and that I, the said A. B., [and the said other owners, *if any,*] am [*or are*] truly and bona fide a subject [*or subjects*] of Great Britain, and that [I, the said A. B., have not, nor have any of the other owners, to the best of my knowledge and belief,] taken the oath of allegiance to any foreign State whatever, [*except under the terms of some capitulation, describing the particulars thereof,*] or that since my taking [*or* his *or* their taking] the oath of allegiance to [*naming the foreign States respectively to which he or any of the said owners shall have taken the same,*] I have [*or* he *or* they hath *or* have] become a denizen, [*or* denizens, *or* naturalized subject, *or* subjects, *as the case may be,*] of the United Kingdom of Great Britain and Ireland, by her Majesty's letters patent, [*or* by an act of Parliament, *or* by or under or by virtue of an act or ordinance of the legislature of ———, *or* have been authorized by an act or ordinance of the legislature of ———, to hold shares in British shipping within the said colony, and since the passing of such act or ordinance,] I have [*or* he *or* they hath *or* have] taken the oath of allegiance to her Majesty Queen Victoria, [*naming the times when such letters of denization have been granted, respectively, or the year or years in which such act or acts of naturalization, or such colonial acts or ordinances, have passed, respectively,*] and that no foreigner, directly or indirectly, hath any share or part interest in the said ship or vessel:" *Provided always,* That if it shall become necessary to register any ship or vessel belonging to any corporate body in the United Kingdom, the following declaration, in lieu of the declaration hereinbefore directed, shall be made and subscribed by the Secretary or other proper officer of such corporate body—(that is to say:)

"I, A. B., secretary *or* officer of [*name of company or corporation,*] do truly declare: That the ship or vessel [*name,*] of [*port,*] whereof [*master's name,*] is at present master, being [*kind of build, burden, &c., as described in the certificate of the surveying officer,*] was [*when and where built, or, if prize or forfeited, capture and condemnation as such,*] or [*if the vessel be foreign-built, and that such secretary or officer does not know when and where built,*] that the said vessel is foreign-built, and that I do not know the time and place of the building, and that the same doth wholly and truly belong to [*name the company or corporation.*"]

XX. *And be it enacted,* That notwithstanding that by the said recited act for the registering of British vessels it is enacted, that in case any ship, not being duly registered, shall exercise any of the privileges of a British vessel, the same shall be forfeited, nevertheless all boats or vessels under fifteen tons burden, wholly owned and navigated by British subjects, although not registered as British ships, shall be admitted to be British vessels in all navigation in the rivers and upon the coasts of the United Kingdom, or of the British possessions abroad, and not proceeding over sea, except within the limits of the respective colonial governments, within which the managing owners of such vessels respectively reside; and that all boats or vessels wholly owned and navigated by British subjects, not exceeding the burden of thirty tons, and not having a whole or fixed deck, and being employed solely in fishing on the banks and shores of Newfoundland, and of the parts adjacent, or on the banks and shores of the provinces of *Canada, Nova Scotia,* or *New Brunswick,* adjacent to the *Gulf of Saint Lawrence,* or on the north of *Cape Canso,* or of the islands within the same, or in trading coastwise within the said limits, shall be admitted to be British boats or vessels, although not registered, so long as such boats or vessels shall be solely so employed.

XXI. *And be it enacted,* That this act shall come into operation on the first day of *January,* one thousand eight hundred and fifty.

"An Act to amend the laws relating to the customs."—[1st *August*, 1849.]

[Extract.]

Whereas several acts were passed in the session of Parliament holden in the 8th and 9th years of the reign of her present Majesty Queen *Victoria*, for consolidating the laws of customs; and whereas, since the passing of the said act, divers acts for the amendment thereof have from time to time been passed; and whereas certain further amendments of the same acts are now required: *Be it enacted, &c.*, That from and after the passing of this act, the same shall, except so far as is otherwise provided by this act, come into and be and continue in full force and operation for the purposes herein mentioned.

II. And whereas by one of the said acts, intituled "*An act for the general regulations of the customs*," snuff is prohibited to be imported into the United Kingdom, unless in hogsheads, casks, chests, or cases containing three hundred pounds weight of snuff each at least, not being separated or divided in any manner within the cask or package; and whereas it is expedient to amend the said act: *Be it therefore enacted*, That it shall be lawful to import into any port of the United Kingdom into which the importation of tobacco is or may hereafter be permitted, any snuff the produce of, and coming directly from, the *United States* in *America*, in packages, each containing at least one hundred and fifty pounds net weight of such snuff.

III. *And be it enacted*, That it shall and may be lawful to import into the United Kingdom cigarillos or cigarettos in any packages containing seventy-five pounds weight each, at the least, of such cigarillos or cigarettos.

IV. *And be it enacted and declared*, That where the importation of tobacco or snuff is required by law to be made in packages of a certain weight, such tobacco or snuff shall not be separated or divided in any manner within such packages, except in such manner as is provided by the said last-mentioned act, under penalty of forfeiture of the same.

V. *And be it enacted*, That if any dispute shall arise as to the proper duty payable in respect of any goods imported into the United Kingdom, and admissible for home consumption, the importer or consignee, or his or their agent, shall deposite in the hands of the collector of the customs at the port of importation the amount of duty demanded by such collector; and such deposite shall be deemed and taken to be the proper duty payable in respect of such goods, unless an action or suit shall be brought or commenced by the importer of such goods, within three calendar months from the time of making such deposite, in some or one of her Majesty's courts of law at *Westminster*, *Dublin*, or *Edinburgh*, against such collector, for the purpose of ascertaining whether any and what amount of duty is due and payable upon such goods; and, upon payment of such deposite, and passing a proper entry for such goods by the importer, consignee, or agent, such collector shall thereupon cause the said goods to be delivered in virtue of such entry.

VI. *And be it enacted*, That where such deposite shall have been made as aforesaid, the same shall be paid by the said collector to the receiver general of her Majesty's customs, to be by him carried to the consolidated fund of the United Kingdom of *Great Britain* and *Ireland;* and in case no action shall be brought within the time hereinbefore limited for that purpose, such deposite shall be retained and applied to the use of her Majesty, in the same manner as if the same had been originally paid and received as the duties due and payable on such goods; and in case such action shall be so brought, and it shall thereupon be determined by due course of law that the duty so demanded and deposited was not the proper duty due and payable upon such goods, but that a less duty, or no duty, was payable thereon, then the difference between the sum so deposited and the duty so found to be due, or the whole sum so deposited, as the case may require, shall forthwith be returned to such importer, with interest thereon after the rate of five pounds *per centum per annum* for the period during which the sum so paid or returned shall have been so deposited; and such payment shall be accepted and taken by such importer in satisfaction of all claims and demands in respect of the importation of such goods, and the duties payable thereon, and of all or any damages and expenses incident thereto.

VII. *And be it enacted,* That if the proper officers of the customs shall place any lock, mark, or seal upon any stores on board any ship or vessel arriving in the United Kingdom, and such lock, mark, or seal be wilfully opened, altered, or broken, or if any such stores be secretly conveyed away, either while the ship remains in the port at which she shall have so arrived, or before she shall have arrived at any other port in the United Kingdom to which she may then be about to proceed, the master of such ship shall forfeit the sum of twenty pounds.

VIII. *And be it enacted,* That if the proper officer of the customs shall place any lock, mark, or seal upon any goods taken from the warehouse without payment of duty, as stores on board any ship or vessel departing from any port in the United Kingdom, and such lock, mark, or seal be wilfully opened, altered, or broken, or if any such stores be secretly conveyed away, either while such ship or vessel remains at her first port of departure, or at any other port or place in the United Kingdom, or on her passage from one such port or place to another, before the final departure of such ship or vessel on her foreign voyage, the master shall forfeit the sum of twenty pounds.

IX. And whereas by the said last-mentioned act it is enacted that no ship shall be cleared from any port of the United Kingdom, either for a coasting or a foreign voyage, laden with coals or culm, or cinders, which had not been previously brought into such port, until the fitter or coal-owner, or his agent, vending or shipping the same, shall have delivered to the collector or comptroller two certificates, under his hand, expressing the total quantities of coals, culm, and cinders, respectively, shipped or intended to be shipped by him in such ship: *Be it enacted,* That so much of the said act as is hereinbefore recited shall be repealed.

X. *And be it enacted,* That no ship shall be cleared from any port in the United Kingdom, either for a coasting or a foreign voyage, laden with coals or coal, or culm or cinders, which had not been previously brought coastwise into such port, until the fitter or coal-owner, or his agent, vending or shipping the same, or the purchaser of such coals or coal, or culm or cinders, or the master or owner of the vessel in which such coals or coal, or culm or cinders, are shipped or intended to be shipped, or the agent to such vessel, shall have delivered to the collector or comptroller two certificates, under his hand, expressing the total quantities of coals or coal, or culm and cinders, respectively, shipped or intended to be shipped by him in such ship, and the collector or comptroller shall retain one of such certificates, and shall deliver the other, signed by him, to the master of the ship; and every fitter, coal-owner or agent, purchaser, master, owner, or agent of and for the vessel on board of which such coals or coal, or culm or cinders, are shipped or intended to be shipped, who shall refuse to give such certificate, shall forfeit and pay the sum of one hundred pounds; and if any such fitter, coal owner or his agent, purchaser, master, owner, or agent of the vessel, or any other person, shall give a false certificate, he shall forfeit the sum of one hundred pounds; and the master of such ship shall keep such certificate and produce the same to any officers of the customs demanding such production, and shall, before bulk be broken, deliver such certificate to the collector or comptroller of any port of the United Kingdom to which such coal, culm or cinders, shall be carried in such ship; and if such master shall refuse to produce or deliver such certificate in manner aforesaid, he shall forfeit the sum of twenty pounds.

XI. And whereas by the said last-mentioned act it is enacted that no goods cleared for drawback or bounty, or from the warehouse, shall be carried or water-borne to be put on board any ship for exportation from the United Kingdom by any person, unless such person shall be authorized for that purpose by license under the hands of the commissioners of her Majesty's customs; and whereas such goods are frequently so carried and water-borne by unlicensed persons:

*Be it enacted*, That if, after the passing of this act, any person not so licensed as aforesaid, or not being in the employ of some person so licensed and approved of for that purpose by the said commissioners, shall so carry or water-bear any goods so cleared for drawback or bounty, or from the warehouse, he shall for every such offence forfeit the sum of twenty pounds.

XII. And whereas by the said last-mentioned act it is enacted that every importer of any goods shall, within fourteen days after the arrival of the ship importing the same, make perfect entry inwards of such goods, or entry by bill of sight, in the manner therein provided, and shall within such time land the same; and that in default of such entry and landing, it shall be lawful for the officers of the customs to convey such goods to the Queen's warehouse: and whereas it is expedient to extend the provisions of the said act to goods subject to the performance of quarantine: *Be it therefore enacted*, That the importers of all goods which shall be liable to the performance of quarantine shall, within fourteen days after such goods shall have been released from quarantine, make perfect entry inwards of such goods, and shall within such time remove the same from the Lazarette, and land them; and in default of such entry, removal, and landing, within the said period of fourteen days, it shall be lawful for the officers of the customs to convey such goods to the Queen's warehouse; and if the duties due upon any goods so conveyed to the Queen's warehouse shall not be paid within three months after the same shall have been lodged in such warehouse, together with all charges of removal and warehouse rent, the same shall be sold, and the produce thereof shall be applied, first, to the payment of freight and charges; next, of duties; and the overplus, if any, shall be paid to the proprietors of the goods.

XIII. And whereas it is expedient to amend the regulations for the landing of goods from importing vessels, in the manner following: *Be it enacted*, That when any goods shall be unshipped or removed from any vessel in which they shall have been imported from foreign parts for the purpose of being landed after due entry thereof, such goods shall be thereupon with all convenient speed removed to and landed at the wharf, quay, or other place at which the same are intended to be landed; and if such goods are not so removed and landed, the same shall be forfeited, together with the barge, lighter, boat, or other vessel employed in removing the same.

XIV. And whereas by the said act it is enacted that all bonds relating to the customs required to be given in respect of goods or ships, except bonds given for securing the due exportation of, or payment of duty upon, goods warehoused according to law, shall be taken by the collector and comptroller for the use of her Majesty; and that after the expiration of three years from the date thereof, or from the time, if any, limited for the performance of the condition thereof, every such bond upon which no prosecution or suit shall have been commenced shall be void, and may be cancelled or destroyed:

*Be it enacted*, That so much of the said act as is above recited shall be repealed, and that all bonds relating to the customs required to be given in respect of goods or ships shall be taken by the collector and comptroller for the use of her Majesty; and after the expiration of three years from the date thereof, or from the time, if any, limited for the performance of the condition thereof, all such bonds, except such as are given for securing the due exportation of or payment of duty upon goods warehoused according to law, upon which no prosecution or suit shall have been commenced, shall be void, and may be cancelled and destroyed.

* * * * * * * *

XVI. And whereas by another of the said acts, intituled "*An act for the prevention of smuggling*," certain vessels therein mentioned are rendered liable to forfeiture unless the owners thereof shall have obtained a license from the commissioners of her Majesty's customs in the manner therein described, and it is expedient to alter and amend the same as hereinafter is mentioned:

*Be it enacted*, That so much of the said act as regards the licensing of vessels and boats shall be repealed, except so far as relates to any penalty or forfeiture which shall have been incurred under the said act.

XVII. *And be it enacted*, That it shall be lawful for said commissioners, by order under their hands, to make such general regulations, and to revoke, alter, and vary the same from time to time, as they shall deem expedient, in respect of vessels and boats not exceeding one hundred and seventy tons burden, for the purpose of defining and prescribing with reference to the tonnage, build, or description of such vessels or boats, the limits within which the same may be employed, the mode of navigation, the manner in which such vessels or boats shall be so employed, and, if armed, the number and description of arms, the quantity of ammunition, and such other terms, particulars, conditions, and restrictions as the said commissioners may think fit; and also from time to time to revoke, alter, or vary such regulations.

XVIII. *And be it enacted*, That every vessel or boat which shall be used or employed in any manner contrary to the regulations so to be prescribed by the said commissioners shall be liable to forfeiture, and shall and may be seized by * * * *, unless the same shall have been specially licensed by the commissioners of her Majesty's customs to be so used or employed, as next hereinafter provided.

XIX. *And be it enacted*, That the said commissioners shall and may, if they shall so think fit, grant licenses in respect of any vessels or boats not exceeding one hundred and seventy tons burden, upon such terms and conditions and subject to such restrictions and stipulations as in such licenses shall be mentioned or contained, notwithstanding any general regulations made in pursuance of this act, and whether the said regulations shall be revoked or not: *Provided always*, That if any vessel or boat which shall be so licensed as aforesaid shall not comply with the conditions imposed by or expressed in any such license, or if such vessel or boat shall be found without having such license on board, such vessel or boat shall be forfeited.

XX. *And be it enacted*, That it shall be lawful for the said commissioners to revoke, alter, or vary any license or licenses already or hereafter to be granted under the laws now in force, or which may hereafter be granted under this or any other act relating to the customs.

XXI. *And be it enacted*, That all licenses for vessels or boats granted in pursuance of any former act relating to the customs, or for the prevention of smuggling, shall continue valid for all the purposes for which such licenses were required (unless the same shall, in the mean time, be revoked, altered, or varied) until the said commissioners shall make such general regulations as aforesaid; and all bonds given on the granting of any such license as aforesaid shall continue valid, and may be put in force.

XXII. *And be it enacted*, That if any such vessel or boat, of whatever tonnage or description it may be, shall be made use of in the importation, landing, removal, carriage, or conveyance of any uncustomed or prohibited goods, the same shall be liable to forfeiture, and shall and may be seized by * * *; and the owner and master of every such vessel or boat shall forfeit and pay a penalty equal to the value of such vessel or boat, provided such penalty shall not, in any case, exceed one thousand pounds.

XXIII. *And be it enacted*, That all the regulations which shall be so made by the said commissioners relating to vessels and boats, and the power to grant, revoke, alter, or vary such licenses, shall extend to the islands of *Guernsey*, *Jersey*, *Alderney*, *Sark*, and *Man*.

* * * * * * * *

XXV. *And be it enacted*, That every person who shall be in any way concerned in importing or bringing into the United Kingdom or the *Isle of Man* any goods which, under any law now in force or hereafter to be made, may be in any way prohibited or restricted, shall forfeit either treble the value of the said goods or the penalty of one hundred pounds, at the election of the commissioners of her Majesty's customs, notwithstanding such goods may not have been unshipped from the vessel in which they may have been imported or brought into the said United Kingdom or into the *Isle of Man*.

* * * * * * * *

XXVIII. *And be it enacted,* That so much of another of the said acts, intituled "*An act for the registering of British vessels,*" as relates to the issue of *Mediterranean* passes, shall be, and the same is hereby, repealed.

XXIX. *And be it enacted,* That in lieu and instead of the duties of customs now payable upon the articles mentioned in the table to this act annexed, marked B, there shall be raised, levied, collected, and paid to her Majesty, her heirs and successors, upon the said articles already or hereafter to be imported into the United Kingdom, the several duties of customs respectively inserted and set forth in figures in the said table.

XXX. *And be it enacted and declared,* That such of the several sorts of goods as are by this act charged with duty as shall have been warehoused without payment of duty upon the importation thereof, and which shall be in the warehouse at the commencement of the duties imposed by this act, shall be deemed and taken to be liable to such duties.

* * * * * * * *

XXXII. *And be it enacted,* That in all cases where any new duties of customs or other duties under the management, collection, or control of the commissioners of her Majesty's customs, are or may be imposed by any act or acts in lieu of any former duties payable at the time of passing of such act or acts, such former duties shall be and continue payable until such new duties imposed in lieu thereof shall become chargeable, save and except in cases where the provision hereby made shall, in the act or acts imposing such new duties, be specially repealed or declared to be inapplicable thereto.

XXXIII. And whereas by another of the said acts, intituled "*An act for the warehousing of goods,*" a certain abatement of duty is made upon spirits (other than *rum* of the *British* plantations) when taken out of warehouse for home use, on account of deficiency of the quantity or strength first ascertained in the mode prescribed by the said act, after the several rates of allowance therein mentioned: and whereas the importers of such spirits or other agents frequently require to have the same regauged, in order to ascertain the rates of allowance to which such spirits may be entitled * * *: *Be it therefore enacted,* That no such spirits shall be regauged except when required for actual delivery; and when such regauging shall take place, it shall be deemed to be made for the purpose of such spirits being so delivered, and the duty shall be charged upon the quantity then ascertained, whether the delivery of such spirits shall take place immediately upon their being so regauged or not: *Provided always,* That if such spirits shall not be delivered within three months from the time of their being so regauged, it shall be lawful for the importer or his agent again to have them re-gauged, and so on for every period of three months during which such spirits shall remain in the warehouse.

XXXIV. And whereas corn, grain, meal, and flour, may, upon importation thereof into the United Kingdom, upon due entry thereof, be deposited in warehouses or places of security without payment of duty upon such entry and deposite: and whereas it is expedient that the duties imposed upon such goods should be immediately paid upon the importation and entry thereof: *Be it enacted*, That from and after the passing of this act, the duties imposed upon corn, grain, meal, and flour, imported or brought into the United Kingdom, shall be paid immediately upon the importation and entry of all such corn, grain, meal, and flour, whether the same be entered to be warehoused or not.

XXXV. *And be it enacted*, That all goods whatsoever, which now are or may be deposited in any warehouse or place of security, under any act of Parliament passed or to be passed for the warehousing of goods, without payment of duty upon the first importation thereof, or which may be imported and on board any ship or vessel, shall, upon being entered for home consumption, be subject and liable to such and the like duties as may, at the time of passing such entry, be due and payable on the like sort of goods under any act or acts passed for imposing any duty or duties of customs which shall or may be in force at the time of passing such entry, save and except in cases where special provisions shall be made in any such act or acts to the contrary.

XXXVI. *And be it enacted*, That when any goods deposited in any warehouse for security of duties shall remain unclaimed for a period of seven years from the date of importation, and the owner of such goods cannot be found, it shall be lawful for the commissioners of her Majesty's customs to direct sale thereof for payment of the duties due thereon; and after payment of such duties, together with the freight and charges, warehouse rent and other incidental expenses, to retain the surplus, if any, arising from such sale, to abide the claim of the owner of such goods; or if such goods shall not be found to be worth the duty, then it shall be lawful for the said commissioners to direct or cause the same to be destroyed.

XXXVII. *And be it enacted*, That any act, matter, or thing required by any law relating to the customs to be done or performed by, to, or with the collector and comptroller, or by, to, or with any officer of customs in any of her Majesty's possessions abroad, shall and may be done and performed by, to, and with any officer of customs appointed by the commissioners of her Majesty's customs to do and perform such acts, matters and things in any such possession; and every such act, matter and thing done or performed by, to, and with such officer, shall be as valid and effectual in law, as if the same had been done and performed by, to, and with any such collector, or any such collector and comptroller, or by, to, and with any officer of customs, under any law now in force or hereafter to be made.

XXXVIII. *And be it enacted*, That from and after the passing of this act, Muscovado sugar shall be admissible into the *Isle of Man*, upon the payment of a duty of one shilling for every hundred weight, and so in proportion for any greater or less quantity than a hundred weight; and that all tea imported or brought by sea into the said island shall be admissible into the said island, and be charged with a duty of one shilling per pound. * * * * * *

XLI. And whereas, by an act passed in the 39th year of the reign of his Majesty King *George* the Third, intituled "*An act for rendering more commodious and for better regulating the port of London*," and also by several subsequent acts, certain rates or duties of tonnage were imposed on ships or vessels frequenting the port of London, to be applied in manner therein directed: and whereas, by the said act and by several subsequent acts, certain sums of money were advanced out of the consolidated fund upon the credit of the said rates or duties for the purposes of the said act: and whereas the said sums of money so advanced * * * have been fully paid and replaced:

*Be it therefore enacted*, That from and after the passing of this act, so much of an act passed in the fourth and fifth years of the reign of his Majesty King *William* the Fourth, as directs that the duties imposed by that act shall be under the management of the commissioners of his Majesty's customs, and shall be received and recovered in the same manner as any duties of customs are or can be received or recovered, shall be repealed. * * * * * *

XLIII. And whereas: * * * *Be it enacted*, That no goods which shall be brought into any such docks,* shall be landed and warehoused without due entry thereof.

## B.

*Table of duties referred to in the foregoing act.*

| Articles. | Of or from foreign countries. | | | Of or from British possessions. | | |
|---|---|---|---|---|---|---|
| | £ | *s.* | *d.* | £ | *s.* | *d.* |
| Embroidery and needle-work, for every 100*l.* value | 15 | 0 | 0 | 5 | 0 | 0 |
| Articles of green or common glass, the cwt | | | 9 | | | 9 |
| Leather, manufactures of— | | | | | | |
| Men's boots and shoes. If the quarter do not exceed 2¾ inches or the vamp 4 inches in height from the sole, inside, the dozen pairs | | 7 | 0 | | 7 | 0 |
| Men's boots and shoes. If either the quarter or vamp exceed the above dimensions, but do not exceed 6 inches in height from the sole, inside, the dozen pairs | | 10 | 6 | | 10 | 6 |
| Men's boots and shoes. If either the quarter or vamp do exceed 6 inches in height from the sole, inside, the dozen pairs | | 14 | 0 | | 14 | 0 |
| Wild nutmegs, not in the shell, the pound | | | 5 | | | 5 |
| Wines, of any description, not enumerated or otherwise charged with duty in any act or acts relating to the customs, the gallon | | 0 | 0 | | 2 | 9 |
| The lees of such wines, the gallon | | 0 | 0 | | 2 | 9 |
| Coffee, kiln-dried, roasted or ground, on and after the 1st day of January, 1850, the pound | | | 8 | | | 5 |

* Docks established and regulated by certain local acts.

"AN ACT to amend the laws relating to the customs."—[*14th August*, 1850.]

[Extract.]

Whereas several acts were passed in the session of Parliament holden in the eighth and ninth years of the reign of her present Majesty Queen Victoria, for consolidating the laws of the customs; and whereas, since the passing of the said acts, divers acts for the amendment thereof have from time to time been passed: and whereas certain further amendments of said acts are now required:

*Be it therefore enacted, &c.*, That from and after the passing of this act, the same shall, except so far as is otherwise provided by this act, come into and be and continue in full force and operation, for the purposes herein mentioned.

II. And whereas divers rules, orders and regulations, have from time to time been made by the commissioners of her Majesty's customs, in pursuance of the powers conferred upon them by certain acts passed in various sessions of Parliament, some of which acts have since been repealed, and doubts have arisen whether such rules, orders and regulations, are still of legal force and efficacy:

*Be it therefore enacted*, That all rules, orders and regulations, already made or issued by or under the authority of the said commissioners, under or in pursuance of any act or acts relating to the customs, or to trade or navigation, although such act or acts may have been repealed, shall be and continue in full force and effect, so far as such rules, orders and regulations, are consistent with the provisions of the laws in force relating to the customs, or to trade or navigation, unless and until the same shall be revoked or rescinded; and that all acts whatsoever to be done in pursuance of any such orders, rules and regulations, shall be valid and effectual. * * * * *

IV. *And be it enacted*, That the owner or consignee of all goods free of duties imported into the United Kingdom from parts beyond the seas shall, within twenty-four hours after the due entry and landing of such goods, deliver, or cause to be delivered, to the collector of the customs, or other proper officer, at the port where the goods shall be discharged, a true account of all such free goods so landed; and in default thereof every such owner or consignee shall forfeit and pay a penalty of five pounds.

V. *And be it enacted*, That any goods the growth of the islands of *Guernsey*, *Jersey*, *Alderney*, *Sark* or *Man*, and any goods manufactured in the said islands, or either of them, from materials not subject to duty in the United Kingdom, or from materials upon which the duty shall have been paid in the United Kingdom, and upon which no drawback or bounty shall have been subsequently granted, and any manufactures of linen or cotton made in and imported from the *Isle of Man*, may be imported into the United Kingdom from the said islands, respectively, without payment of any duty; and that such goods shall not be deemed to be included in any charge of duties imposed by any act hereafter to be made on the importation of goods generally from parts beyond the seas: *Provided always*, That such goods may nevertheless be charged with any proportion of such duties as shall fairly countervail any duties of excise or inland revenue, or any coast duty payable on the like goods the produce or manufacture of the part of the United Kingdom into which they shall be imported, or payable upon any of the materials from which such goods are manufactured: *Provided also*, That all goods manufactured in any of the said islands from any other materials than the materials aforesaid, except manufactures of linen and cotton made in and imported from the *Isle of Man* as aforesaid, shall be deemed and taken to be foreign goods.

VI. *And be it enacted*, That all manufactured goods shall be deemed to be the produce of the country of which they are the manufacture.

VII. *And be it enacted*, That no abatement of duties shall be made on account of any damage received by any corn, grain, meal, or flour imported into the United Kingdom or the *Isle of Man*.

VIII. *And be it enacted*, That it shall be lawful to import into the islands of *Guernsey*, *Jersey*, *Alderney*, or *Sark*, from the United Kingdom, in vessels of not less than sixty tons burden, any cigars, tobacco, or snuff, in packages of such cigars, tobacco, or snuff, respectively, of the same weight at least in which the like sorts of goods may be legally imported into the United Kingdom: *Provided always*, That no such cigars, tobacco, or snuff shall be separated or divided in any manner within any such package; and all cigars, tobacco, or snuff imported into the said islands respectively, or found within one league of the coasts thereof, contrary hereto, shall be forfeited.

IX. And whereas, by one of the said acts, intituled "*An act for the general regulation of the customs*," certain restrictions are imposed upon the importation of tobacco into the United Kingdom; and whereas, by another act, passed in the session of Parliament holden in the ninth and tenth years of the reign of her said Majesty, intituled "*An act to amend the laws relating to the customs*," the said restrictions are thereby altered and amended; and whereas it is expedient to further alter and amend the said restrictions:

*Be it therefore enacted*, That so much of the said last-mentioned act as alters and amends the said restrictions as to the importation of tobacco into the United Kingdom shall be repealed.

X. *And be it enacted*, That it shall be lawful to import into any of the ports of the United Kingdom, into which tobacco may be lawfully imported, any tobacco from *Malta*, or any tobacco the produce of *Porto Rico*, *Mexico*, *South America*, *Saint Domingo*, *Cuba*, or the *British possessions in America*, and imported direct from any of those places, in packages each containing at least eighty pounds net weight of such tobacco.

XI. *And be it enacted*, That so much of the said act passed in the session of Parliament holden in the eighth and ninth years of the reign of her present Majesty, intituled "*An act for the general regulation of the customs*," as prohibits the re-importation of *tea* for home use, shall be repealed.

XII. *And be it enacted*, That so much of an act passed in the session of Parliament holden in the third and fourth years of the reign of his late Majesty King William the Fourth, intituled "*An act to provide for the collection and management of the duties on tea*," as prohibits the importation of tea into any of the islands of *Guernsey*, *Jersey*, *Alderney*, or *Sark*, or into the *British possessions in America*, from any other place than the *Cape of Good Hope*, and places eastward of the same to the *Straits of Magellan*, or from the United Kingdom, shall be repealed.

XIII. *And be it enacted*, That it shall be lawful to import into the United Kingdom, into any of such ports, any tobacco the produce of the *Philippine islands*, and imported direct from *Manilla*, in bales or packages containing three hundred pounds weight of tobacco each, at least, not being separated or divided in any manner within such bale or package; and all such tobacco imported contrary hereto shall be forfeited.

XIV. And whereas, by an act passed in the session of Parliament holden in the ninth and tenth years of the reign of her present Majesty, intituled "*An act for consolidating and amending the laws relating to wreck and salvage*," certain acts and parts of acts therein mentioned are thereby repealed; and whereas, by the said act it is enacted that the same shall extend to all parts of the United Kingdom except *Scotland;* and whereas doubts are entertained whether such acts and parts of acts are still in force as regards *Scotland:*

*Be it therefore enacted and declared*, That the said acts and parts of acts mentioned and recited in the said act shall, so far as the same are applicable to *Scotland*, be deemed to be and continue in full force and effect.

XV. *And be it enacted*, That the importation into the United Kingdom of any extracts, essences, or other concentrations of coffee, chiccory, tea, or tobacco, or any admixture of the same, shall be prohibited.

XVI. *And be it enacted*, That every person who shall be in any way concerned in importing or bringing into the United Kingdom or the *Isle of Man*, or who shall unship, carry, convey, harbor, or conceal, or be aiding, assisting, or concerned in the unshipping, carrying, conveying, harboring, or concealing any tobacco stalks, or tobacco stalk flour, or to whose hands or possession the same shall come, shall and may be dealt with in like manner as if such tobacco stalks or tobacco stalk flour were tobacco; and the value thereof shall be estimated, in the adjudication of any penalty, as if the same were unmanufactured tobacco of the best description, upon which the duty had been paid.

* * * * * * * *

XX. And whereas it is expedient that the original names of all foreign vessels purchased by *British* subjects, and registered as *British* vessels, should be recorded on the registry thereof, in order to maintain the identity of such vessels:

*Be it enacted*, That before any foreign-built vessel shall be registered as a *British* vessel, the owner or owners thereof shall state in writing to the collector or comptroller of the port, at which such vessel is intended to be registered, the foreign name of such vessel, and the same shall be inserted in the declaration now required by law to be made previous to the registry of any vessel, and also in the certificate of registry of such vessel. * * * * *

XXI. *And be it enacted*, That if any passenger or passengers shall be carried by any foreign ship or vessel, contrary to the provisions of the law of navigation, the master of such ship or vessel shall forfeit the sum of five pounds for each any every passenger so carried.

* * * * * * * *

XXIII. *And be it enacted*, That no duties of customs shall be chargeable upon the importation of the following articles; that is to say:

WOOD.—Stringy bark wood and blue gum wood for ship-building, and shaped for treenails, not exceeding three feet in length.
Locust treenails for ship-building.
Green heart, mora wood, and locust wood, for ship-building.
Shovel-hilts.

XXIV. And whereas by one other of the said acts, intituled "*An act for granting duties of customs*," a duty of four shillings per ton is imposed upon coals, culm, or cinders, exported to foreign countries in a foreign ship; and whereas it is expedient to repeal the said duty: *Be it therefore enacted*, That from and after the passing of this act the said duty shall be repealed.

XXV. *And be it enacted*, That so much of an act, passed in the session of Parliament holden in the eighth and ninth years of the reign of her present Majesty, intituled "*An act for the warehousing of goods*," as enacts that before goods shall be delivered to be removed from one warehousing port to another port to be there warehoused due entry of the same shall be made, and a proper bill of such entry, with duplicates thereof, shall be delivered to the collector or comptroller, shall be and the same is hereby repealed.

XXVI. *And be it enacted*, That no entry shall, from and after the passing of this act, be received for, or in respect of, any timber or wood goods deposited in any warehouse, yard, or other bonded premises, for security of duties, for any less quantity at any one time than five loads of such timber or wood goods, unless such wood goods shall be delivered by tale, in which case such entry may be passed for any quantity thereof, not less than two hundred and forty pieces, or two great hundreds of such wood goods; and that no less quantity of such timber or wood goods shall be delivered in virtue of any such entry, at any one time, than five loads of such timber or wood goods, or two hundred and forty pieces of such wood goods if delivered by tale.

---

"AN ACT to alter certain duties of customs, &c."—[*7th August*, 1851.]

[Extract.]

Whereas it is expedient to alter the duties of customs now payable by law upon the importation of the goods, wares, and merchandise enumerated and described in the table to this act annexed: *Be it therefore enacted*—

I. That in lieu and instead of the duties of customs now payable by law upon the goods, wares, and merchandise enumerated and described in the said table, there shall, from and after the fifteenth day of *April*, one thousand eight hundred and fifty-one, be raised, levied, collected, and paid unto her Majesty, her heirs and successors, upon the said goods, wares, and merchandise respectively, when imported into the United Kingdom, the several duties of customs only as inserted and set forth in figures in the said table to this act annexed.

II. That such of the several sorts of goods as are by this act charged with duty, as shall have been warehoused without payment of duty upon the importation thereof, and which shall be in the warehouse on the sixteenth day of *April*, one thousand eight hundred and fifty-one, shall be deemed, and taken to be, liable to such duties only.

III. That the duties by this act imposed shall be under the management of the commissioners of her Majesty's customs, and shall be ascertained, raised, levied, collected, paid, recovered, and applied or appropriated under the provisions of any act or acts now in force or hereafter to be passed relating to the customs.

* * * * * * * *

*Table referred to in this act.*

| | £ | s. | d. |
|---|---|---|---|
| Coffee, the pound | 0 | 0 | 3 |
| kiln-dried, roasted, or ground, the pound | | | 6 |
| Upon timber and wood goods not otherwise charged with duty: | | | |
| Timber or wood, not being deals, battens, boards, staves, handspikes, oars, lathwood or other timber, or wood sawed, split, or otherwise dressed, except hewn, and not being timber or wood otherwise charged with duty, the load of 50 cubic feet | | 7 | 6 |
| Deals, battens, boards, or other timber, or wood, sawed or split, and not otherwise charged with duty, the load of 50 cubic feet | | 10 | 0 |
| Staves, if exceeding 72 inches in length, 7 inches in breadth, or 3½ inches in thickness, the load of 50 cubic feet | | 9 | 0 |
| Handspikes, not exceeding 7 feet in length, the 120 | | 6 | 0 |
| exceeding 7 feet in length, the 120 | | 12 | 0 |
| Knees, under 5 inches square, the 120 | | 3 | 0 |
| 5 inches and under 8 inches square, the 120 | | 12 | 0 |
| Lathwood, the fathom of 216 cubic feet | | 12 | 0 |
| Oars, the 120 | 2 | 5 | 0 |
| Spars or poles, under 22 feet in length, and under 4 inches in diameter, the 120 | | 6 | 0 |
| 22 feet in length and upwards, and under 4 inches in diameter, the 120 | | 12 | 0 |
| of all lengths, 4 inches and under 6 inches in diameter, the 120 | 1 | 4 | 0 |
| Wood planed, or otherwise dressed or prepared for use, and not particularly enumerated or otherwise charged with duty, per foot of cubic contents | | | 2 |
| And further for every 100*l.* value | 10 | 0 | 0 |

Or, in lieu of ascertaining the cubical contents in pile, the importer may have the option, at the time of passing the first entry, in respect of planks, deals, deal-ends, battens, and batten-ends, of entering the same by tale upon a computation of their cubic contents, calculated according to the under-mentioned scale, specifying in such entry the number and dimensions of the several pieces included therein; and the duties imposed thereon by this act shall be ascertained, computed, and charged upon the planks, deals, deal-ends, battens, and batten-ends included in such entry, on the cubical contents thereof, computed in conformity with the said scale.

| | PLANKS. | DEALS. | BATTENS. | | |
|---|---|---|---|---|---|
| | 3 by 11 inches and not above $3\frac{1}{4}$ by $11\frac{1}{2}$ inches. | 3 by 9 inches and not above $3\frac{1}{4}$ by $9\frac{1}{2}$ inches. | 3 by 7 inches and not above $3\frac{1}{4}$ by $7\frac{1}{4}$ inches. | $2\frac{1}{2}$ by 7 inches and not above $2\frac{5}{8}$ by $7\frac{1}{4}$ inches. | $2\frac{1}{2}$ by $6\frac{1}{2}$ inches and not above $2\frac{5}{8}$ by $6\frac{5}{8}$ inches. |
| | *Cub. ft.* | *Cub. ft.* | *Cub. ft.* | *Cub. ft.* | *Cub. ft.* |
| Not above 4 feet in length ............the 120.. | 115 | 95 | 73 | 61 | 57 |
| Above 4 ft. and not above 5 ft. in length....do.... | 144 | 118 | 91 | 77 | 71 |
| Above 5.......do.......6 ....do.........do.... | 173 | 142 | 110 | 92 | 86 |
| Above 6.......do.......7 ....do.........do.... | 202 | 165 | 128 | 107 | 100 |
| Above 7.......do.......8 ....do.........do.... | 231 | 189 | 146 | 123 | 114 |
| Above 8.......do.......9 ....do.........do.... | 260 | 213 | 165 | 138 | 128 |
| Above 9.......do......10 ....do.........do.... | 288 | 236 | 183 | 153 | 143 |
| Above 10......do......11 ....do.........do.... | 317 | 260 | 201 | 169 | 157 |
| Above 11......do......12 ....do.........do.... | 346 | 284 | 220 | 184 | 171 |
| Above 12......do......13 ....do.........do.... | 375 | 307 | 238 | 200 | 185 |
| Above 13......do......14 ....do.........do.... | 404 | 331 | 256 | 215 | 200 |
| Above 14......do......15 ....do.........do.... | 433 | 354 | 274 | 230 | 214 |
| Above 15......do......16 ....do.........do.... | 462 | 378 | 293 | 246 | 228 |
| Above 16......do......17 ....do.........do.... | 490 | 402 | 311 | 261 | 242 |
| Above 17......do......18 ....do.........do.... | 519 | 425 | 329 | 276 | 257 |
| Above 18......do......19 ....do.........do.... | 548 | 449 | 348 | 292 | 271 |
| Above 19......do......20 ....do.........do.... | 577 | 473 | 366 | 307 | 285 |
| Above 20......do......21 ....do.........do.... | 606 | 496 | 384 | 322 | 300 |

## SYNOPSIS OF GENERAL ORDERS, &C., OF THE BOARD OF CUSTOMS, TRANSMITTED WITH DESPATCHES OF THE U. S. MINISTERS IN LONDON.

*November* 14, 1849.—Regulation that spirits required as stores in larger quantities than five gallons be shipped in one entire cask is dispensed with, and one cask, under the legal size, of *each description or sort of spirits*, is allowed to be shipped on board a vessel as stores.

*November* 12, 1849.—"Manna croup," or wheat ground by a particular arrangement of the stones, is liable to a duty of $4\frac{1}{2}$*d.* per cwt.

*December* 29, 1849.—Goods warehoused, under the act of 8 & 9 Vict., c. 88, for exportation only, are not to be admitted to entry for home use.

*February* 18, 1850.—Coffee, kiln-dried, roasted, or ground, may be shipped as stores from the bonded warehouse in the same proportions as raw coffee, viz: one oz. per day, per man, and under the like regulations.

*April* 18, 1850.—Duty is to be paid, at the port of arrival, on any deficiency which may have occurred in transit, in goods removed under bond, before a certificate is to be issued to cancel the bond given on the removal of the goods.

*April* 23, 1850.—Stringy bark wood, and blue gum wood, used in ship-building, and shaped for treenails of three feet in length, are to be admitted free of duty from the Australian colonies.

*April* 30, 1850.—All sheep's wool, entered for exportation, is to be described in the shipping bills either as the produce of a British colony, or the produce of a foreign country, as the case may be.

*August* 26, 1850.—Empty glass bottles of British manufacture, which, when exported from England, contained merchandise, are to be admitted to entry duty free.

*July* 31, 1850.—All articles of silk or velvet, made up, such as mantles, cloaks, and other articles of millinery, not specifically rated, are to be charged with the ad valorem duty of 15 per cent., without reference to weight.

*October* 29, 1850.—Glass chemical apparatus is to be charged with a duty of one penny per pound, only. Rough ground-glass stoppers and caps, and punty marks, are to be charged with the same.

*November* 15, 1850.—Deteriorated butter, delivered at ports to which it is removed under bond, is not to be dealt with at such ports as unsound, should it have left the port of removal in a sound state.

*Regulation relating to London only.*

*November* 9, 1850.—The regulations of the minute of July 19, 1850, for assessing the duty on rice upon an average to be ascertained by weighing one bag in ten of each entry or mark, is to be rescinded so far as regards cargoes of rice landed on warehousing entries in the docks of London; and the practice of weighing packages of rice in warehouse, &c., is to be reverted to until *further orders.*

*Regulation relating to London only.*

*October* 12, 1850.—In case of samples of sugar taken from packages brought to England from foreign parts for transhipment only, the samples upon which the duties shall not exceed one shilling on each export entry are to be delivered duty free; but, if exceeding that sum, the duty is to be paid thereon.

*May* 3, 1850.—Scale of charges for rent on surplus stores deposited in the Queen's warehouse:

| | | |
|---|---|---|
| Wine, spirits, and cordials— | | |
| Under two gallons | *Nil.* | |
| Two gallons, and under six | 1*d.* | per week. |
| Six gallons and upwards | 2*d.* | per week. |
| Dry goods— | | |
| Not exceeding one cubic foot of space | 1*d.* | per week. |
| Exceeding one cubic foot of space | 2*d.* | per week. |

*May* 9, 1850.—Locust wood is to be admitted duty free.

*July* 6, 1850.—Iodine is to be admitted at the duty of 10 per cent. ad valorem.

*July* 25, 1850.—Duty is to be charged on the *setting* of pearls only, when imported.

*July* 31, 1850.—Quantity of cigars or manufactured tobacco under the weight of half a pound, being the unconsumed stores of a passenger, who is not a frequent visitor, and when there is no cause of suspicion, is to be delivered duty free; but cigars and manufactured tobacco brought by passengers, of the weight of half a pounds and upwards are to be charged with duty on the actual quantity.

*July* 17, 1850.—Spirits, coffee, cocoa, and other articles subject to differential duties, to be taken out of warehouse for exportation, are allowed to be described in the bonds as "spirits," "coffee," &c., only, instead of by their proper denominations according to the tariff.

*July* 19, 1850.—Casks of rice, imported at London and Liverpool, are to be assessed for duty on an average of one in ten of each entry or mark.

*September* 4, 1850.—British biscuit, being surplus stores, is to pass duty free.

*September* 13, 1850.—Tobacco may be imported *direct from Turkey* in packages of 100 pounds each.

*January* 16, 1851.—In cases of emigrant ships, one cask, under the legal size, of each description or sort of spirits, is allowed to be shipped on board a vessel, not only as stores, for the use of the vessel, but as "medical comforts."

*January* 28, 1851.—Bars of steel are to be admitted to entry as "unwrought steel."

*January* 29, 1851.—Extract of logwood is to be admitted to entry duty free.

*April* 30, 1851.—Allowance of raw sugar and molasses for ships' stores is extended to 16 ounces per week for each person on board.

*Regulation for the port of London only.*

*April* 2, 1851.—Orders of 5th March, 1851, and 9th September, 1850, (that tallow, the produce of and imported from the British possessions, being subject to the duty of 1*d.* per cwt., be delivered on duty-paid entries, according to the *weight* by the wharfinger's account, in the same manner as free goods,) are *continued* until further orders.

*May* 8, 1851.—Tobacco, *direct* from Egypt, may be imported in packages of 100 pounds each.

*February* 28, 1851.—All treenails from British possessions are to be admitted duty free, in like manner as locust treenails from the United States.

*June* 5, 1851.—Pepper is to be shipped as stores, duty free.

*September* 8, 1851. Charge of lower rates of duty (under the act 8 & 9 Vict., c. 90) on timber and wood goods, the produce of, and imported from the British possessions, is continued.

*September* 9, 1851.—Practice of restricting the claims for drawback (under act of 8 & 9 Vict., c. 86, s. 99) on wine and tobacco to three years from the date of payment of duty, is to be discontinued.

*Regulation relating to London only.*

*September* 6, 1851.—Card and paper cuttings, fit only to be re-manufactured, are to be admitted free of duty.

*Regulation relating to London only.*

*September* 19, 1851.—Samples of tobacco exported to the continent are to be retained, without payment of duty, in charge of customs officers, on condition that, within 12 months from the date of the exportation of the tobacco, the samples be either taken out for home consumption, on payment of duty, or be packed into legal sized packages and duly exported under the usual regulations.

*October* 29, 1851.—Soups preserved from fresh meats imported into England from a British possession, are to be admitted duty free.

*October* 30, 1851.—Any deficiency, not exceeding one pound, ascertained, at the port of arrival, on the gross re-weight of each package of tobacco removed under bond, is not to be charged with duty, in cases in which there shall be no reason to suspect fraudulent or improper tampering with the packages.

*November* 15, 1851.—Fir wood, sawed, not exceeding 2 feet 7 inches long, 7 inches wide, and $\frac{3}{4}$ inch thick, is to be admitted free of duty, if intended solely for making herring barrels.

*November* 17, 1851.—Tobacco may be imported from British East India possessions, in bales containing not less than 100 pounds.

*November* 18, 1851.—Tobacco may be imported from west coast of Africa in packages containing not less than 80 pounds.

## EXTRACTS FROM TREATIES.*

From a "treaty of friendship and commerce between her Majesty and the republic of *Liberia*," signed November 21, 1848. Ratifications exchanged August 1, 1849.

"Art. 2. There shall be reciprocal freedom of commerce between the British dominions and the republic of Liberia. The subjects of her Britannic Majesty * * * shall be allowed to buy from and to sell to whom they like, without being restrained or prejudiced by any monopoly, contract, or exclusive privilege of sale or purchase whatever. * * * The citizens of the republic of Liberia shall, in return, enjoy similar protection and privileges in the dominions of her Britannic Majesty.

"Art. 3. No tonnage, import, or other duties or charges, shall be levied in the republic of Liberia on British vessels, or on goods imported or exported in British vessels, beyond what are or may be levied on national vessels, or on the like goods imported or exported in national vessels; and in like manner, no tonnage, import, or other duties or charges, shall be levied in the British dominions on vessels of the republic, or on goods imported or exported in those vessels, beyond what are or may be levied on national vessels, or on the like goods imported or exported in national vessels.

"Art. 4. Merchandise or goods coming from the British dominions in any vessel, or imported in British vessels from any country, shall not be prohibited by the republic of Liberia, nor be subject to higher duties than are levied on the same kinds of merchandise or goods coming from any other foreign country, or imported in any other vessels.

"All articles, the produce of the republic, may be exported therefrom by British subjects and British vessels, on as favorable terms as by the subjects and vessels of any other foreign country.

---

* Transmitted with despatches of United States ministers in London.

"Art. 5. It being the intention of the government of the republic of Liberia to trade in certain articles of import, with a view to raising a revenue by selling them at a fixed advance upon the cost price, it is hereby agreed, that in no case shall private merchants be absolutely prohibited from importing any of such articles, or any article in which the government of the republic may at any time see fit to trade; nor shall such articles, or any article in which the government of the republic may at any time see fit to trade, be subject to a duty of a greater amount than the amount of the advance upon the cost price at which the government may from time to time be bound to sell the same.

"In case the government of the republic shall, at any time, fix the price of any article of native produce, with a view to such article being taken in payment for any articles in which the government may trade, such article of native produce shall be received into the treasury at the same fixed price, in payment of taxes, from all persons trading with the republic.

* * * * *

"Art. 7. It being the intention of the two contracting parties to bind themselves by the present treaty to treat each other on the footing of the most favored nation, it is hereby agreed between them, that any favor, privilege, or immunity, whatever, in matters of commerce and navigation, which either contracting party has actually granted, or may hereafter grant, to the subjects or citizens of any other State, shall be extended to the subjects or citizens of the other contracting party, gratuitously, if the concession in favor of that other State shall have been gratuitous, or in return for a compensation as nearly as possible of proportionate value and effect, to be adjusted by mutual agreement, if the concession shall have been conditional.

"Art. 8. Each contracting party may appoint consuls for the protection of trade, to reside in the dominions of the other. * * *

"Art. 9. Slavery and the slave trade being perpetually abolished in the republic of Liberia, the republic engages that a law shall be passed declaring it to be piracy for any Liberian citizen or vessel to be engaged or concerned in the slave trade.

"The republic engages to permit any British vessel-of-war which may be furnished with special instructions under the treaties between Great Britain and foreign powers for the prevention of the slave trade, to visit any vessels sailing under the Liberian flag which may, on reasonable grounds, be suspected of being engaged in the slave trade; and if, by the result of the visit, it should appear to the officer in command of such British vessel-of-war that the suspicions which led thereto are well grounded, the vessel shall be sent, without delay, to a Liberian port, and shall be delivered up to the Liberian authorities, to be proceeded against according to the laws of the republic.

"Art. 10. The republic of Liberia further engages to permit any British vessel-of-war which may be furnished with special instructions as aforesaid, to visit on the coast within the jurisdiction of the republic, or in the ports of the same, any vessel which may be suspected of being engaged in the slave trade, and which shall be found sailing under any flag whatever, or without any flag; and if the suspicions which led to the visit should appear to the officer in command of such

British vessel-of-war to be well grounded, to detain such vessel, in order to send it as soon as possible before the competent court for adjudication.

"Duly constituted ports of entry in the republic of Liberia shall be excepted from the operation of the stipulations of the present article, and no vessel shall be visited by a British cruiser within the limits of such ports, except on permission specially granted by the local authorities."

From a "treaty of friendship, navigation and commerce, between her Majesty and the republic of Costa Rica," signed November 27, 1849. Ratifications exchanged February 20, 1850.

"Art. 5. No higher nor other duties shall be imposed on the importation into the territories, dominions, or settlements of her Britannic Majesty of any article being of the growth, produce, or manufacture of the republic of Costa Rica, and no higher or other duties shall be imposed on the importation into the territories of the republic of Costa Rica of any articles being the growth, produce, or manufacture of the territories, dominions, and settlements of her Britannic Majesty, than are or shall be payable on the like articles, being the growth, produce, or manufacture of any other foreign country; nor shall any other or higher duties or charges be imposed in the territories, dominions, or settlements of either of the high contracting parties, on the exportation of any articles to the territories, dominions, or settlements of the other, than such as are or may be payable on the exportation of the like articles to any other foreign country; nor shall any prohibition be imposed upon the exportation or importation of any articles the growth, produce, or manufacture of the territories, dominions, or settlements of her Britannic Majesty, or of the republic of Costa Rica, to or from the said territories, dominions, or settlements of her Britannic Majesty, or to or from the republic of Costa Rica, which shall not equally extend to all other nations.

"Art. 6. No higher nor other duties or payments on account of tonnage, of light or harbor dues, of pilotage, of salvage in case either of damage or shipwreck, or on account of any other local charges, shall be imposed in any of the ports of the republic of Costa Rica on British vessels, than those payable in the same ports by Costa Rican vessels; nor in any of the territories, dominions, or settlements of her Britannic Majesty on Costa Rican vessels, than shall be payable in the same ports on British vessels.

"Art. 7. The same duties shall be paid on the importation into the territories of the republic of Costa Rica of any article being of the growth, produce, or manufacture of the territories, dominions, or settlements of her Britannic Majesty, whether such importation shall be made in Costa Rican or in British vessels; and the same duties shall be paid on the importation into the territories, dominions, or settlements of her Britannic Majesty, of any article being the growth, produce, or manufacture of the republic of Costa Rica, whether such importation shall be made in British or in Costa Rican vessels.

"The same duties shall be paid, and the same bounties or drawbacks allowed, on the exportation to the republic of Costa Rica of any articles being the growth, produce, or manufacture of the territories, dominions, or settlements of her Britannic Majesty, whether such exportation shall be made in Costa Rican or in British vessels; and the same duties shall be paid, and the same bounties and drawbacks allowed, on the exportation of any articles being the growth, produce, or manufacture of the republic of Costa Rica, to the territories, dominions, or settlements of her Britannic Majesty, whether such exportation shall be made in British or in Costa Rican vessels.

"ART. 8. * * * Absolute freedom shall be allowed, in all cases, to the buyer and seller, to bargain and fix the price of any goods, wares, or merchandise imported into, or exported from, the republic of Costa Rica, as they shall see good, observing the laws and established usages of the country. The same privileges shall be enjoyed in the territories, dominions, and settlements of her Britannic Majesty, by the citizens of the republic of Costa Rica, under the same conditions.

* * * * * *

"ART. 14. The government of the republic of Costa Rica, in order to co-operate with her Britannic Majesty for the total abolition of the slave trade, engages to execute perfectly the laws of the said republic, which prohibit in the most effectual manner all persons inhabiting within the territories of the republic of Costa Rica, or in places subject to their jurisdiction, from taking any share in such trade."

From a "convention of navigation between her Majesty and the King of Sardinia, additional to the treaty of September 6, 1841," signed 23d January, 1851. Ratified February 3, 1851.

"ART. 1. No duties of tonnage, harbor, light-house, pilotage, quarantine, or other or similar or corresponding duties, of whatever nature or under whatever denomination, shall be imposed in the ports of either country upon the vessels of the other country, from whatever port or place arriving, which shall not be equally imposed in the like cases on national vessels; and in neither country shall any duty, charge, restriction, or prohibition be imposed upon, nor any drawback, bounty, or allowance be withheld from, any goods imported into or exported from such country in vessels of the other, which shall not be equally imposed upon or withheld from such goods when so imported or exported in national vessels."

From a "convention of navigation between her Majesty and the King of the Netherlands, additional to the treaty of October 27, 1837," signed March 27, 1851. Ratifications exchanged 16th April, 1851.

"ART. 1. No duties of tonnage, harbor, light-house, pilotage, quarantine, or other similar or corresponding duties, of whatever nature or under whatever denomination, shall be imposed in the ports of either country upon the vessels of the other country, from whatever port or place arriving, which shall not be equally imposed in the like cases on national vessels; and in neither country shall any duty, charge, restriction, or prohibition be imposed upon, nor any drawback, bounty, or allowance be withheld from, any goods imported into or exported from such country in vessels of the other, which shall not be equally imposed upon or withheld from such goods when so imported or exported in national vessels."

### HELIGOLAND.

"No import or export duties are levied in this island."

### CANADA.

*A table* showing the present amount of duties payable on articles imported into the province of Canada. (The act imposing these duties was passed 25th April, 1849, and is not limited in its duration.†)*

| Articles subject to duty. | Amount of duty in currency. | | |
|---|---|---|---|
| | £ | s. | d. |
| Sugar: | | | |
| Refined, in loaves, or crushed, or candy, the cwt | 0 | 14 | 0 |
| And further for every £100 value | 12 | 10 | 0 |
| Bastard, and other kinds, the cwt | | 9 | 0 |
| And for every £100 value | 12 | 10 | 0 |
| Molasses, the cwt | | 3 | 0 |
| And further for every £100 value | 12 | 10 | 0 |
| Coffee: | | | |
| Raw or green, the cwt | | 4 | 8 |
| And further for every £100 value | 12 | 10 | 0 |
| Other kinds, the cwt | | 14 | 0 |
| And further for every £100 value | 12 | 10 | 0 |
| Tobacco: | | | |
| Manufactured, the pound | | | 1 |
| And further for every £100 value | 12 | 10 | 0 |
| Unmanufactured, the pound | | | ½ |
| And further for every £100 value | 12 | 10 | 0 |
| Cigars, the pound | | 1 | 6 |
| And further for every £100 value | 12 | 10 | 0 |

* According to returns made in August, 1851, to British House of Commons.

† A subsequent act, cap. 5, 10th August, 1850, makes it lawful for the governor in council, from time to time, to order any article not enumerated in this schedule, and thereby made subject to a duty of 12½ per centum ad valorem, to be placed among the articles subjected to a duty of 2½ per centum ad valorem, which last-mentioned duty, and no other, shall be payable on such articles so long as such order shall be in force. The same act directs that no duty shall be payable on military clothing imported into Canada for the use of her Majesty's troops, nor upon wine so imported for the use of any officers' mess; nor upon salt imported into the district of Gaspe for the use of the fisheries in that district; provided such regulations as the governor in council shall make for the purpose of preventing fraud or abuse, under pretext of such exemption from duty, be duly complied with, and not otherwise.

TABLE—Continued.

| Articles subject to duty. | Amount of duty in currency. | | |
|---|---|---|---|
| | £ | s. | d. |
| Snuff, the pound | 0 | 0 | 4 |
| And further for every £100 value | 12 | 10 | 0 |
| Wine: | | | |
| In wood, the value of £15 the pipe of 126 gallons or under, the gallon | | | 6 |
| In wood, for every £100 value | 25 | 0 | 0 |
| In wood, value over £15 the pipe, the gallon | | 1 | 6 |
| And further for every £100 value | 25 | 0 | 0 |
| In bottles or other vessels not made of wood, the gallon | | 4 | 0 |
| And further for every £100 value | 25 | 0 | 0 |
| Spirits, and strong waters of all sorts, for every gallon of any strength not exceeding the strength of proof by Sykes's hydrometer, and so in proportion for any greater strength than the strength of proof, and for any greater or less quantity than a gallon, viz: | | | |
| Whiskey, the gallon | | | 3 |
| And further for every £100 value | 12 | 10 | 0 |
| Rum, the gallon | | 1 | 3 |
| And further for every £100 value | 25 | 0 | 0 |
| Geneva, brandy, and other spirits or strong waters, except rum and whiskey, the gallon | | 2 | 0 |
| And further for every £100 value | 25 | 0 | 0 |
| Spirits, cordials, and liqueurs, sweetened or mixed with any article so that the strength cannot be ascertained by Sykes's hydrometer, the gallon | | 3 | 0 |
| And further for every £100 value | 25 | 0 | 0 |
| Salt, the bushel | | | 1 |
| And further for every £100 value | 12 | 10 | 0 |
| Spices and fruits, nuts, vinegar, maccaroni and vermicelli, sweetmeats or fruits preserved in sugar, candy, or molasses, for every £100 value | 30 | 0 | 0 |
| Animals of all kinds, hams, meats of all kinds, (except mess pork,) butter, cheese, flour, barley, buckwheat, bear and bigg, oats, rye, beans and peas, meal of the above grains and of wheat not bolted, bran in shorts, and hops, for every £100 in value | 20 | 0 | 0 |
| Anchors, bark, berries, nuts, vegetables, woods, and drugs used solely in dyeing, and indigo, bristles, burr-stones unwrought, chain cables the iron of the links of which is not less than five-eighths of an inch diameter, and which are not less than 15 fathoms in length, coal and coke, grease and scraps, hemp, flax, and tow undressed, hides, junk or oakum, lard, lead, pig and sheet, marble | | | |

TABLE—Continued.

| Articles subject to duty. | Amount of duty in currency. £ s. d. |
|---|---|
| in blocks unpolished, oil, cocoa-nut and palm only, ores of all kinds of metal, railroad bars, bar and rod-iron not hammered, charcoal, made or refined, boiler-plate, sheet-iron not thinner than No. 16 wire-gauge, and hoop iron not more than two inches broad, spike rods, pig, scrap, and old iron, pipe-clay, resin and rosin, saw-logs, ships' water casks in use, teasels, steel, broom-corn, wood used in making carpenters' and joiners' tools, tallow, tar and pitch, tarred rope when imported by ship-builders for the rigging of their ships, type metal in blocks or pigs, wool, for every £100 value.......... | 2 10 0 |
| All goods, wares, and merchandise not otherwise charged with duty, and not herinafter excepted, for every £100 value.......................................... | 12 10 0 |

*Exemptions.*

Ashes, pot and pearl, and soda; cotton-wool, anatomical preparations, philosophical instruments and apparatus, printed books, (not foreign reprints of British copyright works;) maps, busts and casts of marble, bronze, alabaster, or plaster of Paris; paintings, drawings, engravings, etchings, and lithographs; cabinets of coins, medals or gems, and other collections of antiquities; specimens of natural history, mineralogy or botany; trees, shrubs, bulbs and roots; wheat and Indian corn; animals specially imported for the improvement of stock.

Models of machinery, and other inventions and improvements in the arts.

Coin and bullion.

Manures of all kinds.

Arms, clothing, cattle, provisions, and stores of every description, which any commissary or commissaries, contractor or contractors, shall import or bring, or which may be imported or brought, by the principal or other officer or officers of her Majesty's ordnance, into the province, for the use of her Majesty's army or navy, or for the use of the Indian nations in this province, provided the duty otherwise payable thereon would be defrayed or borne by the treasury of the United Kingdom, or of this province.

Horses and carriages of travellers, and horses, cattle, and carriages, and other vehicles, when employed in carrying merchandise, together with the necessary harness and tackle, so long as the same shall be *bona fide* in use for that purpose; except the horses, cattle, carriages, vehicles and harness of persons hawking goods, wares and merchandise, through the province, for the purpose of retailing the same; and the horses, cattle, carriages and harness, of any circus or equestrian troop for exhibition; the horses, cattle, carriages and harness, of any menagerie, to be free.

Donations of clothing, specially imported for the use of, or to be distributed gratuitously by, any charitable society in this province.

Seeds of all kinds, farming utensils, and implements of husbandry, when specially imported in good faith by any society incorporated or established for the encouragement of agriculture.

The following articles, in the occupation or employment of persons coming into the province for the purpose of actually settling therein, viz: Wearing apparel in actual use, and other personal effects, not merchandise; horses and cattle; implements and tools of trade of handicraftsmen.

The personal household effects, not merchandise, of inhabitants of this province, being subjects of her Majesty, and dying abroad.

And the following articles, when imported directly from the United Kingdom, or from any British North American province, and being the growth, produce, or manufacture of the said United Kingdom, or of such province, respectively, viz: Animals, beef, pork, biscuit, bread, butter, cocoa-paste, corn or grain of all kinds, flour, fish, fresh or salted, dried or pickled; fish oil, fins or skins, the produce of fish or creatures living in the sea; gypsum, horns, meat, poultry, plants, shrubs and trees, potatoes and vegetables of all kinds, seeds of all kinds, skins, pelts, furs, or tails undressed; wood, viz: boards, plank, staves, timber, and fire-wood.

## NEWFOUNDLAND.

*Table of duties on imports in* 1850.* *(Compiled from returns made in* 1851 *for British House of Commons.)*

| Articles. | Amount of duty in sterling. | | |
|---|---|---|---|
| | £ | *s.* | *d.* |
| Apples, the barrel | 0 | 1 | 6 |
| Bacon and hams, the cwt. | | 5 | 0 |
| Beef, salted and cured, the barrel, not exceeding 200 lbs. | | 2 | 0 |
| Bread or biscuit, the cwt. | | | 3 |
| Butter, the cwt. | | 2 | 0 |
| Calves, sheep, and pigs, each | | 1 | 0 |
| Cheese, the cwt. | | 5 | 0 |
| Cigars, the 1,000 | | 5 | 0 |

* The latest return received at the Colonial Office, August 8, 1851.

TABLE—Continued.

| Articles. | Amount of duty in sterling. | | |
|---|---|---|---|
| | £ | s. | d. |
| Cocoa, the cwt | 0 | 5 | 0 |
| Coffee, the cwt | | 5 | 0 |
| Coals, the ton | | 1 | 0 |
| Flour, the barrel, not exceeding in weight 196 lbs | | 1 | 6 |
| Horses, mares, and geldings, each | | 10 | 0 |
| Lumber, the 1,000 feet, 1 inch thick | | 2 | 6 |
| Molasses, the gallon | | | 1½ |
| Oatmeal or Indian meal, the barrel, not exceeding in weight 200 lbs | | | 6 |
| Pork, the barrel, not exceeding in weight 200 lbs | | 3 | 0 |
| Salt, the ton | | | 6 |
| Shingles, the 1,000 | | 1 | 0 |
| Spirits— | | | |
| Brandy, whiskey, gin, cordials, and other spirits, not herein defined or enumerated, and not exceeding the strength of proof by Sykes's hydrometer, and so in proportion for any greater strength, and for any greater or less quantity than a gallon, the gallon | | 3 | 0 |
| Rum, not exceeding the strength of proof by Sykes's hydrometer, and so in proportion for any greater strength, and for any greater or less quantity than a gallon, the gallon | | | 9 |
| Sugar— | | | |
| Loaf and refined, the cwt | | 7 | 6 |
| Bastard, the cwt | | 5 | 0 |
| Unrefined, the cwt | | 5 | 0 |
| Tea, the pound | | | 3 |
| Timber, including balk and scantling, the ton | | 1 | 6 |
| Tobacco, manufactured and leaf, the lb | | | 2 |
| Tobacco stems, the cwt | | 2 | 0 |
| Wines, in bottles, the gallon | | 3 | 0 |
| All other wines, the gallon | | 2 | 0 |
| Clocks and watches; furniture manufactured of wood; ale, porter, beer, cider, perry; oil, blubber, fins, and skins, the produce of creatures living in the sea; for every £100 of the value | 10 | 0 | 0 |
| Candles of all kinds, for every £100 of the value | 7 | 10 | 0 |
| Goods, wares, and merchandise, not otherwise enumerated, described, or charged with duty in this act, and not otherwise exempt from duty, and neat cattle, for every £100 of the value | 5 | 0 | 0 |

In addition to the foregoing duties, £10 per cent. is levied on every £100 of duties paid on all goods, wares, and merchandise, imported into the town of St. John.

*Exemptions.*

Printed books and pamphlets, maps and charts; coin and bullion; hemp, flax, and tow; lime and limestone; manures of all kinds; provisions of every description imported or supplied for her Majesty's land or sea forces; passengers' personal luggage; rice (freed,) refuse of rice, seed of all kinds intended to be used for agricultural purposes; vegetables of all sorts, fresh; mules and asses; and fish, fresh or salted, dried or pickled.

No duties are levied on *exports.*

NEW BRUNSWICK.

*A table* of colonial duties and exemptions from duties imposed under an act passed in the province on the 28th March, 1851; the act to continue in force till the 31st December, 1854.*

| Articles subject to duty. | Amount of duty. | | |
|---|---|---|---|
| | £ | *s.* | *d.* |
| Apples, per bushel | | 0 | 6 |
| Axes, each, of 3 pounds weight and upwards | | 1 | 6 |
| Butter, per cwt | | 9 | 4 |
| Beans and peas, per bushel | | 1 | 6 |
| Barley, per bushel | | | 6 |
| Barley-meal, per cwt | | 2 | 0 |
| Buckwheat, per bushel | | | 6 |
| Buckwheat-meal, per cwt | | 2 | 6 |
| Candles, of all kinds, except sperm and wax, per pound | | | 1 |
| sperm and wax, per pound | | | 4 |
| Cattle of all kinds over one year old, each | 2 | 0 | 0 |
| Cheese, per cwt | | 14 | 0 |
| Cider, per gallon | | | 3 |
| Clocks or clock-cases of all kinds, each | | 15 | 0 |
| Coffee, per pound | | | 1½ |
| Coals, per ton | | 1 | 0 |
| Chairs, per dozen, (in addition to any duty imposed on chairs and parts of chairs by this act) | | 10 | 0 |
| Corn-meal, per barrel of 196 pounds | | 1 | 0 |
| Fruit, dried, per cwt | | 9 | 4 |
| Horses, mares, and geldings, each | 2 | 0 | 0 |
| Lard, per pound | | | 1 |
| Leather, sole, upper, harness, and belt, per pound | | | 2½ |

* According to returns made to the British House of Commons August 8, 1851.

TABLE—Continued.

| Articles subject to duty. | Amount of duty. | | |
|---|---|---|---|
| | £ | s. | d. |
| Leather, sheepskins, tanned and dressed, per dozen... | 0 | 3 | 0 |
| calfskins, tanned, per dozen................ | | 6 | 0 |
| Malt liquors of every description, (not being aqua vitæ, otherwise charged with duty,) whether in bottles or otherwise, per gallon.................. | | | 6 |
| Meats, fresh, per cwt.................. | | 9 | 4 |
| salted and cured, per cwt.................. | | 7 | 0 |
| With an additional duty of 1*s.* 2*d.* per cwt. on and after the 1st day of April, 1852, and a further increase of duty of 1*s.* 2*d.* per cwt. on and after the 1st day of April, 1853. | | | |
| Molasses and treacle, per gallon.................. | | | 1 |
| Oats, per bushel.................. | | | 3 |
| Oat-meal, per barrel of 196 pounds.................. | | 2 | 4 |
| Rye, per bushel.................. | | | 2 |
| Rye-flour, per barrel of 196 pounds.................. | | 1 | 0 |
| Soap, per pound.................. | | | ½ |
| Spirits and cordials, viz: | | | |
| brandy, per gallon.................. | | 3 | 4 |
| rum, for every gallon thereof of any strength under and not exceeding the strength of proof of 26 by the bubble.................. | | 1 | 0 |
| and for every bubble below 26 in number, by the bubble, an additional, per gallon, of.......... | | | 1 |
| lemon-syrup, per gallon.................. | | 1 | 0 |
| gin, whiskey, and all other spirits, (not herein-before enumerated,) per gallon.............. | | 1 | 6 |
| Sugar, refined, in loaves, per pound.............. | | | 1½ |
| refined, crushed, and white bastard, per cwt.... | | 9 | 4 |
| of all kinds, except refined crushed and white bastard, per cwt.................. | | 6 | 0 |
| Tea, per pound.................. | | | 2 |
| Tobacco, manufactured, except snuff and cigars, per pound.................. | | | 1½ |
| Wines, per gallon.................. | | 2 | 6 |
| and on every £100 of the true and real value thereof, in addition.................. | 10 | 0 | 0 |
| Wheat, per bushel.................. | | | 2 |
| Wheat-flour, per barrel of 196 pounds.............. | | 3 | 0 |

TABLE—Continued.

| Articles subject to duty. | Amount of duty. | | |
|---|---|---|---|
| | £ | s. | d. |
| *Ad valorem.* | | | |
| On the following articles, for every £100 of the true and real value thereof, viz: | | | |
| Anchors; ashes; barilla; burr-stones; canvass; cordage, (except Manilla rope;) chain cables, and other chains for ships' use; cotton-wool and cotton warp; copper and patent metal in sheets, bars, and bolts, for ship-building; dye-wood; felt; hemp, flax, and tow; hides, green and salted; iron, in bolts, bars, plates, sheet, and pig-iron; oakum; ores of all kinds; pitch; sails and rigging for new ships; sheathing-paper; silk plush, for hatters' purposes; tallow; tar; tobacco, unmanufactured; wool | 1 | 0 | 0 |
| Bread; biscuit; bricks; Manilla rope; ready-made clothing | 10 | 0 | 0 |
| Castings, viz: steam-engines and boilers, and parts thereof; mill-machinery; ships' castings; composition rudder-braces, &c.; machinery of every description; square stoves, known and designated as Canada stoves | 7 | 10 | 0 |
| On the following articles, for every £100 of the true and real value thereof, viz: | | | |
| Boots, shoes, and other leather manufactures; chairs, and prepared parts of, or for chairs; clock-wheels, machinery, and materials for clocks; household furniture, (except baggage, apparel, household effects, working-tools, and implements used and in the use of persons and families arriving in this province, if used abroad by them, and not intended for any other person or persons, or for sale;) looking-glasses; oranges and lemons; whale-oil, (except the return-cargoes of vessels fitted out for fishing voyages from ports in this province;) brushes, hats and hat-bodies, piano-fortes, snuff and cigars | 20 | 0 | 0 |
| Carriages, wagons, sleighs, and other vehicles; veneer and other mouldings for looking-glasses, picture and other frames made of wood; wooden wares of all kinds; matches, corn-brooms, and all agricultural implements, except ploughs | 30 | 0 | 0 |

TABLE—Continued.

| Articles subject to duty. | Amount of duty. |
|---|---|
| | £ s. d. |
| Iron castings, viz: cooking, close, box, and round stoves; Franklin stoves, register grates, fire-frames, and parts thereof; kitchen-ranges, boilers, cast-iron furnaces, and parts thereof; cast-iron ploughs...... | 15 0 0 |
| And all other goods, wares, and merchandise not herein otherwise charged with duty, and not hereafter declared to be free from duty, for every $100 of the true and real value thereof.......................... | 7 10 0 |

* All articles of which any component part or parts is or are subject to duty, to be liable to the highest rate of duty to which any one of the said component parts will be liable under this act.

*Articles exempt from duty.*

Baggage, apparel, household effects, working-tools and implements used and in the use of persons or families arriving in this province, if used abroad by them, and not intended for any other person or persons, or for sale; books, printed; carriages of travellers and not intended for sale; coins and bullion; corn-broom brush; Indian corn; rice, ground and unground; eggs; manures of all kinds; oil, blubber, fins, and skins, the produce of creatures living in the sea; the return of vessels fitted out in this province for fishing-voyages; oil, seal, cod, hake, porpoise, palm, and rape; plants, and shrubs, and trees; printing-paper, types, printing-presses, and printers' ink; rags, old rope and junk; rock salt; sails and rigging saved from vessels wrecked; salt; soap; grease; wood and lumber of all kinds, (except cedar, spruce, pine, and hemlock shingles;) block-tin, zinc, lead, tin-plate, bar and sheet steel; lines and twines for the fisheries.

## BAHAMAS.

**[From a despatch of the United States consul at Nassau, N. P., August 20, 1849.]**

"I enclose a copy of the tariff of duties levied on articles brought to this port either from England or America. This tariff is in lieu of all other duties heretofore collected by the officers of the imperial customs, that office having been abolished in this colony by an act of the Bahama assembly, confirmed by her Majesty in council."

* **Note.—By a subsequent act, cap. 9, 9th April, 1851, this clause was repealed.**

*Tariff under an act for regulating the trade of the Bahama islands.—No.* 158, 11*th Victoria, chap.* 22, *passed April* 19, 1848; *confirmed May* 1, 1849.

| | £ | s. | d. |
|---|---|---|---|
| Ale and porter, in wood, per gallon | 0 | 0 | 3 |
| Ale and porter, in quart bottles, per dozen | | | 9 |
| Apples, per barrel | | 1 | 0 |
| Asses, each | 1 | 0 | 0 |
| Beets, per barrel | | 1 | 0 |
| Beans, per bushel | | | 6 |
| Biscuit and bread, per cwt | | 2 | 0 |
| Brandy, per gallon | | 3 | 6 |
| Butter, per cwt | | 12 | 0 |
| Cabbages, per dozen | | 9 | 0 |
| Candles, adamantine or any composition of tallow and other substances other than wax or spermaceti, per cwt | | 10 | 0 |
| Candles, tallow, per cwt | | 5 | 0 |
| Candles, sperm and wax, per cwt | | 12 | 0 |
| Calves, each | | 2 | 0 |
| Cattle, cows, bulls, and oxen, each | | 8 | 0 |
| Carrots, per barrel | | 1 | 0 |
| Cheese, per cwt | | 9 | 0 |
| Cocoa, per cwt | | 6 | 0 |
| Colts and foals, each | 1 | 0 | 0 |
| Coffee, per cwt | | 8 | 0 |
| Cordials, per gallon | | 5 | 0 |
| Cider, in the wood, per gallon | | | 3 |
| Cider, in bottles, per dozen | | | 9 |
| Cordage, hemp and manilla, per cwt | | 4 | 0 |
| Corn (Indian) and oats, per bushel | | | 3 |
| Corn-meal, per barrel | | 2 | 0 |
| Currants, per cwt | | 8 | 0 |
| Copper and composition in bars, rods, sheets or nails, per cwt | | | 8 |
| Drugs, medicines, and perfumery, ad valorem, 10 per cent. | | | |
| Flour, wheat, per barrel of 196 lbs. net | | 5 | 0 |
| Flour, rye, per barrel | | 3 | 0 |
| Figs, per cwt | | 5 | 0 |
| Fish, dried or salted, per cwt | | 5 | 0 |
| Fish, pickled salmon, mackerel, and shad, per barrel | | 8 | 0 |
| Fish, herring, alewives, and others not enumerated, per barrel | | 4 | 0 |
| Gin, whiskey, and other spirits not enumerated, per gallon | | 2 | 6 |
| Geese, per dozen | | 8 | 0 |
| Horses, mares, and geldings, each | 2 | 0 | 0 |
| Honey and syrup, per gallon | | | 3 |
| Hulks and materials of vessels, ad valorem, 15 per cent. | | | |
| Iron, in bars, rods, sheets, or nails, per cwt | | 3 | 0 |
| Lard, per cwt | | 6 | 0 |
| Lead and zinc, per cwt | | 4 | 0 |
| Lumber, per thousand feet | | 8 | 0 |
| Materials of vessels, ad valorem, 15 per cent. | | | |

| | £ | s. | d. |
|---|---|---|---|
| Meal, corn, per barrel | 0 | 2 | 0 |
| Meat, salted or cured, per cwt. | | 7 | 0 |
| Medicines, ad valorem, 10 per cent. | | | |
| Molasses, per gallon. | | | 3 |
| Mules, each. | 1 | 0 | 0 |
| Nails, of copper or composition, per cwt. | | 8 | 0 |
| Nails, of iron, per cwt. | | 3 | 0 |
| Oils, almond and olive, per gallon | | 1 | 6 |
| Oils, sperm and lard, per cwt. | | 2 | 0 |
| Oils, all other kinds, per gallon | | | 6 |
| Oakum, per cwt. | | 2 | 0 |
| Onions, per barrel. | | 1 | 0 |
| Onions, not in barrels, per 100 bunches. | | 1 | 6 |
| Oats, corn (Indian) per bushel. | | | 3 |
| Paints, white lead and other colors, in oil, per cwt. | | 4 | 0 |
| Peas and beans, per bushel. | | | 6 |
| Perfumery, ad valorem, 10 per cent. | | | |
| Pitch, per barrel. | | 2 | 0 |
| Porter, in wood, per gallon | | | 3 |
| Porter, in quart bottles, per dozen. | | | 9 |
| Potatoes, per bushel. | | | 6 |
| Poultry, (except geese and turkeys,) per dozen | | 4 | 0 |
| Prunes, per cwt. | | 8 | 0 |
| Raisins, per cwt. | | 8 | 0 |
| Rice, per cwt. | | 1 | 6 |
| Rosin, per barrel. | | 2 | 0 |
| Rope, mahoa and bale, per cwt. | | 2 | 0 |
| Rum, stronger than 18 per bubble, per gallon. | | 3 | 0 |
| Rum, 18 and not weaker than 24 per bubble, per gallon. | | 2 | 6 |
| Rum, weaker than 24 degrees per bubble, per gallon. | | 2 | 0 |
| Segars, per thousand. | | 9 | 0 |
| Sheep and lambs, each | | 1 | 6 |
| Shingles, cypress, per thousand. | | 4 | 0 |
| Shingles, other than cypress, per thousand | | 2 | 0 |
| Soap, per cwt. | | 4 | 0 |
| Sugar, unrefined, per cwt. | | 9 | 0 |
| Sugar, white clayed, per cwt. | | 12 | 0 |
| Sugar, refined, per cwt. | | 17 | 0 |
| Swine, per cwt. | | 4 | 0 |
| Syrup, (cane) and honey, per gallon. | | | 3 |
| Tar, per barrel | | 2 | 0 |
| Tea, hyson and other green, per lb. | | | 9 |
| Tea, congo, and other black, per lb. | | | 6 |
| Tobacco, manufactured, per cwt. | | 14 | 0 |
| Tobacco, unmanufactured, per cwt. | | 5 | 0 |
| Turnips, per barrel. | | 1 | 0 |
| Turpentine, per barrel. | | 2 | 0 |
| Turpentine, spirits of, per gallon. | | | 3 |
| Turkeys, per dozen | | 8 | 0 |
| Turtle, (live) per cwt. | | 1 | 0 |

| | £ | s. | d. |
|---|---|---|---|
| Wines, the growth of the continent of Europe and island of Madeira, per gallon | 0 | 2 | 6 |
| Wines, (all other,) per gallon | | 1 | 0 |
| Zinc and lead, per cwt | | 4 | 0 |

Articles not enumerated, except such as are comprised in the table of exemptions set forth in this act, five per cent. ad valorem.

Articles subject to ad valorem duty, when found derelict, wrecked or stranded, will be charged in lieu of such duty, on the value at the port or place of entry, a duty of fifteen per centum.

In addition to the foregoing duties, a duty of five pounds per centum will be imposed on the said duties respectively.

The following articles may be imported without the payment of any duty whatever—that is to say: coin, bullion, diamonds, printed books and pamphlets, metalline ores, tallow and raw hides, dye goods and stuffs, mahogany, lignumvitæ, cedar and yellow wood, ice, wax, tannin, hemp, flax and tow, cotton-wool, tortoise-shell, manures of all kinds, trees imported for planting, old copper and iron fit only to be remanufactured; provisions and stores of every description imported or supplied from a bonded warehouse for the use of her Majesty's land or sea forces; articles imported or supplied out of a bonded warehouse for the colonial service; articles of every description imported or supplied out of a bonded warehouse for the use of the governor or commander-in-chief of the colony; wine, spirits, wearing apparel, and military or naval equipments, and other articles imported or supplied out of a bonded warehouse for the use or accommodation of any officer of her Majesty's army or navy, on full pay and doing duty within these islands.

If any of the before-mentioned articles exempted from the payment of import duties be wrecked, stranded, or found derelict, and brought into any port or place of this colony, and here sold at public auction, whether such sale shall take place by order of a court of law, or otherwise, there shall be imposed and paid upon the gross amount of such sales, in addition to any other auction duty chargeable on such sales, an auction duty or tax of five pounds per centum.

A credit of six calendar months is allowed for payment of duties (except articles from the warehouse) when the amount exceeds £20.

On the exportation of any article shipped in the original package, a drawback of ninety per centum is allowed.

*Export duty.*

Five per cent. on Bahama produce, produce of fishery excepted.

*Tonnage duty*—(one shilling.)

Vessels arriving in ballast, and taking away a full and entire cargo of Bahama produce, and vessels arriving with part cargo, and filling up with Bahama produce, without landing any part of their original cargo, will be allowed a drawback of one-half of such tonnage dues.

The following vessels shall be totally exempt from the payment of such duty, viz: steam-vessels; vessels arriving in ballast and departing in ballast, or arriving with cargo and not landing any part thereof; as also vessels which may put into any port within these islands through stress of weather, or for the purpose of refitting and repairing damages sustained during the voyage on which any such vessel may be then proceeding, or to obtain supplies of provisions and water, or any articles necessary for the safety of the said vessel, or the comfort of the persons on board; and whether the cargo or lading of such vessel, or any part thereof, shall have been landed or not; provided, that if landed, the same be reshipped without any part thereof being sold or disposed of in the way of trade, or any other cargo being shipped on board of such vessel.

*Anchorage and harbor fees.*

ANCHORAGE.

| | £ | s. | d. |
|---|---|---|---|
| 100 tons, or under | 0 | 5 | 0 |
| 100 to 150 | | 10 | 0 |
| 100 to 200 | | 15 | 0 |
| 200 and upwards | 1 | 0 | 0 |

HARBOR.

| | £ | s. | d. |
|---|---|---|---|
| Vessels drawing 8 feet, or under | | 10 | 0 |
| Upwards of 8 and below 10 | | 15 | 0 |
| 10 feet or upwards, and below 12 | 1 | 0 | 0 |
| 12 feet or upwards, but below 14 | 1 | 5 | 0 |
| 14 feet, or upwards | 1 | 10 | 0 |

On every removal from one part of the harbor to another, one-half of the above fees are chargeable.

N. B.—In case of vessels proceeding from the port of Nassau, in ballast, to any of the out-islands of this government, for the purpose of loading with salt or fruit, and returning with such cargo to the said port of Nassau for a temporary purpose, before proceeding therewith to some port or place abroad, such vessels, on leaving the said port of Nassau for such out-island port, and on returning as aforesaid to such port, shall be liable only to half pilotage and harbor fees. Entrance fee, 12*s.* 6*d.*

*Clearance fees.*

| | £ | s. | d. |
|---|---|---|---|
| On the clearance of every vessel of 100 tons burden, and over | 1 | 0 | 0 |
| 60 tons, and less than 100 | | 15 | 0 |
| 30, and less than 60 | | 10 | 0 |
| Under 30 tons | | 5 | 0 |

*Fees on wrecking licenses.*

| | £ | s. | d. |
|---|---|---|---|
| On the renewal of the annual permit of wrecking, coasting, and droghing vessels, viz: on vessels of 30 tons burden and upwards | 0 | 16 | 0 |
| 20 tons, and under 30 | | 10 | 0 |
| All under 20 tons | | 5 | 0 |

## JAMAICA.

[From despatch of United States consul at Kingston, Jamaica, March —, 1851.]

Having adverted to a decision of the United States Supreme Court January, 1850, against him, in a case in which a Captain Vose refused to deliver to him his ship-papers, he proceeds:

"As far back as 1794, when in command of a vessel, I always deposited the registers and other papers immediately, or as soon as practicable, with our consuls; which, according to my interpretation of the act, and hundreds of other persons, I have felt it my duty to do; and for the last forty years, as a consul myself, I have never failed to compel others to do so likewise.

"As the deposite of papers by many of our shipmasters always has been a stumbling-block to those engaged in illicit trade to Africa, and the commission of frauds on the revenue, &c., I have often been consulted by our consular agents, as well as these men themselves, concerning this matter in England and many other parts of Europe as well as the West Indies. And I have also taken the opinion of some of the ablest jurists and men of information in those countries, who have invariably declared that the act for the deposite of papers appeared too clear to admit of any other interpretation or meaning, but that they should be immediately, or as soon as may be, deposited with the consuls, if our government wished to do away with the foul opprobrium which has often been heaped upon our flag for covering vessels engaged in the African trade, &c.

"In submitting these facts to your consideration, I pray you to believe that I do not presume to set up my own opinion, or that of those I have consulted, in opposition to the Supreme Court of the United States.

"My object is to show the bad policy and evil that may result by not depositing the registers, as heretofore, with our consuls. In the first place, a pirate, or slaver, or any other freebooter, may come in here, with impunity, for the vilest purposes, (and lie as long as he pleases, without my knowledge, as some masters of vessels have already done,) of which, from their known reputation, I have had reason to suspect them.

"Secondly. How am I to report the names of vessels, or their masters, &c., touching here, as required by the consul's instructions, and for the information of owners and underwriters, if no report is made to me on their arrival?

"I feel most assured that the only objection of shipmasters who are engaged in lawful trade is the charge of four dollars. The legislature of this island has passed an act to oblige all shipmasters to deposite their registers, &c., with their consuls.

* * * * * * * *

"I have before informed you that the Danes, Swedes, Prussians, Hamburgers, Bremeners, and Dutchmen, are now the carriers of all, or most of, the supplies required from the United States, for this and other colonies; in consequence of which, my fees have dwindled into *mere nothing*."

*Registers of United States vessels.*

Act of the Jamaica legislature. [Not dated: received with Consul Harrison's despatch of March —, 1851.]

"Whereas it is expedient to amend certain laws of this island, in order to facilitate the commerce between this island and the United States of America:

"*Be it enacted, &c.*, That the registers of all vessels belonging to the United States of America, arriving in this island, shall henceforth be deposited with the consul or agent of the United States for the time being resident here, and duly accredited, any law or usage to the contrary notwithstanding: *Provided*, That no vessel belonging to the United States shall be permitted to quit any of the ports of this island before all dues and duties, payable by such vessel or her cargo, shall have been actually paid or secured: *Provided*, That this shall not be in force unless there be some accredited agent of the United States resident in this island: *And provided also*, That at every port of entry of this island where there is no vice-consul or agent of the United States duly appointed, the deputy receiver-general of such port shall continue to hold such registers of vessels, as heretofore, till a vice-consul or agent be duly appointed, and such appointment be notified to his excellency, the governor, for the time being."

*Steamers and vessels importing coals for steamers exempted from all tonnage dues.*

Act of the Jamaica legislature, approved 23d May, 1851.

"*Be it enacted, &c.*, That from and after the passing of this act, the following acts shall be, and the same are hereby, repealed: that is to say, three several acts made and passed in the thirteenth year of the reign of her present Majesty Queen Victoria, entitled, respectively, 'An act to promote and encourage steam navigation between this island and other countries;' 'An act to declare certain vessels exempt from tonnage dues, upon the exportation in them of fruit or vegetables, ground provisions, and preparations thereof, the growth and produce of this island;' and 'An act to exempt steam-vessels from the duty of gunpowder, payable on tonnage, and from all tonnage dues.'

II. "*And it be further enacted*, That from and after the passing of this act, all steam-vessels shall be permitted to enter the ports of this island, and again to depart therefrom, free and exempt from all tonnage dues, whether such vessels shall or shall not import or export cargo.

III. "*And it be further enacted*, That all vessels employed in importing coals for the use of such steam-vessels aforesaid, shall be free and exempt from all tonnage dues: *Provided*, That such vessels importing coals import no other cargo whatever, and that they take no cargo of any description whatever from the island, other than fruit, vegetables, ground provisions, or preparations thereof, the growth of this island: *And provided further*, That proof be given, to the satisfaction of the receiver-general and officers of customs, that the coals so imported have been imported solely for the use of steam-vessels, and that they are deposited in a depôt, to be appropriated exclusively to that purpose.

IV. "*And be it further enacted,* That on the arrival of any such steam-vessel, the commander of such steam-vessel, or the next chief officer, shall deliver to the collector and controller of her Majesty's customs at the port, a manifest of all goods, wares, and merchandise on board the said steam-vessel, specifying the marks and numbers, the nature and contents of the packages, so far as he is able to ascertain the same, together with the names of the shippers, and the party to whom consigned; and that no goods be landed from the said steam-vessels but by an order from the collector and controller of her Majesty's customs, and under such regulations as shall be established by the collector and controller of her Majesty's customs at the port of Kingston, subject to the approval of his excellency, the governor."

### ST. VINCENT.

[According to returns compiled for the British House of Commons, in 1851.]

*Table of imports.*

| Articles subject to duty. | Duties in sterling money. | | |
|---|---|---|---|
| | £ | s. | d. |
| Ale, beer, cider, porter, or perry, in wood, per tun | 1 | 5 | 0 |
| Ale, bottled, for every dozen quart bottles | | | 4 |
| Asses, per head | | 4 | 0 |
| Beef and pork, salted or cured, per barrel, not exceeding 200 lbs. weight | | 8 | 4 |
| Bread or biscuit, per cwt | | 1 | 0 |
| Bricks, per 1,000 | | 4 | 0 |
| Butter, per cwt | | 6 | 0 |
| Candles— | | | |
| Wax, sperm, or composition, per cwt | | 10 | 0 |
| Tallow, per cwt | | 1 | 6 |
| Cattle, neat, per head | | 10 | 0 |
| Cocoa, per cwt | | 2 | 0 |
| Coffee, per cwt | | 2 | 0 |
| Cheese, per cwt | | 4 | 4 |
| Cordage, per cwt | | 1 | 6 |
| Canvass, per bolt, not exceeding 43 yards | | 1 | 0 |
| Corks, per gross | | | 1 |
| Currants and raisins, dried, per cwt | | 2 | 0 |
| Flour, wheat, per barrel of 196 lbs. weight | | 4 | 0 |
| Fish— | | | |
| Dried or salted, per cwt | | 1 | 0 |
| Pickled, per barrel | | 1 | 0 |
| Salmon, wet or salted, per cwt | | 1 | 6 |
| Herrings, smoked, per box not exceeding 10 lbs | | | 3 |

TABLE—Continued.

| Articles subject to duty. | Duties in sterling money. | | |
|---|---|---|---|
| | £ | s. | d. |
| Hams, bacon, dried beef, dried or pickled tongues, per cwt. | 0 | 4 | 2 |
| Horses, mares, and geldings, per head | 1 | 0 | 0 |
| Lard, per cwt | | 2 | 0 |
| Lead, sheet or pipe, per cwt | | 2 | 0 |
| Lime, per hogshead | | | 6 |
| Meal or other flour, not wheat, per barrel | | 1 | 3 |
| Mules, per head | | 10 | 0 |
| Naval stores—tar and pitch, crude turpentine and rosin, per barrel | | 1 | 0 |
| Oil— | | | |
| Common fish, per barrel | | 1 | 6 |
| Sperm, neatsfoot, and any other kind, not above enumerated, per gallon | | | 6 |
| All other, per gallon | | | 3 |
| Peas, beans, and all description of grain, per bushel | | | 1 |
| Pepper, black and white, per cwt | | 4 | 0 |
| Powder, (gun,) coarse, per cwt | | 3 | 0 |
| Rice, per cwt | | 1 | 0 |
| Sheep, goats, and swine, per head | | 1 | 0 |
| Soap— | | | |
| Common yellow, per cwt | | 1 | 0 |
| All other | | 2 | 0 |
| Spirits— | | | |
| Brandy, per gallon | | 2 | 0 |
| Gin, per gallon | | 1 | 0 |
| And all other spirits and cordials, except rum, per gallon. | | 3 | 0 |
| Rum, the produce of any British possession, per gallon | | 1 | 0 |
| Sugar— | | | |
| Unrefined, the produce of any British possession, per cwt. | | 5 | 0 |
| Refined, per cwt | | 10 | 0 |
| Shooks, red or white oak, per bundle not exceeding 35 staves | | | 3 |
| Slates and tiles, for covering roofs, per 1,000 | | 4 | 2 |
| Sago, tapioca, and oatmeal, per cwt | | 1 | 0 |
| Tea, per lb | | | 3 |
| Tobacco, unmanufactured, per cwt | | 6 | 0 |
| Snuff, and all other manufactured tobacco, per cwt | 1 | 5 | 0 |
| Tallow, per cwt | | 1 | 0 |
| Turpentine, spirits of, per gallon | | | 2 |
| Vinegar, per barrel, 30 gallons | | 2 | 0 |
| Wine, in wood and bottle, for every £100 value | 12 per ct. | | |

TABLE—Continued.

| Articles subject to duty. | Duties in sterling money. | | |
|---|---|---|---|
| | £ | s. | d. |
| Wood— | | | |
| For every 1,000 feet of pitch-pine lumber, by superficial measure of one inch thick | 0 | 7 | 0 |
| For every 1,000 feet of white pine or other lumber, per superficial measure of one inch thick | | 4 | 0 |
| Shingles, cypress and wallaba, per 1,000 | *2 *shingles.* | | |
| All other kinds of shingles, per 1,000 | | 1 | 0 |
| Wood-hoops, per 1,000 | | 1 | 0 |
| Staves and headings of all kinds, per 1,000 | | 2 | 0 |
| Cedar, per 1,000 feet superficial, 1 inch thick | | 15 | 0 |
| Mahogany, per 1,000 feet superficial | 1 | 0 | 0 |
| Other woods not here enumerated, per 1,000 feet superficial | | 15 | 0 |
| Cedar or other posts, or timbers, per 100 | | 5 | 0 |
| Zinc, per cwt | | 2 | 0 |
| Glass manufactures, being ornamental, not included in the description of glass-ware herein enumerated; clocks, looking-glasses, watches, jewelry, toys, paintings, engravings, prints, furniture, carpets, floor-cloths, perfumery, china, porcelain wares, and plate | 5 per cent. | | |
| Silk manufactures, being articles of dress, either wholly or in part made up, and millinery | 5 per cent. | | |
| Cotton, linen, woolen, leather and paper manufactures; window and other glass, such as decanters, tumblers, wine-glasses, and other articles of household use, (not ornamental,) earthenware, hardware | 2 per cent. | | |
| On all other goods, wares, merchandise, plantation supplies, clothing, and effects of every description, not previously enumerated, for every £100 value | 2 per cent. | | |

*Except* the following, which shall not be liable to any duty under this act:

Coin, bullion, diamonds, coal, fresh fruits and vegetables, ice, salt, hay and straw, printed books and papers; all manures imported for agricultural purposes. And the following:

Military clothing and accoutrements, imported under the authority of her Majesty's treasury, for the use of her Majesty's forces; and all building materials and supplies for the use of her Majesty's army and navy;

All arms and accoutrements imported for the use of the militia of this island; and

*Intended to be 2*s.*, but made 2 shingles, owing to a clerical error in the act.

Machinery imported to be erected in this island, and driven by water, wind, steam, cattle, or horse power:

*Provided always*, That no goods of any description liable to duty under this act, (cattle excepted,) entered as imported for the use of her Majesty's forces, shall be exempted from the duty laid by this act, unless the party claiming such exemption shall give bond to the treasurer, at the time of entry of such goods, conditioned for the payment of the amount of duty payable on such goods under the provisions of this act, in default of producing to the said treasurer, within three months after importation, a certificate from the commissariat, or other proper officer, that the same goods have been used for the forces, or received by the commissariat or other official and proper department for the same; or unless, at the time of entry and permit granted for landing the same goods, a certificate from the proper official military authority shall be produced, to the satisfaction of the treasurer, that such goods are for the use of her Majesty's forces, in which case the treasurer is hereby authorized to grant permit for landing the same without the payment of duty, and without bond being given.

### *Exports.*

No export duties are levied in this island; but, by the annual tax act, an impost is laid upon its produce.

## TRINIDAD.

[With despatch of United States consul at the island of Trinidad, February 1, 1849.]

"I enclose a table of duties payable on imports from the 1st of January, 1849."

### *Tables of duties from 1st January, 1849.*

Table 1.

Upon all goods, wares, and merchandise imported into this colony, the following duties:

| | £ | s. | d. |
|---|---|---|---|
| Flour, per barrel of 196 pounds | 0 | 5 | 0 |
| Meal or other flour, not wheaten, per barrel | | 1 | 0 |
| Do..........do..............per puncheon | | 4 | 0 |
| Crackers and other breadstuffs, per barrel | | | 7½ |
| Corn, per bushel | | | 2½ |
| Black-eyed peas, per bushel | | | 2½ |
| Meat, salted or cured, per 100 pounds | | 4 | 2 |
| Fish, dried or salted, per 100 pounds | | 1 | 0 |
| pickled, per 100 pounds | | 2 | 6 |
| Lard, per 100 pounds | | 2 | 6 |
| Cheese, per 100 pounds | | 5 | 0 |
| Soap, per 100 pounds | | 1 | 0 |

| | £ | s. | d. |
|---|---|---|---|
| Candles, tallow, per 100 pounds | 0 | 2 | 1 |
| wax, sperm, composition, and all others, per 100 pounds | | 6 | 0 |
| Sugar, refined or not, per 100 pounds | | 5 | 0 |
| Cocoa, per 100 pounds | | 5 | 0 |
| Coffee, per 100 pounds | | 5 | 0 |
| Chocolate, per pound | | | 1 |
| Molasses, per gallon | | | 6 |
| Rice, per 100 pounds | | 2 | 0 |
| Butter, per pound | | | ¾ |
| Tea, per pound | | | 2 |
| Olive oil, per dozen bottles | | 1 | 0 |
| per dozen half bottles | | | 6 |
| per dozen flasks | | | 4 |
| Spirits and strong waters, per gallon | | 2 | 0 |
| Oats, per bushel | | | 2½ |
| Tobacco, manufactured or unmanufactured, per pound | | | 3 |
| Malt liquor, in wood, per sixty-four gallons | | 5 | 4 |
| in bottles, per dozen quart bottles, and so in proportion | | | 6 |
| Wines, in wood, French wines, (except Bordeaux, Vin de Cote, and Muscat,) per gallon | | | 6 |
| Vin de Côte, per gallon | | | 1 |
| Teneriffe, Canary, dry and sweet Malaga, Fayal and Cicilian, and Muscat, per gallon | | | 4 |
| Bordeaux, Sherry, Madeira, Port, and all other wines not above enumerated, per gallon | | | 6 |
| (except Muscat,) in bottles, per dozen quart bottles, and so in proportion | | 3 | 0 |
| Muscat, in bottles, per dozen bottles | | 2 | 0 |
| Spirits of turpentine, per gallon | | | 1 |
| Tar, per barrel | | | 6 |
| Pitch, per barrel | | | 6 |
| Coals, per hogshead | | 1 | 0 |
| Building lime, per hogshead | | 1 | 0 |
| Bricks, per thousand | | 1 | 0 |
| Tan tiles, and other roofing tiles, per thousand | | 2 | 1 |
| Paving tiles, per hundred | | 1 | 0 |
| Marble tiles, per hundred | | 2 | 1 |
| Lumber, white, spruce, and pine, per 1,000 feet | | 6 | 3 |
| Shingles, per thousand | | 1 | 0 |
| Shooks, per bundle | | | 6 |
| Staves, per thousand | | 10 | 0 |
| Neat cattle, each | | 2 | 1 |
| Horses, mares, geldings, and foals, each | 2 | 0 | 0 |
| Mules, each | | 10 | 0 |
| Asses, each | | 2 | 1 |
| Carriages, on springs, four-wheeled, each | 7 | 0 | 0 |
| Do......do.....two-wheeled, each | 4 | 0 | 0 |
| Muskets, guns, and fowling-pieces | | 5 | 0 |

| | £ | s. | d. |
|---|---|---|---|
| Gunpowder, loose in kegs, per pound | 0 | 0 | 2 |
| in canister | | | 5 |
| Articles of silk manufacture, per £100 ad valorem | 7 | 10 | 0 |
| Non-enumerated articles, per £100 ad valorem | 3 | 10 | 0 |

*Exemptions.*

Coins, bullion, and diamonds; printed books; guano or other manure; steam-engines and appurtenances; sugar pans, and apparatus used for the manufactures of sugar or other produce; temper lime and draining tiles; all live stock, except horses, mares, geldings, colts, foals, mules, asses, and neat cattle.

Provisions and stores of every description imported for the use of her Majesty's land and sea forces.

Table 2.

Upon all sugar, molasses, rum, cocoa, coffee, cotton, indigo, and other produce exported from this colony, per £100 ad valorem, £3 10*s.*

Table 3.

Upon all ships and vessels coming to and entering at this colony the following duties or tonnage, namely:

Upon every ship or vessel of 50 tons and upwards, for every ton of the registered tonnage of such ship or vessel, 1*s.* 6*d.*

Upon every ship or vessel of 25 tons and upwards, but under 50 tons, for every ton of the registered tonnage of such ship or vessel, 1*s.* 3*d.*

And upon every ship or vessel under 25 tons, for every ton of the registered tonnage of such ship or vessel, 3*d.*

*Provided always,* That no such duty or tonnage shall be payable in respect to any vessel entering and clearing in ballast: *And provided,* That where any ship or vessel, of which the registered tonnage shall be less than 50 tons, shall enter more than twice in one and the same year, the tonnage payable upon or in respect of every entry after the second in the same year, shall be 3*d.* sterling per ton, and no more.

Table 4.

And upon the following goods landed upon any public wharf or quay in the town of Port of Spain the following rates of wharfage to be paid by the importer:

|  |  |
|---|---|
| On every thousand feet of lumber | 1*s.* |
| On every thousand staves, or staves in shook | |
| On every thousand bricks | |
| On every thousand tiles | |
| On every thousand slates | |
| On every thousand shingles | |
| On every hogshead of lime | |
| On every hogshead of coal | |

DOMINICA.

*A table of duties, payable under an act of this island, entitled "An act to repeal two acts of this island, imposing duties on the importation of goods, wares, and merchandise, and to impose duties in lieu thereof." (Compiled from returns made in 1851, for British House of Commons.)*

| Articles subject to duty. | Amount of duty. | | |
|---|---|---|---|
| | £ | s. | d. |
| Ale, beer, porter, perry, and cider, per gallon | 0 | 0 | 5 |
| Animals, living, viz: horses, mares, geldings, foals, per head | 2 | 2 | 0 |
| Beef. (*Vide* Meats.) | | | |
| Bran, per bushel | | | 5 |
| Navy bread and biscuit, per cwt | | 2 | 0 |
| Bread and biscuit, other kinds | | 3 | 0 |
| Bricks, building or common, per 1,000 | | 6 | 0 |
| Butter, per cwt | | 6 | 0 |
| Candles: | | | |
| Tallow, per cwt | | 4 | 6 |
| All other kinds per lb | | | 3 |
| Cheese, per cwt | | 6 | 0 |
| Corn and grain of all kinds, unground, per bushel | | | 4½ |
| Corks, per gross | | | 2 |
| Cigars. (*Vide* Manufactured Tobacco.) | | | |
| Fish: | | | |
| Dried, salted, or smoked, per cwt | | 1 | 6 |
| Pickled, per barrel | | 3 | 0 |
| Flour: | | | |
| Wheat, per barrel | | 4 | 0 |
| All other kinds, and meal, per barrel | | 2 | 0 |
| Fruit: | | | |
| Dried, per lb | | | 3 |
| Preserved in syrup or brandy, per gallon | | 1 | 6 |
| Goods, produce of places within the limits of the East India Company's charter, viz: | | | |
| Silk bandannas and corahs, per piece of 7 handkerchiefs | | 1 | 9 |
| Cotton Madrasses and Ventapollams, per piece of 8 handkerchiefs | | 2 | 3 |
| Glass, per cwt | | 3 | 9 |
| Hams and tongues. (*Vide* Meats.) | | | |
| Lard, per cwt | | 3 | 0 |
| Lumber: | | | |
| Pitch pine, per 1,000 feet, superficial | | 11 | 6 |
| White pine, and all other kinds, per 1,000 feet, superficial | | 7 | 3 |
| Lime, building, per bushel | | 2 | 0 |

TABLE—Continued.

| Articles subject to duty. | Amount of duty. | | |
|---|---|---|---|
| | £ | s. | d. |
| Meats or tongues, dried, salted, or cured, per cwt | 0 | 3 | 9 |
| Nuts, cocoa, per 1,000 | | 15 | 0 |
| Oil: Of olives, per gallon | | | 9 |
| All other kinds, per gallon | | | 4 |
| Oats. (*Vide* Corn.) | | | |
| Pepper, per cwt | | 3 | 0 |
| Pearl barley, per cwt | | 3 | 0 |
| Pitch, per barrel | | 3 | 0 |
| Peas, Beans. (*Vide* Corn, unground.) | | | |
| Rice, per cwt | | 1 | 6 |
| Rosin, per barrel | | 3 | 0 |
| Salt, per barrel | | 1 | 0 |
| Sausages. (*Vide* Meats.) | | | |
| Soap, per cwt | | 3 | 0 |
| Starch, per lb | | | 2 |
| Sugar, refined, and sugar-candy, per cwt | | 6 | 0 |
| Shingles, viz: | | | |
| Over 16 inches, per 1,000 | | 4 | 6 |
| Under 16 inches, per 1,000 | | 2 | 4 |
| Spirits, viz: | | | |
| Brandy, per gallon | | 3 | 9 |
| Gin, per gallon | | 2 | 0 |
| Rum, per gallon | | 3 | 9 |
| Sweetened, per gallon | | 3 | 9 |
| All other kinds, per barrel | | 3 | 9 |
| Tar, per barrel | | 2 | 4 |
| Tea, per lb | | 1 | 6 |
| Tiles, of earthenware, and slates, per 1,000 | | 6 | 0 |
| Marble, per 1,000 | | 9 | 0 |
| Tobacco: | | | |
| Unmanufactured, per lb | | | 2 |
| Manufactured, per lb | | | 3 |
| Vermicelli and maccaroni, per lb | | | 2 |
| Vinegar, per gallon | | | 3 |
| Wines, viz: | | | |
| Madeira, sercial, tinta, port, and sherry, per gallon | | 2 | 6 |
| Teneriffe wine, per gallon | | | 4 |
| Other wines not enumerated, in bottles, per gallon | | 1 | 6 |
| Other wines, in wood, per gallon | | | 4 |
| Champagne, per gallon | | 4 | 6 |
| Goods not enumerated, (except those that are comprised or referred to in the subjoined table of exemptions,) for £100 of the value thereof | 7 | 10 | 0 |

*Table of exemptions.*

Provisions and stores of every description imported or supplied for the use of her Majesty's land and sea forces.
Mules, asses, neat cattle, and all other live stock.
Coin, bullion, and diamonds.
Specimens, illustrative of natural history.
Fresh meat, fresh fish.
Fruit and vegetables, fresh.
Ice.
Manures of all kinds.
Fire-bricks.
Coals.
Wood-hoops.
Truss-hoops.
White and red-oak staves and heading.
All other kinds of staves and heading.
Machinery for agricultural purposes.
Printed books.
Ploughs.
Harrows.
Top-cutters.
Sugar-boilers.
Stills.
Worms.
Furnaces.
Carts.
Wains.
Trucks and carriages for agricultural purposes.
Brass and iron work for agricultural purposes.
Iron, pewter, and lead pipes for agricultural purposes.
Iron, for railing, &c.
Tramways.
Implements and utensils used in the manufacture of sugar, rum, molasses, coffee, and cocoa.

There are no duties leviable on *exports*.

## GRENADA.

[According to return made to British House of Commons, in 1850.]

*Table of import duties, under act number 438, of 16th March, 1849. (This act is not limited in its duration.)*

| Articles subject to duty. | Amount of duty. £ | s. | d. |
|---|---|---|---|
| Ale, porter, beer, cider and perry, per hogshead | 0 | 6 | 0 |
| Ale, ditto, per dozen quart bottles | | | 3 |
| Asses, per head | | 5 | 0 |
| Beef and pork, salted or cured, per barrel, 200 lbs | | 8 | 0 |
| Bread and biscuit, per 100 lbs | | 1 | 0 |
| Bricks and paving tiles, per 1,000 | | 5 | 0 |
| Butter, per 100 lbs | | 8 | 0 |
| Candles, wax, sperm, or composition, per 100 lbs | | 8 | 0 |
| Tallow, per 100 lbs | | 5 | 0 |
| Cattle, neat, per head | | 10 | 0 |
| Cheese, per 100 lbs | | 10 | 0 |
| Cigars, per 1,000 | | 8 | 0 |
| Cocoa, per 100 lbs | | 3 | 0 |
| Coffee, per 100 lbs | | 6 | 0 |
| Flour, wheaten, per barrel, 196 lbs | | 4 | 0 |
| Fish, dry or salted, per quintal | | 1 | 0 |
| Pickled, per barrel, 200 lbs | | 2 | 0 |
| Hams, bacon, dried beef, or tongues, per 100 lbs | | 5 | 0 |
| Horses, per head | 1 | 0 | 0 |
| Lard, per 100 lbs | | 4 | 0 |
| Meal, and other flour, not wheaten, per barrel, 196 lbs. | | 2 | 0 |
| Mules, per head | | 10 | 0 |
| Oil, olive, per gallon | | | 8 |
| Peas, beans, barley, calavances, Indian corn, per bushel. | | | 3 |
| Puncheon and hogshead packs, with heading | | | 6 |
| Do. do. without heading | | | 4 |
| Rice, per 100 lbs | | 2 | 0 |
| Soap, per 100 lbs | | 1 | 0 |
| Shingles, cypress or wallaba, per 1,000 | | 4 | 0 |
| cedar or white pine do. | | 2 | 0 |
| Staves, white oak, and heading | | 7 | 6 |
| red oak, and others | | 5 | 0 |
| Spirits and cordials, per gallon | | 3 | 0 |
| Sugar, refined, per 100 lbs | | 12 | 0 |
| Muscovado, do. | | 8 | 0 |
| Tea, per lb | | | 4 |
| Tiles and slates, per 1,000 | | 6 | 0 |
| Tobacco, leaf, per 100 lbs., including snuff | | 12 | 0 |
| Wines, bottled or not, ad valorem | 20 per cent. | | |

TABLE—Continued.

| Articles subject to duty. | Amount of duty. | | |
|---|---|---|---|
| | £ | s. | d. |
| Wood, white, spruce, or yellow pine, per 1,000 feet | 0 | 5 | 0 |
| other descriptions, per 1,000 feet | | 7 | 6 |
| hoops, per 1,000 | | 5 | 0 |
| And after the above rates for any greater or less quantity of every such articles. | | | |
| Articles of any sort, not above specifically mentioned, not exempted from duty under this act, 5 per cent. ad valorem. | | | |

ST. LUCIA.

*A tariff of duties levied on articles imported into this colony for the year* 1850, *(according to returns made to the British House of Commons, in* 1851.)

| Articles subject to duty. | Amount of duty. | | |
|---|---|---|---|
| | £ | s. | d. |
| Ale, beer, cider, and perry, per gallon | 0 | 0 | 1 |
| Do........do......do... per dozen | | | 4 |
| Asses, per head | | 5 | 0 |
| Beef and pork, per barrel | | 8 | 0 |
| Bread and biscuit, per barrel | | 1 | 0 |
| Bricks, per thousand | | 3 | 0 |
| Butter, per pound | | | ½ |
| Casks, empty, each | | | 6 |
| Candles: | | | |
| Sperm, wax, or composition, per pound | | | 1 |
| Tallow, per pound | | | ½ |
| Cattle, neat, per head | | 10 | 0 |
| Champagne, per dozen | | 8 | 0 |
| Cheese, per pound | | | 1 |
| China, porcelain images, musical instruments | 20 per cent. | | |
| Coals, per ton | | | 6 |
| Chairs: | | | |
| First quality, per dozen | | 12 | 0 |
| Second quality, per dozen | | 6 | 0 |
| Flour, per barrel | | 3 | 0 |
| Fish: | | | |
| Dry and salted—cod 1*s*., scale 9*d*., per quintal. | | | |
| Pickled, (except salmon,) per barrel | | 2 | 0 |

TABLE—Continued.

| Articles subject to duty. | Amount of duty. | | |
|---|---|---|---|
| | £ | s. | d. |
| Salmon, per barrel | 0 | 6 | 0 |
| Herrings, smoked, per box of 10 pounds | | | 3 |
| Glass | 10 per cent. | | |
| Grindstone, per inch diameter | | | ¼ |
| Horses, each | 1 | 0 | 0 |
| Hams, bacon, dried beef, dried and pickled tongues, and sausages, per pound | | | ¾ |
| Lard, per pound | | | ½ |
| Liqueurs, per dozen | | | 6 |
| Lime: | | | |
| Building, per hhd | | 1 | 0 |
| Temper, per jar | | | 6 |
| Locust, mahogany, and other hard wood, per cubic foot | | | 1 |
| Meal, and other flour, not wheaten, per barrel | | 1 | 0 |
| Mules, each | | 5 | 0 |
| Oil: | | | |
| Produce of creatures living in the sea, per gallon | | | 3 |
| Linseed or cocoanut, per gallon | | | 4 |
| Olive, per dozen | | 1 | 6 |
| In paubans, per dozen | | | 6 |
| Pepper, black, per pound | | | 1 |
| Pickles of all sorts, per dozen | | 1 | 6 |
| Pitch, tar, and rosin, per barrel | | 1 | 0 |
| Preserved fruits, per lb | | | 2 |
| Peas, beans, calavances, per bushel | | | 3 |
| Barley, oats, and corn, per bushel | | | 3 |
| Raisins and other dried fruits, per lb | | | 1 |
| Rice, per cwt | | 1 | 6 |
| Rum and other spirits, (as may be fixed by the annual tax ordinance,) per gallon. | | | |
| Slates, per thousand | | 6 | 0 |
| Salt, per barrel | | 1 | 0 |
| Sago, tapioca, arrowroot, per pound. | | | |
| Sheep and goats, per head | | 1 | 0 |
| Silk manufactures, (articles merely lined or covered with silk not to come under this head,) | 10 per cent. | | |
| Swine, per head | | 4 | 0 |
| Stones or flags for paving squares, per square foot | | | 1 |
| Soap, per cwt | | 1 | 0 |
| Sugar, refined, per cwt | | 4 | 8 |
| Turpentine, spirits, per gallon | | | 6 |
| Do......do..per barrel | | 2 | 0 |
| Tea, per pound | | | 6 |
| Tiles, per thousand | | 6 | 0 |

TABLE—Continued.

| Articles subject to duty. | Amount of duty. | | |
|---|---|---|---|
| | £ | s. | d. |
| Tobacco: | | | |
| Cigars, per thousand | 0 | 4 | 0 |
| Boutes, per thousand | | 2 | 0 |
| Snuff, per pound | | | 4 |
| Ditto, manufactured and not enumerated, per pound | | | 4 |
| Ditto, unmanufactured, per pound | | | 2 |
| Tallow and mill grease, per pound | | | ¼ |
| Vermicelli and maccaroni, per pound | | | 2 |
| Vinegar, per gallon | | | 3 |
| On all wines, 10 per cent. ad valorem. | | | |
| Wood: | | | |
| Pitch pine, per thousand feet | | 8 | 0 |
| White pine, and all others, per thousand feet | | 5 | 0 |
| Hoops, per thousand | | 3 | 0 |
| Ditto, truss, per set | | 1 | 0 |
| Wallaba and cypress shingles, per thousand | | 3 | 0 |
| Cedar and Boston chips, per thousand | | 1 | 0 |
| Masts and spars, per inch in the average diameter | | | 2 |
| Staves, red and white oak, shooks, and others, per thousand | | 6 | 0 |
| All other articles not enumerated, 3 per cent. | | | |
| Exemptions from the foregoing: | | | |
| Coin, bullion, diamonds, fresh fruits and vegetables, hay and straw, printed books, ice, fresh fish, fresh meats and poultry; and also all agricultural and manufacturing machinery, manure, military clothing and accoutrements imported from the United Kingdom, under authority of her Majesty's treasury, for the use of her Majesty's troops, and all uniforms directed to be worn by the superior civil officers of her Majesty's colonies, by the regulations of the colonial service, and all building materials and supplies imported *bona fide* for the use of her Majesty's army and navy, and actually applied to such uses. | | | |

*Statement of duties levied on articles exported from this colony, for* 1850.

| Articles subject to duty. | Amount of duty. | | |
|---|---|---|---|
| | £ | s. | d. |
| Charcoal, per barrel | 0 | 2 | 0 |
| Logwood, per ton | | 2 | 0 |
| Fire-wood, per cord | | 4 | 0 |
| Hides, each | | 1 | 0 |
| Coffee, per hundred pounds | | 1 | 0 |
| Cocoa, per hundred pounds | | | 9 |
| N. B.—The above duties are levied in virtue of an ordinance, of date 17th July, 1848, No. 5, entitled "An ordinance for the promotion of education and agricultural science," and are solely applied for educational purposes. | | | |

### TURK'S AND CAICOS ISLANDS.

[From despatch of the United States consul at Turk's Island, February 20, 1850.]

"I have to inform you that the tonnage duties on United States vessels trading with the Turk's and Caicos islands have ceased since the 1st of January, 1850, and that in lieu thereof, one cent per bushel export duty has been levied on salt shipped from the same.

"I also enclose herewith the tariff of duties levied on imports into these islands, which will remain in full force for five years from the 1st of January, 1850."

*Tariff of duties on imports into the presidency of the Turk's and Caicos islands.—(In force for five years from* 1st *January,* 1850.)

| | £ | s. | d. |
|---|---|---|---|
| Ale and porter, in quart bottles, per dozen | 0 | 0 | 6 |
| Beans, per bushel | | | 3 |
| Biscuit and bread, per cwt | | 1 | 6 |
| Brandy, per gallon | | 3 | 3 |
| Bulls, cows, and oxen, each | | 6 | 0 |
| Butter, per cwt | | 9 | 4 |
| Calves, each | | 2 | 0 |
| Candles, (tallow) per cwt | | 3 | 0 |
| Candles, sperm and wax, per cwt | | 12 | 0 |
| Candles, adamantine, or any composition of tallow and other substances other than wax or spermaceti, per cwt | | 6 | 3 |
| Cheese, per cwt | | 8 | 0 |
| Cider, in quart bottles, per dozen | | | 9 |
| Cigars, per M | | 10 | 0 |
| Cocoa, per cwt | | 1 | 0 |
| Chocolate, per cwt | | 6 | 0 |
| Coffee, per cwt | | 6 | 0 |
| Colts, each | 1 | 0 | 0 |
| Copper and composition, (new,) per cwt | | 8 | 0 |

| | £ | s. | d. |
|---|---|---|---|
| Copper and composition, (old,) ad valorem | 7 per cent. | | |
| Cordials, per gallon | | 5 | 0 |
| Cordage, (new,) per cwt. | | 4 | 0 |
| Corn and other grain not enumerated, per barrel | | | 2 |
| Cows, (see *Bulls*,) each | | 6 | 0 |
| Currants, raisins, figs, and prunes, per cwt. | | 8 | 0 |
| Fish, dried or salted, per cwt. | | 2 | 0 |
| Fish, pickled salmon, shad, mackerel, per barrel | | 5 | 0 |
| Fish, in kits, per cwt | | 4 | 0 |
| Fish not enumerated, per barrel | | 4 | 0 |
| Flour, wheat, per barrel | | 3 | 9 |
| Flour other than wheat, per barrel | | 1 | 6 |
| Geese and turkeys, per dozen | | 6 | 0 |
| Geldings and horses, each | 2 | 0 | 0 |
| Gin, per gallon | | 3 | 0 |
| Honey, (see *Syrup*,) per gallon | | | 2½ |
| Horses, mares and geldings, each | 2 | 0 | 0 |
| Hulks and materials of vessels, ad valorem | 15 per cent. | | |
| Iron, unmanufactured, per cwt | | 2 | 0 |
| Lambs, (see *Sheep*,) each | | 1 | 0 |
| Lard, per cwt | | 4 | 0 |
| Lumber, per M | | 6 | 0 |
| Meal, or flour, except wheat flour, per barrel | | 1 | 6 |
| Meat, salted or cured, per cwt | | 4 | 8 |
| Metallic ores, ad valorem | 9 per cent. | | |
| Molasses, per gallon | | | 2 |
| Nails, iron, per cwt. | | 3 | 0 |
| Nails, copper or composition, per cwt. | | 8 | 0 |
| Oakum, per cwt. | | 2 | 0 |
| Oxen, (see *Bulls*,) each | | 6 | 0 |
| Oil, olive and almond, per gallon | | 1 | 6 |
| Oil, sperm, per gallon | | 2 | 0 |
| Oil, lard, per gallon | | | 6 |
| Oil, all other, per gallon | | | 4 |
| Paints, in oil, per cwt. | | 4 | 0 |
| Peas, per bushel | | | 2 |
| Pitch, tar, rosin, and tupentine, per barrel | | 2 | 0 |
| Porter, (see *Ale*.) | | | |
| Poultry, other than geese and turkeys, per dozen | | 3 | 0 |
| Perfumery, ad valorem | 10 per cent. | | |
| Prunes, (see *Currants*,) per cwt. | | 8 | 0 |
| Raisins, (see *Currants*,) per cwt. | | 8 | 0 |
| Rice, per cwt | | 1 | 0 |
| Rope, mahoa or bale, per cwt. | | 2 | 0 |
| Rum, 24 degrees proof, per gallon (and one penny per gallon for every degree stronger.) | | 3 | 0 |
| Rum, of weaker proof, per gallon | | 2 | 6 |
| Sheep and lambs, each | | 1 | 0 |
| Shingles, (cypress,) per thousand | | 2 | 0 |
| Shingles other than cypress, per thousand | | 1 | 0 |

| | £ | s. | d. |
|---|---|---|---|
| Soap, per cwt | 0 | 3 | 0 |
| Spirits of wine, per gallon | | 4 | 0 |
| Spirits of turpentine, per gallon | | | 3 |
| Steel, per cwt | | 5 | 0 |
| Sugar, refined, per cwt | | 17 | 0 |
| Sugar, unrefined, per cwt | | 4 | 8 |
| Sugar, clayed, per cwt | | 7 | 0 |
| Swine, per cwt | | 4 | 8 |
| Syrup (cane) and honey, per gallon | | | 2½ |
| Tar, (see *Pitch.*) | | | |
| Tea, green, per lb | | | 7 |
| Tea, black, per lb | | | 3 |
| Tobacco, manufactured, other than cigars, per cwt | | 8 | 4 |
| Tobacco, unmanufactured, per cwt | | 4 | 2 |
| Turkeys, (see *Geese.*) | | | |
| Turpentine, (see *Pitch.*) | | | |
| Turtle, alive, per cwt | | 8 | 4 |
| Wines, when imported in bottles, commonly called whole bottles: | | | |
| Champagne, per dozen | | 5 | 0 |
| Barsac, Claret, Hock, Madeira, Port, Sherry, Sauterne, — The growth of the continent of Europe and the island of Madeira, per dozen | | 4 | 0 |
| The wines enumerated and specified above, when imported in wood, per gallon | | 1 | 6 |
| All other wines imported either in wood or bottles, per gallon | | 2 | 6 |
| Articles not enumerated in the above scale of duties, except such as are comprised in the table of exemptions set forth in this ordinance, shall pay a duty of £7 10*s.*—per cent. ad valorem | 7½ per ct. | | |

*Exemptions.*

Ale and porter, in wood.

Articles imported or supplied, out of a bonded warehouse, for the colonial service.

Articles, of every description, imported or supplied out of a bonded warehouse, for the use of the President.

Asses; bullion; carts and cart harness; cart-wheels, arms and boxes for cart-wheels; cedar and yellow wood; cider, in wood; coin; cotton-wool; diamonds; drugs; dye-woods and stuffs; flax and tow; fruits, (fresh) vegetables, and roots of all kinds; hemp; hay; ice; lead and zinc; lignumvitæ; mahogany; manures of all kinds; medicines; mules; oats; osnaburgs and baggings; printed books and pamphlets; provisions and stores of every description, imported or supplied from a bonded warehouse, for the use of her Majesty's land or sea forces; tallow and raw-hides; tannin; tortoise-shell; trees imported for planting; vegetables of all kinds.

## TOBAGO.

[According to the returns made to the British House of Commons, in 1851.]

*Tabular statement of duties levied on articles imported into this colony, under the act called the "tariff act," proclaimed 2d May,* 1850.

| Articles subject to duty. | Amount of duty. | | |
|---|---|---|---|
| | £ | *s.* | *d.* |
| Asses, each | 0 | 5 | 0 |
| Almonds, raisins, prunes, and currants, per cwt | | 8 | 0 |
| Beef and pork, per 200 lbs | | 6 | 0 |
| Bran, per bushel | | | 3 |
| Bread and biscuits— | | | |
| Navy, per cwt | | 2 | 0 |
| Other kinds, per barrel | | 2 | 0 |
| Bricks: | | | |
| Building, per 1,000 | | 3 | 0 |
| Fire, except for estates' use, per 1,000 | | 4 | 0 |
| Brandy, and other spirits, per imperial gallon | | 1 | 6 |
| Butter, per lb | | | 1 |
| Boats, per foot keel | | 1 | 6 |
| Candles, tallow, per lb | | | ¾ |
| composition, per lb | | | 1 |
| wax and sperm, per lb | | | 1½ |
| Cheese, per lb | | | 1 |
| Cigars, per 1,000 | | 10 | 0 |
| Corn, and grain of all kind, unground, per bushel | | | 3 |
| Cattle, neat, each | | 10 | 0 |
| Champagne, per dozen quarts | | 6 | 0 |
| China, porcelain images, clocks, and musical instruments, 20 per cent. ad valorem. | | | |
| Coals: | | | |
| Unless imported for estates' purposes, per hogshead | | 1 | 6 |
| Or, if landed in bulk, per ton | | 2 | 0 |
| Coffee and cocoa, per 100 lbs | | 3 | 0 |
| Chocolate, per 100 lbs | | 4 | 0 |
| Cordials, per dozen quarts | | 6 | 0 |
| Fish: | | | |
| Dried or salted, per quintal | | 1 | 0 |
| Smoked, unless salmon, per quintal | | 1 | 0 |
| Pickled, unless salmon, per barrel | | 1 | 8 |
| Flour: | | | |
| Wheat, per barrel of 196 lbs | | 3 | 6 |
| All other kinds, and meal, per barrel | | 1 | 6 |
| Furniture, 10 per cent. ad valorem. | | | |
| Fruits, preserved, per dozen quarts | | 1 | 6 |

TABLE—Continued.

| Articles subject to duty. | Amount of duty. | | |
|---|---|---|---|
| | £ | s. | d. |
| Glass, 15 per cent. ad valorem. | | | |
| Gunpowder: | | | |
| Sporting, per lb. | 0 | 0 | 2 |
| Blasting, per lb. | | | 1 |
| Horses, mares, geldings, colts, and foals, each | 1 | 0 | 0 |
| Hams, bacon, dried-beef, dried and pickled tongues, and sausages, per lb. | | | 1 |
| Hoops: | | | |
| Wood, per 1,000 | | 4 | 0 |
| Truss, per set | | 1 | 0 |
| Indigo, per lb. | | | 6 |
| Lard, per lb. | | | ½ |
| Lumber: | | | |
| White, yellow, and spruce, per 1,000 feet | | 6 | 0 |
| Pitch-pine, per 1,000 feet | | 8 | 0 |
| Lime, building, per hogshead | | 1 | 6 |
| Mahogany, locust, and other hard wood, per cubic foot | | | 3 |
| Malt liquor, perry and cider: | | | |
| In wood, per hogshead | | 5 | 0 |
| In bottles, per dozen quarts | | | 3 |
| Muskets, guns, and fowling-pieces, 15 per cent. ad valorem. | | | |
| Mules, each | | 10 | 0 |
| Marble squares, (12 inches,) per 1,000 | | 10 | 0 |
| Nuts, cocoa, per 1,000 | 1 | 0 | 0 |
| Oil: | | | |
| Produce of creatures living in the sea, unless spermaceti, per gallon | | | 2 |
| Linseed, or cocoanut, per gallon | | | 3 |
| Spermaceti, per gallon | | | 4 |
| Olive, per dozen quarts | | 1 | 0 |
| Olive, per dozen pints | | | 6 |
| Olive, per dozen flasks | | | 4 |
| Oats. (*Vide* Corn, unground.) | | | |
| Oars, per running foot | | | 1 |
| Pepper, per lb. | | | ½ |
| Pitch, tar, rosin, and turpentine, per barrel | | | 9 |
| Rice, per 100 lbs. | | 1 | 0 |
| Sheep, goats, and pigs, each | | 2 | 0 |
| Salmon: | | | |
| Pickled, per barrel | | 5 | 0 |
| Smoked, per 100 lbs. | | 8 | 4 |
| Slates, per 1,000 | | 6 | 0 |
| Salt, per barrel | | | 4 |
| Stones, or flags, for paving squares, per square foot | | | 1 |

TABLE—Continued.

| Articles subject to duty. | Amount of duty £ | s. | d. |
|---|---|---|---|
| Shooks, hogshead, rum and molasses puncheon, each | 1 | 0 | 3 |
| Staves: | | | |
| Red oak, per 1,000 pieces | | 6 | 0 |
| White oak and heading, per 1,000 pieces | | 8 | 0 |
| Spices, per lb. | | | 3 |
| Sugar: | | | |
| Refined, and sugar-candy, per cwt. | | 5 | 0 |
| Slave, per cwt. | | 12 | 0 |
| Muscovado, per cwt. | | 5 | 0 |
| Spars, per cubic foot | | | 2 |
| Shingles: | | | |
| Wallaba, per 1,000 | | 2 | 6 |
| Cypress, per 1,000 | | 2 | 6 |
| Cedar and white pine, per 1,000 | | 1 | 6 |
| Soap, per cwt. | | 1 | 6 |
| Silk manufactures, 20 per cent. ad valorem. | | | |
| Turpentine, spirits of, per gallon | | | 3 |
| Tea: | | | |
| Hyson, per lb. | | | 3 |
| Black, per lb. | | | 2 |
| Turkeys and geese, each | | | 1 |
| Tobacco: | | | |
| Unmanufactured, per lb. | | | 1 |
| Manufactured, except cigars, per lb. | | | 2 |
| Tiles: | | | |
| Pan and roofing, per 1,000. | | 2 | 6 |
| Paving, per 1,000 | | 5 | 0 |
| Vermicelli and maccaroni, per lb. | | | 2 |
| Vinegar, per gallon | | | 3 |
| Wines, as follows: | | | |
| Madeira, sercial, tinta, claret, port, and sherry, per gallon | | 1 | 6 |
| Teneriffe, per gallon | | | 6 |
| Other wines, not enumerated, in bottles, per gallon | | 1 | 0 |
| Other wines, in wood, per gallon | | | 4 |
| All other articles, not enumerated, 5 per cent. | | | |

*Schedule of duties imposed by the supply bill of 1849, on sugar, rum, and molasses, shipped from or sold in this island.*

| Articles subject to duty. | Amount of duty. | | |
|---|---|---|---|
| | £ | s. | d. |
| Sugar— | | | |
| On each hogshead | 0 | 7 | 0 |
| On each tierce | | 3 | 6 |
| On each half tierce | | 1 | 9 |
| On each barrel | | | 11 |
| Rum— | | | |
| On each puncheon | | 3 | 0 |
| On each hogshead | | 1 | 6 |
| On each quarter cask | | | 9 |
| Molasses— | | | |
| On each puncheon | | 1 | 8 |
| On each hogshead or cask | | | 10 |

[*Duties levied on articles exported from this colony—Nil.*]

## BARBADOES.

[According to returns made to the British House of Commons, in 1851.]

*Table of import duties.*

| Articles subject to duty. | Amount of duty. | | |
|---|---|---|---|
| | £ | s. | d. |
| Bacon, the cwt | 0 | 2 | 1 |
| Beef: for every barrel wet salted, weighing not more than 200 lbs | | 2 | 1 |
| Dried, the cwt | | 2 | 1 |
| Beer, viz: | | | |
| Malt liquors of all sorts, for every cask not exceeding 64 gallons | | 4 | 2 |
| For every dozen bottles | | | 3 |
| Bread: for every barrel of white bread or biscuits | | | 8 |
| For every cwt. of brown bread or biscuits | | | 6 |
| Bricks, for every 1,000 | | 2 | 1 |
| Butter, for every cwt. salted | | 4 | 2 |
| Barley, per bushel | | | 6 |

TABLE—Continued.

| Articles subject to duty. | Amount of duty. | | |
|---|---|---|---|
| | £ | s. | d. |
| Candles: for every cwt. of tallow candles | 0 | 4 | 2 |
| For every cwt. of wax, spermaceti, or other candles | | 8 | 4 |
| Cider: for every 100 gallons cider, or perry, in wood | | 4 | 2 |
| For every dozen bottles cider or perry | | | 3 |
| Coffee, per cwt | | 2 | 1 |
| Coals, the ton | | 2 | 1 |
| Cocoa, the cwt | | 1 | 4 |
| Cocoanuts, the 1,000 | | 2 | 1 |
| Corn—Indian, Guinea, or other description of corn, beans, calavances, or peas, per bushel | | | 3 |
| Cheese, per cwt | | 4 | 2 |
| Cattle, neat or horned, per head | | 8 | 4 |
| Cement, per cwt | | | 3 |
| Copper, per cwt | | 1 | 0 |
| Cordage, per cwt | | 1 | ½ |
| Canvass, per bolt of 43 yards | | | 6 |
| Fish: for every barrel of pickled fish, except salmon, the cwt | | | 6 |
| Dried or salted, except salmon, the cwt | | | 4 |
| For every box of smoked herrings | | | 2 |
| For every cwt. of dried or smoked salmon | | 1 | 6 |
| For every barrel of wet salted salmon, weighing not more than 200 lbs | | 2 | 1 |
| Flour: for every barrel of wheat flour, weighing not more than 196 lbs | | 1 | 6 |
| For every barrel of meal, or other flour, not weighing more than 196 lbs | | 1 | ½ |
| Gunpowder, blasting, the keg of 25 lbs | | 1 | 0 |
| Hams, the cwt | | 2 | 1 |
| Hoops, of wood, the 1,000 | | 2 | 1 |
| Ice, the ton | | 2 | 1 |
| Lard, the cwt | | 2 | 1 |
| Lead: sheet and pipe, the cwt | | | 3 |
| White, the cwt | | 1 | ½ |
| Lumber, viz: | | | |
| White pine, per 1,000 feet, one inch thich | | 2 | 1 |
| Pitch or yellow pine, per 1,000 feet, one inch and a quarter thick | | 2 | 1 |
| Shingles: cedar, the 1,000 | | 1 | ½ |
| Deal or juniper, the 1,000 | | 1 | 6 |
| Cypress, the 1,000 | | 2 | 0 |
| Staves: red oak, the 1,000 | | 2 | 1 |
| White oak, the 1,000 | | 2 | 1 |

TABLE—Continued.

| Articles subject to duty. | Amount of duty. | | |
|---|---|---|---|
| | £ | s. | d. |
| Staves: beech, ash, or any other description, the 1,000... | 0 | 2 | 1 |
| All other woods, not specified, one inch thick, the 1,000. | | 2 | 1 |
| Marble paving-squares, the foot superficial measure...... | | | 1 |
| Oil: cocoanut, the 100 gallons.......................... | | 4 | 2 |
| Common lamp or fish-oil, the 100 gallons............ | | 2 | 1 |
| Linseed, the 100 gallons........................... | | 4 | 2 |
| Paving-squares, not of marble, the 100 feet, superficial measurement.................................... | | 2 | 1 |
| Pork, wet salted, for every barrel not weighing more than 200 lbs....................................... | | 2 | 1 |
| Rice, the cwt........................................ | | | 6 |
| Soap, the cwt........................................ | | 1 | 0 |
| Sugar: refined, the cwt.............................. | | 4 | 2 |
| Crushed, or bastard sugar, the cwt................ | | 4 | 2 |
| Tiles, for covering houses, the 1,000................ | | 1 | 8 |
| Tallow, the cwt...................................... | | | 5 |
| Tea, per lb.......................................... | | | 2 |
| Tongues: dried, the cwt.............................. | | 2 | 1 |
| Wet salted, the cwt................................ | | 2 | 1 |
| Turpentine, the 100 gallons.......................... | | 4 | 2 |
| Zinc, the cwt........................................ | | | 8 |

And after these rates for any greater or less quantity of such goods respectively; and on all goods, wares, and merchandise, plantation supplies, clothing, and effects of every description not herein previously enumerated, at the rate of £3 for every £100 of the value thereof, except the following articles, which shall not be subject to duty under this act, viz: Spirits, wine, tobacco, cigars, bullion or coin, diamonds, fruit, vegetables, hay or straw, fuel, wood or charcoal; fresh fish, fresh meats, live or dead stock, horses, mules, sheep, manure, salt, blubber, heads or offals of fish, machinery used for agricultural purposes; printed or manuscript books or papers, military clothing, accoutrements or appointments exported from the United Kingdom, under the authority of her Majesty's treasury, for the use of her Majesty's forces; all building materials and supplies for the use of her Majesty's army and navy, and all articles of clothing, accoutrements, and appoint ments imported for the use of the militia, police force, and fire companies of this island, by the commissioners appointed under the militia, police, and fire company acts of this island.

*A list of duties levied on articles exported from the Island of Barbadoes.*

| Articles subject to duty. | Amount of duty. | | |
|---|---|---|---|
| | £ | s. | d. |
| For every cask of sugar, 42 inches truss, and upwards | 0 | 4 | 6 |
| For every cask of sugar, 40 inches, and under 42 inches | | 3 | 10½ |
| For every cask of sugar, 38 inches, and under 40 inches | | 3 | 2½ |
| For every cask of sugar, 36 inches, and under 38 inches | | 2 | 7 |
| For every cask of sugar, 34 inches, and under 36 inches | | 1 | 11 |
| For every cask of sugar, 32 inches, and under 34 inches | | 1 | 0 |
| For every barrel of sugar, and all other packages in proportion | | | 4 |
| For every cwt. net of ginger | | | 3¼ |
| For every cwt. net of aloes | | | 8 |
| For every cwt. net of arrowroot | | | ¾ |
| For every 100 gallons of molasses | | | 8 |

## ANTIGUA.

[According to returns made to the British House of Commons, in 1851.]

*Schedule of import duties levied under tariff act of 14th January, 1850.*

| Articles subject to duty. | Amount of duty. | | |
|---|---|---|---|
| | £ | s. | d. |
| Asses, per head | 0 | 4 | 2 |
| Ale, beer, perry, cider, and porter: | | | |
| Per dozen quart bottles | | | 9 |
| In bulk, per tun | 1 | 10 | 0 |
| Beef and pork, salted and cured, per barrel of 200 lbs | | 16 | 0 |
| Bread or biscuit, per cwt | | 2 | 6 |
| Bricks and tiles of all descriptions, per 1,000 | | 4 | 2 |
| Butter, per cwt | | 10 | 0 |
| Candles: | | | |
| Tallow, per lb | | | 1 |
| Other than tallow, per lb | | | 3 |
| Cheese, per cwt | | 8 | 0 |
| Cigars, per 1,000 | | 10 | 0 |
| Cattle, horned, per head | | 10 | 0 |
| Fish: | | | |
| Dried, per quintal | | 1 | 0 |
| Pickled, per barrel | | 2 | 0 |
| Flour, wheat, per barrel of 196 lbs | | 5 | 0 |
| Fruits, dried and preserved, per lb | | | 2 |

TABLE—Continued.

| Articles subject to duty. | Amount of duty. | | |
|---|---|---|---|
| | £ | s. | d. |
| Hams, bacon, dried beef, and tongues, pickled or dried, per cwt | 0 | 8 | 0 |
| Horses, mares, and geldings, per head | 1 | 10 | 0 |
| Lard, per cwt | | 5 | 0 |
| Mules, per head | 1 | 0 | 0 |
| Meal, or other flour, not wheat: | | | |
| Per puncheon | | 8 | 0 |
| Per barrel of 196 lbs | | 2 | 0 |
| Meal, oil-cake or linseed, per cwt | | 1 | 0 |
| Oil of all kinds, per gallon | | | 6 |
| Peas, beans, barley, calavances, oats, Indian corn, and all other grain or pulse, per bushel | | | 3 |
| Potatoes, not sweet, per barrel | | 1 | 0 |
| Rice, per cwt | | 2 | 0 |
| Sheep, goats, and swine, per head | | 1 | 0 |
| Soap, per lb | | | ½ |
| Spirits: | | | |
| Brandy, per imperial gallon | | 2 | 6 |
| Gin, and all other spirits not sweetened, per imperial gall. | | 2 | 0 |
| Sweetened, and all cordials and liqueurs, per imp. gall. | | 4 | 0 |
| Sugar, refined, in bond, in the United Kingdom, not being of the growth of any of the British possessions in America, or of the Mauritius, or of any of the British possessions within the limits of the East India Company's charter, per lb | | | 6 |
| Teas of all descriptions, per lb. | | | 4 |
| Tobacco, leaf, unmanufactured, per lb. | | | 2 |
| Tobacco, manufactured, per lb. | | | 4 |
| Wines, whether bottled or not, on each £100 value | 15 | 0 | 0 |
| Wood: | | | |
| Pitch pine, for every 1,000 feet by superficial measure of an inch thick | | 12 | 6 |
| White pine, per same measure | | 8 | 4 |
| Spruce, per same measure | | 8 | 4 |
| Shingles, cypress and wallaba, per 1,000 | | 6 | 3 |
| Shingles, cedar, pine, or spruce, per 1,000 | | 2 | 1 |
| Wood-hoops, per 1,200 | | 6 | 3 |
| Staves, per 1,000 | | 10 | 5 |
| Shooks, hogshead or puncheon, each | | | 9 |
| And after these rates for any greater or less quantity of such goods, respectively. | | | |
| Packages, viz: butts, hogsheads, puncheons, tierces, and trunks, on their invoice value, per value of £100 | 4 | 10 | 0 |
| All non-enumerated articles, per value of £100 | 4 | 10 | 0 |

*Table of exemptions.*

Personal baggage of passengers; bullion; books, not being foreign reprints of English copyrights; coin; fresh fish; fresh meat; fruit, not being dried or preserved; ice; maps and charts; machinery and apparatus for mills, steam-engines, and for the manufacture of sugar, rum, or other produce; green vegetables; poultry; plants and shrubs; seeds of all kinds, for planting; turtle; provisions and stores of every description, imported or supplied for the use of her Majesty's land and sea forces.

No export duty of any description.

## ST. CHRISTOPHER'S.

[According to returns made to the British House of Commons, in 1851.]

*Schedule showing the rates levied on each article imported into this island under act* 690.

| Articles subject to duty. | Amount of duty. | | |
|---|---|---|---|
| | £ | s. | d. |
| Asses, each | 0 | 4 | 2 |
| Beef, pork, and salted meats, 100 lbs | | 4 | 2 |
| Butter, pound | | | 1 |
| Beans and peas, bushel | | 1 | ½ |
| Bread and biscuit, barrel | | 1 | ½ |
| Cedar post, 100 | | 8 | 4 |
| Square cedar, 1,000 feet | | 12 | 6 |
| Corn and oats, bushel | | | 3 |
| Candles: | | | |
| Tallow, pound | | | ¾ |
| Other, pound | | | 1½ |
| Cattle, neat, each | | 4 | 2 |
| Cheese, 100 lbs | | 8 | 4 |
| Cigars, 1,000 | | 12 | 6 |
| Cocoa, 100 lbs | | 5 | 0 |
| Coffee, 100 lbs | | 5 | 0 |
| Currants, raisins, and figs, 100 lbs | | 8 | 4 |
| Flour: | | | |
| Wheat, barrel | | 4 | 2 |
| Not wheat, barrel | | 2 | 1 |
| Fish, pickled and dry, 100 lbs | | 1 | ½ |
| Hard wood and other wood, 1,000 feet | 1 | 13 | 4 |
| Hoops, wood, 1,200 | | 8 | 4 |
| Horses, each | 1 | 0 | 10 |

TABLE—Continued.

| Articles subject to duty. | Amount of duty. £ | s. | d. |
|---|---|---|---|
| Lumber: | | | |
| White pine, 1,000 feet | 0 | 8 | 4 |
| Pitch pine, 1,000 feet | | 12 | 6 |
| Lard, pound | | | ½ |
| Meal, barrel | | 2 | 1 |
| Mules, each | | 10 | 5 |
| Malt liquors, hogshead | | 8 | 4 |
| Malt liquors, dozen | | | 7 |
| Oil cake, 100 lbs. | | | 10 |
| Rice, 100 lbs. | | 1 | ½ |
| Shingles; | | | |
| Cypress, &c., 1,000 | | 4 | 2 |
| Cedar, 1000 | | 2 | 1 |
| Staves, 1,000 | | 8 | 4 |
| Shooks, bundle | | | 4 |
| Sugar: | | | |
| Refined, pound | | | 1 |
| Muscovado, 100 lbs. | | 5 | 0 |
| Snuff, 100 lbs. | | 6 | 0 |
| Soap, 100 lbs. | | 2 | 1 |
| Tobacco: | | | |
| Unmanufactured, 100 lbs. | | 6 | 0 |
| Manufactured, 100 lbs. | | 10 | 0 |
| Spirits and cordials, gallon | | 1 | 6 |
| Vinegar, gallon | | | 2 |
| Wines, 15 per cent. ad valorem. | | | |
| All other goods, 8 per cent. ad valorem. | | | |

*Schedule showing the rates of export tonnage paid by vessels taking produce from this island, levied by virtue of act* 515.

| Articles subject to duty. | Amount of duty. £ | s. | d. |
|---|---|---|---|
| On each hogshead of sugar | 0 | 2 | 0 |
| On each tierce of sugar | | 1 | 8¾ |
| On each barrel of sugar | | | 4 |
| On each puncheon of rum | | 1 | 6 |
| On each hogshead of rum | | | 9 |
| On each puncheon of molasses | | 1 | 6 |
| On each hogshead of molasses | | | 9 |

## NEVIS.

[According to returns compiled for the British House of Commons, in 1851.]

*Table of import duties.*

| Articles subject to duty. | Amount of duty. | | |
|---|---|---|---|
| | £ | s. | d. |
| Ale, beer, and porter, per gallon | 0 | 0 | 1½ |
| Beef, pork and hams, per cwt. | | 5 | 0 |
| Biscuit, per barrel | | 2 | 0 |
| Brandy, rum, Geneva and other spirits, per gallon | | 1 | 6 |
| Butter, per cwt. | | 5 | 0 |
| Candles— | | | |
| Sperm, wax, or composition, ad valorem | 10 per cent. | | |
| Tallow, ad valorem | 5 per cent. | | |
| Cattle, (horned,) and asses, each | | 4 | 2 |
| Cheese, per cwt. | | 5 | 0 |
| Cider, per gallon | | | 6 |
| Coffee, and cocoa, per cwt. | | 5 | 0 |
| Cordials, per gallon | | 1 | 6 |
| Corn and grain, unground, per bushel | | | 3 |
| Corn-meal and rye-meal, per barrel | | 2 | 0 |
| Fish— | | | |
| Pickled, per barrel | | 2 | 0 |
| Salted or dried, per quintal | | 1 | 0 |
| Flour, per barrel | | 4 | 0 |
| Hard wood, and all wood not enumerated, ad valorem | 10 per cent. | | |
| Horses— | | | |
| Under 12 hands in height, each | | 12 | 0 |
| Above 12 hands in height, each | 1 | 0 | 0 |
| Lard, per cwt. | | 4 | 0 |
| Lumber— | | | |
| White, yellow, and spruce pine, per 1,000 feet | | 8 | 0 |
| Pitch pine, per 1,000 feet | | 12 | 0 |
| Mules, each | | 12 | 0 |
| Packages of intrinsic value, containing goods, ad valorem | 4 per cent. | | |
| Peas and beans, per bushel | | | 6 |
| Raisins, prunes, and currants, per cwt. | | 8 | 0 |
| Rice, per cwt. | | 1 | 0 |
| Sheep, goats, and pigs, each | | 1 | 0 |
| Shingles— | | | |
| Cypress and wallaba, per 1,000 | | 6 | 0 |
| Pine, cedar, and Boston, per 1,000 | | 2 | 6 |
| Soap, per cwt. | | 2 | 0 |
| Staves, heading, and shooks, per 1,000 | | 10 | 0 |
| Sugar, refined, per cwt. | | 5 | 0 |

TABLE—Continued.

| Articles subject to duty. | Amount of duty. | | |
|---|---|---|---|
| | £ | s. | d. |
| Tea, per lb | 0 | 0 | 3 |
| Tobacco— | | | |
| Manufactured, ad valorem | 10 per cent. | | |
| Unmanufactured, per cwt. | | 5 | 0 |
| Wine, ad valorem | 10 per cent. | | |
| Wood-hoops, per 1,000 | | 5 | 0 |

*Table of exemptions.*

Coin, coals, bullion and diamonds; fresh fish; fresh fruit; fresh meat; hay; straw; manures of all kinds; salt; fresh vegetables; printed books and pamphlets; specimens illustrative of natural history; goods, wares, and merchandise imported for the use of her Majesty's land or sea forces, or for the public uses of this island; seeds and trees imported for planting.

By section VI. Upon all goods, wares and merchandise which shall be imported or brought into this island, other than those specified in the two preceding tables, there is charged a duty of four per cent. ad valorem on the price which they shall have cost at the place from whence they were last exported.

Also, by authority of an act (No. 448) of this island, passed on the 12th of February, 1850, and to be in force for two years from that date, there is charged an additional duty of two per cent. ad valorem on all goods which are not specified in the "table of exemptions."

*Export duty.*—(Act No. 448.)

| | £ | s. | d. |
|---|---|---|---|
| Upon every hogshead of sugar | 0 | 6 | 0 |
| Upon every puncheon of rum | | 2 | 6 |
| Upon every puncheon of molasses | | 1 | 3 |

And upon all other packages of the same articles, in proportion.

VIRGIN ISLANDS.

*Import duties under the imperial act* 8 & 9 *Vict.*, *c.* 93, *October* 1, 1851.

| Articles subject to duty. | Amount of duty. | | |
|---|---|---|---|
| | £ | s. | d. |
| Wheat flour, the barrel, 196 lbs | 0 | 2 | 0 |
| Fish of foreign taking or curing, dried or salted, the cwt | | 2 | 0 |
| Fish of foreign taking or curing, pickled, the barrel | | 4 | 0 |
| Meat, salted or cured, per cwt | | 3 | 0 |
| Butter, the cwt | | 8 | 0 |
| Cheese, the cwt | | 5 | 0 |
| Coffee, the cwt | | 5 | 0 |
| Cocoa, the cwt | | 1 | 0 |
| Molasses, the cwt | | 3 | 0 |
| Sugar, unrefined | | 5 | 0 |
| Refined sugar, the produce of, and refined in, foreign countries, ad valorem | 20 per cent. | | |
| Tea, unless imported direct from China, or unless imported from the United Kingdom or from any of the British possessions, per lb | | | 1 |
| Rum, per gallon | | | 6 |
| Other spirits and cordials | | 1 | 0 |
| Silk manufactures and spermaceti, ad valorem | 15 per cent. | | |
| Wine, whether bottled or not ... do | 7 per cent. | | |
| Cotton manufactures ... do | do. | | |
| Linen manufactures ... do | do. | | |
| Woolen manufactures ... do | do. | | |
| Leather manufactures ... do | do. | | |
| Paper manufactures ... do | do. | | |
| Hardware, clocks and watches, manufactured tobacco, soap, candles (other than spermaceti,) corks, cordage, and oakum, ad valorem | do. | | |
| Oil, blubber, fins, and skins, the produce of fish and creatures living in the sea, of foreign fishing, ad val. | 15 per cent. | | |
| Articles not enumerated, except such as are comprised or referred to in the subjoined table of exemptions | 4 per cent. | | |

And if any of the goods hereinbefore charged with duty, except sugar, shall be imported through the United Kingdom, (having been warehoused therein, and being exported from the warehouse, or the duties thereon, if there paid, having been drawn back,) such goods shall only be charged with three-fourths of the duties hereinbefore imposed. Sugar refined, in bond, in the United Kingdom, not being the produce of any of the British possessions in America, or of the Mauritius, or of any of the British possessions within the limits of the East India Company's charter, 10 per cent. ad valorem.

*Table of exemptions.*

Coin, bullion, and diamonds; horses, mules, asses, neat cattle, and all other live stock; hay and straw; tallow and raw hides; salt, rice, corn, and grain, unground; biscuit or bread; meal, or flour, except wheat flour; fresh meat; fresh fish; fruit and vegetables, fresh; carriages of travellers; wood and lumber; cotton, wool, hemp, flax, and tow; drugs; gums and resins; tortoise-shell; manure of all kinds; specimens illustrative of natural history; herrings taken and cured by the inhabitants of the Isle of Man, and imported from thence; tea imported direct from China, or from the United Kingdom, or from any British possession; provisions and stores of every description imported or supplied for the use of her Majesty's land or sea forces. All goods imported from the United Kingdom after having there paid the duties of consumption, and imported from thence without drawback; and also such of the following articles as shall be imported for the use of the British fisheries in America into any place at or from whence any such fishery is carried on: salted or cured meats, flour, butter, cheese, molasses, cord-wood, cordage, oakum, pitch, tar, turpentine, leather and leather-ware, fishermen's clothing and hosiery, fishing-craft utensils, implements, and bait.

*Duties under the colonial import duty act, passed December 5,* 1850.

| Articles subject to duty. | Amount of duty. | | |
|---|---|---|---|
| | £ | s. | d. |
| Wheat-flour, the barrel | 0 | 1 | 0 |
| Other flour than wheat flour, the barrel | | 1 | 6 |
| Corn-meal, the barrel | | 1 | 6 |
| Meat or tongues, dried, salted, or cured, per cwt | | 1 | 0 |
| Butter, per cwt | | 2 | 0 |
| Candles, tallow, per cwt | | 3 | 0 |
| Candles, all other kinds, per lb | | | 2 |
| Soap, per cwt | | 2 | 0 |

Upon all goods not enumerated in the foregoing schedule, a duty at and after the rate of five per cent. ad valorem.

*Table of exemptions.*

Goods, the property of her Majesty's government, imported or supplied for the use of her Majesty's land and sea forces; fruits and vegetables; fresh meat, and fish, fresh; poultry of all kinds; coin and bullion; manure; ice, and drugs.

BRITISH GUIANA.

*Tabular statement of the duties levied on articles imported into the colony of British Guiana. (Compiled from returns made in 1851 for the British House of Commons.)*

| Articles subject to duty. | Amount of duty. |
|---|---|
| Bread, pilot, navy biscuit, and crackers, and all other kinds, per 100 pounds, English | $0 50 |
| Beef, pickled, per barrel of 200 pounds, English | 2 75 |
| dried or smoked, per pound, English | 2 |
| Bacon, per pound, English | 2 |
| Butter, per pound, English | 3 |
| Corn; grains of every kind and description; beans, peas, and pulse of every kind and description, whether whole or split, per bushel, English | 15 |
| Corn-meal and oat-meal, per 100 pounds, English | 50 |
| Candles, tallow, per pound, English | ½ |
| spermaceti, wax, adamantine, hydraulic press, or any kind of composition other than simple tallow, per pound, English | 5 |
| Cigars, per 1,000 | 2 00 |
| Cocoa, per pound, English | 1 |
| Chocolate, per pound, English | 4 |
| Coffee, per cwt | 2 50 |
| Clapboards, per 1,000 | 1 50 |
| Cheese, per pound, English | 1½ |
| Cattle, say, bulls per head | 4 00 |
| oxen, per head | 1 50 |
| Flour, wheat, per barrel of 196 pounds | 1 75 |
| rye, per barrel of 196 pounds | 50 |
| Fish, dried, per 112 pounds, English | 50 |
| pickled, say, salmon per barrel of 200 pounds, English | 2 00 |
| mackerel, per barrel of 200 pounds, English | 1 00 |
| and all other sorts, per barrel of 200 pounds, English | 75 |
| smoked, per pound, English | 2 |
| Hams, and all other dried or smoked meats, per pound, English | 2 |
| Horses, per head | 7 00 |
| Lard, per pound, English | 1 |
| *Lumber of all kinds, per 1,000 feet, board measure | 2 00 |
| Liquors, spirituous, liqueurs, bitters and cordials, proof 24 or weaker, per gallon | 1 00 |

* Spruce and white lumber subject to a deduction of 5 per cent. for splits.

TABLE—Continued.

| Articles subject to duty. | Amount of duty. |
|---|---|
| Liquors, for every degree of proof stronger than 24 of every gallon of spirituous liquors, liqueurs, bitters, and cordials, in addition to the duty of $1 per gallon | $0 05 |
| Malt, in wood, per hogshead | 1 50 |
| in bottles, each bottle containing not more than a quart, per dozen | 8 |
| in bottles, each bottle containing not more than a pint, per dozen | 4 |
| Matches, for every gross boxes of, each box not to contain more than 100 matches; or if imported in any other kind of packages than boxes, then for every 14,000 matches | 50 |
| Mules, per head | 5 00 |
| Molasses, per gallon | 7½ |
| Oats, per bushel | 5 |
| Oil, spermaceti, per gallon | 25 |
| other descriptions, per gallon | 12½ |
| Pork, pickled, per barrel of 200 pounds, English | 2 75 |
| Pepper, per pound | 5 |
| Pitch, per barrel | 50 |
| Potatoes, per bushel of 64 pounds, English | 8 |
| Plantains, per bunch | 10 |
| Rice, per 100 pounds, English | 50 |
| Rosin, per barrel | 50 |
| Soap, per pound, English | 1¼ |
| Sugar, per cwt | 4 00 |
| Staves and heading, white-oak, per 1,000 | 2 00 |
| Staves of every other description, per 1,000 | 1 50 |
| Shingles of all kinds, per 1,000 | 50 |
| Sago, per pound, English | 5 |
| *Tobacco, in packages not less than 800 pounds, per pound English | 10 |
| in packages less than 800 pounds, manufactured or otherwise, per pound, English | 15 |
| Tea, per pound, English | 15 |
| Turpentine, crude, per barrel | 50 |
| spirits, per gallon | 15 |
| Tongues, pickled, dried, or smoked, per pound, English | 2 |
| Tapioca, per pound, English | 5 |
| Tar, per barrel | 50 |
| Wine, bottled, of all descriptions, per dozen quarts | 1 00 |
| bottled, of all descriptions, per dozen pints | 50 |
| in wood of all kinds, per gallon | 45 |

* Duty on tobacco to be paid on certificate of weight by weighmaster.

## FALKLAND ISLANDS.

No import duties are levied in this colony.

## GIBRALTAR.

[According to a return made to the British House of Commons, August 8, 1851.]

*Duties levied on articles imported into Gibraltar under the order in council of 23d June, 1841. (Period of duration not limited.)*

No spirits, strong waters, or cordials, of a greater strength than 9 in 100 over-proof by Sykes's hydrometer, can be admitted for consumption within the garrison or territory of Gibraltar, *save* and except rums and spirits the produce of Great Britain, British colonies, or plantations.

A quantity not exceeding the proportion of seven gallons of spirits to one pipe of wine is allowed, free of duty, to be infused into a pipe of wine, under certain regulations.

Of all wines, spirits, strong waters, cordials, and other liquids in casks, landed at Gibraltar, whether in bottles or otherwise, if the full contents of the cask shall gauge to exceed ten gallons:

| | £ | *s.* | *d.* |
|---|---|---|---|
| For every botassa | 0 | 2 | 2 |
| For every pipe, or butt, or puncheon | | 1 | 10 |
| For every hogshead | | | 11 |
| For every tierce | | | 7¼ |
| For every quarter cask | | | 5½ |
| For every cask less than a quarter cask, being liable to the wharfage toll | | | 3 |
| On all tobacco landed at Gibraltar, being in hogsheads or in kegs, as commonly imported from the United States of America, or being in rolls, as commonly imported from the Brazils: | | | |
| For every hogshead | | 1 | 10 |
| For every keg or roll not exceeding 1¼ cwt | | | 2 |
| For every keg weighing more than 1¼ cwt., but not exceeding 2 cwt | | | 3 |
| For every roll weighing more than 1¼ cwt., but not exceeding 5 cwt | | | 7 |
| Kegs exceeding 2 cwt. and rolls exceeding 5 cwt., to pay wharfage each as half a hogshead; and in case of dispute as to weight, the tobacco is to be weighed at the expense of the merchant. | | | |

### *Duty on wines.*

| | | | |
|---|---|---|---|
| On all wines consumed in taverns, wine-houses, retail wine and spirit stores, eating-houses, and canteens, per gallon | | | 5 |

| | £ | s. | d. |
|---|---|---|---|
| Duty on spirits, strong waters, or cordials admitted for consumption in the garrison: | | | |
| For every gallon, being of the strength of proof by Sykes's hydrometer, and so in proportion for any greater strength than the strength of proof, and for any greater quantity than a gallon | 0 | 4 | 0 |

MALTA.

[According to a return made to the British House of Commons, August 8, 1851.]

*Table showing the amount of duties levied on articles imported into Malta under local ordinances* 5 *and* 6, *of* 1846. *(Period of duration not limited.)*

| | £ | s. | d. |
|---|---|---|---|
| Beer, per Maltese barrel | 0 | 2 | 0 |
| Cattle: | | | |
| Bullocks, and other animals of the kind, per head | | 10 | 0 |
| Horses and mules, per head | 1 | 0 | 0 |
| Grain: | | | |
| Wheat, per salm | | 10 | 0 |
| Indian corn, per salm | | 6 | 0 |
| Barley, per salm | | 4 | 0 |
| Saggina, per salm | | 3 | 0 |
| Other inferior grain, per salm | | 5 | 0 |
| Manufactured grain, per cantar | | 6 | 0 |
| Wheat, Indian corn, barley, or other inferior grains, if damaged so as to be unfit for the food of man, commonly called frumentazzo, per salm | | 2 | 0 |
| Manufactured grain, if damaged so as to be unfit for the food of man, per cantar | | 2 | 0 |
| Oil, olive, per caffiso | | | 6 |
| Potatoes, per cantar | | | 10 |
| Pulse and seeds: | | | |
| Beans, calavances, chick-peas, kidney-beans, lentils, lupins, peas, and vetches, per salm | | 2 | 0 |
| Carob beans, and cotton-seed, per cantar | | | 6 |
| Spirits, viz: For every Maltese barrel of such spirits of any strength not exceeding the strength of proof by Sykes's hydrometer, (namely, London proof,) and so in proportion for any greater strength than the strength of proof | 1 | 2 | 0 |
| Vinegar, per Maltese barrel | | 2 | 0 |
| Wines, the value of which shall exceed £15 per pipe of 11 Maltese barrels, per Maltese barrel | | 11 | 0 |
| All other wines, per Maltese barrel | | 2 | 0 |

*Observations.*

1. The duties payable by the salm on grain, pulse, and seed, (except large Sicilian beans,) to be charged by the strike measure; the duties on large Sicilian beans to be charged by the heap measure.

2. Every liquid, compounded of spirit and any other ingredient or ingredients, and containing more than 25 per cent. of spirits of the strength of proof, to be liable to the duty on spirits which is imposed by the present tariff.

*Store-rent on articles lodged in bond.*

| | £ | s. | d. |
|---|---|---|---|
| On beer, per Maltese barrel | 0 | 0 | 1 |
| On oil, olive, per caffiso | | | 1 |
| On other articles above enumerated, (cattle excepted) | | | 2 |

CEYLON.

*Duties on imports: compiled from returns made in* 1851 *for the British House of Commons.*

| | £ | s. | d. |
|---|---|---|---|
| Ale, porter, and all other malt liquors, per imperial gallon | 0 | 0 | 3 |
| Cigars, per thousand | | 5 | 0 |
| Fish, dried or salted, and fins and skins, the produce of creatures living in the sea, per cwt. | | 1 | 6 |
| Guns and rifles, each | | 5 | 0 |
| Gunpowder, per pound | | | 4 |
| Opium, per pound | | 2 | 0 |
| Paddy, per bushel | | | 3 |
| Pistols, per pair | | 5 | 0 |
| Rice, per bushel | | | 7 |
| Spirits and cordials, per imperial gallon | | 5 | 0 |
| Sugar, unrefined, per cwt. | | 2 | 6 |
| refined, or candy, per cwt. | | 5 | 0 |
| Tea, per pound | | | 6 |
| Tobacco, unmanufactured, per cwt. | | 10 | 0 |
| manufactured, other than cigars, per cwt. | 1 | 0 | 0 |
| Snuff, per pound | | 1 | 6 |
| Wheat, grain, peas, beans, and other grain, (except paddy,) per bushel | | | 7 |
| Wine, in bottles, per imperial gallon | | 2 | 6 |
| not in bottles ........do | | 1 | 6 |
| Goods, wares, and merchandise not otherwise charged with duty or prohibited, and not comprised in the table of exemptions hereinafter set forth, for every £100 of the value thereof in this market | 5 | 0 | 0 |

*Table of exemptions.*

|  |  |
|---|---|
| Books and maps, printed | Free. |
| Bullion, coin, pearls, and precious stones | Free. |
| Coal and coke | Free. |
| Copperah | Free. |
| Garden seeds and plants | Free. |
| Horses, mules, asses, and all other live-stock | Free. |
| Ice | Free. |
| Manures | Free. |
| Regimental accoutrements | Free. |
| Specimens of natural history | Free. |

*Export duties.*

|  |  |
|---|---|
| Cinnamon, per pound | 4*d.* |
| All other articles | Free. |

*Prohibitions and restrictions inward.*

Arms, ammunition, and utensils of war, by way of merchandise, except by license of her Majesty for furnishing her Majesty's public stores only, or under special authority of the governor.

Cinnamon, cinnamon oil, cassia, or cassia buds.

Coin, viz:

False money, or counterfeit sterling;

Silver of the realm, or any money purporting to be such, not being of the established standard in weight or fineness.

Gunpowder, except by license from her Majesty, such license to be granted for the furnishing her Majesty's public stores, or under special authority of the governor.

Salt, except by license under authority of the governor.

Coffee, foreign sugar, and rum, or rum-shrub, except to be warehoused for exportation.

*Port duties.*

| | £ | *s.* | *d.* |
|---|---|---|---|
| Entry inward with cargo, per ton | 0 | 0 | 2 |
| Entry inward in ballast | | Free. | |
| Clearance outward with cargo, per ton | | | 2 |
| Clearance outward in ballast | | Free. | |
| And in no case to exceed | 5 | 0 | 0 |

## BENGAL.

[With a despatch of the United States consul at Calcutta, January 2, 1852.]

"BENGAL, *December* 12, 1849.

"Notice is hereby given that the honorable the deputy governor of Bengal, under the authority conferred on him by section 3d, act 16, of 1837, has this day approved and established the following revised table of fixed valuations for the articles therein mentioned of import and export, and that the said respective values shall, from the 1st of February next, be the valuations of the said articles for assessment of customs duty thereon, at the ports of this presidency, until other notice.

"By order of the honorable the deputy governor of Bengal."

*Import tariff.*

| Names of goods. | Rate of valuation. | | |
|---|---|---|---|
| Akurburra or pellitory, per md | 25 | 0 | 0 |
| Ale, beer, and porter, Bass and Allsop's, per hhd | 50 | 0 | 0 |
| Do. Saunders's, Hodgson's, and Worthington's, per hhd | 40 | 0 | 0 |
| Ale, beer, and porter, other marks, per hhd | 30 | 0 | 0 |
| Do. in quart bottles, per dozen | 4 | 0 | 0 |
| Aloes, per md | 9 | 0 | 0 |
| Almonds, per md | 8 | 0 | 0 |
| Aloe-wood, per seer | 3 | 0 | 0 |
| Alum, per md | 2 | 0 | 0 |
| Ambergris, per sa. wt | 5 | 0 | 0 |
| Anise-seed, star, per md | 16 | 0 | 0 |
| Antimony, per md | 13 | 0 | 0 |
| Arsenic, white, per md | 16 | 0 | 0 |
| yellow, per md | 14 | 0 | 0 |
| Gulf and Red Sea, of sorts, per md | 30 | 0 | 0 |
| red, per md | 18 | 0 | 0 |
| orpiment, per seer | 1 | 0 | 0 |
| orpiment, from China, per md | 18 | 0 | 0 |
| Assafœtida, (Hing,) per md | 60 | 0 | 0 |
| (Hingra,) per md | 9 | 0 | 0 |
| Animal charcoal, per md | 5 | 8 | 0 |
| Beads, common, per lb | | 4 | 0 |
| seed, per lb | | 12 | 0 |
| red, per lb | | 14 | 0 |
| small scarlet and red, per lb | 1 | 0 | 0 |
| glass, white and colored, per 1,000 beads | | 14 | 0 |
| China, per box | 50 | 0 | 0 |
| Bdellium, per md | 6 | 0 | 0 |
| Bedannah or quince seed, per md | 28 | 0 | 0 |

TABLE—Continued.

| Names of goods. | Rate of valuation. | | |
|---|---|---|---|
| Betelnut, per md | 3 | 0 | 0 |
| Blacking, quarts, per dozen | 3 | 0 | 0 |
| Bottles, wine, quarts, British, per 100 | 8 | 0 | 0 |
| pints, British, per 100 | 6 | 8 | 0 |
| pints, foreign, per 100 | 3 | 8 | 0 |
| soda-water, glass, per 100 | 5 | 0 | 0 |
| soda-water, stone, per 100 | 2 | 0 | 0 |
| Brimstone, stick, roll, and prepared, per md | 3 | 10 | 0 |
| crude, per md | 2 | 0 | 0 |
| medicinal, per md | 25 | 0 | 0 |
| Bugloss, per md | 8 | 0 | 0 |
| Cider and perry, quarts, per dozen | 5 | 0 | 0 |
| Camphor, per md | 18 | 0 | 0 |
| refined, per md | 50 | 0 | 0 |
| Candles, wax, spermaceti, and composition, per lb | | 9 | 6 |
| wax, eastward, per md | 36 | 0 | 0 |
| Canvass, sail, per bolt | 14 | 0 | 0 |
| Cardamoms, per md | 75 | 0 | 0 |
| bastard, per md | 15 | 0 | 0 |
| Cassia, per md | 16 | 0 | 0 |
| Chanks, green, per 100 | 6 | 0 | 0 |
| white, per 100 | 3 | 0 | 0 |
| Cheeses, per lb | | 8 | 0 |
| China root, per md | 3 | 12 | 0 |
| Chocolate, per lb | 1 | 0 | 0 |
| Chrome yellow, per lb | | 12 | 0 |
| Cloves, per md | 20 | 0 | 0 |
| Cochineal, per seer | 6 | 0 | 0 |
| Cocoanuts, per 1,000 | 18 | 0 | 0 |
| Cocoanut shell, per 1,000 | 50 | 0 | 0 |
| Cocoanut kernel, per md | 3 | 2 | 0 |
| Coffee, Gulf and Red Sea, per md | 16 | 0 | 0 |
| other places, per md | 8 | 8 | 0 |
| Coir, per md | 4 | 0 | 0 |
| Coir rope, per md | 4 | 8 | 0 |
| China ginger syrup, in quart bottles, per dozen | 12 | 0 | 0 |
| China candied fruits, in small tubs of 5 catty, per tub | 2 | 8 | 0 |
| in large tubs of 10 catty, per tub | 5 | 0 | 0 |
| China preserves, in boxes of 6 small jars, per box | 9 | 0 | 0 |
| Copperas, per md | 2 | 0 | 0 |
| Cordage, hemp, per cwt | 16 | 0 | 0 |
| Manilla, per cwt | 10 | 0 | 0 |
| Corks, French, per gross | 2 | 4 | 0 |
| English and other, per gross | | 12 | 0 |

TABLE—Continued.

| Names of goods. | Rate of valuation. | | |
|---|---|---|---|
| Corrosive sublimate, per seer | 7 | 0 | 0 |
| Cotton, coast, per md | 9 | 0 | 0 |
| other places, per md | 14 | 0 | 0 |
| mule twist, or cotton yarn, per morah | | 3 | 7 |
| *Cotton, foreign, Turkey red or German dye red, per lb | 1 | 4 | 0 |
| *Cotton twist, British, Turkey red and imitation German dye red, per lb | 1 | 2 | 0 |
| *Cotton, orange and red, per lb | | 10 | 6 |
| *Cotton, of other colors, per lb | | 10 | 0 |
| Cotton sewing-thread, per lb | | 14 | 0 |
| Cotton in reels, per dozen reels | | 3 | 0 |
| Cowries, maldive, per md | 16 | 0 | 0 |
| bazar, per md | 4 | 0 | 0 |
| Cubebs, per md | 16 | 0 | 0 |
| Cummin seed, per md | 8 | 0 | 0 |
| Currants, per lb | | 8 | 0 |
| Chamois skins, per dozen | 5 | 0 | 0 |
| Damar, per md | 4 | 0 | 0 |
| Dates, wet, in pots, per md | 5 | 0 | 0 |
| in bag, per md | 2 | 8 | 0 |
| dry, per md | 4 | 0 | 0 |
| Deal planks, (of all sizes) per plank | 2 | 0 | 0 |
| Dried snails, per md | 40 | 0 | 0 |
| Ebony, per md | 2 | 8 | 0 |
| Elephant's teeth or tusks, per md | 125 | 0 | 0 |
| grinders, per md | 12 | 0 | 0 |
| Felt, per piece | | 8 | 0 |
| Figs, per lb | | 4 | 0 |
| Fish maw, per md | 50 | 0 | 0 |
| Flints, gun, per 1,000 | 3 | 0 | 0 |
| Flour, per barrel | 18 | 0 | 0 |
| per half barrel | 9 | 0 | 0 |
| American, per barrel | 10 | 0 | 0 |
| American, per half barrel | 5 | 0 | 0 |
| Frankincense or olibanum, per md | 7 | 8 | 0 |
| Galangal, per md | 2 | 8 | 0 |
| Gall nuts, per md | 30 | 0 | 0 |
| Gambier, per md | 2 | 0 | 0 |
| Gamboge, per md | 70 | 0 | 0 |
| Ghee, per md | 14 | 0 | 0 |

*N. B.—Duty to be charged on the gray weight of colored yarn; when not ascertainable' the actual wharf weight or invoice weight to be taken.

TABLE—Continued.

| Names of goods. | Rate of valuation. | | |
|---|---|---|---|
| Glass, crown, of sizes, per 100 feet | 5 | 0 | 0 |
| plate, per foot | | 11 | 0 |
| broken, per md | 4 | 0 | 0 |
| Glue, per seer | 1 | 0 | 0 |
| Grease and tallow, per md | 9 | 8 | 0 |
| Guernsey shirts, per dozen | 20 | 0 | 0 |
| Gum copal, per md | 24 | 0 | 0 |
| Gum arabic, per md | 14 | 0 | 0 |
| Gum myrrh, per md | 12 | 0 | 0 |
| Gunpowder, sporting, per lb | 1 | 8 | 0 |
| cannon, per lb | | 3 | 0 |
| Gum, bamboo, or bunslochun, per md | 40 | 0 | 0 |
| Hemp, Manilla, per md | 6 | 0 | 0 |
| Hides, dry American, per corge | 60 | 0 | 0 |
| wet do., salted, per hide | 10 | 0 | 0 |
| do. do. British, per hide | 14 | 0 | 0 |
| Cape, per hide | 10 | 0 | 0 |
| Horns, buffalo, per 100 | 9 | 0 | 0 |
| stag, or deer, per md | 8 | 0 | 0 |
| Horse-hair, per lb | 8 | 0 | 0 |
| Kutch, or katechu, per md | 3 | 4 | 0 |
| Lampblack, per md | 8 | 0 | 0 |
| Liquorice root, per md | 5 | 0 | 0 |
| Lithographic stones, per lb | | 4 | 0 |
| Musk, per sa. wt | 5 | 0 | 0 |
| in pod, per sa. wt | 2 | 0 | 0 |
| Macaroni, per lb | | 8 | 0 |
| Mace, per seer | 1 | 12 | 0 |
| Mahogany, in logs, per superficial square foot of one inch thickness | | 3 | 0 |
| Morocco skins, per skin | 4 | 0 | 0 |
| imitation, or roan, per skin | 1 | 4 | 0 |
| American, per skin | 1 | 8 | 0 |
| Mother-o'-pearl shells, per md | 5 | 8 | 0 |
| Bird-shot, per bag | 3 | 8 | 0 |
| Brass, per md | 25 | 0 | 0 |
| Brass leaf, China, per box of 100 bundles | 90 | 0 | 0 |
| China, white copper ware, per catty | 3 | 8 | 0 |
| Copper, sheet, sheathing and plate, per md | 36 | 0 | 0 |
| bolt, per md | 36 | 0 | 0 |
| nails, and composition nails, per md | 32 | 0 | 0 |
| tiles, ingots, cakes, and bricks, per md | 34 | 0 | 0 |
| Japan, per md | 36 | 0 | 0 |
| pigs and slabs, (foreign,) per md | 29 | 0 | 0 |

TABLE—Continued.

| Names of goods. | Rate of valuation. | | |
|---|---|---|---|
| Copper, old, per md | 34 | 0 | 0 |
| China, cash, per md | 17 | 0 | 0 |
| Iron, flat, square, and bolt, per md | 2 | 6 | 0 |
| rod, under half-inch diameter, per md | 3 | 12 | 0 |
| nail rod, per md | 3 | 4 | 0 |
| nails, per cwt | 12 | 0 | 0 |
| pump tacks, per 1,000 | | 10 | 0 |
| rivets, per cwt | 14 | 0 | 0 |
| hoop, plate, and sheet, per md | 4 | 0 | 0 |
| rice bowls, per set of 10 | 4 | 0 | 0 |
| do. per set of 6 | 2 | 0 | 0 |
| Swedish, flat and square, per md | 5 | 0 | 0 |
| pig, per md | 1 | 4 | 0 |
| kentledge, per md | | 10 | 0 |
| anchors, per cwt | 10 | 0 | 0 |
| anchors, for wooden stocks, per cwt | 9 | 0 | 0 |
| cables, per cwt | 8 | 0 | 0 |
| Lamitta, single, per corge | 2 | 8 | 0 |
| double, per corge | 5 | 0 | 0 |
| Lead, pig and sheet, per md | 7 | 0 | 0 |
| thin sheet, for tea canisters, per md | 16 | 0 | 0 |
| pipes, per md | 10 | 0 | 0 |
| Leaf, gold, per 100 leaves | 4 | 8 | 0 |
| mock, per packet of 10 books | 2 | 8 | 0 |
| Orsidue, foreign Europe, per corge | | 12 | 0 |
| per lb | 1 | 8 | 0 |
| Patent metal, per md | 32 | 8 | 0 |
| Quicksilver, per seer | 4 | 8 | 0 |
| Iron bottles, per bottle | 1 | 0 | 0 |
| Spelter, sheet, per md | 13 | 0 | 0 |
| nails, per md | 13 | 0 | 0 |
| plate, per md | 7 | 0 | 0 |
| Steel, British, per md | 6 | 0 | 0 |
| blistered, per md | 7 | 0 | 0 |
| cast, per md | 20 | 0 | 0 |
| spring, per md | 12 | 0 | 0 |
| Swedish, per md | 6 | 0 | 0 |
| Tin, block, per md | 25 | 0 | 0 |
| Tin plates, per box | 16 | 0 | 0 |
| Wire, copper, per lb | 1 | 0 | 0 |
| brass, per lb | | 12 | 0 |
| iron, per lb | | 3 | 0 |
| Nutmegs, per seer | 1 | 8 | 0 |
| in shell, per seer | 1 | 0 | 0 |

TABLE—Continued.

| Names of goods. | Rate of valuation. | | |
|---|---|---|---|
| Nutmegs, wild, per md | 14 | 0 | 0 |
| Ochre, red, per md | 1 | 0 | 0 |
| yellow, per md | 1 | 8 | 0 |
| Oil, sandalwood, per seer | 16 | 0 | 0 |
| cassia, per seer | 20 | 0 | 0 |
| cocoanut, per md | 6 | 8 | 0 |
| linseed, per wine gallon | 1 | 12 | 0 |
| turpentine, per wine gallon | 1 | 4 | 0 |
| whale and fish, per md | 10 | 0 | 0 |
| grass, per seer | 7 | 0 | 0 |
| earth, per md | 5 | 0 | 0 |
| wood, per md | 8 | 0 | 0 |
| peel, per md | 7 | 0 | 0 |
| koiapotic, per quart bottle | 2 | 0 | 0 |
| attar of roses, per sa. wt | 5 | 0 | 0 |
| Paints of all sorts, per lb | | 1 | 6 |
| Pepper, black, per md | 7 | 0 | 0 |
| long, per md | 6 | 12 | 0 |
| white, per md | 15 | 0 | 0 |
| Pimento, or alspice, per md | 40 | 0 | 0 |
| *British white and gray cotton piece goods, viz:* | | | |
| Long-cloth and shirting, white, not exceeding 45 inches in width ... per yard | | 2 | 0 |
| Long-cloth and shirting, gray, not exceeding 45 inches in width ... per yard | | 1 | 9 |
| Madapolams, white, 26 yards long and under, 35 inches wide and under ... per piece | 2 | 4 | 0 |
| Madapolams, gray, ditto ditto ... do | 2 | 1 | 0 |
| Cambric, white, of 12 yards ... do | 2 | 8 | 0 |
| white, double, 12 yards ... do | 5 | 0 | 0 |
| gray, of 12 yards ... do | 2 | 2 | 0 |
| gray, double, 12 yards ... do | 4 | 8 | 0 |
| Mulls and mediums, white, of 20 yards, not exceeding 45 inches wide ... do | 2 | 12 | 0 |
| Mulls and mediums, gray, ditto ditto ... do | 2 | 2 | 0 |
| Jaconets, white, of 20 yards ... do | 3 | 0 | 0 |
| gray ... do ... do | 2 | 0 | 0 |
| Lappets, of 10 yards ... do | 1 | 10 | 0 |
| Lenoes, plain, ditto ... do | 1 | 6 | 0 |
| Checks, spots, and stripes, of 10 yards ... do | 2 | 2 | 0 |
| Book muslin, plain, of 10 yards, not exceeding 45 inches wide ... do | 1 | 12 | 0 |

TABLE—Continued.

| Names of goods. | Rate of valuation. | | |
|---|---|---|---|
| Net, common, of 10 yards....................per piece.. | 1 | 0 | 0 |
| Dhootees and sarrees....................per pair... | 2 | 4 | 0 |
| Ditto, printed borders....................do..... | 1 | 8 | 0 |
| Scarfs....................per scarf.. | | 7 | 6 |
| Ditto, Dacca pattern....................do..... | 1 | 12 | 0 |
| Figured lenoes and mountain gauze, 10 yds., per piece.. | 2 | 8 | 0 |
| Twills, gray and imitation gray, American drilling....................per yard.. | | 2 | 6 |
| Ditto, white....................do..... | | 3 | 0 |
| Gray and white twilled shirtings, not exceeding 40 inches in width....................do..... | | 2 | 0 |
| Pocket handkerchiefs, per piece of 1 dozen.......... | 2 | 4 | 0 |
| Scotch cambric, of 7½ yards....................per piece.. | 2 | 12 | 0 |
| Brocades, not exceeding 42 inches wide...per yard.. | | 5 | 0 |
| Woorney....................per piece.. | 1 | 8 | 0 |
| Jean satin, jean and drills, white and col'd..per yard.. | | 4 | 0 |
| Moleskins, cartoons, and corduroy, white and colored....................do..... | | 5 | 0 |
| Quilting, white and colored, and embossed....do..... | | 7 | 0 |
| *Printed and dyed cotton piece goods, viz:* | | | |
| Bandannas and printed handkerchiefs.....per dozen.. | 1 | 6 | 0 |
| Chintz and prints, not exceeding 28 yards..per piece.. | 3 | 0 | 0 |
| Chintz twills..........do.......do.........do..... | 4 | 8 | 0 |
| Colored book muslin, of 10 yards...........do..... | 2 | 4 | 0 |
| Cotton velvet, plain, printed, and embossed..per yard.. | | 7 | 0 |
| Ginghams, of 12 yards....................per piece.. | 2 | 4 | 0 |
| Gros de Naples gingham....................per yard.. | | 3 | 0 |
| Gros de Naples checked gingham...........do..... | | 4 | 0 |
| Plates and Bengal stripes, not exceeding 28 yards, per piece.................... | 2 | 4 | 0 |
| Printed muslin....................per yard.. | | 3 | 6 |
| Printed garments, or Turkey red chintz and prints, per yard.................... | | 5 | 0 |
| Red cambric and red twills, of 36 inches wide and under....................per yard.. | | 4 | 3 |
| Red cambric and red twills, above 36 inches wide, per yard.................... | | 5 | 9 |
| Ticking....................per yard.. | | 3 | 6 |
| Zebra dresses....................per piece.. | 2 | 0 | 0 |
| Colored mulls, of 20 yards....................do..... | 3 | 6 | 0 |
| Red mulls, of 20 yards....................do..... | 5 | 0 | 0 |
| Red jaconets, of 20 yards....................do..... | 5 | 0 | 0 |

TABLE—Continued.

| Names of goods. | Rate of valuation. | | |
|---|---|---|---|
| *British linen piece goods, silk piece goods, and mixed piece goods, viz:* | | | |
| Linen dowlas, per yard | | 4 | 0 |
| drills and ducks, per yard | | 9 | 0 |
| Irish ... do | | 12 | 0 |
| sheeting ... do | | 12 | 0 |
| ticking ... do | | 7 | 0 |
| Scotch Holland ... do | | 5 | 0 |
| thread, per pound | | 12 | 0 |
| Silk velvet, per yard | 6 | 8 | 0 |
| Printed corahs or handkerchiefs, per piece of 7 handkerchiefs | 4 | 8 | 0 |
| Bombasins, per yard | | 9 | 0 |
| *American cotton piece goods, viz:* | | | |
| Drilling, per yard | | 2 | 6 |
| Jean ... do | | 3 | 0 |
| Sheeting .. do | | 2 | 0 |
| Shirting ... do | | 2 | 6 |
| Flannel ... do | | 3 | 6 |
| *Foreign Europe cotton piece goods, viz:* | | | |
| Printed muslin, per metre | | 8 | 0 |
| Printed muslin handkerchiefs and printed shawl handkerchiefs, per dozen | 5 | 0 | 0 |
| Printed muslin garments, or Turkey red prints and chintz, per yard | | 6 | 0 |
| Red cambric and red twills, of 36 inches wide and under, per yard | | 5 | 0 |
| Red cambric and red twills, above 36 inches, per yard | | 7 | 0 |
| Red cambric mulls and jaconets, of 20 yards, per piece | 6 | 0 | 0 |
| Printed velvet, plain, figured, and embossed, per yard | | 12 | 0 |

N. B.—Madapolams to be confined to the above dimensions: when exceeding those dimensions, to be classed as shirting or cambric, as the case may be. Other piece goods of the above descriptions, herein enumerated, exceeding the specified length and width, to be rated in proportion. Unenumerated to be rated at the actual wholesale market value of the day.

TABLE—Continued.

| Names of goods. | Rate of valuation. | | |
|---|---|---|---|
| *China cotton and grass-cloth piece goods, viz:* | | | |
| Cotton nankeens, broad, per corge | 30 | 0 | 0 |
| narrow, per corge | 10 | 0 | 0 |
| Grass cloth, single, per piece | 10 | 0 | 0 |
| double, per piece | 20 | 0 | 0 |
| Grass cloth handkerchiefs, per piece of 10 handkerchiefs | 3 | 8 | 0 |
| *Foreign Europe silk piece goods, viz:* | | | |
| Crape lise, per metre | | 10 | 0 |
| Crape, single, per piece | 6 | 8 | 0 |
| double, per double piece | 13 | 0 | 0 |
| Gauze, per metre | 1 | 0 | 0 |
| Gros-de-Naples, plain and figured, and other silks, per metre | 1 | 4 | 0 |
| Sarsenet, per metre | | 12 | 0 |
| Satin, plain and figured, per metre | 1 | 4 | 0 |
| Waistcoating, per metre | 3 | 0 | 0 |
| Velvet, plain, per metre | 5 | 0 | 0 |
| figured, per metre | 6 | 12 | 0 |
| *Eoreign mixed piece goods, viz:* | | | |
| Velvet, silk and cotton mixed, per yard | 3 | 12 | 0 |
| *China silk piece goods, viz:* | | | |
| Camlets, of eighteen yards, per piece | 24 | 0 | 0 |
| narrow, per piece | 18 | 0 | 0 |
| Gros-de-Naples, per yard | 2 | 0 | 0 |
| Curtain gauze, plain single, per piece | 4 | 8 | 0 |
| plain double, per piece | 9 | 0 | 0 |
| figured single, per piece | 6 | 0 | 0 |
| figured double, per piece | 12 | 0 | 0 |
| Damask, per piece | 34 | 0 | 0 |
| Damask camlet, per piece | 40 | 0 | 0 |
| Lutestring, of eighteen yards, per piece | 13 | 0 | 0 |
| of thirty yards, per piece | 24 | 0 | 0 |
| Ponjee, per piece | 20 | 0 | 0 |
| Sarsenet, of eighteen yards, per piece | 14 | 0 | 0 |
| of thirty yards, per piece | 26 | 0 | 0 |
| Colored handkerchiefs, per piece of 20 handkerchiefs | 12 | 0 | 0 |
| per piece of 10 handkerchiefs | 6 | 0 | 0 |

TABLE—Continued.

| Names of goods. | | Rate of valuation. | | |
|---|---|---|---|---|
| Satin, plain, of 18 yards, per piece | | 20 | 0 | 0 |
| figured, of 18 yards, per piece | | 20 | 0 | 0 |
| Velvet, per piece | | 28 | 0 | 0 |
| N. B.—All foreign silk, cotton, and mixed piece goods, not enumerated, to be ad valorem. | | | | |
| Pitch, per barrel | | 8 | 0 | 0 |
| American, per barrel | | 2 | 8 | 0 |
| coal, per barrel | | 2 | 8 | 0 |
| Pine boards, American, per 1,000 superficial square feet, and one inch thickness | | 45 | 0 | 0 |
| Staves, pipe, per 100 staves | | 6 | 4 | 0 |
| barrel, per 100 staves | | 3 | 0 | 0 |
| Packs, hogshead, complete, per pack | | 2 | 12 | 0 |
| puncheon, complete, per pack | | 4 | 8 | 0 |
| butt and pipe, complete, per pack | | 4 | 8 | 0 |
| Water casks, of sizes, per cask | | 5 | 0 | 0 |
| Pistachio nuts, per md | | 25 | 0 | 0 |
| *Provisions, salted, viz:* | | | | |
| Bacon, joles and cheeks | per pound | | 8 | 0 |
| Beef and pork | per tierce | 40 | 0 | 0 |
| Do. do. | per barrel | 25 | 0 | 0 |
| Do. do. American | per tierce | 35 | 0 | 0 |
| Do. do. do. | per barrel | 20 | 0 | 0 |
| Hams | per pound | | 8 | 0 |
| Do. in canister | do | | 12 | 0 |
| American | do | | 6 | 0 |
| Butter | do | | 12 | 0 |
| Salted tongues | per keg of 6 | 9 | 0 | 0 |
| Prunes, Bussorah | per md | 20 | 0 | 0 |
| foreign Europe | per pound | | 12 | 0 |
| Pump-leather | do | | 12 | 0 |
| Panchopaut | per md | 6 | 0 | 0 |
| Patent fuel | per ton | 13 | 0 | 0 |
| Raisins, Gulf and Red Sea | per md | 10 | 0 | 0 |
| Monocka, do. | do | 5 | 0 | 0 |
| Muscatel or Bloom | per box | 7 | 0 | 0 |
| Do. do. | per half box | 4 | 0 | 0 |
| Ratans | per md | 3 | 0 | 0 |
| Red lead | do | 10 | 0 | 0 |
| Rose-water | do | 20 | 0 | 0 |
| Rosin | per barrel | 3 | 0 | 0 |
| Rhubarb | per md | 35 | 0 | 0 |

TABLE—Continued.

| Names of goods. | Rate of valuation. | | |
|---|---|---|---|
| Saffron...per seer.. | 25 | 0 | 0 |
| Do. inferior, in cakes or lumps...do.... | 10 | 0 | 0 |
| Sago...per md.. | 4 | 0 | 0 |
| Sandal wood...do.... | 13 | 0 | 0 |
| Sandal wood, bastard...do.... | 3 | 4 | 0 |
| Sapan wood and root...do.... | 2 | 12 | 0 |
| Segars, Havana...per 1,000.. | 40 | 0 | 0 |
| Do. ...per pound.. | 5 | 12 | 0 |
| Manilla...per 1,000.. | 26 | 0 | 0 |
| American...do..... | 20 | 0 | 0 |
| Senna leaf...per md.. | 6 | 8 | 0 |
| Silk sewing-thread, China...per catty.. | 8 | 0 | 0 |
| Snuff, Europe...per pound.. | 3 | 0 | 0 |
| American in small bottles...per dozen.. | 3 | 0 | 0 |
| Soap, bar...per pound.. | | 2 | 0 |
| cake...do..... | | 12 | 0 |
| cake...per dozen.. | 1 | 8 | 0 |
| Stick lac...per md.. | 4 | 8 | 0 |
| Sunchal, or black medicinal salt...do.... | 4 | 0 | 0 |
| Sulphuric acid...per pound.. | | 2 | 6 |
| Sugar, loaf...do.... | | 4 | 0 |
| soft...per md.. | 8 | 0 | 0 |
| Storax, liquid...do.... | 20 | 0 | 0 |
| Tar, Swedish...per barrel.. | 10 | 0 | 0 |
| American...do.... | 7 | 0 | 0 |
| coal...do.... | 7 | 0 | 0 |
| Thread, gold...per ounce.. | 3 | 12 | 0 |
| silver...do.... | 2 | 12 | 0 |
| mock gold and silver...do.... | | 8 | 0 |
| Tobacco, leaf, Sandoway...per md.. | 10 | 0 | 0 |
| leaf, China...do.... | 18 | 0 | 0 |
| cut, do. ...do.... | 22 | 8 | 0 |
| leaf, Gulf and Red Sea...do.... | 20 | 0 | 0 |
| cut, do. do. ...do.... | 25 | 0 | 0 |
| American...do.... | 22 | 8 | 0 |
| Tortoise-shell...per seer.. | 14 | 0 | 0 |
| Turpentine...per barrel.. | 10 | 0 | 0 |
| Twine, sail...per pound.. | | 7 | 0 |
| Turmeric...per md.. | 2 | 4 | 0 |
| Verdigris...do.... | 30 | 0 | 0 |
| Vermillion, China...per box of 90 bundles.. | 120 | 0 | 0 |
| Vermicelli...per pound.. | | 8 | 0 |
| Vinegar, in wood...per wine-gallon.. | | 9 | 0 |
| Umbrellas, cotton...each.. | 1 | 0 | 0 |

TABLE—Continued.

| Names of goods. | Rate of valuation. | | |
|---|---|---|---|
| Wax.................................per md... | 35 | 0 | 0 |
| White-lead..........................do..... | 10 | 0 | 0 |
| *Woolens, British and foreign, viz:* | | | |
| Blankets............................per pair... | 12 | 0 | 0 |
| Bombazette..........................per yard.. | | 5 | 0 |
| Broadcloth, and ladies' cloth, fine.............do..... | 6 | 0 | 0 |
| medium..........................do..... | 2 | 0 | 0 |
| coarse..........................do..... | 1 | 1 | 0 |
| Pelisse-cloth, Spanish stripes, ladies' cloth, ordinary, and kerseymere..........do..... | 2 | 4 | 0 |
| Bunting.............................per piece.. | 10 | 0 | 0 |
| Camlet, not exceeding 28 yards..............do..... | 17 | 0 | 0 |
| Flannel.............................per yard.. | | 8 | 0 |
| Shalloons, not exceeding 28 yards........per piece.. | 20 | 0 | 0 |
| Serge, or long ells, white, not exceeding 24 yards..............................do..... | 16 | 0 | 0 |
| Serge and purpet, colored, not exceeding 24 yards..............................do..... | 14 | 0 | 0 |
| Merino..............................per yard.. | | 14 | 0 |
| Do. foreign.........................do..... | 1 | 8 | 0 |
| Wools, for embroidery.................per pound.. | 6 | 0 | 0 |

*Export tariff.*

| Names of goods. | Rate of valuation. | | |
|---|---|---|---|
| Ajwan, or lovage.....................per md... | 2 | 4 | 0 |
| Korisan.............................do..... | 5 | 0 | 0 |
| Aloe-wood...........................per seer.. | 2 | 0 | 0 |
| Arrowroot, in canister...............per md... | 40 | 0 | 0 |
| common..........................do..... | 10 | 0 | 0 |
| Anise-seed..........................do..... | 5 | 0 | 0 |
| Bran................................do..... | | 12 | 0 |
| Biscuits, white, cabin.................do..... | 7 | 0 | 0 |
| brown...........................do..... | 3 | 0 | 0 |
| Butter..............................do..... | 20 | 0 | 0 |
| Blankets, Patna......................per corge.. | 14 | 0 | 0 |
| country.........................do..... | 9 | 0 | 0 |

TABLE—Continued.

| Names of goods. | Rate of valuation. | | |
|---|---|---|---|
| Borax........per md.. | 12 | 0 | 0 |
| Brass and composition brass ware........do.... | 40 | 0 | 0 |
| Bahurra, or myrabolans........do.... | 1 | 12 | 0 |
| Copper ware........do.... | 50 | 0 | 0 |
| Calleejeerah, or black cummin seed........do.... | 2 | 0 | 0 |
| Canvass, hemp or cotton, and mixed........per bolt.. | 6 | 0 | 0 |
| Cardamoms........per md.. | 15 | 0 | 0 |
| Cheyratah........do.... | 5 | 0 | 0 |
| Chillies........do.... | 3 | 8 | 0 |
| Cinnabar........per seer.. | 5 | 8 | 0 |
| Coffee........per md.. | 10 | 0 | 0 |
| Coriander........do.... | 1 | 8 | 0 |
| Cotton-twist, Gloster........per morah.. | | 4 | 0 |
| Cow-tails, white........per md.. | 110 | 0 | 0 |
| black........do.... | 70 | 0 | 0 |
| Cummin seed........do.... | 8 | 0 | 0 |
| Coals........do.... | | 5 | 0 |
| Caoutchouc or India-rubber........do.... | 14 | 0 | 0 |
| Cowries........do.... | 12 | 0 | 0 |
| Elephants' teeth or tusk........do.... | 130 | 0 | 0 |
| Flour........do.... | 2 | 8 | 0 |
| Do. Soojee........do.... | 5 | 0 | 0 |
| Fish-maw........do.... | 50 | 0 | 0 |
| Ghee........do.... | 14 | 0 | 0 |
| Gum tragacanth........do.... | 8 | 0 | 0 |
| Ginger, dry........do.... | 3 | 8 | 0 |
| Gum babool........do.... | 7 | 0 | 0 |
| *Gunnies, viz:* | | | |
| Doffally........per 100.. | 13 | 0 | 0 |
| Fatiah........do.... | 7 | 8 | 0 |
| Cheekun........do.... | 9 | 0 | 0 |
| Gunny-bags........do.... | 11 | 0 | 0 |
| Jail gunny-bags........do.... | 25 | 0 | 0 |
| Gunny-cloth bags........do.... | 17 | 0 | 0 |
| Gunny-sacks........per sack.. | | 12 | 0 |
| Gunny-cloth, of 20 yards, and 36 inches wide and under........per piece.. | 2 | 0 | 0 |
| Gunny-cloth, of 30 yards, above 36 inches wide........do.... | 4 | 0 | 0 |
| Gunny-cloth, Kanchoony........per 100.. | 8 | 0 | 0 |
| Mootabariah........do.... | 12 | 0 | 0 |
| Gunjah, crude and cakes........per md.. | 12 | 0 | 0 |

TABLE—Continued.

| Names of goods. | Rate of valuation. | | |
|---|---|---|---|
| Honey ... per md. | 2 | 8 | 0 |
| Hemp ... do. | 2 | 0 | 0 |
| Hides, ox and cow, all round ... per corge | 20 | 0 | 0 |
| buffalo ... do. | 30 | 0 | 0 |
| Horns, buffalo ... per 100 | 10 | 0 | 0 |
| deer or stag ... per md. | 7 | 0 | 0 |
| Horn tips ... do. | 7 | 0 | 0 |
| Hurrah ... do. | 1 | 8 | 0 |
| Jaggry ... do. | 1 | 12 | 0 |
| Jute ... per bale of 300 pounds | 9 | 0 | 0 |
| Jute rope ... per md. | 2 | 0 | 0 |
| Kutch, or catechu ... do. | 3 | 0 | 0 |
| Kutkey, or hellebore ... do. | 12 | 0 | 0 |
| Karree noon ... do. | 1 | 4 | 0 |
| Lac dye ... do. | 20 | 0 | 0 |
| cake ... do. | 2 | 0 | 0 |
| seed ... do. | 4 | 0 | 0 |
| shell ... do. | 9 | 0 | 0 |
| stick ... do. | 4 | 0 | 0 |
| Lard, hogs' ... do. | 14 | 0 | 0 |
| Lines, of sizes and sorts ... do. | 7 | 0 | 0 |
| Loodh ... do. | 2 | 0 | 0 |
| Minium ... per seer | 3 | 0 | 0 |
| Mathee ... per md. | 1 | 8 | 0 |
| Molasses ... do. | | 12 | 0 |
| Munjeet, or madder ... do. | 3 | 0 | 0 |
| Musk ... per sa. wt. | 5 | 0 | 0 |
| Musk, in pod ... do. | 2 | 0 | 0 |
| Oil, castor ... per md. | 10 | 0 | 0 |
| cocoanut ... do. | 6 | 8 | 0 |
| croton ... per pint | 6 | 0 | 0 |
| grass ... per quart | 8 | 0 | 0 |
| linseed ... per md. | 7 | 0 | 0 |
| mustard ... do. | 7 | 0 | 0 |
| poppy ... do. | 7 | 0 | 0 |
| teel ... do. | 7 | 0 | 0 |
| Oil-seeds ... do. | 2 | 0 | 0 |
| Otter skins ... per skin | 1 | 8 | 0 |
| Ounlah ... per md. | 1 | 0 | 0 |
| Pepper, long ... do. | 10 | 0 | 0 |
| Patchuck, or orris root ... do. | 7 | 0 | 0 |
| Peplamool, or long pepper root ... do. | 14 | 0 | 0 |

TABLE—Continued.

| Names of goods. | Rate of valuation. | | |
|---|---|---|---|
| *Piece goods, silk, viz:* | | | |
| Korahs, 14 by 2........................per piece.. | 5 | 8 | 0 |
| Bandannas, choppahs, moomee choppahs, 14 by 2 ...........per piece of 7 hdkfs.. | 5 | 8 | 0 |
| Do. do., 13 by 1-14...............do......... | 4 | 8 | 0 |
| Do. do., 12 by 1-12...............do......... | 3 | 0 | 0 |
| Do. do., 10 by 1-6 ...............do......... | 2 | 0 | 0 |
| Tussur..............................per yard.. | | 10 | 0 |
| *Piece goods, cotton, viz:* | | | |
| Baftahs ...........................per corge.. | 26 | 0 | 0 |
| Gurrah ..............................do...... | 16 | 0 | 0 |
| Kharwah .............................do...... | 15 | 0 | 0 |
| Mamoodie ............................do...... | 32 | 0 | 0 |
| Mirzapore chintz ....................do...... | 11 | 0 | 0 |
| Patna ...............................do...... | 25 | 0 | 0 |
| Sahns ...............................do...... | 40 | 0 | 0 |
| Tunjebs, Oude........................do...... | 26 | 0 | 0 |
| [N. B. Silk piece goods of the above description herein enumerated, exceeding the prescribed length and width, to be rated in proportion; unenumerated to be rated at the wholesale market value of the day.] | | | |
| Rose-water, per seer.......................... | | 8 | 0 |
| Rum, country, per wine gallon ................ | | 5 | 0 |
| Suet, per md ................................. | 20 | 0 | 0 |
| Safflower, per md............................. | 30 | 0 | 0 |
| Sal ammoniac, per md.......................... | 14 | 0 | 0 |
| Saltpetre, per md............................. | 5 | 12 | 0 |
| Sapan wood, per md............................ | 3 | 0 | 0 |
| Silk, Chussum, per md......................... | 10 | 0 | 0 |
| Skins, goat, per 100 ......................... | 30 | 0 | 0 |
| Soap, in balls, per md........................ | 6 | 0 | 0 |
| Sugar, soft......do .......................... | 6 | 8 | 0 |
| candy....do .................................. | 12 | 0 | 0 |
| balls.....do ................................. | 16 | 0 | 0 |
| loaf......do ................................. | 14 | 0 | 0 |
| crushed.. do ................................. | 10 | 0 | 0 |
| Khaur... do .................................. | 4 | 0 | 0 |
| Sajee muttee, or crude soda, per md........... | 2 | 0 | 0 |
| Sulphuric acid, per lb........................ | | 2 | 6 |
| Tamarinds, per md............................. | 1 | 0 | 0 |
| Tapioca.....do ............................... | 40 | 0 | 0 |

TABLE—Continued.

| Names of goods. | Rate of valuation. | | |
|---|---|---|---|
| Talc, per md | 20 | 0 | 0 |
| Tallow and grease, per md | 10 | 0 | 0 |
| Tallow candles, per md | 13 | 0 | 0 |
| Tincal, per md | 9 | 0 | 0 |
| Tootiah, or blue vitriol, per md | 20 | 0 | 0 |
| Turmeric, per md | 2 | 8 | 0 |
| Twine, jute, per md | 4 | 0 | 0 |
| hemp, per md | 10 | 0 | 0 |
| Vermillion, or sindoor, per md | 8 | 0 | 0 |
| Wax, per md | 40 | 0 | 0 |
| black or inferior, per md | 28 | 0 | 0 |
| candles, per md | 45 | 0 | 0 |

## COLONIAL ACTS.

[Transmitted with despatches of the United States ministers in London.]

*Passed by the Governor-General of India, in council, on the 8th March*, 1850.

[Extract.]

AN ACT for freedom of the coasting trade of India.

"I. Goods and passengers may be conveyed from one part of the territories under the government of the East India Company to another part thereof, in other than British ships, without any restriction other than is or shall be equally imposed on British ships, for securing payment of duties of customs or otherwise."

*Passed by the Governor-General of India, in council, on the 15th of March*, 1850.

AN ACT to declare Aden a free port.

I. The port and settlement of Aden, in Arabia, is a free port and settlement, and no duty of customs is payable there on any ship or other vessel, or on any goods lawfully carried by sea or land, to or from the said port and settlement.

II. The said port of Aden shall not be taken to be within the provisions of act VI, 1848.

*Passed by the president of the council of India, in council, on the 8th June, 1850, with the assent of the Governor-General of India.*

An Act for better defining the special duty levied on tobacco in Bombay.

I. Regulations XXXIII, 1827, and XV, 1828, of the Bombay code, and so much of act I, 1838, as relates to the customary or special duty levied on the import of tobacco into the island of Bombay, are rescinded and repealed.

II. All tobacco imported into the island of Bombay, either by sea or across any of the causeways, from whatever port or place it is brought, is and shall continue to be liable to the payment of a special duty levied at the rate of seven rupees and eight annas for the Indian maund, which duty shall be paid over and above the customary duty of one rupee and eight annas, at the option of the importer, either on importation or after being warehoused in the custom-house warehouse, on being delivered out for internal consumption.

III. No drawback of the said duty shall be allowed on exportation, unless the tobacco has been warehoused in and is exported direct from the custom-house warehouse; in which case a drawback of the whole of the special duty shall be allowed, if claimed at the time of re-exportation.

IV. This act shall not be taken to affect the provisions and penalties of any act or regulation for enforcing payment of the special duty, which shall continue in force for compelling payment of the duty as declared payable by this act, and for punishing any evasion of such payment.

*Passed by the president of the council of India, in council, on the 9th August, 1850, with the assent of the Governor-General of India.*

An Act for protecting the salt revenue in Bombay.

I. A duty of customs shall be levied on salt passing by land into or out of foreign European settlements, or territories declared to be foreign under section VIII, act I, 1838, at the same rate as the excise duty leviable on salt within the territories subject to the presidency of Bombay.

II. The said duty of customs shall be levied in the same manner, and under the same rules and restrictions, and subject to the same penalties, as is prescribed for the levy of duties of customs on goods imported and exported by land by act I, 1838.

III. Any person who shall be concerned in passing salt, either by land or sea, contrary to the provisions of this or any other act, shall be punishable with imprisonment for a term not exceeding three months, or fine not exceeding five hundred rupees, or both.

IV. All salt passed, or attempted to be passed, or removed, contrary to the provisions of this or any other act, and all vessels, carriages and animals used in so passing or removing such salt, and the contents of any package in which such salt may be concealed, shall be liable to confiscation at the discretion of the governor of Bombay in council; but may be redeemed on payment of such fine as the governor in council, or any officer or officers of the revenue department to whom the governor in council shall think fit, from time to time, to delegate this power, may think reasonable.

OCTOBER 14, 1848.

The president of the council of India in council, with the concurrence of the Governor-General, is pleased to resolve, in modification of the rate prescribed in schedule A, annexed to act VI, of 1844, that from and after the date of publication of a notification to that effect in the Fort St. George Gazette, the duty chargeable on the import of tobacco by sea into any port of the presidency of Fort St. George shall be five per cent.* ad valorem.

*Notification of the Board of Customs—salt and opium.*

FORT WILLIAM, *October* 21, 1848.

In further modification of the rules in force for warehousing imported salt under bond, it is hereby notified, that in settling for the import duty on clearance of the salt, a deduction will be allowed on account of wastage, at a rate not exceeding 4 per cent. upon the quantity delivered over the ship's side: Provided, however, that if the collector of customs have reason to believe that any portion of the salt has been clandestinely or fraudulently removed, he will be at liberty to levy duty on the entire quantity so delivered.

The duty upon bonded salt will be levied at the rate in force at the time of clearance.

The collector of customs may, at his discretion, allow parties to whom salt stored in bond may be transferred, to enter into a new engagement for the payment of duty upon the entire quantity weighed over the ship's side; and upon execution thereof, to cancel the bond of the first owner, importer, or consignee, and release him from further responsibility.

NOVEMBER 4, 1848.

The president of the council of India, in council, has resolved to remove the existing prohibition against the importation into the Tenasserim provinces, of foreign sugar, rum, and rum-shrub, or sugar-rum and rum-shrub, the produce of any British territory into which foreign sugar, rum, and rum-shrub can be legally imported; and it is hereby declared, that the resolutions of the 18th July, 1846, making such importation illegal, are rescinded accordingly.

MARCH 31, 1849.

The deputy governor of Bengal, with the concurrence of the government of India, has now been pleased to determine, that on and after the 1st April, 1849, the rate of duty to be charged on salt imported by sea into any part of the presidency of Fort William, in Bengal, shall be 2 rupees and 8 annas upon every maund of 3,200 tolahs. On and after the same date, the whole of the salt in store, at the several public

* N. B.—Malabar and Canara are excepted in the notification of the government of Fort St. George.

depots, will be available at the following wholesale prices, subject in other respects to the rules and conditions now in force, the price in each instance being equal to the fixed duty above mentioned, added to the cost of production:

| | | | | |
|---|---|---|---|---|
| Hidgellee salt, at the agency depots.... | 310 | rupees | per | 100 maunds. |
| Do..do..at Sulkea.............. | 323 | " | per | " " |
| Tumlook salt.......................... | 322 | " | per | " " |
| 24 Pergunnahs salt, at Baugundee...... | 347 | " | per | " " |
| Do.....do.at Sulkea........... | 354 | " | per | " " |
| Chittagong salt....................... | 329 | " | per | " " |
| Arrakan salt, at Kyack Ghyas......... | 302 | " | per | " " |
| Do...do..at Chittagong............. | 330 | " | per | " " |
| Cuttack salt, at Sulkea............... | 343 | " | per | " " |
| Balasore salt, at Sulkea.............. | 328 | " | per | " " |
| Khurda and Chilka salt, at Sulkea..... | 341 | " | per | " " |
| Madras salt, at Sulkea................ | 306 | " | per | " " |

The government reserves to itself the power of reimposing the full amount of duty authorized by law, if circumstances should arise to render such a measure necessary. There will be no alteration, however, in the duty now fixed on all salt, whether imported on private account or sold by wholesale on account of government, before the 1st April, 1854; but the price of salt sold on account of government, so far as it depends upon the cost of production as calculated upon an average of three years, will be subject to annual adjustment.

JUNE 21, 1850.

The president in council is pleased to resolve, that sugar and rum be henceforth exempted from any demand on account of export duty throughout India.

*From Under-Secretary of the Government of Bengal to the Officiating Secretary of the Board of Customs.*

SEPTEMBER 6, 1850.

I am directed by the deputy governor of Bengal to inform you, that on the recommendation of the board, his honor has been pleased to allow articles, the private property of parties residing in this conntry, which are sent to Europe for the purpose of being repaired, to pass inwards free of duty through the custom-house on their re-importation.

### HONG KONG.

No duties on imports are levied in this colony.

### LABUAN.

No import duties are levied in this colony.

## WESTERN AUSTRALIA.

[According to a return made to the British House of Commons, August 8, 1851.]

*Table of duties of customs payable on goods, wares, and merchandise imported into Western Australia under the local ordinance No.* 8, *of May* 9, 1849 *: also of duty-free goods.*

| Articles subject to duty. | Amount of duty. | | |
|---|---|---|---|
| | £ | s. | d. |
| Spirits: | | | |
| The production and manufacture of any part of the British Empire, not exceeding the strength of hydrometer proof, and in proportion for any greater strength, imperial gallon | 0 | 8 | 0 |
| Of foreign production imported from any part of the British Empire, imperial gallon | | 10 | 0 |
| Of foreign production imported from any foreign place, imperial gallon | | 12 | 0 |
| Wine: | | | |
| The produce of any part of the British Empire, imperial gallon | | | 6 |
| The produce of any other place, imperial gallon | | 1 | 6 |
| Cigars and snuff: | | | |
| For every pound weight | | 5 | 0 |
| Tobacco: | | | |
| Leaf, for every pound weight | | | 3 |
| All other kinds | | 1 | 0 |
| Boiled down in bond for the purpose of being used as a sheep-wash, every pound weight | | | 1 |
| Live stock: | | | |
| Imported from any part of the British Empire, for every £100 value | 5 | 0 | 0 |
| From any other place, for every £100 value | 10 | 0 | 0 |
| On all goods not otherwise charged with a specific duty, and not set forth as free of duty, being the produce, &c., of any part of the British Empire, for every £100 value | 5 | 0 | 0 |
| On all goods, the produce, &c., of any foreign State, for every £100 value | 10 | 0 | 0 |

*Free of duty.*

All military or naval stores, or provisions, or stores required for he Majesty's service.

All bottles imported full.

All bullion and coin.

All staves and hoops for casks.

All trees and rooted plants.

All personal baggage of emigrants.

All articles of naval and military uniform, and appointments, imported by officers stationed in this colony for their own use.

Goods specially exempted by the governor.

## SOUTH AUSTRALIA.

[According to a return made to the British House of Commons, 8th August, 1851.]

*Statement of duties on imports levied in South Australia under the local ordinance No.* 11, *of* 1848, *passed* 23*d of November*, 1848. *(The ordinance is not limited in its duration.)*

| Articles subject to duty. | Rate of duty. |
|---|---|
| | £ s. d. |
| Alkali, per cwt. | 0 0 6 |
| Arms, ad valorem | 5 per cent. |
| Annatto, per cwt. | 3 0 |
| Apparel and slops, ad valorem | 5 per cent. |
| Arrowroot, per cwt. | 3 0 |
| Bacon and hams, per cwt. | 2 6 |
| Bags and sacks: | |
| Corn, per 100 | 5 0 |
| Ore, gunny, and returned, per 100 | 2 6 |
| Bales for wool, each | 2 |
| Baskets, ad valorem | 5 per cent. |
| Beef and pork, per cwt. | 1 6 |
| Beer, porter, ale, cider, and perry, per gallon | 3 |
| Blacking, per gallon | 4 |
| Blacking paste, per lb. | 1 |
| Boats, ad valorem | 5 per cent. |
| Books, printed, per cwt. | 6 0 |
| Barrows and trucks, each | 1 0 |
| Boots and shoes, viz: | |
| Boots, per dozen pairs | 6 0 |
| Half do., per dozen pairs | 3 0 |
| Shoes, per dozen pairs | 2 0 |
| Children's, per dozen pairs | 1 0 |
| Brass manufactures, ad valorem | 5 per cent. |
| Bread and biscuit, per cwt. | 7 |
| Bottles, glass and stone, per dozen | 1 |
| Bricks: | |
| Fire and Bath, per 1,000 | 5 0 |
| Other bricks, per 1,000 | 2 0 |
| Brimstone, per cwt. | 6 |
| Butter, per cwt. | 3 0 |

TABLE—Continued.

| Articles subject to duty. | Rate of duty. |
|---|---|
| | £ s. d. |
| Brooms and brushes, ad valorem | 5 per cent. |
| Cables, chain, per cwt | 1 6 |
| Candles: | |
| Tallow, per cwt | 3 0 |
| Wax, composition, sperm, &c., per cwt | 6 0 |
| Canvass, per bolt | 2 0 |
| Carts and drays, each | 10 0 |
| Wheeled wagons and timber carriages, each | 1 0 0 |
| Carriages, ad valorem | 5 per cent. |
| Casks, empty, per ton | 2 0 |
| Cement, per cwt | 4 |
| Chalk, per ton | 1 6 |
| Cheese, per cwt | 3 0 |
| Chocolate and cocoa, per lb | 1 |
| Clocks and watches, ad valorem | 5 per cent. |
| Coals, per ton | 9 |
| Coke, per ton | 2 0 |
| Coffee, per cwt | 4 0 |
| Confectionery, per lb | 2 |
| Copper: | |
| Sheathing and nails, per cwt | 5 0 |
| Manufactures, ad valorem | 5 per cent. |
| Cordage and rope, viz: | |
| Europe, per cwt | 2 0 |
| Manilla, per cwt | 1 6 |
| Coir and jute, per cwt | 9 |
| Unenumerated, per cwt | 1 6 |
| Cord, small, and twine, per cwt | 5 0 |
| Cork, per cwt | 2 0 |
| Corks, per gross | 1 |
| Corn, meal, and flour, viz: | |
| Wheat, per quarter | 1 6 |
| Barley, per quarter | 1 3 |
| Oats, per quarter | 1 3 |
| Maize and millet, per quarter | 1 0 |
| Peas, beans, and pulse, per quarter | 1 6 |
| Malt, per quarter | 3 0 |
| Flour and meal, per 100 lbs | 1 0 |
| Bran and pollard, per 100 lbs | 3 |
| Cotton manufactures, ad valorem | 5 per cent. |
| Cutlery, ad valorem | 5 per cent. |
| Drapery, ad valorem | 5 per cent. |

TABLE—Continued.

| Articles subject to duty. | Rate of duty. | | |
|---|---|---|---|
| | £ | s. | d. |
| Drugs, viz: | | | |
| Corrosive sublimate, per lb | 0 | 0 | 2 |
| Spirits, tar, per gallon | | | 1 |
| Vitriol, per gallon | | | 1 |
| Unenumerated drugs, ad valorem | 5 per cent. | | |
| Earthenware and china, ad valorem | 5 per cent. | | |
| Feathers, bed, per lb | | | 1 |
| Fish, dry and pickled, per cwt | | 1 | 0 |
| Flax, per cwt | | 1 | 0 |
| Fruit: | | | |
| Dried, of all sorts, per cwt | | 2 | 0 |
| In bottles, per dozen quarts | | | 6 |
| Preserved in sugar, succades and jams of all sorts, per pound | | | 1 |
| Fresh, per bushel | | | 6 |
| Furniture, ad valorem | 5 per cent. | | |
| Glass: | | | |
| Plate, in squares exceeding 600 inches, per lb | | | 4 |
| Plate, in squares not exceeding 600 inches, per lb | | | 3 |
| Crown and sheet, in squares exceeding 200 inches, per 100 feet | | 2 | 0 |
| Crown and sheet, in squares not exceeding 200 inches, per 100 feet | | 1 | 6 |
| Flint, cut, cast, mirrors, and manufactures, ad valorem | 5 per cent. | | |
| Gloves, ad valorem | 5 per cent. | | |
| Glue, per cwt | | 1 | 6 |
| Grease, per cwt | | 1 | 0 |
| Gunpowder, sporting, in canisters, per cwt | | 5 | 0 |
| blasting, per cwt | | 2 | 3 |
| Grindery, ad valorem | 5 per cent. | | |
| Groceries, ad valorem | 5 per cent. | | |
| Haberdashery and millinery, ad valorem | 5 per cent. | | |
| Hosiery, ad valorem | 5 per cent. | | |
| Hair: | | | |
| Curled for upholsterers' use, per lb | | | 1 |
| Manufactured, ad valorem | 5 per cent. | | |
| Hardware, ad valorem | 5 per cent. | | |
| Hats and caps, ad valorem | 5 per cent. | | |
| Hay, per ton | | 2 | 0 |
| Hemp: | | | |
| Dressed, per cwt | | 1 | 6 |
| Undressed, tow and oakum, per cwt | | 1 | 0 |

TABLE—Continued.

| Articles subject to duty. | Rate of duty. £ | s. | d. |
|---|---|---|---|
| Hides: | | | |
| Dressed, per cwt. | 0 | 3 | 0 |
| Raw, salt, and dried, per cwt. | | 1 | 0 |
| Honey, per cwt. | | 4 | 0 |
| Hops, per lb | | | 2 |
| Ink, per gallon | | | 3 |
| printing, per lb | | | 1 |
| Iron, bar and rod, per ton | | 10 | 0 |
| sheet and hoop, per ton | | 14 | 0 |
| pig, per ton | | 5 | 0 |
| sledges, anchors, anvils, plates, cart-arm moulds, and articles of wrought-iron, heavy, and in the rough, per cwt. | | 1 | 0 |
| cart arms and boxes, finished; chain articles of wrought-iron, finished, per cwt | | 1 | 6 |
| camp-ovens, pots, boilers, and castings, per cwt. | | | 10 |
| manufactures enumerated, ad valorem | 5 per cent. | | |
| Isinglass: | | | |
| Refined, per lb | | | 6 |
| Common, for manufacture, per lb | | | 2 |
| Implements and tools, ad valorem | 5 per cent. | | |
| Jewelry, ad valorem | 5 per cent. | | |
| Junk, old, per cwt | | 1 | 0 |
| Lard, per cwt | | 2 | 6 |
| Lead: | | | |
| Pig, sheet, and shot, per cwt | | 1 | 0 |
| Manufactures, ad valorem | 5 per cent. | | |
| Leather: | | | |
| Sole, per cwt | | 3 | 0 |
| Kip, and harness, per cwt | | 6 | 0 |
| Calf, per lb | | | 1 |
| Patent bazils, per dozen | | 5 | 0 |
| Kangaroo, per dozen | | 1 | 0 |
| Hogskin, each | | 1 | 0 |
| Bazils, per dozen | | | 6 |
| Enamel, per hide | | 3 | 6 |
| Other unenumerated, and manufactures, ad valorem | 5 per cent. | | |
| Lime, and lemon juice, and syrup of all sorts, per gallon | | | 3 |
| Linen manufactures, ad valorem | 5 per cent. | | |
| Lucifers, gross boxes | | | 4 |
| Maccaroni and vermicelli, per lb | | | 1 |
| Machinery, ad valorem | 5 per cent. | | |
| Mats, and matting, ad valorem | 5 per cent. | | |
| Musical instruments, ad valorem | 5 per cent. | | |

TABLE—Continued.

| Articles subject to duty. | Rate of duty. | | |
|---|---|---|---|
| | £ | s. | d. |
| Mustard, per lb | 0 | 0 | 1 |
| Needles, per 1,000 | | | 3 |
| Netting, ad valorem | 5 per cent. | | |
| Nuts, viz: | | | |
| Almonds, walnuts, chestnuts, filberts, and small nuts, per cwt | | 2 | 0 |
| Shelled almonds, per cwt | | 4 | 0 |
| Cocoa, per cwt | | | 6 |
| Oil: | | | |
| Black, per gallon | | | 1 |
| Sperm, head matter, and other fish or animal oil, per gallon | | | 3 |
| Linseed, rape, hemp, and cocoanut, per gallon | | | 2 |
| Olive, castor, and other vegetable oils, per gallon | | | 6 |
| Oilman's stores, ad valorem | 5 per cent. | | |
| Onions, per cwt | | 1 | 0 |
| Paints, per cwt | | 1 | 0 |
| Painter's colors, and whiting, per cwt | | | 6 |
| Paper: | | | |
| Stained, and hangings, ad valorem | 5 per cent. | | |
| Brown, wrapping, and blotting, per cwt | | 3 | 0 |
| Writing, per lb | | | 1 |
| Printing, and cartridge, per cwt | | 5 | 0 |
| Other unenumerated, manufactures, ad valorem | 5 per cent. | | |
| Parchment, per roll | | 3 | 0 |
| Perfumery, ad valorem | 5 per cent. | | |
| Percussion caps, per 1,000 | | | 2 |
| Pewter ware, ad valorem | 5 per cent. | | |
| Pickles and fruits, preserved in salt, per gallon | | | 4 |
| Pictures and prints, ad valorem | 5 per cent. | | |
| Pipes, tobacco: | | | |
| Of common clay, per gross | | | 1 |
| Not of common clay, ad valorem | 5 per cent. | | |
| Pitch, per barrel | | 1 | 0 |
| Plate and plated goods, ad valorem | 5 per cent. | | |
| Potatoes, per ton | | 3 | 0 |
| Provisions and preserved meats, per cwt | | 3 | 0 |
| Pins, per lb | | | 1 |
| Rice, per cwt | | | 9 |
| Rosin, per cwt | | | 6 |
| Saddlery and harness, ad valorem | 5 per cent. | | |
| Sago, per cwt | | 1 | 0 |
| Salt, per ton | | 3 | 0 |
| Saltpetre, per cwt | | 1 | 6 |

TABLE—Continued.

| Articles subject to duty. | Rate of duty. |
|---|---|
| | £ s. d. |
| Silk manufactures, ad valorem | 5 per cent. |
| Skins for tanning, per dozen | 4 |
| Soap, per cwt | 1 0 |
| Spices, viz: | |
| Cassia, per cwt | 3 0 |
| Cinnamon, per lb | 2 |
| Cloves, per lb | 1 |
| Mace, per lb | 2 |
| Nutmegs, per lb | 2 |
| Ginger, per cwt | 2 0 |
| Pepper, per cwt | 1 6 |
| Other spices, ad valorem. | |
| Spirits or strong waters, of all sorts, viz: | |
| For every gallon of such spirits or strong waters of any strength not exceeding the strength of proof by Sykes's hydrometer, and so on in proportion for any greater or less strength than the strength of proof, and for any greater or less quantity than a gallon; also perfumed spirits, not being sweetened or mixed with any article so that the degree of strength thereof cannot be exactly ascertained by such hydrometer, per gallon | 10 0 |
| Spirits, cordials, or strong waters, sweetened or mixed with any article so that the degree of strength thereof cannot be exactly ascertained by Sykes's hydrometer, per gallon | 10 0 |
| Starch, per cwt | 2 0 |
| Stationery, ad valorem | 5 per cent. |
| Steel, per cwt | 2 0 |
| Stones: | |
| Millstones, per foot diameter | 2 0 |
| Grindstones, per foot diameter | 1 |
| Roofing-slates, per 1,000 | 3 6 |
| Slates and flagstones, per 100 feet superficial | 1 0 |
| Tomb and wrought stones, per foot superficial | 1 |
| Marble, wrought, per foot, superficial | 6 |
| Stone, blue, per cwt | 5 0 |
| Sugar: | |
| Refined, and candy, per cwt | 4 0 |
| Muscovado, per cwt | 2 0 |
| Molasses, per cwt | 2 0 |
| Tapioca, per cwt | 2 0 |
| Tallow, per cwt | 2 0 |
| Tar, per barrel | 1 0 |

TABLE—Continued.

| Articles subject to duty. | Rate of duty. |
|---|---|
| | £ s. d. |
| Tea, per lb | 0 0 2 |
| Tin: | |
| Plates, per box | 2 0 |
| Ware, ad valorem | 5 per cent. |
| Tobacco: | |
| Manufactured, per lb | 2 0 |
| Unmanufactured, per lb | 1 0 |
| Cigars and cheroots, per lb | 5 0 |
| Snuff, per lb | 2 0 |
| Boiled down, in bond, for sheep-wash, per lb | 1 |
| Toys, ad valorem | 5 per cent. |
| Turnery and wooden ware, ad valorem | 5 per cent. |
| Turpentine, spirits of, per gallon | 2 |
| Vinegar, per gallon | 1 |
| Whalebone, per cwt | 14 0 |
| Wine, per gallon | 1 0 |
| Wood, posts and rails, handspikes and poles, per 100 | 1 6 |
| Paling, per 100 | 6 |
| Shingles and laths, per 1,000 | 6 |
| Treenails and spokes, per 100 | 2 |
| Oars, per 100 feet | 2 0 |
| Square timber and balks, spars, deals, battens, quartering, planks, boards, and sawed, hewn, or split timber of all kinds, not otherwise particularly enumerated or described, per 40 cubic feet | 2 6 |
| Wood, manufactures of, ad valorem | 5 per cent. |
| Wool, manufactures of, ad valorem | 5 per cent. |
| Zinc, and manufactures of ditto, ad valorem | 5 per cent. |
| Unenumerated articles, viz: | |
| Raw, ad valorem | 5 per cent. |
| Manufactured, ad valorem | 5 per cent. |
| Free list: | |
| Animals, living. | |
| Baggage of passengers. | |
| Bottles, imported full. | |
| Bullion and coin. | |
| Plants and trees. | |
| Seeds and roots, garden. | |
| Specimens illustrative of natural history. | |
| Wool, unmanufactured. | |

## NEW SOUTH WALES.

[Colonial ordinance of May 9, 1849.]

*Table of import duties.*

| Articles subject to duty. | | Amount of duty. | |
|---|---|---|---|
| | £ | s. | d. |
| Whiskey and rum ........................per gallon | 0 | 3 | 6 |
| All other spirits ........................per gallon | | 6 | 0 |
| Perfumed spirits........................per gallon | | 3 | 6 |
| All wine.................................per cent. | 15 | 0 | 0 |
| All tea, sugar, flour, meal; wheat, rice, and other grain.................................per cent. | 5 | 0 | 0 |
| Tobacco, unmanufactured.....................per lb. | | 1 | 6 |
| manufactured........................per lb. | | 2 | 0 |
| Unenumerated goods.........................per cent. | 10 | 0 | 0 |

*Free goods.*

Goods, the produce of the United Kingdom and of British India, metallic ores, wine for officers' messes, specimens of natural history, live plants, bullion and coin.

## VAN DIEMAN'S LAND.

*Table of duties on imports levied in the colony of Van Dieman's Land.**

| Acts of Council. | Articles. | Rate of duty. |
|---|---|---|
| Passed January 2, 1834, 4 Will. 4, No. 15; and 12 Vict., No. 3, passed September 25, 1848. | Spirits imported, being the produce and manufacture of the United Kingdom or any of the British possessions. | Nine shillings for each and every gallon not exceed'g the strength of hydrometer proof, and of any greater or less degree of strength an additional or reduced duty in proportion thereto. |
| Ditto | All other spirits imported | Twelve shillings for each and every gallon, to be ascertained and determined as above. |
| 4 Vict., No. 28, passed October 5, 1840. | All tobacco imported | One shilling and sixpence for and in respect of every pound weight. |
| Passed January 2, 1834, 4 Will. 4, No. 15; passed February 28, 1845, 8 Vict., No. 18. 10 Vict., No. 7, passed July 13, 1846; and 12 Vict., No. 8, passed October, 1848. | All other goods imported, not being of the growth, produce, or manufacture of the United Kingdom, excepting wool, coal for steam navigation, metallic ores, garden seeds, grass and clover seeds, hemp seed, linseed, turnip seed, plants, shrubs and trees alive, manures, specimens of minerals or fossils, and all specimens illustrative of natural history, being the produce of any of her Majesty's colonies or possessions. | Fifteen per cent. ad valorem. |

## GAMBIA.

*Duties levied on articles imported into settlements on the river Gambia, in 1850.*

[Compiled from returns made in 1851, for the British House of Commons.]

On all goods imported........................4 per cent. ad valorem.
Extra duty on spirits..............................6*d* per gallon.
Do. wines..............................6*d* per gallon.
Do. tobacco..............................½*d* per pound.
On palm wine imported into the island of St. Mary....6*d* per gallon.

On *exports*, no duties levied.

* The latest return received at the Colonial Office in 1851.

## NATAL.

[According to returns compiled in 1851, for the British House of Commons.]

*A table of the duties of customs payable on goods, wares, and merchandise imported into the district of Natal, on the* 10*th October*, 1849.

| Articles subject to duty. | Amount of duty. | | |
|---|---|---|---|
| | £ | s. | d. |
| Meat— | | | |
| Salted or cured, of all sorts, not being the produce or manufacture of the United Kingdom, or of any British possession, the cwt | 0 | 3 | 0 |
| Salted or cured, of all sorts, being the produce or manufacture of the United Kingdom, or of any British possession, the cwt | | 1 | 0 |
| Fish— | | | |
| Dried or salted, and fins and skins, the produce of creatures living in the sea, of foreign fishing or taking, for every £100 of the value thereof | 12 | 0 | 0 |
| Flour, wheaten, not being of British manufacture, the barrel of 196 lbs | | 3 | 0 |
| Rice, the cwt | | 1 | 6 |
| Sugar— | | | |
| Not refined, the produce of any British possession, the cwt | | 2 | 3 |
| Not refined, the produce of any foreign country, the cwt | | 4 | 6 |
| Refined or candy, not being of British manufacture, the cwt | | 6 | 0 |
| Refined or candy, being of British manufacture, the cwt | | 3 | 0 |
| Coffee— | | | |
| The produce of any British possession, the cwt | | 5 | 0 |
| The produce of any foreign country, the cwt | | 10 | 0 |
| Tea, the lb | | | 4½ |
| Pepper, the cwt | | 4 | 0 |
| Wine, viz: | | | |
| In bottles, each of greater content than twelve to the imperial gallon, but not of greater content than six to the imperial gallon, the produce of any of the British dominions or possessions, the dozen bottles | | 2 | 0 |
| The produce of any foreign country, the dozen bottles | | 4 | 0 |
| In bottles, each of not greater content than twelve to the imperial gallon, the produce of any of the British dominions or possessions, the dozen bottles | | 1 | 0 |
| The produce of any foreign country, the dozen bottles | | 2 | 0 |
| Not in bottles, the produce of any British dominions or possession, the imperial gallon | | | 9 |

TABLE—Continued.

| Articles subject to duty. | £ | s. | d. |
|---|---|---|---|
| Wine, the produce of any foreign country, the imperial gallon | 0 | 1 | 6 |
| Spirits, viz: Spirits of all sorts, not exceeding the strength of proof by Sykes's hydrometer, and so in proportion for any greater strength, the imperial gallon | | 2 | 0 |
| Tobacco, viz: | | | |
| Not manufactured, the cwt | | 12 | 0 |
| Manufactured, the cwt., (not cigars) | 1 | 0 | 0 |
| Cigars, the 1,000 | | 5 | 0 |
| Oil— | | | |
| Spermaceti, of foreign taking, the tun, (imperial measure) | 7 | 10 | 0 |
| Other oil, train and blubber, the produce of fish or creatures living in the sea, of foreign fishing, the tun, (imperial measure) | 3 | 0 | 0 |
| Wood— | | | |
| Manufactured, viz: Mahogany, rosewood, and teak-wood, the cubic foot | | | 3 |
| All other wood, not the produce of the United Kingdom, or of any British possession, the cubic foot | | | 2 |
| Gunpowder, the lb | | | 3 |
| Goods, wares, and merchandise, not otherwise charged with duty, and not herein declared free of duty, being the growth, produce, or manufacture of the United Kingdom, or of any British possession abroad, for every £100 of the value | 5 | 0 | 0 |
| Goods, wares, and merchandise, not otherwise charged with duty, and not herein declared free of duty, being the growth, produce, or manufacture of any foreign country, for every £100 of the value | 12 | 0 | 0 |

*Provided, nevertheless, and it is hereby further ordered,* That no such duty shall be levied on the following goods, viz:

Bottles of common glass, imported full; bullion; casks, staves, hoops, and coopers' rivets; coin; diamonds; horses, mules, sheep, asses, cattle, and all other live stock, and live animals; seeds, bulbs, plants; specimens illustrative of natural history; provisions or stores of every description, imported or supplied for the use of her Majesty's land and sea forces.

*And it is hereby further ordered,* That whenever any article, being the growth, production, or manufacture of any foreign country, hereinbefore charged with any duty, is imported into the said district of Natal from the United Kingdom, (having been there entered for consumption, and re-exported without any drawback of duty having been first paid thereon,) such article shall be liable only to such duty as is hereinbefore charged upon similar articles, being the growth, production, or manufacture of the United Kingdom, or of any British possession abroad.

And if any goods, being the growth, produce, or manufacture of any foreign country, shall be imported into the said district of Natal through the United Kingdom, (having been warehoused therein, and being exported from the warehouse, or the duties thereon, if there paid, having been drawn back,) there shall be charged on such goods, over and above the duties hereinbefore imposed on similar goods, being the growth, produce, or manufacture of the United Kingdom, or of any of the British possessions abroad, three-fourths of the difference (if any) between such duties and the duties hereinbefore charged on goods not being the growth, produce, or manufacture of the United Kingdom, or of any of the British possessions abroad.

## SIERRA LEONE.

[According to returns compiled for the British House of Commons, in 1851.]

*A table showing the present amount of duties levied on articles imported into Sierra Leone under the ordinances of August* 4 *and September* 12, 1846; *December* 31, 1849; *August* 9 *and October* 22, 1850. (*Not limited in duration.*)

| Articles subject to duty. | Amount of duty. £ | s. | d. |
|---|---|---|---|
| Upon all goods, wares, and merchandise, not being the produce of the west coast of Africa, imported or brought into the colony, or landed and transhipped therein, except such as shall be entered for exportation only, or shall be prize goods, upon the invoice price thereof, per cent. | 5 | 0 | 0 |
| Additional duties on tobacco so imported or brought, and so landed or transhipped, except as aforesaid, an additional duty of, per pound | | | 1½ |
| Bottled beer, per dozen | | 1 | 0 |
| Draught beer, per gallon | | | 6 |
| Bottled wine, per dozen | | 3 | 0 |
| Draught wine, per gallon | | 1 | 6 |
| Rum, per gallon | | 1 | 6 |
| Brandy, gin, Geneva, Hollands, whiskey, and other spirits and cordials, such spirits not exceeding the strength of proof by Sykes's hydrometer, and so in proportion for any greater or less strength than the strength of proof, per gallon | | 2 | 6 |

TABLE—Continued.

| Articles subject to duty. | Amount of duty. | | |
|---|---|---|---|
| | £ | s. | d. |
| Amount of net proceeds of sale of all prize vessels and goods, per cent | 4 | 0 | 0 |
| Amount of net proceeds of sale of prize tobacco, per cent | 4 | 0 | 0 |
| *Table of charges on Queen's warehouse rent.* | | | |
| Upon every hogshead of tobacco, for each and every quarter, and so in proportion for any smaller parcel or package | | 7 | 6 |
| Upon every puncheon of rum, for each and every quarter, and so in proportion for any smaller cask or package | | 5 | 0 |
| Upon every cask of ale not containing more than five dozen, per month | | 1 | 0 |
| Upon every cask of ale containing more than five dozen, per month | | 1 | 3 |
| Upon every cask of flour, per month | | 1 | 0 |
| Every bale of bafts, per month | | 1 | 3 |
| Other bales not exceeding 20 cubic feet, per month | | 1 | 3 |
| Other bales exceeding 20 cubic feet, per month | | 2 | 0 |
| Crates of crockery, per month | | 2 | 6 |
| Barrels of beef, fish, pork, &c., per month | | 1 | 3 |
| Iron pots, per ton, per month | | 5 | 0 |
| Iron in bars or rods, per ton, per month | | 2 | 6 |
| Barrels exceeding 20 cubic feet, per month | | 2 | 0 |
| Hams, bacon, sugar, &c., per cwt., per month | | | 4 |
| A chest of guns, per month | | 1 | 6 |
| Packages not specified, for 20 cubic feet, per month | | 2 | 0 |
| *Tonnage duty.* | | | |
| Upon every ship or vessel entering or leaving the port, for each and every voyage on which such ship or vessel shall so enter or leave, for port, anchorage, and waterage duties or dues, per ton | | | 9 |
| *Light-house.* | | | |
| Upon every ship or vessel that shall arrive at or depart from any port or place of or belonging to, or shall come within the jurisdiction of the colony, for each and every voyage on which every ship or vessel shall so arrive or depart, per ton | | | 3 |

*Exports.*—No duties are levied on articles exported from the colony.

## CAPE OF GOOD HOPE.

[According to returns compiled in 1851, for the British House of Commons.]

*A table of the duties of customs payable on goods, wares, and merchandise imported into the colony of the Cape of Good Hope, (not including the district of Natal,) on the* 10*th October*, 1850, *under her Majesty's orders in council of the* 24*th April*, 1847, *and* 31*st October*, 1848.

| Articles subject to duty. | Amount of duty. £ | s. | d. |
|---|---|---|---|
| Coffee, viz: | | | |
| The produce of British possessions, the cwt | 0 | 5 | 0 |
| The produce of foreign possessions, the cwt | | 10 | 0 |
| Fish, dried or salted, and fins and skins, the produce of creatures living in the sea, of foreign fishing or taking, for every £100 of the value thereof | 12 | 0 | 0 |
| Flour, wheaten, not being the manufacture of the United Kingdom or of any British possession, the barrel of 196 pounds | | 3 | 0 |
| Gunpowder, the pound | | | 3 |
| Meat, salted or cured, of all sorts, not being the production or manufacture of the United Kingdom or of any British possession, the cwt | | 3 | 0 |
| Meat, salted or cured, of all sorts, being the production or manufacture of the United Kingdom or of any British possession, the cwt | | 1 | 3 |
| Oil, train and blubber, the produce of fish or creatures living in the sea, of foreign fishing, the tun (imperial measure) | 3 | 0 | 0 |
| Spermaceti, of foreign fishing, the tun (imperial measure) | 7 | 10 | 0 |
| Pepper, the cwt | | 4 | 0 |
| Rice, the cwt | | 1 | 6 |
| Sugar, viz: | | | |
| Not refined, the produce of any British possession, the cwt | | 2 | 3 |
| Not refined, the produce of any other place, the cwt | | 4 | 6 |
| Refined or candy, not manufactured in the United Kingdom or any British possession, the cwt | | 6 | 0 |
| Refined or candy, the manufacture of the United Kingdom or of any British possession, the cwt | | 3 | 0 |
| Spirits, of all sorts, not exceeding the strength of proof by Sykes's hydrometer, and so in proportion for any greater strength, the imperial gallon | | 2 | 0 |
| Tea, per pound | | | 4½ |
| Tobacco, viz: | | | |
| Not manufactured, the cwt | | 12 | 0 |
| Manufactured, (not cigars,) the cwt | 1 | 0 | 0 |
| Cigars, the 1,000 | | 5 | 0 |

TABLE—Continued.

| Articles subject to duty. | Amount of duty. | | |
|---|---|---|---|
| | £ | s. | d. |
| Wood, unmanufactured, viz: | | | |
| Mahogany, rosewood, and teakwood, the cubic foot.. | 0 | 0 | 3 |
| All other wood, not the produce of the United Kingdom or of any British possession, the cubic foot... | | | 2 |
| Wine, viz: | | | |
| In bottles, each not of greater content than six to the imperial gallon, the dozen bottles................ | | 4 | 0 |
| In bottles, each not of greater content than twelve to the imperial gallon, the dozen bottles............ | | 2 | 0 |
| Not in bottles, the imperial gallon................ | | 1 | 6 |
| Goods, wares, and merchandise, not otherwise charged with duty, and not herein declared free of duty, being the growth, produce, or manufacture of the United Kingdom or of any British possessions abroad, for every £100 of the value........................ | 5 | 0 | 0 |
| Not otherwise charged with duty, and not herein declared to be free of duty, being the growth, produce, or manufacture of any foreign state, for every £100 of the value.................................. | 12 | 0 | 0 |

*Free.*

Bottles of common glass, imported full; bullion; casks, staves, hoops, and coopers' rivets; coin; diamonds; horses, mules, asses, sheep, cattle, and all other live stock and live animals; seeds, bulbs, and plants; specimens illustrative of natural history; provisions or stores of every description, imported or supplied for the use of her Majesty's land or sea forces.

*Provided always*, That whenever any article, being the growth, production, or manufacture of any foreign country, hereinbefore charged with any duty, is imported into the said colony from the United Kingdom, having been there entered for consumption and re-exported without any drawback of duty having been first paid thereon, such articles shall be liable only to such duty as is hereinbefore charged upon similar articles being the growth, production, or manufacture of the United Kingdom or of any of the British possessions abroad: *Provided also*, That if any goods being the growth, produce, or manufacture of any foreign country, shall be imported into the said colony through the United Kingdom, (having been warehoused therein, and being exported from the warehouse, or the duties thereon, if there paid, having been drawn back,) there shall be charged on such goods, over and above the duties hereinbefore imposed on similar goods being the growth, produce, or manufacture of the United Kingdom or of any of the British possessions abroad, three-fourths of the difference (if any) between such duties and the duties hereinbefore charged on goods not being the growth, produce, or manufacture of the United Kingdom or of any of the British possessions abroad.

## ISLAND OF ST. HELENA.

*Duties on articles imported, corrected to September* 30, 1850.*

| Articles subject to duty. | Amount of duty. | | |
|---|---|---|---|
| *H. M. Order in Council, July* 11, 1839. | £ | s. | d. |
| Spirits, (excepting Cape brandy, arrack, Bengal rum, and aqua ardente, which are prohibited to be imported,) the gallon | 0 | 10 | 0 |
| Wine: | | | |
| In bottles, the dozen quart bottles | | 2 | 6 |
| Not in bottles, the gallon | | | 11 |
| Beer: | | | |
| In bottles, the dozen quart bottles | | | 6 |
| All other sorts, the hogshead | | 10 | 0 |
| Coffee, cocoa, chocolate, tea, pepper, spices, sugar-candy, sugar, tobacco, cheroots, cigars, curry-powder, sauces, sago, dried fruits, and other groceries; preserves and confectionery; drugs; woolen, cotton, and silk manufactures; toys; ivory manufactures; wood; wearing apparel of all sorts, being the growth, produce, or manufactures of places in Europe or America, not under the dominion of her Majesty of the Cape of Good Hope, and of all places to the eastward thereof, for every £100 of the value | 10 | 0 | 0 |
| All other goods of the growth, produce, or manufacture of places not under the dominion of her Majesty, for every £100 of the value | 6 | 0 | 0 |
| All goods, the growth, produce or manufacture of the United Kingdom, or the British possessions in Europe or America, and imported therefrom, for every £100 of the value | 3 | 0 | 0 |

### *Exceptions.*

Grain, rice, flour, bran ; horses, live-stock ; natural curiosities ; green fruits and goods on account of her Majesty's service ; wearing apparel, and clothing for her Majesty's troops, and passengers' wearing apparel.

* The latest return received at the Colonial Office, August 8, 1851.

| | s. | d. |
|---|---|---|
| All permits for goods being landed........................ | 1 | 0 |
| " for wines or spirits........................ | 5 | 0 |

Wharfage for casks, boxes, packages, &c., from 6*d*. to 1*s*.

[From a despatch of the United States consul at St. Helena, June 30, 1850.]

"I enclose a copy of a law recently put in force by the local authorities of this place, by order of her Britannic Majesty in council, for imposing a tax of one penny per ton upon vessels of all nations touching at this port."

At the court at Windsor, the 8th day of January, 1850.

[Extract.]

It is therefore hereby ordered by the Queen's most excellent Majesty, by and with the advice of her privy council, that in lieu of the duty of one farthing per ton, imposed as aforesaid, a duty of one penny per ton shall hereafter be levied upon all merchant ships or vessels entering the port of James Town for the purposes hereinafter mentioned.

And it is further ordered, that no ship or vessel shall be allowed to depart from the said port until all such tonnage duties as, by virtue of this present order of her Majesty in council, the said ship or vessel shall be liable to, shall have been fully paid to the collector of customs in the said port, who is hereby authorized and required to levy and collect the same.

And it is further ordered, that all sums of money so levied and collected, as aforesaid, shall be applied solely in aid of the funds required for completing the said hospital, and for erecting the new prison, as well as for defraying the expenses of maintaining the efficiency of both the institutions above mentioned.

## MAURITIUS.

[From a despatch of the United States consul at Port Louis, January 22, 1852.]

"With reference to the letter I had the honor to address to you, under date 24th June last, I respectfully beg to report, that ordinance No. 20, of 1851, intituled "to establish new duties of customs on goods, wares, and merchandise imported into Mauritius," has been approved by the supreme government, and, by proclamation under yesterday's date, published this day, is ordered to take effect from the first day of February next.

"I enclose a copy of the tariff of new duties so established, published by the government printer."

*New customs tariff, according to ordinance No.* 20, *of* 1851, *sanctioned by her Majesty's government, in operation from* 1*st February*, 1852.

| | £ | s. | d. |
|---|---|---|---|
| Wine, in casks of fifty gallons each, and the same in proportion for any larger or smaller cask, each | 0 | 16 | 0 |
| Wine, bottled, per dozen bottles | | 2 | 0 |
| Spirits—rum or arrack, being the produce or manufacture of the United Kingdom, or of any British possession in America, or of any of the British possessions within the limits of the East India Company's charter, into which the importation of rum or arrack, the produce of any foreign country or of any British possession, into which foreign sugar or rum may be legally imported, is prohibited: per gallon, of any strength not exceeding the strength of proof by Sykes's hydrometer, and so in proportion for any greater strength | | 6 | 0 |
| ———except rum or arrack, per gallon, of any strength not exceeding the strength of proof by Sykes's hydrometer, and so in proportion for any greater strength | | 6 | 0 |
| ———or cordials, sweetened or mixed with any article, so that the degree of strength thereof cannot be exactly ascertained by Sykes's hydrometer, per gallon in volume | | 6 | 0 |
| Tobacco—leaf, or unmanufactured, per lb | | | 3 |
| manufactured, per lb | | | 4 |
| cigars and snuff, per lb | | 1 | 0 |
| Ale, beer, porter, cider, and perry, bottled, per dozen bottles | | | 9 |
| Ale, beer, porter, cider, and perry, in casks, per hhd | | 15 | 0 |
| Bacon, butter, cheese, hams, tongues, and sausages, per cwt. | | 4 | 0 |
| Silk manufactures | 15 per cent. ad val. | | |
| Jewelry | 15 per cent. ad val. | | |
| Plate, wrought of gold and silver | 15 per cent. ad val. | | |
| Plated ware | 15 per cent. ad val. | | |
| Carriages | 15 per cent. ad val. | | |
| Musical instruments | 15 per cent. ad val. | | |
| Woolen manufactures | 10 per cent. ad val. | | |
| Leather manufactures | 10 per cent. ad val. | | |
| Paper and paper manufactures | 10 per cent. ad val. | | |
| Glass and glass manufactures, except glass bottles | 10 per cent. ad val. | | |
| Clocks and watches | 10 per cent. ad val. | | |
| Hardware and cutlery | 10 per cent. ad val. | | |
| Cabinet and upholstery ware | 10 per cent. ad val. | | |
| Perfumery | 10 per cent. ad val. | | |
| Tea | 10 per cent. ad val. | | |
| Coffee, the produce of any British possession | 10 per cent. ad val. | | |
| Sugar, refined, and sugar candy, the produce of a British possession from which sugar may be legally imported | 10 per cent. ad val. | | |
| Sugar, foreign, refined, in bond in the United Kingdom | 10 per cent. ad val. | | |

| | |
|---|---|
| And on other goods, wares, and merchandise not otherwise charged with duty, and not hereinafter declared to be free of duty.......................... | 6 per cent. ad valorem. |

*Table of exemptions.*

Animals, viz: horses, mules, asses, neat cattle, and all other live stock.

Books and maps, except foreign reprints of British copyright works.

Bread and biscuit.

Bricks and tiles.

Coal and coke.

Coin and bullion.

Corn and grain, unground.

Fish, dried, salted, or pickled.

Fire-wood.

Flour, bran, and pollard.

Fruits and vegetables, fresh.

Glass bottles, imported full.

Hay and straw.

Ice.

Leeches.

Lime.

Machinery and apparatus for mills for the manufacture of sugar, rum, or other produce.

Manures of all kinds.

Meat, salted and cured, except bacon, hams, tongues, sausages, and preserved meats.

Paintings and drawings.

Peas, beans, and lentils.

Rice, dholl, and churrah.

School materials, for the use of free schools.

Sal ammoniac, saltpetre, and phosphate of soda.

Seeds intended for agricultural and horticultural purposes.

Slates and stones for building and paving.

Vacoa bags and leaves.

Provisions and stores of every description imported or supplied for the use of her Majesty's land and sea forces, or for the colonial government.

Objects and specimens—animal, mineral, and vegetable—illustrative of natural history, including live plants and trees, and vegetable productions connected with the study of botany.

Wearing apparel, baggage, and instruments intended for professional use, the property of, and accompanying, persons arriving in the colony, or the property of persons coming to the colony overland, forwarded by vessels direct from Europe.

Articles of naval and military uniform.

Goods the growth, production, or manufacture of the dependencies of Mauritius.

Goods the growth, production, or manufacture of Mauritius and its dependencies; and all goods upon which the full amount of duty (if any be due thereon) shall have been paid on their first importation into Mauritius, legally exported from thence and afterwards returned: provided such goods shall be returned within three years from the date of their exportation, and it be proved to the satisfaction of the collector of customs that they are the identical goods exported from Mauritius, and provided the property of such goods continue in the person by whom or on whose account the same were exported.

[From a despatch of the United States consul at Port Louis, March 31, 1852.]

"I transmit the official copies I have just obtained from the colonial secretary's office of the two following ordinances, viz:

"1st. Ordinance No. 3 of 1852, reducing from and after the 21st February last, to fourpence-half-penny per hundred pounds, French weight, the exportation duty on sugars, produce of this island.

"2d. Ordinance No. 6 of 1852, for reducing the port charges on vessels coming to this port, and amending certain dispositions of previous ordinances relating thereto."

MAURITIUS AND DEPENDENCIES.

ORDINANCE No. 3, of February 18, 1852; to take effect from February 21, 1852.

J. M. HIGGINSON.—*Enacted by the governor of Mauritius, with the advice and consent of the council of government thereof:*

*Title.*—For further reducing the colonial export duty on sugar. *Preamble.*—Whereas it has become expedient to reduce the colonial export duty of customs levied on sugar:

His excellency the governor in council has ordered, and does hereby order:

*Reduction of duty on exportation of sugar.*—ART. 1. The colonial custom duty on the exportation of sugar, the produce of Mauritius, shall be charged, levied, collected and paid at the rate of 4½*d.* for every 100 pounds net, French weight, in lieu of the duty of sixpence imposed by ordinance No. 22 of 1851.

*Promulgation.*—ART. 2. The present ordinance shall take effect from the twenty-first day of February, 1852.

Passed in council at Port Louis, island of Mauritius, this eighteenth day of February, 1852.

MAURITIUS AND DEPENDENCIES.

ORDINANCE No. 6, of February 25, 1852; to take effect from March 1, 1852.

J. M. HIGGINSON.—*Enacted by the governor of Maritius, with the advice and consent of the council of government thereof:*

*Title.*—For reducing and amending the port charges upon vessels in the harbor of Port Louis. *Preamble.*—Whereas it is expedient to amend ordinances 6 and 44 of 1848, and to revise the port dues at present levied, and to provide for the better arrangement of vessels in the harbor of Port Louis:

His excellency the governor in council has ordered, and does hereby order:

*Charges on vessels in the harbor.*—ART. 1.—The following charges shall henceforth be leviable on all vessels entering or clearing from the harbor of Port Louis; that is to say:

*Schedule of charges.*

| | £ | *s.* | *d.* |
|---|---|---|---|
| For Pilotage: | | | |
| Vessels remaing at the bell-buoy, per foot | 0 | 2 | 6 |
| Vessels entering the harbor— | | | |
| Piloting inwards and mooring, per foot | | 5 | 0 |
| Piloting outwards and unmooring, do | | 5 | 0 |
| Vessels under 100 tons of burden, entering the harbor, shall not be required to take a pilot. | | | |
| For the use of warps and boats, viz: | | | |
| Inwards, for each vessel of 100 tons burden and above | 3 | 0 | 0 |
| The same, if the port office steamer be employed | 1 | 0 | 0 |
| Outwards | 3 | 0 | 0 |
| For the use of boats without warps: | | | |
| For each launch (manned) per day | 1 | 10 | 0 |
| Anchorage dues: | | | |
| Vessels trading with Madagascar or the dependencies of Mauritius, per ton of register | | | 3 |
| Such vessels shall not be charged anchorage dues more than twice in any one year. | | | |
| Vessels entering the harbor in distress, or for repairs, provided that they do not receive cargo nor break bulk, or that they discharge cargo solely for the purpose of repairs, and that the whole of the same be reshipped, (excepting any part condemned as damaged) | | Free. | |
| Vessels entering the harbor, but not breaking bulk, nor receiving cargo, per ton of register | | | 4 |
| All other vessels breaking bulk or receiving cargo, per ton of register | | | 8 |
| Vessels breaking bulk at the bell-buoy to the extent of not more than 10 tons, or landing not more than five horses or horned cattle, or twenty sheep, swine, or goats; and immigrant vessels landing coolies and surplus stores | | Free. | |
| For moving from one berth in the harbor to another, or to hulks, each time | 4 | 0 | 0 |
| For swinging alongside hulks | 2 | 0 | 0 |
| For remooring | 2 | 0 | 0 |
| For the use of the mooring-chains, or the anchors, which are placed around the Trou Fanfaron, viz: | | | |

| | £ | s. | d. |
|---|---|---|---|
| For each vessel under 100 tons, per day | 0 | 1 | 0 |
| of 100 tons, not above 200, per day | | 2 | 0 |
| above 200 tons, per day | | 4 | 0 |
| For the use of an anchor from upwards of 3,500 lbs., per day | | 16 | 0 |
| 3,500 to 2,500 do. | | 12 | 0 |
| 2,500 to 2,000 do. | | 8 | 0 |
| 2,000 to 1,500 and under do. | | 4 | 0 |
| For the use of a cable from 14 to 16 inches, per day | 1 | 12 | 0 |
| 11 to 13 do. do. | 1 | 4 | 0 |
| 8 to 10 do. do. | 1 | 0 | 0 |
| 6 to 7 do. do. | | 12 | 0 |
| 4 to 5 do. do. | | 8 | 0 |
| For vessels remaining swung on the warps above 24 hours, or above 48 hours in cases where the pilot in charge has certified in writing that the vessel was prevented by the wind from leaving the harbor at the end of 24 hours after she was so swung: | | | |
| Under 100 tons, per day | 1 | 0 | 0 |
| If 100 tons or upwards | 4 | 0 | 0 |
| Port and police clearance: | | | |
| On vessels trading with Madagascar and the dependencies of Mauritius, each | | 5 | 0 |
| On all other vessels | | 15 | 0 |
| For the dredging service: | | | |
| An additional proportional amount on all other port charges (excepting the charges for the use of the steamer, and for remaining swung upon the warps) levied upon all vessels except those which remain at the bell-buoy, viz: | | | |
| On vessels under 350 tons, per register | 10 per cent. | | |
| Of 350 tons or upwards | 15 per cent. | | |
| For tugging vessels by the port office steamer, inwards or outwards, viz: | | | |
| For vessels under 100 tons, each | 3 | 0 | 0 |
| For vessels from 100 to 150 tons, each | 4 | 0 | 0 |
| For vessels from 150 to 200 tons, each | 5 | 0 | 0 |
| For vessels from 200 to 400 tons, per ton | | | 6 |
| For vessels above 400 tons, per each additional 100 tons | 1 | 0 | 0 |

Art. 2. In order to prevent the crowding of the harbor with hulks, the harbor-master is hereby empowered to grant licenses for such a number of careening hulks as shall be fixed in the port regulations; and every such hulk shall be liable to a charge of £9 quarterly, payable in advance to the harbor-master.

Art. 3. All vessels abandoned at this port and sold shall either be broken up or fitted for sea within six months from the date of sale, subject to a charge of £1 per diem for every day after the six months aforesaid, during the time that the said vessel shall remain not broken up or not fitted for sea.

Art. 4. The owner or owners of all such careening hulks and other vessels abandoned shall be bound to have a keeper and two men on board of each, and to moor the same securely with four bower anchors, two ahead and two astern, in the situation which shall be pointed out by the harbor-master. Any such owner or owners failing to comply with the provisions of this article shall be subject to a penalty not exceeding £50.

Art. 5. Ordinances 6 and 44 of 1848, are hereby repealed.

Art. 6. The present ordinance shall take effect from the 1st day of March, 1852.

Passed in council at Port Louis, island of Mauritius, this twenty-fifth day of February, 1852.

[From a despatch of the United States consul at Port Louis, May 31, 1850.]

"I have the honor to transmit official copies of two ordinances, viz: No. 5 of 1850, for levying certain duties on tobacco, in leaf or manufactured, imported into this colony; No. 7 of 1850, for levying certain license duties on the manufacture of tobacco, and on the sale by retail of tobacco, in leaf or manufactured, in this colony.

"The ordinance No. 7 will not, in my opinion, have any appreciable influence on the marketable value, manufacture, or consumption of the article it relates to; No. 5 will operate as a great stimulus to the cultivation and manufacturing of tobacco in the island. I am already aware that planting of tobacco has been commenced to a considerable extent; and if the ordinance is maintained in force, it is to be apprehended that the colony will eventually be able to supply a sufficient quantity for its consumption. As, however, the object of the ordinance was to raise revenue, and that object would be defeated under the view I have just taken of its effects, it would appear probable that, so soon as those effects shall be fully ascertained, it will be repealed, or its dispositions will be modified."

## MAURITIUS AND DEPENDENCIES.

Ordinance No. 5 of 1850, to take effect on the 5th of April, 1850.

G. W. Anderson.—*Enacted by the governor of Mauritius, with the advice and consent of the council of government thereof:*

*Title.*—For amending ordinance No. 9 of 1848, relating to the import duty on tobacco, and for fixing a special license duty for the manufacturing and selling of that article within the colony. *Preamble.*—Whereas it is expedient to alter the rate of the colonial custom duty now levied on tobacco imported into the colony, and to fix a special license duty for the manufacturing and selling of that article in the colony, his excellency the governor in council has ordered, and does hereby order:

*New duties on tobacco.*—Art. 1. In lieu and instead of the duties now payable under paragraph five of the table of duties contained in article one of ordinance No. 9 of 1848, on all tobacco imported into the colony, the following sums shall, from and after the fifth of April next, be raised, levied, and collected, viz:

On leaf or unmanufactured tobacco, 3*d.* per pound.
On manufactured tobacco, 4*d.* per pound.
On cigars and snuff, 1*s.* per pound.

*License duty.*—Art. 2. There shall be levied on every license for the manufacture of tobacco a duty of £5 per annum.

*Special licenses for retailers.*—Art. 3. There shall not be retailed any cigars, snuff, or any other manufactured tobacco, except under a separate and special license, and upon payment of a duty of £5 per annum.

*Promulgation.*—Art. 4. The present ordinance shall take effect from the fifth of April next.

Passed in council at Port Louis, this twenty-seventh day of March, 1850.

## MAURITIUS AND DEPENDENCIES.

Ordinance No. 7 of 1850, to take effect from the 24th of April, 1850.

*Enacted by the governor of Mauritius, with the advice and consent of the council of government thereof:*

*Title.*—For removing doubts as to the special license to be taken for the retail of tobacco in leaf or unmanufactured. *Preamble.*—Whereas, by an ordinance passed on the twenty-seventh of March last, under No. 5 of 1850, intituled "An ordinance for amending ordinance No. 9 of 1848, relating to the import duty on tobacco, and for fixing a special license duty for the manufacturing and selling of that article in the colony," it was, among other provisions, enacted that "there shall not be retailed any cigars, snuff, or any other manufactured tobacco, except under a separate and special license, and upon payment of a duty of £5 per annum;" and whereas doubts have arisen whether tobacco in leaf was included in this or other provisions of the said ordinance; his excellency the governor in council has ordered, and does hereby order:

Art. 1. That the provision of article three of ordinance No. 5 o 1850, requiring a separate and special license for the retail of cigars, snuff, or any other manufactured tobacco, is, and shall be, extended to the retail of tobacco in leaf or unmanufactured, in the same manner as if the words "tobacco in leaf or unmanufactured" had been inserted in the above said provision.

Art. 2. Any infraction to articles two and three of the said ordinance No. 5 of 1850, and to the present ordinance, shall subject the offender to the fines and penalties directed in the first article of ordinance No. 27 of 1845, and in article nine of ordinance No. 18 of 1849.

*Promulgation.*—Art. 3. The present ordinance shall have effect from this day's date.

Passed in council, at Port Louis, island of Mauritius, this twenty-fourth day of April, 1850.

## NEW ZEALAND.

[From a despatch of the U. S. vice-consul at Auckland, New Zealand, August 9, 1851.]

"Great changes having taken place in the rates of duties chargeable upon imports in this colony, I do myself the honor of enclosing a gazette issued by the colonial government, giving the ordinance applicable to all parts of New Zealand. From this time forward, merchandise from the United States of America, Great Britain, or other nations, will pay equally."

An Ordinance to alter and amend the duties of customs.

Whereas, by an ordinance enacted by the lieutenant-governor o New Zealand, with the advice and consent of the le gislative counci thereof, session 7, No. 14, intituled "An ordinance to alter certain duties of customs," provision is made for imposing duties of customs on goods, wares, and merchandise imported into and landed in the colony of New Zealand: And whereas it is expedient that the scale of duties to be imposed on the importation of goods, wares, and merchandise be amended as follows:

1. *Be it therefore enacted by the Governor-in-chief of New Zealand, with the advice and consent of the legislative council thereof*, That the said recited ordinance shall be, and the same is hereby, repealed.

2. In lieu of the said duties, there shall be raised, levied, collected, and paid unto her Majesty, her heirs and successors, for the public uses of the colony, upon goods, wares, and merchandise which shall be imported into the colony of New Zealand, and landed at any port or place therein, or cleared from any warehouse for home consumption, after this ordinance shall come into operation, the several duties of customs as the same are respectively inserted, described, and set forth in figures in the table to this ordinance annexed, denominated a table of duties of customs.

3. The duties hereby imposed shall be raised, levied, collected, and paid in like manner as if the duties had been imposed by the ordinance, session 1, No. 3, to provide for the collection of duties of customs imposed on goods imported into, and for the general regulation of the revenue of customs in, the colony of New Zealand and its dependencies; and subject, also, to all such provisions and regulations as may, for the time being, be in force under, or by virtue of, any colonial ordinance for the collection of and for the general regulation of the revenue of customs in the colony of New Zealand.

4. This ordinance shall come into operation at the port of Wellington on the day next following the passing thereof; and at every other port of entry within the colony on the day next following the receipt of a copy hereof by the principal officer of customs at any such port, who is hereby required, immediately upon the receipt hereof, to give public notice of the same; and at all other places throughout the colony on the sixth day of August next.

Passed the legislative council this third day of July, in the year of our Lord one thousand eight hundred and fifty-one.

*Table of duties of customs.*

| | £ | s. | d. |
|---|---|---|---|
| Agricultural implements, not otherwise described, for every £100 value | 10 | 0 | 0 |
| Ale, porter, and beer, of all sorts, in casks, per gallon | | | 4 |
| in bottle, per dozen, of two gallons | | 1 | 0 |
| Alkali: | | | |
| Pot and pearl ash, per cwt | | 2 | 4 |
| Soda, per cwt | | 2 | 4 |
| Alum, for every £100 value | 10 | 0 | 0 |
| Animals, (living) | Free. | | |
| Apothecary wares, not otherwise described, for every £100 value | 10 | 0 | 0 |
| Apparel, not otherwise described, for every £100 value | 10 | 0 | 0 |
| Arms and ammunition: Ordnance of brass or iron, muskets, fowling-pieces, pistols, gunpowder, and percussion caps, (importation prohibited except under license from the government,) for every £100 value | 10 | 0 | 0 |
| Arrowroot, per cwt | | 3 | 6 |
| Arsenic, for every £100 value | 10 | 0 | 0 |
| Artificial flowers, for every £100 value | 10 | 0 | 0 |
| Bacon and hams, per cwt | | 2 | 0 |
| Baggage of passengers | Free. | | |
| Bags (empty:) | | | |
| Gunny bags, per dozen | | | 6 |
| Corn sacks, per dozen | | 1 | 0 |
| Bark, for every £100 value | 10 | 0 | 0 |
| Beef, salted—per tierce | | 6 | 0 |
| per barrel | | 4 | 0 |
| Blankets. (See *Woolens.*) | | | |
| Blacking, for every £100 value | 10 | 0 | 0 |
| Blocks, for ships' rigging, and dead-eyes | Free. | | |
| Boats | Free. | | |
| Books, printed, not being account-books | Free. | | |
| account-books, for every £100 value | 10 | 0 | 0 |
| Boots and shoes: | | | |
| Boots, (Wellington and other long,) per dozen pair | | 8 | 0 |
| Half-boots, per dozen pair | | 4 | 0 |
| Shoes, and women's boots and shoes, per dozen pair | | 3 | 0 |
| Children's boots and shoes, per dozen pair | | 2 | 0 |
| Bran and pollard, per bushel | | | 1 |
| Brass manufactures, of all sorts, for every £100 value | 10 | 0 | 0 |
| Bread and buiscuit | Free. | | |
| Bricks, Bath and Flanders, per 100 | | 2 | 0 |
| fire and other, per 1,000 | | 3 | 0 |
| Bottles, glass and stone, (empty,) per dozen | | | 1 |
| full | Free. | | |
| Butter, per pound | | | 1 |
| Bullion and coin | Free. | | |
| Cabinet and upholstery wares, for every £100 value | 10 | 0 | 0 |
| Cables | Free. | | |

| | £ | s. | d. |
|---|---|---|---|
| Candles: | | | |
| Cocoanut, palm, spermaceti, stearine, and wax, per cwt. | 0 | 14 | 0 |
| Tallow, per cwt | | 4 | 8 |
| Canvass duck, per bolt | | 3 | 0 |
| Canes and sticks, for every £100 value | 10 | 0 | 0 |
| Caps: | | | |
| Cloth, per dozen | | 2 | 0 |
| Woolen, per dozen | | | 8 |
| Carpeting. (See *Woolens.*) | | | |
| Carraway seeds, per pound | | | 1 |
| Carriages: | | | |
| Carts and wagons, for every £100 value | 10 | 0 | 0 |
| Carriage wheels of all sorts, for every £100 value | 10 | 0 | 0 |
| Casks. (See *Wood.*) | | | |
| Cement, Roman, per barrel | | 2 | 6 |
| Chalk, per ton | | 2 | 0 |
| Charcoal, animal and vegetable, for every £100 value | 10 | 0 | 0 |
| Cheese, per cwt | | 4 | 8 |
| Chocolate and cocoa, per pound | | | 1 |
| Cider and perry, in bottles, per dozen, of two gallons | | 1 | 3 |
| Clocks and watches, for every £100 value | 10 | 0 | 0 |
| Coals | Free. | | |
| Coal, pitch and tar | Free. | | |
| Coin and bullion | Free. | | |
| Confectionery, for every £100 value | 10 | 0 | 0 |
| Copper and composition sheathing nails and bolts | Free. | | |
| wrought of other sorts, per pound | | | 1 |
| Cordage and cables | Free. | | |
| Coffee, per cwt | | 4 | 8 |
| Corks, for bottling, per gross | | | 3 |
| Corn, grain, meal, flour, viz: | | | |
| Barley, per bushel | | | 4 |
| hulled. (See *Pearl and Scotch Barley.*) | | | |
| Barley meal | Free. | | |
| malt, per bushel | | | 6 |
| Beans, per bushel | | | 8 |
| Oats, per bushel | | | 4 |
| hulled. (See *Groats* or *Grits.*) | | | |
| Oatmeal | Free. | | |
| Peas, per bushel | | | 8 |
| split, per bushel | | 1 | 3 |
| Rye | Free. | | |
| Wheat | Free. | | |
| Wheat flour | Free. | | |
| Maize, per bushel | | | 3 |
| Cotton manufactures: | | | |
| Calicoes and cottons, white or plain, over 36 inches wide, per yard | | | $\frac{3}{4}$ |
| Calicoes and cottons, white or plain, 36 inches and under, per yard | | | $\frac{1}{2}$ |

| | £ | s. | d. |
|---|---|---|---|
| Printed, checked, stained, or dyed, wide, per yard.... | 0 | 0 | ¾ |
| narrow, per yard.. | | | ½ |
| Dimities, ginghams, nankeens, damasks, diaper, quilting, per yard | | | 1 |
| Cotton shawls and handkerchiefs, for every £100 value. | 10 | 0 | 0 |
| Muslins, cambrics, lawns, laces, gauzes, crapes, muslin shawls, and handkerchiefs, for every £100 value.... | 10 | 0 | 0 |
| Velvets, velverets, velveteens, and cords, per yard..... | | | 2 |
| Fustians, jeans, jeanets, &c., per yard | | | 1 |
| Counterpanes, each | | 2 | 0 |
| Bed-quilts, each | | | 6 |
| Lace and patent net, for every £100 value | 10 | 0 | 0 |
| Hosiery, viz: stockings, per dozen pair | | 1 | 0 |
| of all other sorts, for every £100 value | 10 | 0 | 0 |
| Tapes and small wares, for every £100 value | 10 | 0 | 0 |
| Cotton, for stitching or sewing, per pound | | | 1½ |
| on reels, per gross | | 1 | 0 |
| twist and yarn, for every £100 value | 10 | 0 | 0 |
| Earthen and china ware, for every £100 value | 10 | 0 | 0 |
| Engravings, for every £100 value | 10 | 0 | 0 |
| Fish, dried and pickled, per cwt | | 2 | 0 |
| Fishing tackle, including nets, lines, and twines, for every £100 value | 10 | 0 | 0 |
| Fruit: | | | |
| Apples, apricots, peaches, pears, &c., fresh, per bushel. | | 1 | 3 |
| dried, per lb.... | | | ½ |
| Almonds, per pound | | | ½ |
| shelled, per pound | | | 1 |
| Currants, raisins, dates, nuts, walnuts, filberts, figs, and prunes, dried, per pound | | | 1 |
| Oranges, limes, and lemons, fresh, per dozen | | | 2 |
| Glass, crown and sheet, per 100 feet | | 2 | 0 |
| Glasses, looking, and mirrors, for every £100 value | 10 | 0 | 0 |
| Glue, per pound | | | ½ |
| Groats, or grits, per cwt | | 2 | 4 |
| Haberdashery and millinery, not otherwise described, for every £100 value | 10 | 0 | 0 |
| Hardware and cutlery, not otherwise described, for every £100 value | 10 | 0 | 0 |
| Harrows | Free. | | |
| Hats: | | | |
| Beaver, castor and silk, per dozen | | 12 | 0 |
| Chip or willow, felt, leather, and straw | | 1 | 6 |
| Hay, per ton | | 8 | 0 |
| Honey, per pound | | | 1 |
| Hops, per pound | | | 1½ |
| Iron: | | | |
| Bar, bolt, rod, sheet, and hoop, per ton | 1 | 0 | 0 |
| Nails, per cwt | | 3 | 0 |

| | £ | s. | d. |
|---|---|---|---|
| Anchors, chains, and chain cables, for ships | Free. | | |
| Chain, per ton | 2 | 0 | 0 |
| Hollow-ware, per ton | 2 | 0 | 0 |
| Not otherwise described, for every £100 value | 10 | 0 | 0 |
| Jewelry, not otherwise described, for every £100 value | 10 | 0 | 0 |
| Juice of lemons and limes, per gallon | | | 9 |
| Junk | Free. | | |
| Lard, per pound | | | ½ |
| Lead, manufactured, per cwt | | 2 | 0 |
| black, red, and white, per cwt | | 3 | 0 |
| Leather, sole, per cwt | | 7 | 0 |
| kip and calf, per pound | | | 1½ |
| basils, per dozen | | | 9 |
| kangaroo, per dozen | | 3 | 0 |
| all other sorts, for every £100 value | 10 | 0 | 0 |
| Linen manufactures: | | | |
| White or plain, per yard | | | 1 |
| Checked, striped, printed, stained, or dyed, per yard | | | 1 |
| Cambrics and lawns, per yard | | | 2 |
| Damask and diaper, per yard | | | 1½ |
| Sail-cloth and sails | Free. | | |
| Ticking, per yard | | | ½ |
| Hosiery, viz: stockings, per dozen pairs | | 1 | 0 |
| all other sorts, for every £100 value | 10 | 0 | 0 |
| Tape, and swallwares, for every £100 value | 10 | 0 | 0 |
| Thread, for stitching or sewing, per pound | | | 2 |
| Yarn, per pound | | | 1 |
| Litharge of lead, per cwt | | 3 | 0 |
| Maccaroni and vermicelli, per pound | | | 2 |
| Machines, threshing, winnowing, and draining | Free. | | |
| Machinery for mills | Free. | | |
| Matches, Lucifer or Congreve, per gross | | | 8 |
| Vestas, per gross | | 1 | 6 |
| Molasses, per cwt | | 1 | 2 |
| Musical instruments, for every £100 value | 10 | 0 | 0 |
| Mustard, in bulk, per pound | | | 1 |
| in one-pound bottles, per dozen | | 1 | 6 |
| in half-pound bottles...do | | | 9 |
| Mutton, salted, per cwt | | 2 | 0 |
| Oakum | Free. | | |
| Oil-cloth, per square yard | | | 3 |
| Oil, cocoanut, linseed, rape-seed, hemp-seed, neat's foot, per gallon | | | 4 |
| olive, castor, and unenumerated vegetable | | 2 | 0 |
| oil blubber, and bone, the produce of fish or creatures living in the sea | Free. | | |
| of turpentine, per gallon | | | 6 |
| Paints, per cwt | | 3 | 0 |
| Painters' and dyers' colors and materials, not otherwise described, for every £100 value | 10 | 0 | 0 |

| | £ | s. | d. |
|---|---|---|---|
| Paper, brown, wrapping, or blotting, per cwt | 0 | 4 | 0 |
| printing, and cartridge, per cwt | | 7 | 0 |
| writing, per pound | | | 1½ |
| Paper hangings, per dozen yards | | | 1 |
| Parchment, and vellum, per skin | | | 2 |
| Perfumery of all sorts, for every £100 value | 10 | 0 | 0 |
| Perry. (See *Cider.*) | | | |
| Pickles and sauces, in quart bottles, per dozen | | 1 | 6 |
| in pint bottles, per dozen | | | 9 |
| in half-pint and smaller bottles, per doz. | | | 6 |
| Pitch | | Free. | |
| Plants, bulbs, trees, and seeds | | Free. | |
| Ploughs | | Free. | |
| Pork, salted, per barrel | | 5 | 0 |
| Rice, per cwt | | 2 | 0 |
| Rosin, per barrel | | 2 | 0 |
| Saddlery and harness, for every £100 value | 10 | 0 | 0 |
| Sago, per cwt | | 3 | 6 |
| salt, coarse, per ton | | 6 | 0 |
| fine, per ton | | 10 | 0 |
| Saltpetre, per cwt | | 3 | 6 |
| Silk manufactures, (silks and satins,) per yard | | | 6 |
| hosiery, viz: stockings, per dozen pair | | 5 | 0 |
| not otherwise described, for every £100 value | 10 | 0 | 0 |
| stuffs, ribbons, lace, fringe, trimmings, &c., for every £100 value | 10 | 0 | 0 |
| sewing silk, per pound | | 1 | 0 |
| twist and yarn, per pound | | 1 | 6 |
| stockings, of silk and cotton, per dozen pairs | | 2 | 0 |
| of silk and linen, per dozen pairs | | 2 | 0 |
| of silk and worsted, per dozen pairs | | 2 | 0 |
| velvet, per yard | | 1 | 6 |
| Slates. (See *Stones.*) | | | |
| in frame, per dozen | | | 9 |
| Slops, trousers, moleskin and Tweed, per pair | | | 4 |
| shirts, blue and red serge, per dozen | | 4 | 0 |
| regatta, and cotton striped, per dozen | | 1 | 6 |
| white, per dozen | | 2 | 0 |
| Soap, common, per cwt | | 3 | 0 |
| fancy, per cwt | | 6 | 0 |
| Spades and shovels, per dozen | | 3 | 0 |
| Specimens illustrative of natural history | | Free. | |
| Spices: cassia, cinnamon, cloves, mace, pimento, and nutmegs, per pound | | | 6 |
| ginger, per pound | | | 1 |
| pepper, red or Cayenne, per pound | | | 1 |
| pepper, black and white, per pound | | | 1 |
| Spirits of tar, per gallon | | | 6 |
| Spirits of turpentine, per gallon | | | 6 |

| | £ | s. | d. |
|---|---|---|---|
| Spirits: Brandy, gin, rum, and whiskey not exceeding hydrometer proof, and so in proportion for spirits of a greater strength. All cordials, sweetened spirits and liqueurs, being rated as proof spirits, at the rate of, for every gallon imperial measure | 0 | 6 | 0 |
| Pearl and Scotch barley, per cwt | | 2 | 4 |
| Starch, per cwt | | 4 | 8 |
| Stationery, not otherwise described, for every £100 value | 10 | 0 | 0 |
| Steel, per cwt | | 4 | 8 |
| Stones, hearth, flag, and slab, per ton | | 5 | 0 |
| grindstones, per foot | | | 3 |
| slate, ladies', per 1,000 | | 10 | 0 |
| slate, countess and duchess, per 1,000 | | 15 | 0 |
| Stone, blue, per pound | | | 1 |
| Sugar, refined, loaf, crushed, and candy, per cwt | | 4 | 8 |
| raw, per cwt | | 2 | 5 |
| Syrup, in bottles, per dozen | | 1 | 6 |
| Tapioca, per cwt | | 4 | 0 |
| Tar | | Free. | |
| Tea, per pound | | | 2 |
| Tin, in plates, per cwt | | 3 | 0 |
| block, per pound | | | 1 |
| ware, for every £100 value | 10 | 0 | 0 |
| Tobacco, cigars, and snuff, per pound | | 2 | 0 |
| manufactured, per pound | | 1 | 0 |
| unmanufactured, per pound | | | 9 |
| stems | | | 9 |
| for sheep-wash* | | Free. | |
| Tobacco pipes, common clay, per gross | | | 4 |
| other sorts not described, for every £100 value | 10 | 0 | 0 |
| Tongues, per barrel | | 5 | 0 |
| Toys, for every £100 value | 10 | 0 | 0 |
| Treacle. (See *Molasses.*) | | | |
| Turpentine. (See *Oil or spirits of.*) | | | |
| Twine, (except sewing twine,) per pound | | | 1 |
| Varnish, for every £100 value | 10 | 0 | 0 |
| Vinegar, per gallon | | | 2 |
| Watches. (See *Clocks and watches.*) | | | |
| Wines, in casks, per gallon | | 1 | 6 |
| bottled, per dozen of two gallons | | 5 | 0 |
| Wood: | | | |
| Board, plank, and scantling, per 100 feet | | 1 | 0 |
| Cedar, per 100 feet | | 2 | 0 |
| Casks, empty | | Free. | |
| Handspikes, masts, yards, bowsprits, oars, treenails, or trunnels | | Free. | |

* Subject to its being rendered unfit for human consumption, and be only admitted free under such regulations and restrictions as may, from time to time, be made in that behalf by his excellency the governor.

| | £ | s. | d. |
|---|---|---|---|
| Shingles and laths, per thousand | 0 | 1 | 0 |
| Palings, per thousand | | 10 | 0 |
| Wooden ware, for every £100 value | 10 | 0 | 0 |
| Wool, unmanufactured | Free. | | |
| Woolen manufactures: | | | |
| Cloths, broad, per yard | | 1 | 3 |
| Kerseymere, per yard | | | 8 |
| Baizes, of all sorts, per yard | | | 3 |
| Pilot and Flushing, per yard | | | 4 |
| Flannel, per yard | | | 1 |
| Tweeds, per yard | | | 3 |
| Blankets, per pair | | 2 | 0 |
| Blanketing, per yard | | | 9 |
| Carpets and carpeting, per yard | | | 3 |
| Rugs or coverlets for beds, each | | | 4 |
| Stuffs, woolen or worsted, for every £100 value | 10 | 0 | 0 |
| Hosiery, viz: stockings, per dozen pair | | 1 | 0 |
| all other sorts, for every £100 value | 10 | 0 | 0 |
| Tapes and small wares, for every £100 value | 10 | 0 | 0 |
| Woolen or worsted yarn, per pound | | | ½ |
| Woolpacks, each | | | 6 |
| Zinc, per cwt | | 3 | 6 |
| All goods, wares, and merchandise, not otherwise enumerated, for every £100 value | 10 | 0 | 0 |

---

## FRANCE.

[From a despatch of the United States consul at Havre, 31st December, 1850.]

"The repeal of the navigation laws has produced an important change in the direct commerce between France and the United States. English steamers and sailing vessels come to France for freight and steerage passengers, with great advantage of port charges, as English vessels pay only 20 cents the ton duty, American vessels paying 94 cts.

"The Cunard steamers from Liverpool to New York have established a branch line, running weekly to this port, taking freight and passengers for the United States. The past year a number of English sailing vessels have been chartered in England to come to this port for freight and passengers destined for the United States; that has caused several American ships to return home in ballast, principally owing to the advantage of port charges in favor of English bottoms.

"This shows the necessity of a reduction of tonnage duty to enable American ships to compete with English ships in the ports of France."

*Import duties: alterations in the French tariff, according to returns made to the British House of Commons March 26, 1850.*

| Articles. | NEW DUTY. | | Date of alteration. |
|---|---|---|---|
| | Imported in French vessels. | Imported in foreign vessels. | |
| | £ s. d. | £ s. d. | |
| Nankeens from India.................per pound. | 0 0 4½ | 0 0 0 | Dec. 15, 1848. |
| Plate-glass of more than 3 millimetres in thickness, viz: | | | |
| 50 decimetres or under in extent..per cwt.. | 6 3 | 6 3 | Dec. 15, 1848. |
| 50 to 100.......do.......do.........do.... | 9 4½ | 9 4½ | do |
| 100 to 200.......do.......do.........do.... | 11 8 | 11 8 | do |
| 200 to 300.......do.......do.........do.... | 16 8 | 16 8 | do |
| 400 to 500.......do.......do.........do.... | 1 0 10 | 1 0 10 | do |
| Above 500.......do.......do.........do.... | 1 5 0 | 1 5 0 | do |
| Iron, cast, from Algeria.....................do.... | Free. | ............ | do |
| Salt ..........................................do.... | 9 | 11 | July 12, 1849. |
| Salt, refined ...............................do.... | 1 2 | 1 4 | do |
| Iodine ........................................do.... | 5 0 | 5 0 | Dec. 15, 1848. |
| Iodine, refined.............................do.... | 6 3 | 6 3 | do |
| Sarsaparilla from French Guiana.........do.... | 16 8 | ............ | Feb. 14, 1850. |

## SENEGAL AND GOREE.

[Translation of a decree of the President of the French republic of February 8, 1852.]

### *Senegal.—Importations.*

Art. 1. French merchandise of every kind, and such articles of foreign merchandise as are named in the annexed table, will be admitted at the port of St. Louis, in Senegal, at a duty of two per cent. *ad valorem* when imported in French vessels from ports or entrepôts of France only.

Nevertheless, wood, unwrought iron, and unwrought steel, tobacco, and gunpowder, (*les poudres,*) will also be admitted at the port of St. Louis at a duty of two per cent. *ad valorem,* if taken thither from the entrepôt of Gorée in French vessels.

Blue cloths of India, called *guinées,* will continue not to be admitted at Senegal, by paying said duty of two per cent. *ad valorem,* until after they shall have "made a port" *(fait escale)* in the entrepôts of France.

Wines of Madeira and Teneriffe, imported direct under the French flag, will pay sixty francs the liquid *hectolitre.*

Fruits, fresh vegetables, and Canary stones, *(les pierres des Canaries,)* imported direct by French vessels, will be admitted free of all duties.

*Exportations.*

Art. 2. Products of Senegal cannot be exported from the port of St. Louis but in French vessels, nor to ports other than those of France or her colonies, *(pour aucune autre destination que les ports de France ou des colonies Francaises.)*

These exportations will continue to be subject to a duty of two per cent. *ad valorem.*

*Gorée.—Importations and exportations.*

Art. 3. Merchandise of every kind and of every production (except *guinées*, the disposal of which is regulated by article 1 of this decree) can be imported into and exported from the island of Gorée, by vessels of all nations, free of custom duties.

*Navigation.*

Art. 4. Navigation between France and Senegal, (including the island of Gorée,) and intercourse *(les rapports)* between those and other French possessions, Asiatic, African, and American, will continue to be carried on by French vessels only.

Foreign vessels will pay but one navigation duty, at the rate of four francs per ton, not subject to an additional tenth of a franc, *(et non passible du décime additionnel.)*

From this duty will be exempted vessels which shall return to sea without having effected any lading or unlading of merchandise.

Art. 5. All regulations contrary to the preceding are abolished.

Done at the palace of the Tuilleries, February 8, 1852.

*Table annexed to the above decree,* (Article 1.)

Amber, or succinum.

Cloths called *guinées*, *bajulapaux*, *néganépaux*, and others of that description.

Cloths *à carreaux de l'Inde.*

Walking-sticks.

*Barbuts.*

Basins and caldrons.

Baizes, *(bayettes.)*

Woolen caps.

*Cauris*, *(coquillages.)*

Wrought coral.

Knives, sabres, and fusils, dits *de traite.*

Copper, copper nails, round rods, and flat bars of copper.

Unwrought iron and unwrought steel.

Fusees *de traite* and fowling-pieces not ornamented.

Glass vessels, *(flacons de verre.)*

Dried beans of Holland.

Small metallic bells, *(grelots et clochettes en métal.)*

Coarse brown pasteboard.

Coarse hardware.
*Manilles?*
*Moques de faïence?*
Marine charts, *(neptunes.)*
Small German mirrors.
Dutch pipes.
Lead *de deux points.*
Tin (or pewter?) ware, *(poterie d'étain.)*
Gunpowder of every kind.
Products of French colonies.
Leaf and manufactured tobacco.
Trumpets.
Cooking vessels of Saxony, *(vases de cuisine.)*
*Platilles de breslau?*

---

## RUSSIA.

[From a despatch of the United States minister to Russia of December 3, 1850.]

"The new Russian tariff has been at last adopted. I learn that it makes no change upon former duties that will materially affect our trade. The contemplated *increase of the duty upon cotton has been abandoned, and that item remains as before.* The duty upon furs remains the same, operating almost as a prohibition. This far, it is still a concession to the Russian manufacturers of cotton, and to the Russian American fur-traders. In most other respects, it is a concession to the doctrines of free tade."

[From a despatch of the United States consul at St. Petersburg, December 4-16, 1850.]

"The alterations in the new Russian tariff, coming into operation on the 1-13th January, 1851, refer principally to manufactured articles, and cannot materially affect American commerce with this empire, though very favorable to England and France."

## SPAIN.

*Import duties: alterations in the Spanish tariff, according to returns made to the British House of Commons March 26, 1850.*

| Articles. | NEW DUTY. Imported in Spanish vessels. | NEW DUTY. Imported in foreign vessels. | Date of alteration. |
|---|---|---|---|
| | £ s. d. | £ s. d. | |
| Brass manufactures, common........per pound. | 0 0 7½ | 0 0 10 | Oct. 5, 1849. |
| superior ........ .......do.... | 1 0 | 1 2½ | do |
| Butter.................................do.... | 3¾ | 5 | do |
| Cheese..............................per cwt.. | 17 7 | 1 1 1 | do |
| Coal....................................do.... | 4 | 5½ | do |
| Copper, sheet...........................do.... | 2 4 0 | 2 15 0 | do |
| manufactures ..............per pound. | 1 1 | 1 4 | do |
| Cordage, hempen..................per cwt.. | 13 2 | 15 10 | do |
| Cotton thread, spun, Nos. 60 to 80...per pound. | 10 | 1 0 | do |
| No. 80 and upwards..do.... | 11 | 1 1 | do |
| Cotton manufactures, viz: | | | |
| Raw or white, 26 threads and upwards to ¼ inch, per pound. | 1 1 & 1 8 | 1 4 & 2 0 | do |
| Gauze, plain ..................per pound. | 4 2 | 5 0 | do |
| figured...........................do.... | 5 7 | 6 8 | do |
| Handkerchiefs, 20 threads and upwards, per pound.................................. | 2 0 | 2 6 | do |
| Lace.........................per pound. | 8 9 | 10 6 | do |
| Lawns, jaconets, &c................do.... | 3 6 to 5 7 | 4 2 to 6 8 | do |
| Muslins, 15 to 25 threads ...... ....do.... | 2 10 | 3 4 | do |
| 26 and upwards ..............do.... | 4 2 | 5 0 | do |
| Quiltings ..... .....................do.... | 3 6 | 4 2 | do |
| Tulle ...............................do.... | 7 0 | 8 4 | do |
| Velveteens .........................do.... | 1 7 | 1 11 | do |
| Earthenware, common ..............per cwt.. | 1 15 2 | 2 2 2 | do |
| porcelain...... ..........do.... | 2 17 2 | 3 8 7 | do |
| Fish, cod, direct from fisheries..........do.... | 7 8 | 10 6 | do |
| other...............................do.... | 12 3 | 16 3 | do |
| other, fresh.............................do.... | Free. | 3 3 | do |
| salted, smoked, &c ......do.... | 11 0 | 13 2 | do |
| Flax, raw..... ........................do.... | 6 7 | 7 11 | do |
| dressed ................................do.... | 8 9 | 10 6 | do |
| Glass, plate..............................do.... | 1 10 10 | 1 17 0 | do |
| manufactures ..........................do.... | 1 4 8 | 1 9 7 | do |
| mirrors .....................each... | 3 to 11 5 0 | 4 to 15 0 0 | do |
| Iron, pig..........................per cwt.. | 1 9 | 2 1 | do |
| refined metal ......................do.... | 3 11 | 4 8 | do |
| bars, above 1 square inch..........do.... | 8 9 | 10 6 | do |
| under......do........................do.... | 10 6 | 12 7 | do |
| Lead, pig.................................do.... | 3 11 | 4 8 | do |
| manufactured ........................do.... | 6 7 | 7 11 | do |
| Linen manufactures, viz: | | | |
| Plain, according to number of threads, per cwt. | 3 11 6 to 24 15 0 | 4 8 0 to 30 16 0 | do |
| Drills, serges, &c..... .........per cwt.. | 6 12 0 | 3 8 0 | do |
| Damasks, &c.......................do.... | 7 3 0 | 8 16 0 | do |
| Lace..........................per ounce. | 1 2 | 1 5 | do |
| Machinery, locomotives, &c........ad valorem. | 2 per cent. | 3 per cent. | do |
| spinning, weaving, &c........do.... | 3 per cent. | 4 per cent. | do |

*Import duties*—Continued.

| Articles. | NEW DUTY. | | Date of alteration. |
|---|---|---|---|
| | Imported in Spanish vessels. | Imported in foreign vessels. | |
| | £ s. d. | £ s. d. | |
| Pewter........per pound. | 0 0 8½ | 0 0 11 | Oct. 5, 1849. |
| Silk, manufactures of, viz: | | | |
| Plain........do.... | 10 0 | 12 0 | do |
| Plain, in shawls, &c........do.... | 10 0 | 12 0 | do |
| Figured........do.... | 10 0 | 12 0 | do |
| Figured, in shawls, &c........do.... | 10 0 | 12 0 | do |
| Embroidered........do.... | 12 0 | 14 5 | do |
| Embroidered, in shawls, &c........do.... | 12 0 | 14 5 | do |
| Gauze........do.... | 10 0 | 12 0 | do |
| Gauze, in shawls, &c........do.... | 10 0 | 12 0 | do |
| Ribbons, satin........do.... | 6 0 | 7 2 | do |
| velvet........do.... | 7 2 | 8 7 | do |
| gauze, &c........do.... | 8 9 | 10 6 | do |
| Tulle, &c........do.... | 16 0 | 19 2 | do |
| embroidered........do.... | 1 0 0 | 1 4 0 | do |
| Velvets........do.... | 13 6 | 16 2 | do |
| Velvets, in shawls, &c........do.... | 13 6 | 16 2 | do |
| Steel, in bars, unwrought........per cwt.. | 6 8 | 8 10 | do |
| cast, in bars........do.... | 10 0 | 13 4 | do |
| Sugar, refined........do.... | 1 6 5 | 1 13 5 | do |
| Tar........do.... | 6½ | 8½ | do |
| Thread, flax, unbleached........do.... | 13 2 | 17 8 | do |
| bleached........do.... | 16 5 | 1 2 0 | do |
| twisted........do.... | 4 2 6 | 4 19 0 | do |
| Tin, in bars........do.... | 6 7 | 7 11 | do |
| in plates........do.... | 13 2 | 17 8 | do |
| Wire, copper........do.... | 2 4 0 | 2 19 5 | do |
| iron........do.... | 7 11 | 10 7 | do |
| Wool, sheep's........do.... | 1 6 4 | 1 15 4 | do |
| Woolen manufactures, viz: | | | |
| Plain, common, &c., per yard, according to width........per sq. yd. | 8½ | 10 | do |
| Superior, &c., per yard, according to width........do.... | 1 1½ | 1 4 | do |
| Double cassimeres and beavers, per yard, according to width........do.... | 3 2 | 4 3 | do |
| Brocades, per yard, according to width........do.... | 1 0 | 1 4 | do |
| Plushes, velvets, &c., per yard, according to width........do.... | 1 0 | 1 4 | do |
| Worsted, unbleached........per pound. | 8¼ | 10¼ | do |
| bleached........do.... | 1 0 | 1 2½ | do |
| dyed........do.... | 1 5½ | 1 8½ | do |
| Zinc, plates........per cwt.. | 1 1 0 | 1 6 3 | do |

Remarks in the British return.—"In addition to the articles enumerated in the above list, which includes all of importance to British industry, a general reduction of duties has been made in almost all articles in the most voluminous and detailed tariff of Spain."

[From a despatch of the United States minister to Spain, May 1, 1849.]

"This decree, [of April 11, 1849,] as you will observe, abolishes the duty for light-houses and farols of twenty-four mervadies per ton on merchant vessels, and, in lieu thereof, establishes a greatly augmented duty for the same object. By the 3d article, foreign merchant vessels entering the Spanish ports of the peninsula and adjacent islands are to pay two reals of velon (or 68 mervadies) per ton. There are a few exceptions as to vessels arriving and departing in ballast, but these do not at all change the character of the decree."

*Decree of April* 11, 1849.

[Translation.]

Art. 1. In place of the dues established for the ports of the peninsula and the adjacent islands, under the name of light and lantern, there shall be charged hereafter in the ports where there are custom-houses, and at the same time with the other navigation fees, one light-house duty or fee, according to the rules contained in the following articles:

Art. 2. Spanish merchant vessels arriving from our possessions beyond the seas, or from foreign ports, shall pay one real for each ton.

Art. 3. Foreign merchant vessels from same destination as above, shall pay two reals for each ton. The government is hereby authorized to alter or change this fee, so as to conform to that charged on Spanish vessels in foreign ports.

Art. 4. The following exceptions are made to the preceding in favor of—

1st. Spanish vessels returning in ballast from the afore-mentioned countries.

2d. The flags of all nations which may enter and depart from our ports in ballast.

3d. All vessels arriving in distress, in case only that they do not receive or discharge cargo. If, however, they should do so, they shall pay the entire duty, and be thereafter exempt from again paying said duty at any port at which they may arrive with any part of said cargo. The foregoing disposition will be likewise applicable to those vessels arriving, not in distress, at two or more ports to discharge the effects marked in their registers.

Art. 5. Spanish vessels of the coasting trade shall pay for every voyage, going or returning, half a real for each ton.

Shall be *excepted:*

1st. Those vessels which do not measure more than twenty tons.

2d. Of more than twenty tons, but whose voyage does not extend to a greater distance than twenty marine leagues.

3d. Vessels in those ports at which they may touch in route previously to arriving at their destination, no matter what may be the distance between the said port and the one from which its register was issued.

4th. Those returning in ballast from the ports to which they were destined.

Art. 6. The light-house dues shall bear the character of being temporary, and shall be applied to the preservation and maintenance thereof, when the expenses of their establishment are covered.

[From a despatch of the United States minister to Spain, July 20, 1851.]

"I transmit herewith a copy of a communication from the Marquis of Miraflores, her Majesty's Minister of State, under date of the 30th June last, informing me that her Majesty's government have decreed that the manifests of all goods and merchandise liable to sanitary duties in the ports of Mahon or Vigo, while the vessels containing them are performing quarantine at those stations, shall be made out in the Spanish language, instead of that of their respective nations, as heretofore.

"I also transmit herewith a copy of a communication from the Spanish Minister of State, in reply to my note of the 9th April, 1850, complaining of the manner in which the quarantine regulations of the island of Cuba had been administered, and of the pernicious effects of the same on our commercial interests in those seas. The complaints which were of a general or important character have been met by a reform of the objectionable features of the regulations, or the manner of their administration.

"Three new ports of quarantine have been named, viz: Nuevitas, Cienfuegos, and Masio; and that of Trinidad will be, as soon as a convenient edifice for a lazaretto can be built. Also the time of quarantine will be counted hereafter, not from the time of the vessel's arrival at the quarantine port, but from the time of her touching at any port of the island, upon the certificate of the secretary of the health board or the deputation of such port. And all ports in the island are constituted ports of 'quarantine of observation,' vessels being obliged to proceed to the lazaretto only in cases of '*causas graves*,' which require strict quarantine."

[From a despatch of the United States minister to Spain, January 22, 1852.]

"I have the satisfaction to inform you that, on the 3d instant, her Catholic Majesty, with the advice of her ministers, has been pleased to make and publish a *royal decree* abolishing the differential duties previously existing, and establishing an exact reciprocity in navigation and port duties in this peninsula, and the islands adjacent, with all foreign nations who may concede like benefits in their respective territories to Spanish vessels. A copy (translated) of this *royal decree* is herewith transmitted."

*Royal decree of January* 3, 1852.

Art. 1. In the peninsula, and islands adjacent, there shall be put upon the same footing with Spanish vessels for the exaction of navigation and port duties, or, and that is to say, for those of light-houses, anchorage, and of loading and unloading cargo, established in the law of the 11th of April, 1849, and in my royal decree of the 16th of December last, the vessels of all nations who may concede a like benefit in their respective territories to the vessels of the Spanish marine.

Art. 2. The government will give account of this order to the Cortes.

[From a despatch of the United States minister to Spain, March 23, 1852.]

"With my despatch of 22d January last, I had the honor to transmit a copy of the recent *royal decree* of the 3d January ultimo, abolishing the differential port and navigation duties exacted in *this peninsula*, and the *islands adjacent*, on foreign vessels, and offering reciprocity in the same in favor of *all* nations who concede like benefits to vessels of the Spanish marine, in their respective ports.

"Since the date of that despatch, I have had a correspondence with her Majesty's Minister of State, in which, under and by virtue of our acts of Congress of the 24th May, 1828, and the 13th July, 1832, I have endeavored to obtain from her Majesty's government a royal order placing the *American* flag and vessels on the same footing, in regard to such duties, with *Spanish* vessels in the Spanish ports of this peninsula and the islands adjacent.

"To this request the Spanish government are very willing to accede; and the only difficulty was the designation of a given day when this reciprocity or assimilation of the two flags in the respective countries shall take effect in each. I have suggested the 1st day of May next.

"It will be perceived that the reciprocity proposed under said decree is confined to vessels of foreign nations entering the Spanish ports of *this peninsula and the adjacent islands*, and, of course, does not extend to the Spanish West India or other colonial possessions."

[From a despatch of the United States minister to Spain, June 9, 1852.]

"I transmit, herewith, a copy of a communication from his excellency her Majesty's Minister of State, under date of the 24th ultimo, on the subject of quarantine and sanitary regulations in Spanish ports, from which it will be seen that, in certain cases, quarantines of observation have been abolished by order of her Majesty's government."

[Translation.—Extract.]

MAY 24, 1852.

"The government of her Majesty has instructed the governors of the maritime provinces, that the maritime boards of health cease to subject to any quarantine of observation those vessels whose bills of health ought not to be considered unclean or suspicious; and that, with respect to arrivals from points where the yellow fever prevails habitually, and from those where it may accidentally prevail, as also from those which do not guard themselves against the said disease, the said boards shall observe with all scrupulousness what is ordered in the royal decree of the 28th September last, and in its explanatory decree of the 26th of January last."

## PORTUGAL.

[From a despatch of the United States chargé d'affaires to Portugal, May 26, 1852.]

"By the treaty between this government and the United States, of August 26, 1840, vessels of the United States are entitled to the same facilities and privileges, in the ports of the kingdom, as are enjoyed by the flag of Portugal. But, although this treaty has been in force nearly twelve years, a system of regulations in regard to the salt trade of St. Ubes has been in operation all this while, and was made a law of the kingdom by a decree, dated November 20, 1851, which makes important distinctions between the Portuguese and all foreign flags.

"In pursuance of these regulations, public officers have set apart one-third of the product of the 'salt-pans' of St. Ubes for sale to foreign vessels. Of the other two-thirds they could not buy; and, in buying even of the designated third, they have been obliged to take of the several salt proprietors in rotation, and at a price fixed by the 'Junta' of St. Ubes. The 'Junta' have also had entire control of the lighters of the ports, and have determined the lighterage.

"The price of salt in the pans, as thus fixed for foreigners, has been 1,000 Rs. per moyo, twenty-two and a half bushels.

"For lighterage and other incidental expenses, they have been charged 320 Rs. per moyo.

"For salt and lighterage, 1,320 Rs. per moyo. Portuguese vessels have, at the same time, paid but 400 Rs. per moyo for the salt, and 200 Rs. per moyo lighterage—in all, 600 Rs. per moyo.

"The decree of November, 1851, allowed Portuguese ships to buy of whomsoever they chose, and at prices that may be agreed upon by the parties.

"Thus you will perceive that, during the whole time of the existence of the treaty, guarantying to American ships the same privileges as Portuguese ships enjoy in the trade of the country, American merchants have actually been obliged, by law, to pay double the price charged to the Portuguese for the salt of St. Ubes. A cargo of 300 moyos, about 200 tons, costs a Portuguese vessel 180 mill-reis; the same cargo, in the same port, costs an American vessel 396 mill-reis.

"The consequence has been, that our ships have nearly deserted St. Ubes and gone to Cadiz, some hundreds of miles further, and paid something more than the current price of St. Ubes salt, to the Portuguese merchants, for an inferior article.

"My attention having been called to the subject, and seeing this palpable violation of the treaty of 1840, under the cover of law, I immediately made arrangements to bring the matter before her Majesty's Minister of State."

[Here follows his correspondence with that officer, &c.]

"The tone of this correspondence, on the part of the Secretary for Foreign Affairs, leaves no room to doubt either the good will of her Majesty's government towards the United States, or their determination to execute the duty imposed on them by the existing treaty in its fullest extent.

"No American ship need fear, in future, the slightest opposition or embarrassment in loading with salt at this port, at such rates as may be agreed upon in a fair and open market. St. Ubes is now overflowing with salt; and the best quality may be bought, in abundance, at 400 Rs. per moyo; lighterage, 200 Rs. per moyo."

## NETHERLANDS.

### *Steam navigation.—Royal decree of February* 15, 1850.

[Translation.]

"1. It is not needful hereafter to require a permission for the *steam navigation* as long as it is practised *directly* either from a Netherland port to a foreign port, or from a foreign to a port in the Netherlands: provided, however, that permission be asked and granted in cases in which these steamboats are also, at stipulated periods, previously announced; or, in the event of regular service, from one to another place in this country, either for the transportation of passengers or goods, or jointly, as the towing of other vessels or craft, according to the decree of the 31st July, 1841, or the royal decree of May 9, 1846.

"2. That the permission hitherto granted, in this country, to the ocean steam navigation, with the customary conditions thereunto attached, be, and hereby is abrogated, except where it should conflict with the stipulations in the preceding article.

"3. That, notwithstanding the admission of foreign steamers without permission from this kingdom, set forth in article 1 of this decree, it is intended that it should be based upon a principle of reasonable reciprocity, to wit: that in the event of Netherland steamers being, in their regular passages to said foreign ports, subjected to any formalities or onerous exactions, in like manner the steamers of foreign nations shall be compelled to comply, in Netherland, with the same formalities and exactions."

### *Laws of the Netherland government relaxing restrictions on trade with Holland and her colonial possessions, August* 8, 1850.

[Translation.]

"LAW LIT. A."

[*Respecting the abolition of regulations by which privileges are granted to the Netherland flag above the foreign; the reduction of import duties on ship-building materials; and fixing certain regulations respecting the trade and navigation in the colonies and possessions of the kingdom in other parts of the world.—August* 8, 1850.]

We, William III, &c., having taken into consideration the necessity to repeal the different regulations contained in the laws of June 19,

1845, and August 26, 1822; and also, that the interest of Netherland ship-building requires a reduction of the duties levied on the import of the principal ship-building materials, conformably to the law of June 19, 1845; and, lastly, that, in combination with the above, a necessity exists for legal regulations relative to the trade and shipping in the colonies and possessions of the kingdom in other parts of the world:

We, after having heard our Council of State, and in concert with the State's General, have thought proper to decree:

ARTICLE 1. At the close of article 3, § 1, of the law of June 19, 1845, the following is to be added:

"Similar freedom is granted by us, if the import takes place by vessels of those States which—

"*a.* Place the Dutch flag on the same footing with the national one trading to and from their own ports (coasting trade and fisheries excepted;)

"*b.* Which place the Dutch flag on the same footing with the national one trading to and from their colonies, if they possess any; and,

"*c.* Which do not levy other differential duties to the disadvantage of the produce of the Netherland colonies, or to the prejudice of produce imported from other parts of the world, from Netherland ports, than those which are levied in favor of the produce of their own colonies, when imported direct."

ART. 2. The words "by Dutch vessels," contained in article 3, §§ 4 and 14, of the law of June 19, 1845, are repealed.

ART. 3. Articles 4 and 5 of the law of June 19, 1845, are abolished.*

ART. 4. The tariff of duties added to the law of June 19, 1845, is to be modified, by omitting the articles enumerated under Litt. A, and by inserting the articles under Litt. B, as mentioned hereafter.

---

* The regulations above abolished were the following:

"*Article* 4. All articles imported or exported by sea under Dutch flag are subject to a reduction of 10 per cent. on the import or export duties, excepting those to which, by the tariff itself, any special favor, if imported under Dutch flag, is granted. On the duties on wheat, rye, spelter, buckwheat, barley, malt, and oats, imported by Netherland vessels, a reduction of 2f. per last (of 30 mud) is granted.

"*Article* 5. The reduction or exemption of duty stipulated by law in the tariff in favor of Netherland vessels is enjoyed for all goods imported or exported by sea in vessels possessed f Dutch registers."

*Tariff A.—Repealed regulations of the law of June* 19, 1845.

| Articles. | Standard. | Import. | Export. |
|---|---|---|---|
| Almonds, by Netherland vessels, from ports in the Mediterranean | 100 pounds. | *f.* *c.* 1 75 | Free. |
| Ashes— | | | |
| Pot ashes, pearl ashes (1) | do | 60 | do |
| By Netherland vessels | do | 30 | do |
| Weed ashes and soda | do | 40 | do |
| By Netherland vessels | do | 20 | do |
| Manufactory and steam-engines (2) | Value | 6 per cent. | do |
| Yarns of hemp, flax, or tow—cable, rope, and sail yarn, and all other yarns spun on the small yard | 100 pounds. | 3 00 | do |
| Spirits, rum, arrack, and liquors, on cask, by Netherland vessels | Cask | 50 | do |
| Rosin | 100 pounds. | 20 | do |
| Hemp, not hackled | do | 50 | do |
| By Netherland vessels | do | 25 | do |
| Timber— | | | |
| All sorts of timber for ship and house building, with unbroken bulk, from Norway, Sweden, the Baltic, and Russia, not sawed (3) | Ton | 25 | do |
| All sorts of timber for ship and house building, with unbroken bulk, from Norway, Sweden, the Baltic, and Russia, whether sawed, not entirely sawed, or not sawed | Ton | 1 50 | do |
| With broken bulk or from other parts, all (4) kinds of sawed timber not specifically rated | Value | 2½ per cent. | do |
| With broken bulk or from other parts, all kinds of timber entirely sawed or not sawed | Cubic ell | 1 50 | do |
| Hides— | | | |
| Skins and leather—all unprepared hides not specifically rated, whether fresh, salted, or dried, imported direct from ports in South America | Value | ½ per cent. | do |
| Skins and leather from other ports | Value | 1 per cent. | do |
| By Netherland vessels | Value | ½ per cent. | do |
| Iron— | | | |
| Cast in rough blocks or pieces, the so-called slabs, for ballast; also, ore and forged, staff, bar, sheath and plate iron, and rails for railroads | Value | 1 per cent. | do |
| By Netherland vessels | Value | ½ per cent. | do |
| Ironware and utensils, cast, forged, mould, flattened, ships' anchors included | Value | 6 per cent. | do |
| Cotton, not spun | 100 pounds. | 50 | do |
| By Netherland vessels | do | Free. | do |
| Coals, pit— | | | |
| Dust, or measured (5) coals | 10 mud | 1 50 | do |
| Large or scale coals | 1000 pounds. | 2 00 | do |
| Without any specification, imported by sea or along the rivers and canals, by Netherland vessels | (6) | Free. | do |
| Copper, beaten or flattened, excepting that which is specifically rated, round or square, and also the basins and kettles as they leave the mill, plates and sheathing for coppering ships, copper wire, and copper nails | 100 pounds. | 4 00 | do |
| Currants, by Netherland vessels, from ports in the Mediterranean | do | 75 | do |
| Manufactures—linen, and stuffs of hemp, flax, and tow, sail cloth (7) | Roll | 50 | do |
| Oil— | | | |
| Olive oil, by Netherland vessels, from ports in the Mediterranean | Cask | 1 00 | do |

*Tariff A*—Continued.

| Articles. | Standard. | Import. | Export. |
|---|---|---|---|
| Oil— | | *f. c.* | |
| Bergamot, lemon, and other scented oils, from ports in the Mediterranean, and imported by sea in brass or tin bottles containing not less than 10 pounds | Value | 1 per cent. | Free. |
| Oil of orange blossoms, (oleum neroli,) imported in the natural state, and not prepared to be used as scent | Value | 1 per cent. | do |
| Raisins, by Netherland vessels, from ports in the Mediterranean | 100 pounds. | 40 | do |
| Zinc, flattened, also wire and nails | do | 1 50 | do |
| Syrup— | | | |
| Molasses, unprepared, imported direct by Netherland vessels from ports beyond Europe | do | 3 00 | do |
| Molasses, unprepared, imported from other parts, also prepared molasses, kitchen treacle, and all other kinds of syrup | do | 10 00 | do |
| Sugar, raw, formed, and clayed (8) | do | 1 00 | do |
| By Netherland vessels | do | 20 | do |
| Tobacco, cigars— | | | |
| From ports in Europe | do | 40 00 | do |
| From other parts | do | 30 00 | do |
| Tea (9)— | | | |
| Imported direct from China or the East Indian possessions, with unbroken bulk— | | | |
| Bohea and coarse Congou | do | 18 00 | do |
| All other sorts | do | 34 00 | do |
| By Netherland vessels— | | | |
| Bohea and coarse Congou | do | 7 00 | do |
| All other sorts | do | 12 00 | do |
| From other parts or with broken bulk— | | | |
| Bohea and coarse Congou | do | 27 00 | do |
| All other sorts | do | 51 00 | do |
| Tow, ropes or ships' rigging, and all other kinds of tow | do | 6 00 | do |
| Figs, by Netherland vessels, from ports in the Mediterranean or Portugal | do | 75 | do |
| Fruit—all kinds of fresh and dried fruit, not specifically rated, by Netherland vessels | Value | 1 per cent. | do |
| Wine, in casks, by Netherland vessels | Cask | 50 | do |
| Seed—cole, rape, linseed, vetches, and hemp seed, and all other oil seeds not specially enumerated, by Netherland vessels | Last | 1 00 | do |
| Salt (10)— | | | |
| Raw, imported by sea | 100 pounds. | 2 00 | do |
| By Netherland vessels | do | Free. | do |
| Imported by land | do | 2 00 | do |
| Sulphur, unrefined, by Netherland vessels, from ports in the Mediterranean | do | Free. | do |

## EXPLANATORY REMARKS ON TARIFF A.

[See numbers in the preceding table referring to these remarks.]

1. Under this head are also included all kinds of ashes not specifically enumerated—such as are derived from wood or plants; or calcined ashes—such as straw ashes, vine ashes, and such like.

2. It is reserved to the King to admit, free of duty, machinery of recent invention, or such which is not manufactured in this country, when it is required for the interests of industry, ship-building, or agriculture.

3. Under this head are included deals imported with unbroken bulk from Sweden, Russia, the Baltic, and Norway, of not less than 5 inches thick, 30 inches broad, and 4 ells long. By "unbroken bulk" is meant, wherever half of the capacity of the vessel, as stated in the certificate of measurement for the tonnage duty, is loaded with timber. The duty is to be paid for the full tonnage stated in the certificate of measurement, whether the cargo consists only partly of timber, or even if there be timber on deck.

In case of mixed cargoes, such as of sawed and not sawed timber, the principle of levying duty for the full tonnage of the ships will be applied as follows: the existing amount of tons of sawed timber will be deducted from the number of tons stated in the certificate of measurement, and the difference considered to be the cargo of unsawed timber. All this over and above the payment of duty according to the regulations in the tariff for such goods as form part of the cargo besides the timber for ship and house building.

4. Under this head can be included deals of which the floors and huts on the rafts are made, but in no other proportion than of 4 cubic ells for every 100 cubic ells which the raft measures.

5. See the law on pit coals. It is reserved to the King to grant freedom or reduction of duties on coals imported by way of land, along a prescribed route, for the interest of the inhabitants on the frontiers.

6. For dust or measure coals, 10 mud; for scale coals, 1,000 pounds.

7. By the "roll" is understood a roll of 42 ells, or less; measuring more than that, it will be considered a double roll, and double the duty (1 fl.) will be paid accordingly.

8. Tare for sugar: imported in boxes from Havana, 13 per cent.; in boxes from Rio Janeiro, Pernambuco, East India, 18 per cent.; in boxes from other parts, 15 per cent.; in casks, 14 per cent.; in leather, mats, baskets, or linen, and such like packages, 5 per cent., (5 of such packages, if possible, always to be weighed together;) in kannassers and kranjangs, 10 per cent.—all gross weight.

9. Tare of tea: of ordinary tea chests, weighing 55 Netherland pounds, and above, 18 per cent.; ordinary tea chests, weighing less than 55 pounds, 25 per cent. On entering tea coming direct from China or the Netherland East India possessions, the original manifest, or other ship's or lading documents, sufficiently showing the origin of the cargo, must be exhibited to identify the cargo; and the functionaries can also claim a legal declaration by the captain, mate, and part of the crew.

As tea, Bohea or coarse Congou, can only be admitted such tea which is imported unmixed, in whole chests of about 180 to 200 Netherland pounds, and without being packed or incased in smaller chests or packages.

As coarse Congou, is not to be admitted such tea, which, although being in whole chests, has at the time of entry a value of 2 f. per Netherland pound, or above, according to the current price of the day in this country; and is liable to seizure all tea entered as coarse Congou, when it has less value than 2 f. per Netherland pound, including the augmentation and restitutions specified by article 263, and as per general law of import, export, and transit, and excise duties, and in conformity with the regulations thereof in as far as they are applicable to this case.

10. See the law on salt. On importing pickle, the salt therein contained will be reduced in pounds according to the Netherland hydrometer, and in compliance with the existing or afterwards-to-be-made regulations in the excise law on salt, and be subject to the same duties as the raw salt.

*References.*—Bohea tea, Congou tea, see *Tea*. Cinders, see *Pit coals*.

*Tariff B.—New regulations.*

| Articles. | Standard. | Import. | Export. |
|---|---|---|---|
| Ashes— | | *f. c.* | |
| Pot and pearl ashes (1) | 100 pounds. | 0 30 | Free. |
| Weed ashes and soda | ....do.... | 20 | do |
| Manufactory and steam-engines | Value | 1 per cent. | do |
| Yarns of hemp, flax, and tow— | | | |
| Cable and rope and sail yarn | 100 pounds. | 1 00 | do |
| Twine and all other yarns spun on the small yard | ....do.... | 3 00 | do |
| Rosin | ....do.... | 10 | do |
| Hemp, not hackled | ....do.... | 25 | do |
| Timber— | | | |
| For ship and house building, imported by sea, with unbroken bulk, unsawed (2) | Ton | 25 | do |
| Sawed | Ton | 1 50 | do |
| For ship and house building, not specifically enumerated, unsawed (3) | Value | 1 per cent. | do |
| Sawed | Cubic ell | 1 50 | do |
| Hides, skins, and leather—all hides unprepared, either fresh, salted, or dried, not specifically rated | Value | ½ per cent. | do |
| Iron— | | | |
| Cast, in rough blocks or pieces, likewise the so-called slabs for ballast and ore, forged, staff, bar, band, and sheath iron, and rails for railroad | Value | ½ per cent. | do |
| Ironware and utensils cast, forged, beaten, or flattened, not specifically rated | Value | 6 per cent. | do |
| Ironware and utensils, ships' anchors, chains, and capstans | Value | 1 per cent. | do |
| Cotton, not spun | Value | Free. | do |
| Coals, pit, including cinders (4) | Value | Free. | do |
| Copper— | | | |
| Beaten or flattened, (excepting that which is specifically rated,) round or square, likewise the basins and kettles as they leave the mill, wire | 100 pounds. | 4 00 | do |
| Beaten or flattened, plates and sheaths of yellow and red copper for sheathing ships' bottoms, bolts, and nails | ....do.... | 1 00 | do |
| Manufactures—linen, and stuffs of hemp, flax, and tow—sail cloth (5) | Roll | 30 | do |
| Oil, bergamot, lemon oil, oil of orange blossoms, (oleum neroli,) and all other scented oils, in as far as imported in their natural state, and not prepared to be used as scent | Value | 1 per cent. | do |
| Zinc— | | | |
| Flattened, (excepting that which is specifically rated,) likewise wire | 100 pounds. | 1 50 | do |
| Plates and sheaths for coppering ships, also nails | ....do.... | 30 | do |
| Syrup— | | | |
| Molasses, unprepared, by which is only to be understood those obtained from the cane after the first crystallization (6), | ....do.... | 3 00 | do |
| Molasses, prepared and all other unprepared, kitchen and all other treacle | ....do.... | 10 00 | do |
| Sugar, raw, formed and clayed (7) | ....do.... | 20 | do |
| Tobacco, cigars | ....do.... | 40 00 | do |
| Tea (8) | ....do.... | 20 00 | do |
| Tow—ropes, ships' rigging, and all other rope work | ....do.... | 2 00 | do |
| Salt, raw (9) | ....do.... | Free. | do |

## EXPLANATORY REMARKS ON TARIFF B.

[See numbers in the preceding table referring to these remarks.]

1. Under this head are included all kinds of ashes not specifically enumerated—such as are derived from wood or plants; or calcined ashes—such as straw ashes, vine ashes, and such like.

2. Under this head are included deals imported with unbroken bulk from Sweden, Russia, the Baltic, and Norway, of not less than 5 inches thick, 30 inches broad, and 4 ells long. By "unbroken bulk" is meant, whenever half of the capacity of the vessel, as stated in the certificate of measurement for the tonnage duty, is loaded with timber, duty is to be paid for the full amount of tonnage stated in the certificate of measurement, whether the cargo consists only partly of timber, or even if there be timber on deck. In case of mixed cargoes, such as of sawed and unsawed timber, the principle of levying duty for the full tonnage of the ships will be applied as follows: the existing amount of the tons of sawed timber will be deducted from the number of tons stated in the certificate of measurement, and the difference considered to be the cargo of unsawed timber.

3. Under this head are included deals of which the floors and huts are made on the rafts, but in no other proportion than of 4 cubic ells per every 100 cubic ells which the raft measures.

4. See the law on pit coals. On entering measure coals, the standard measure is by mud; for scale coals, by pounds.

5. By the "roll" is understood a roll of 42 ells, or less; measuring more, it will be considered a double roll, and duty at 60 cents paid accordingly.

6. At the entry, the nature of the molasses must be stated.

7. Tare for sugar: imported in boxes from Havana, 13 per cent.; in boxes from Rio Janeiro, Pernambuco, East India, 18 per cent.; in boxes from other parts, 15 per cent.; in casks, 14 per cent.; in packages of leather, mats, baskets, linen, and such like, 5 per cent., (5 of such packages always, if possible, to be weighed together;) in kannassers or kranjangs, 10 per cent.—all gross weights.

8. Tare of tea: of ordinary tea chests, weighing 55 Netherland pounds, and above, 18 per cent.; of ordinary tea chests, weighing less than 55 Netherland pounds, 25 per cent.

9. See the law on salt. On importing pickle the salt therein contained will be reduced to pounds, according to the Netherland hydrometer, and according to the still existing or afterwards-to-be-made regulations in the excise law on salt, and must be entered as such.

*References.*—Twine, see *Yarn;* Bohea tea, see *Tea;* Bolts, copper, see *Copper;* Congou tea, see *Tea;* Chains, ships', see *Iron;* Cinders, see *Pit coals;* Capstans, ships', see *Iron.*

Art. 5. In the existing colonial import, export, and transit duties, no alteration is to be made than by legal enactment.

The governor general has power only in cases of emergency to modify temporarily the duties. Of such modification immediate notice is to be given to both the chambers of the States General.

Art. 6. The flags of such States which comply with the conditions enumerated in article 1 of this law are placed on the same footing with the Dutch flag in the colonies and possessions of this kingdom in other parts of the globe. The above exemption does not apply to the coasting trade in Netherland India. Netherland vessels only, and vessels belonging to ports in Netherland India, as also the native vessels enjoying equality with the above vessels, are entitled to carry on the coasting trade in Netherland India, as exercised according to the existing regulations.

Art. 7. By chapter 25 of the law of August 26, 1822, the following modifications are to be inserted:

Article 292 is to be read as follows:

"On all vessels which, after the period mentioned in article 1, enter or leave this kingdom, either by sea or along the marshes between the islands and the coasts of Friesland and Groningen, a duty is to be paid under the designation of tonnage duty, calculated on the number of tons which the vessels are measured at.

"Every ton is to be calculated at the rate of 1,000 Netherland pounds represented by one cubic and a half of the Netherland ell.

"The tonnage duty is to be 45 cents per ton at the first outward clearance, and a like sum at the first arrival in each year, from January 1st to 31st December."

Articles 293, 294, 295 are repealed.

Article 298 is repealed.

Article 299 is to be read as follows:

"The owners, skippers, or commanders of vessels subject to tonnage duty, are under obligation to have them measured by functionaries thereto expressly appointed at the port where the vessels may be lying at the time, when such metage is necessary."

Article 301 is to be read as follows:

"The meter has to provide the skipper or commander with a certificate of measurement duly signed in duplicate, containing, besides the description of the flag under which the vessel navigates, and all that is further necessary to identify the vessel, the length, width, depth, and number of tons."

Article 305 is to be read as follows:

"On exhibiting the certificate of measurement at the office of the collector of the port, the payment of the tonnage duty is to be made in conformity, after the calculation shall have been found to be correct, in exchange for a tonnage register, expressing receipt of the payment, the name of the port, and date of certificate of measurement.

"Each payment, together with the date of the year, has to be inserted in the certificate of measurement, which is always to be returned to the parties interested, until the day of expiry, and then be returned in order to be repeated, on exhibiting the new certificate of measurement, issued as per article 303. At the first payment, the duplicate of the certificate of measurement must be returned, and kept at the collector's office."

Article 306 is to be altered as follows: "At each new payment of the tonnage duty, the previous tonnage register is to be annulled."

Art. 8. We reserve to ourselves the right of retaliation on vessels of those nations where the Netherland vessels, or the goods imported or exported by Netherland vessels, are subject to higher duties or charges (of whatsoever denomination) than the national ships, or the goods of the same description imported or exported by national ships, or where the import or export of any goods permitted by national ships are prohibited to Netherland vessels, whenever circumstances may render such measures necessary, and shall be deemed to be desirable for the interest of Netherland trade and shipping, either by refusing to vessels of said nations admission of certain articles, whether by subjecting said vessels to a higher tonnage duty, or the goods imported by the same to higher import duties; but always in such degree, that in the application of such retaliation, as much as possible, absolute reciprocity be maintained.

Art. 9. The day on which the present is to come into operation will be further fixed.

## Litt. B.

*Law respecting the repeal of navigation dues on the Rhine and Yssel, and the repeal of transit duties.*—[*August* 8, 1850.]

We, William III, &c., having taken into consideration that the necessity exists to repeal navigation dues on the Rhine and Yssel, and likewise to repeal the transit duties; so we, having heard our Council of State, and in concert with the States General, have thought proper to decree:

Article 1. The navigation dues, regulated by tariffs B and C, of the convention concluded on the 31st of March, 1831, between the States on the borders of the Rhine, and established by royal decree of 28th June, 1831, as well as of the water-tolls on the Guilderland Yssel, established by royal decree of 14th May, 1835, are repealed.

We reserve to ourselves to bring said duties again in operation with regard to the vessels of those States which may treat the Dutch flag, in this respect, less favorably than the national one.

Art. 2. At the same time, all transit dues are repealed.

Art. 3. We reserve to ourselves to make such regulations respecting the transit of salt, as shall be necessary to prevent the evasion of the excise on salt.

Art. 4. The day on which this law is to come into operation will be further fixed.

## Litt. C.

*Law repealing the interdiction on vessels built abroad, from navigating under Dutch registers.*—[*August* 8, 1850.]

We, William III, &c., having taken into consideration that the necessity exists to grant also to vessels built abroad, Dutch ships' registers, so we, after having heard our Council of State, and in concert with the States General, have thought proper to decree:

Article 1. Both the last sentences of article 2 of the law of 14th March, 1819, as well as the words, "and not navigating under a foreign flag," contained in article 3, 2°, of the same law, are repealed.*

Art. 2. At the close of article 8 of the same law, the following phrase is to be added:

"On demanding a first Netherland certificate for a vessel built beyond this kingdom or its colonies, the above-mentioned owner's warrant, before the register can be granted, must be furnished with a proof of registration.

"The duty to be paid for this is four per cent. of the value, over and

---

* Both the repealed phrases of article 2, were of the following import:

"Registers will only be granted to vessels built and fitted out in this country, with the exception, however, of vessels built abroad, which, previous to the promulgation of the present law, had obtained Netherland registers.

"We reserve to ourselves to grant registers to vessels built abroad, in as far as such may be for the interest of the trade and shipping, and provided the same stamp and registration dues shall have been paid in this kingdom for such vessels, although bought abroad, as if they had been bought within the kingdom."

The modified article 3, 2°, is now to be read as follows: "2°. All Netherland inhabitants which have had, for the space of one year at least, their fixed residence in this kingdom, although they be, at the same time, subjects of a foreign State."

above the amount which is stipulated by the law for registration of all other cases, which for that purpose, conformably with the instructions of article 10 of the law of June 16, 1832, must be expressed by the applicants at the foot of the above warrant.

"If the functionaries charged with levying the registration duty are not satisfied with this declaration, it will be left to the decision of three arbiters, of whom one is to be appointed by the owners of the vessel, the second by government, and the third by both last mentioned, or, in case of difference of opinion, by the president of the district court of justice.

"Article 56 of the law of 22 Frimaire, year VII, is in this case not applicable.

"The charges of valuation are for account of the owner or joint-owners, in case the determined value shall exceed the declared value by at least one-eighth.

"The amount of the above-named duty will be revised at the same time as the tariff of import and export duties."

ART. 3. The day on which this law is to come into operation will be further fixed.

*General law of August* 26, 1822.—*Revised according to Law Litt. A, of August* 8, 1850, *(see preceding pages,) respecting the regulation of the interest of Netherland shipping.*

CHAPTER XXV.—*Of the tonnage-duty of sea-vessels.**

ARTICLE 292, (article 292 before, but now modified.) Of all vessels entering or leaving this kingdom after the period fixed in article 1, by sea or along the marshes between the islands and the coasts of Friesland and Groningen, a duty will be levied, under the denomination of tonnage-duty, calculated according to the number of tons which the vessels measure.

Every ton will be equal to 1,000 Netherland pounds, represented by one and a half cubic of the Netherland ell.

The tonnage-duty is 45 cents per ton at the first outward clearance, and a like sum at the first entry of each year (from 1st January to the 31st December.)

ARTICLE 293, (the same as before, article 296.) Free of tonnage-duty are:

1. Netherland vessels, in as far and as long as they are only used for the fresh fisheries, the large fisheries or herring fisheries, the haberdine fisheries, and the whale fisheries, including those of Davis's straits, and also, as long as we shall consider it necessary, those which are trading to and from the coast of Guinea.

2. Netherland vessels leaving the kingdom, laden only with turf and coals, and entering again in ballast. Entering with cargo, the inward tonnage-duty is to be paid.

3. All vessels putting in to lie-to for orders, through stress of weather, or to winter, without entirely or partly breaking bulk, or taking cargo, and with reservation or intention of the commander to leave again with

---

* With a new order of articles, and with reference to the former articles now either altered or retained.

unbroken cargo; and it will not be considered having broken bulk if some goods have to be landed for a short time, for repairs of the vessel, or for purifying the goods, or such like, as is before mentioned in chapter 4, neither the discharge or sale against payment of the duty and excise of goods spoiled or heavily damaged during the voyage, except on a written permission of the director of customs.

We reserve, however, to ourselves to extend this freedom on foreign vessels lying-to, no further than to vessels belonging to kingdoms, States, or ports, where to Dutch vessels, in similar case, a like or similar freedom is or will be granted.

4. Vessels used as pilot-boats, and only as such.

Article 294, (same contents as before, article 297.) Coasting-trade mentioned in chapter 17, does not subject Dutch vessels employed in that trade to tonnage duty; but a bond may be required, the same as on inland permits, when the vessels leave, to prevent that under pretence of coasting trade, a sea-voyage to any port beyond the kingdom be undertaken.

Article 295, (before article 299, now modified.) The owners, skippers, or commanders of vessels subject to tonnage duty, must cause them to be measured by functionaries appointed expressly for that purpose, at the ports where the vessels are at the time when such is required.

Article 296, (the same as article 300 before.) Fractions less than a quarter of a cubic ell are not to be reckoned at the measurement; those of a quarter ell and above are reckoned for half an ell.

Article 297, (before article 301, now modified.) The meter has to provide the skipper or commander with a duly signed certificate of measurement in duplicate, showing, over and above the flag under which the vessel navigates, and what is further necessary to identify the same, the length, width, and depth, and the number of tons.

Article 298, (the same as before, article 302.) Owners, skippers, or commanders of vessels can claim, within three times twenty-four hours after the issue of the certificate of measurement, a remeasurement by two other functionaries or two impartial arbitrators.

Article 299, (same contents as before, article 303.) The certificates of measurement are no longer of value than two years after the date of issue. When, after the termination of this period, the Dutch vessels make their first voyage outward, or the foreign vessels enter inward, a remeasurement shall have to take place, and, in conformity of the result thereof, a new certificate of measurement will be granted.

Article 300, (same contents as article 304 before.) Every functionary charged with the measurement is qualified, and in case of suspicion of breach of faith, obliged to verify by remeasurement, or in any other way, all former measurements done by others, when the vessels are empty, without any expense to the commander; and in case of difference, to note the same on the certificate of measurement. In case of a larger room, the excess will have immediately to be supplied for as many times as previous payments have taken place on the certificate of measurement.

The right granted to owners, skippers, or commanders, by article 298, applies equally to such verifications.

ARTICLE 301, (before article 305, now modified.) On exhibiting the certificate of measurement at the office of the comptroller at that port, the payment of the tonnage duty must be made accordingly, after having found the account to be correct, in exchange for a tonnage register, showing receipt of the payment, and mentioning the date of entry and the date of certificate of measurement.

Every payment, and also the date of the year, has to be mentioned on the certificate of measurement, which always must be returned to the applicants, until it has become due, and be handed over to be repealed on exhibiting, as before, the new certificate of measurement issued as per article 299. At the first payment, the duplicate of the certificate of measurement must be returned and deposited at the office of the comptroller.

ARTICLE 302, (before article 306, now modified.) At every new payment of the tonnage duty, the former tonnage register must be repealed.

ARTICLE 303, (the same as before, article 307.) No vessels subject to tonnage duty will be cleared outward, or entitled to positive or negative acts of settlements, than after proof of the payment of tonnage duty, by exhibiting the certificate of measurement and tonnage register at the public office, where the same in proof thereof must be signed.

ARTICLE 304, (the same as before, article 308.) The above signed certificates of measurements and tonnage registers must always remain on board of outgoing ships, to be exhibited, on their demand, to the searching officers, under a penalty of 25 florins, to be paid by the captains.

ARTICLE 305, (the same as before, article 309.) On total absence of said documents, or when they are found not to belong to the ship, the captain shall have to pay a penalty of one florin per every ton which the vessel measures over and above the payment of what is due, for which latter the vessel may, if necessary, be detained.

ARTICLE 306, (the same as article 310 before.) Vessels in ballast which, on their arrival, are still indebted for any part of the duty, may be detained for the tonnage-duty, and until such payment shall have taken place or security have been given for the same.

*Law of June* 19, 1845, *by which a new tariff of import, export, and transit duties is established, (modified after the law Litt. A,* of August* 8, 1850, *for the regulation of Netherland shipping.)*

We, William II, &c., having taken into consideration the necessity to revise the tariff of import, export, and transit duties, so we, after having heard, &c., decree:

*General regulations.*

ARTICLE 1. Of all goods which are imported or exported, or passing transit, and which are not expressly exempted from duty, the import, export, or transit duties are to be paid according to the tariff added to this law.

---

*See law Litt. A, in the preceding pages.

Of the goods not named in the tariff, and which by their nature cannot be classified under the enumerated articles, is to be paid on the import one per cent.; transit $\frac{1}{10}$th per cent. of the value, or 10 cents per 100 lbs., at the option of the importer. Such goods are free of export duty.

Art. 2. We reserve to ourselves, in certain cases, to raise or to reduce, for the interest of trade or industry, the import, export, and transit duties; and also the fixed duty and the navigation dues, and even to repeal entirely, or make restitution of the transit, fixed, and navigation dues.

With reference to the regulations to which the above reservation applies, notice will have to be given to the States General within thirty days after the opening of the first following session, accompanied by a project of law relative thereto.

Should such regulations be necessary in urgent circumstances, during a session of the States General, the projected law will be presented in the course of the same session, within thirty days after the date of our decree.

If the projected law is not accepted by the States General, the regulations made by us retain their power of law till the twentieth day, included from the day on which the law has been rejected.

*Respecting freedom and exemption.*

Art. 3. Over and above the articles which, by the tariff itself, have freedom of import, export, or transit duties, are further exempted therefrom—

A. At the import:

§ 1. The produce of the ultramarine possessions of the kingdom (with the exception of refined sugar, molasses, and tea) imported with unbroken bulk, and in Dutch vessels, direct from there, provided the origin thereof be proved, and that in said possessions the fixed export duties of that produce have been paid. Similar freedom will be also granted by us when that importation takes place by vessels of those States which—

*a.* Place the Dutch flag on the same footing as the national one trading to and from their own ports, (coasting trade and fisheries excepted;)

*b.* Place the Dutch flag on the same footing as the national one trading to and from their colonies, if they possess any colonies; and which—

*c.* Levy no other differential duties to the prejudice of the produce of Dutch colonies, or to the prejudice of the import of produce from other parts of the world out of Netherland ports, than those which are levied in favor of the produce of their own colonies and the direct importation thereof.

§ 2. *a.* Goods returned from the ultramarine possessions of the kingdom.

*b.* Goods of admitted Dutch origin, which are returned unsold from foreign markets.

*c.* All goods which, after having been exported, are reimported from ports where the same, on account of prohibition, or in consequence of a considerable increase of import duties, unknown in this country, during the export, have either not been admissible, or not admissible without considerable loss.

As far as regards the articles above enumerated under *b* and *c*, this freedom is subject to the condition that the same reimport shall take place within two years after the goods have left this country.

The duties paid on the export of such goods will also be returned.

The above, nevertheless, only applies to cases where the fact and the identification of the goods can be sufficiently proved.

This freedom and restitution of duties cannot be granted to goods in transit.

§ 3. Instruments used for rafts, (including cables,) which are imported and reimported as used articles, provided at the import, on exhibiting an inventory at the office of discharge, this use be proved to the satisfaction of the custom-house.

B. At the export:

§ 4. Goods which are transmitted to the ultramarine possessions of the kingdom, under the needful measures of security respecting the destination; and with the exception of the articles glass-dust, offal for glue, ashes, soap-boilers' and salt-refiners' ashes.

By this regulation no breach is made on the prohibition of the export of certain goods stipulated by the tariff.

C. At the import and export:

§ 5. Ammunition, provisions, and other necessaries which are sent by or on account of the Department of War, to our armies or fortresses occupied by the same, or which are returned from there.

By the Department of Finance the thereto-required free passes will be granted.

§ 6. The victuals and ships' stores which are furnished for the service of our ships of war and transports, or to ships employed in fishing, of merchant ships, to be determined by the first functionary at the port of loading, in proportion to the number of souls on board, and to the nature and length of the voyage; provided the provisions for the use of the ships, then on board of vessels inward-bound, are given up and admitted as such by the custom-house, provided that they remain on board.

Those goods enjoy, also, freedom of excise, with exception of what in the special laws of excise is, or afterwards shall have been, determined with regard to the restitution of excise on goods exported to other countries.

The duties and excise must be paid on every excess which is found on board the vessels on entering, unless when the same are housed in a government warehouse till the departure of the vessel, or when, for the satisfaction of the custom-house, a proper bond be given against all change of destination or unloading, and likewise until permission shall have been given for the goods to remain on board.

§ 7. All goods which are exported for account of the government to the ultramarine possessions of the kingdom, or to our squadron or men of war, being abroad, or are imported from thence into the kingdom.

The requisite free passes will be granted thereto by the Department of Finance, on demand of the Department of Colonies and Marine.

§8. The goods belonging to our ambassadors at foreign courts, and which are exported for the first time.

With respect to the goods belonging to ambassadors of foreign courts residing in this country, similar freedom of duties and excise will be granted to them as is or will be granted to the goods of our ambassadors by those courts.

To enjoy this freedom, free passes are given by the Department of Finance, and the holders thereof have to fulfil certain formalities which are prescribed by the laws for levying the duties and excise.

§9. The horses and carriages employed for foreign travelling, in entering as in leaving the country, by land or by sea: provided, always, those regulations taken by us to prevent fraud, and also the common luggage which travellers carry for their own use, in distinction of articles of trade.

§10. Removal of house-furniture, respecting which we reserve to ourselves to determine what may be considered to rank under the following paragraph:

§11. Horses, oxen, sheep, pigs, and other cattle, which are taken to pasture by Dutch inhabitants on their lands out of the kingdom, but situated on the frontiers of the same, or from neighboring lands on the frontiers of the kingdom.

For them, grazing permits will be granted, under bond for the amount of the duties for the re-import or export before the close of every year, and subject to the requisite precautions for the identification of the imported or exported cattle.

With regard to the grazing cattle, which from time to time, or every evening, return to the stables, to return to pasture, special regulations are made by the custom-house for the interest of agriculture, and to prevent fraud.

§12. Fruit of trees or fields, and plants raised on grounds on the frontiers of the kingdom, within a distance of 5,500 ells from the limit, and in use by Dutch inhabitants, the seeds and manure for the cultivation of those lands, as well as the carriages and boats necessary for the transport of the same. This exemption is only granted on condition that the import and export always take place between sunrise and sunset, and in the ordinary season of the harvest, or of the gathering of every kind of produce; and, further, that the possession or use of aforesaid lands be annually proved at the respective offices, by a declaration of the receiver of taxes where the aforesaid lands are registered, or by a duly registered contract of lease.

The exemption of duties named in this and the former paragraph will also be granted (subject to the above conditions) to inhabitants of neighboring States who have in use lands on the frontiers of the kingdom, and within the same distance from the limit as before stated, provided the Dutch inhabitants enjoy similar freedom on entering and leaving the territory of neighboring States.

§13. Ballast, consisting of brick-dust, sand, and such like stuffs, having no value for trade; and, further, all ballast of iron or stone which remains on board the ship.

§14. Goods landed from sea and transhipped in other vessels at the first clearance office, on a previously written permit of the acting functionary higher in rank than the collector, for the purpose of being exported along the same route, either immediately or after a temporary housing, on the footing as is granted by article three of the law of 31st March, 1828.

*Respecting the calculation of duties.*

Art. 4. Duty is paid in proportion to the quantities really imported, exported, or transported, in such a manner, however, that in calculating the amount of duty due for the entered or existing quantity, or value, the subdivisions of the pound, kop, kan, cubic palm, and florin, are considered to be a full pound, kop, kan, cubic palm, and a whole florin. The subdivisions of cents, which may be the product of the calculation of duty on the entered or existing quantities or value, are taken as whole cents.

Art. 5. The importer will have choice to pay transit duty on all goods (horses, cattle, and fish excepted) of which the transit duties are levied in the tariff, according to the value, the number, or the measure, according to that standard measure, or the weight at 10 cents per 100 pounds, provided this be settled at the time of entry.

Art. 6. Import, export, or transit duty, for each document for which any duty is to be paid, will be in no case less than 5 cents, the quantity or value imported, exported, or transported, being ever so small.

*Of tare.*

Art. 7. No tare is to be given on transit of all goods on which duty is paid by the weight, but for which no tare is fixed in the tariff; at the importation or exportation the tare will be paid as follows:

For all casks, cases, &c., made of wood, 15 of 100 lbs. gross weight.

For all packages of leather, mats, baskets, kannassers or linen, and such like, 8 of 100 lbs. gross weight.

Art. 8. In case the importers are not satisfied with the tare fixed by the tariff, or by the previous article, they can pay the tare according to the net weight of the goods, in such a way as it will be settled by the functionaries, at the expense of the importers.

In case there are a great number of casks and cases of the same size, the tare of the goods can be fixed by weighing a part of the empty casks, cases, &c., to be pointed out by the functionary, and the tare for the whole quantity will then be reckoned according to the average weight.

In case of mixed packages, and if the duty on one part of the goods is to be paid by the weight and the other by the value, the net weight of the first can be taken by the functionaries at the expense of the importers, according to the result of which duty then is to be paid.

Art. 9. For all liquids free of excise, rated by the measure, and not being stipulated in article 122 of the general law of August 26, 1822, on importation by sea, a reduction will be granted for leakage, as follows:

Coming from England, Embden, Bremen, Hamburgh, and the Lower Baltic, also from France, Belgium, Spain, Portugal, on this side of the Straits of Gibraltar, 6 per cent.; from other parts, imported by sea, 12 per cent.

Art. 10. If the importers think that the reduction for leakage fixed in the previous articles be not sufficient, or if they should assert a claim to a reduction in those cases in which the law does not grant it, they will be at liberty to pay duty according to the existing quantity, which at their expense will be determined by the functionaries.

*Of transit.*

Art. 11. We reserve to ourselves to modify the regulations of the existing laws with regard to the formalities respecting the goods entered for transit, in cases where such will be more convenient for the trade, reserving the regulations for the payment of import duties.

*Respecting the repeal of former laws.*

Art. 12. At the period when this law and the thereunto appertaining tariff shall come into operation, article 5 of the law of August 26, 1822, the law of August 26, 1822, January 8, 1824, January 10, 1825, March 24, 1826, April 11, 1827, March 31, 1828, December 24, 1828, June 1, 1830, June 8, 1831, and the law of May 31, 1843, will be repealed.

Given at the Hague, this 19th July, 1845.

---

## BELGIUM.

*Export duties.*

"By a royal ordinance of 28th September, 1849, the export duty was taken off the greater number of articles comprised in the tariff; and, out of the 511 headings into which it is divided, the articles contained in 50*, only, now appear to be subject to this duty."—*Return made to British House of Commons, 26th March*, 1850.

---

## AUSTRIA.

[From a despatch of the United States chargé d'affaires to Austria, December 6, 1851.]

"The new tariff has at last been published. It takes effect on the first of February next. The principal change favorable to our country is in the article of cotton. The present duty is 1 florin and 40 kreutzers per 100 pounds. The next year it will pay 1 florin, and after that but 5 kreutzers (about 4 cents) per 100 pounds.

"Tobacco is a government monopoly, but it may now be entered by individuals for their own use at reduced rates. In the leaf it *has* paid 15 florins per 100 pounds; it will now pay but 10 florins. Manufactured, it *has* paid 40 florins per 100 pounds; it will now pay but 25 florins.

"The duties have also been reduced on rice, whale oil and the products of the whale fishery, wooden-ware, tools, implements and machinery for agricultural and household purposes, India rubber fabrics, &c."

---

* Not enumerated in the document from which the preceding remark is taken.

[From a despatch of the United States consul at Vienna, May 29, 1852.]

"On the 1st February of this year the new tariff came into operation. It is of much importance to the trade of the United States, and the considerable reduction made in the duties on furs, skins, on salt fish from 2½ florins to 1½ florin, whalebone from 1½ to ¾, and so on, deserves particular attention. On the importation of cotton the duty for the first year—that is, from 1st February, 1852, to 31st January, 1853—is fixed at 1 florin per hundred, gross weight; from the 1st February, 1853, the duty is then only $\frac{1}{12}$ florin. In the first year, also, common twists pay 8 florins; in the following, only 7 florins. The rates in the first year may be borne the easier, as the duties are payable in paper money, which stands 20 to 25 per cent. under par.

"It may not be superfluous to remark that, in order to bring about a conformity with the German Customs Union, the Prussian Zoll centner, (hundred weight,) equal to 50 French kilograms, has been also here adopted; consequently, 110.27 English or American pounds.

"I may also mention that several articles when imported by sea are admitted at rates still more moderated; for instance, alum, in general rated at 1½ florin per centner, pays only ⅙ florin on being brought in by sea. As by virtue of the treaty of the 27th August, 1829, the United States stand on the footing of one of the most favored nations, the provisions of the new tariff may contribute much to the employment of the United States shipping.

"Allow me also to direct your attention to the treaty of trade and navigation between Austria and Sardinia, dated 18th October, 1851. It contains many concessions that will also turn out to the advantage of the United States."

---

## PRUSSIA.

[From a despatch of the United States chargé d'affaires to Prussia, June 24, 1851.]

"A treaty has lately been concluded between Prussia, for herself and the States of the Zollverein, and Sardinia, by which the duty on rice imported into the former States is to be reduced—on shelled rice from two Prussian thalers, the present duty, to one thaler the centner (110 lbs.,) and on other rice from two thalers to two-thirds of a thaler. I have had an interview with the Minister of Finance, in order to make sure that this reduction of duty on rice would apply as well to rice imported from the United States, as that imported from or through Sardinia. It is to be a reduction on all rice, from what country soever imported, and takes effect from the first of August next."

[From a despatch of the United States consul at Stettin, 26th July, 1851.]

"The duty on rice has been reduced from two to one dollar, (Prussian,) and that on paddy to ⅔ dollar, per cwt.; the former, I fear, will not have much influence upon the consumption of it, and the latter is not low enough in proportion to induce the establishment of rice mills, and I shall get the chambers of commerce here, and in the other Baltic ports, to petition for a further reduction at the next meeting of the Commissioners of the Zollverein."

[From a despatch of the United States chargé d' affaires at Berlin, 9th September, 1851.]

"By an official order for the alteration of the tariff, the duty on cigars and snuff has been raised from 15 thalers the centner to 20 thalers or 35 florins. Raw tobacco is not touched. The law takes effect on the 1st of October."

---

## DENMARK.—St. Croix.

[With despatch of the United States consul at St. Croix.—Translation.]

*Law of* 30*th June*, 1850.—*Published at St. Croix*, 15*th August*, 1850.

We, Frederick the Seventh, by the grace of God King of Denmark, &c., make known: The Diet has passed, and we, by our royal assent, sanctioned the following law:

### A.—*Navigation.*

Sec. 1. All vessels, native or foreign, both from native and foreign ports, may trade to St. Croix, and there discharge and load at the two ports of entry, Christiansted and Frederiksted.

Sec. 2. Vessels belonging to the Danish West India islands, trading between Denmark and the colonies, shall enjoy, in future, the same rights and privileges as vessels belonging to the mother country. Colonial vessels shall, however, as hitherto, take out a sea-pass.

Sec. 3. Every vessel is to pay tonnage-dues according to its tonnage, both on entering and on leaving, at the following rate: if the vessel discharge or load to the amount of one-half its tonnage and above, per commercial last, 30 cents; if it discharge or load from one-quarter to one-half of its tonnage, per commercial last, 20 cents; if it discharge or load less than one-quarter of its tonnage, per commercial last, 10 cents.

All vessels not discharging or loading are exempt from tonnage dues, as well as vessels belonging to the Danish West India islands, when trading between St. Croix and the two other islands.

If tonnage-dues are paid at one of the custom-houses of this island, or at St. Thomas, additional tonnage-dues are to be paid only in case the vessel should again discharge or load, during the same voyage, goods to such an amount that, together with the previous amount discharged or loaded, it shall reach a quantity on which a higher tonnage due is fixed.

At Christiansted, vessels are further to pay one-half the amount of tonnage-dues, at the above rate, for keeping the harbor with wharves and other appurtenances in repairs.

### B.—*Imports.*

Sec. 4. All goods, without exception, may be imported as well from Danish as foreign ports. Fire-arms and ammunition can only be landed on special permission from the governor-general, and subject to such control as he may deem proper.

Sec. 5. Within twenty-four hours after the vessel has been brought to an anchor, the whole cargo, whether intended to be discharged or not, shall be entered at the custom-house, specified and in writing. If the whole cargo is not to be discharged, the remainder shall, on the vessel's clearing out, be entered for export in the same manner.

Sec. 6. On imports, the following duties and exemptions are fixed:

I. In general:

*a.* Free of duty are: Sugar-rum and molasses puncheons, staves, headings, hoops, agricultural implements; all implements used for the manufacture of sugar, the distilling of rum, and for cane-mills; mill-timber, fire-bricks, and fire-stone; machinery, and parts thereof; fresh fish and turtles; greens and vegetables; coals; mules and asses; manure; printed books and papers; and used furniture, when imported as the property of a person going to *reside* in the island.

*b.* A fixed duty to be paid on flour of wheat, per 100 lbs. 60 cents; flour of rye, barley, oats, maize, and all other kinds of flour, per 100 lbs. 25 cents; bread of wheat, per 100 lbs. 75 cents; bread of other corn, per 100 lbs. 35 cents; peas dried, of any kind, per barrel 25 cents; beans, likewise, per barrel 25 cents; beef, tongues, hams, sausages, pickled, smoked, or dried, per 100 lbs. $1 25; pork, pickled or smoked, per 100 lbs. 80 cents; fish, dried or salted, per 100 lbs. 25 cents; fish, pickled or smoked, per 100 lbs. 40 cents; butter, per 100 lbs. $1 50; cheese, per 100 lbs. $1 50; lard, per 100 lbs. 40 cents.

*c.* Five per cent. duty to be paid on iron, steel, lead, copper, zinc in bars, rolls, or plates, sheet-iron, spelter, rope, tar, pitch, rosin, chalk, lime, temperline, cement, gypsum, bricks and tiles, flagstones, earthen pipes; lumber of every kind, except those mentioned in sub-letter A; nails, screws, spikes, tools of every description, ships' anchors and chains, blocks, mule harness, raw leather, wooden yokes, live cattle, except mules and asses, which are free of duty, and horses, which are to pay a higher duty; oats, Indian corn, bran, hay, charcoal, salt, tallow, cart-wheels, axles and boxes for carts and sugar-wagons; canvass for sails.

*d.* Twelve and a half per cent. duty to be paid on all other goods, of whatsoever name, origin, and description, which are not enumerated in sub-letters A, B, and C.

II. Exceptions:

*a.* Free of duty are: All productions of the mother country, and all goods on which duties have been paid in Denmark, imported into this island in Danish vessels, from a Danish port not a free port. Such goods shall be accompanied with a clearance, proving they are of Danish product or manufacture, or that duties have been paid on them in Denmark.

*b.* One-half of the duty above mentioned to be paid on all foreign goods on which duties have not been paid, imported in Danish vessels, provided such goods are shipped from a Danish port not a free port, and accompanied with a clearance. The transit duty, proved to have been paid at such port on the goods, will be deducted in the half-duty.

*c.* A deduction of duty will be made on all goods on which duties have been paid in St. Thomas, which duty will be here deducted; provided such goods be accompanied with a clearance from the custom-house at St. Thomas, showing the duty there paid, and this clearance be produced within fourteen days from its date.

III. With respect to the importation of cards, the directions given in the enactment of the 9th of February, 1849, remain in force, with the only difference that the duties are to be paid in conformity with section 6, I, *d*, and II, *a*, *b*, and *c*, of this law, instead of in conformity with the ordinance of the 6th of June, 1833, section 5 *a*, *c*, *d*, and *e*.

### C.—*Exports.*

SEC. 7. All goods, without exception, may be exported at the two ports of entry.

SEC. 8. On the produce of this island being exported, the following duties are to be paid:

1. Sugar:

A. In Danish vessels to a Danish port, not a free port, 5 per cent.; to a foreign place, 10 per cent.

B. In foreign vessels, in all cases, 10 per cent.

2. Rum and molasses:

A. In Danish vessels to a Danish port, not a free port, 3 per cent.; to a foreign place, 6 per cent.

B. In foreign vessels, in all cases, 6 per cent.

SEC. 9. On sugar, rum, and molasses, imported into this island from St. Thomas, or St. Johns, when exported from here, will be deducted the duty which the clearance from either of said islands shows to have been paid there.

SEC. 10. All other goods, whether the produce of this island or imported, may be exported free of duty. On coffee, tobacco, and on the articles specified in section 6, I, *b*, will be given a drawback of the import duty proved to have been paid, provided the drawback on the goods exported by one clearance amounts to at least $10.

### D.—*Conditional privileges of foreign vessels.*

SEC. 11. The same rights and privileges which, under this law, are granted to Danish vessels, shall also be enjoyed by vessels of those foreign States which are in possession of colonies, and grant the same rights and privileges to Danish vessels as to their own in the trade to and from their colonies.

### E.—*Common rules.*

SEC. 12. The duty stated in the preceding, includes all that is to be paid to the custom-house on imports or exports of goods. All other hitherto existing charges, viz: weigh-money, and ten per cent. fees on the duty, are hereby abolished.

SEC. 13. All persons, natives or foreigners, owning, despatching, or possessing goods to be imported or exported, are at liberty to enter them, and make out the manifest themselves. If required, a verbal entry at the custom-house shall be sufficient; and the collector of customs shall be bound, without remuneration, to make out the manifest in due form for the signature of the concerned.

Sec. 14. The custom-house offices shall be open for transaction of business every day except Sundays, and festival days of the church, from 7 o'clock a. m. to 3 o'clock p. m.; but discharging and loading can be carried on at all times of the day from 6 o'clock morning, to 6 o'clock evening. Before any loading or unloading can take place, special notice shall be given in writing, the same day or the day previous, to the inspector of customs, of what goods are to be landed or taken on board that day, whereon the inspector shall attest that such notification has been made. This certificate shall be given on the notification and clearance being produced at any time between 6 o'clock in the morning and 6 o'clock in the evening.

Sec. 15. Loading or unloading taking place without a certificate from the inspector of customs, or at other hours than specified in the preceding paragraph, is illegal and punished with the confiscation of the goods in question, or of their value, if they are not brought forward.

Sec. 16. This ordinance is in force from the day of its publication, and from the same day all prior ordinances regarding trade and navigation at St. Croix, not in conformity herewith, are hereby repealed.

---

## SWEDEN.

[From a despatch of the U. S. chargé d'affaires to Sweden, December 10, 1848.]

"The new tariff will go into operation, *retaining* the prohibitory clause, [on the import of sugar,] and the five skillings duty [4½ cents per pound] is to commence only in 1850."

[From a despatch of the U. S. chargé d'affaires to Sweden, December 31, 1848.]

"The tariff which goes into operation to-morrow, was published yesterday, and I have hastened to make an examination of its contents.

"Its general arrangement is far more simple than was the case with the former one, and presents separate tables of articles as they are charged with import or export duties, or are entitled to free admission. The changes it contains—which in general are *reductions*—are few in number, and of little importance to the commerce of the United States. I have concluded to present them in detail, however, as they will correct the tariff heretofore forwarded, and place the department, at once, in possession of the duties levied for the next three years.

"The most remarkable feature in this new document is the rejection of those *fixed* and *erroneous valuations* which were assumed as the bases of former taxes, and raised the duties formed upon them to such an unwarrantable height.

"The articles affected by the new tariff are as follows:

| Articles. | Duty. |
|---|---|
| Alum, all kinds, per 17 lispounds* | $2 00 |
| Beef— | |
| Fresh, per lispound | 17 |
| Dried......do | 25 |
| Salted, per barrel | 1 60 |
| Candles, stearine, per pound | 7½ |
| Fish— | |
| Cod......per barrel | 90 |
| Salmon......do | 27 |
| Stromming...do | 25 |
| Other kinds ..do | 35 |
| Grain— | |
| Buckwheat, per barrel | 30 |
| Oats | 20 |
| Wheat | 60 |
| Barley | 30 |
| Flaxseed | 60 |
| Rye | 40 |
| Vetches | 35 |
| Peas | 40 |
| Glass, window, per lispound | 34 |
| Hards— | |
| Of hemp, per shippound† | 1 00 |
| Of linen.......do | 2 00 |
| Horse-hair, per pound | 1¾ |
| Iron— | |
| Cast anchors........per shippound | 1 60 |
| Wrought anchors.........do | 2 00 |
| Spikes, 2 inches and over..do | 3 00 |
| Lamp-black, per 100 pounds | 1 60 |
| Lead— | |
| Painted, per pound | 5 |
| Not painted..do | ¾ |
| Live stock— | |
| Horses, each | 4 00 |
| Oxen...do | 3 20 |
| Cows...do | 1 60 |
| Calves..do | 90 |
| Hogs ...do | 80 |
| Other kinds, each | 60 |

* 1 lispound = 20 Swedish pounds.

† 1 shippound = 20 lispounds = 400 pounds; but the shippound for *iron weight* is different, as, per despatch No. 80, 7½ shippounds = 1 ton.

TABLE—Continued.

| Articles. | Duty. |
|---|---|
| Maize, per barrel | $0 40 |
| Oakum, per shippound | 40 |
| Oil— | |
| Of hemp..........per pound | 5 |
| For apothecaries' use...do | $\frac{3}{4}$ |
| Pork, per lispound | 30 |
| Rice, per barrel | 60 |
| Stockings, of cotton, per pound | 54 |
| Sugar— | |
| Crushed, lump, and Havana, per pound | $4\frac{1}{2}$ |
| Loaf, forbidden until 1850, and then, per pound | $4\frac{1}{2}$ |
| Vitriol— | |
| Green, per 17 lispounds | 1 20 |
| Other sorts, per pound | $\frac{3}{4}$ |
| Cheese, per lispound | 40 |

[From a despatch of the U. S. chargé d'affaires to Sweden, January 24, 1849.]

I herewith forward a copy of the Swedish tariff now in operation, and to the changes contained in which, allusion was made in No. 82.

I regret to state that the intention of the Diet, which was to reject the prohibitions heretofore existing in the tariff, has not met the expected co-operation of his Majesty and council, but that the following articles are still forbidden:

Alcohol and spirits:
from seeds or potatoes, except gin.
from fruits, except French cognac.

Cards:
for playing, of all descriptions.

Clothing:
ready-made of all kinds, except that brought by travellers.

Earthenware:
stone china, printed or painted.

Cast-iron;
pig and Varlast, hoop and flat, or plates not tinned.

Saltpetre:
all kinds.

Syrup:
of brown or white sugar, forbidden until 1850, and then admitted at a high duty.

Sugar:
loaf, candy, and cake, forbidden until 1850, and then admitted as above.

The most important prohibitions, however, are those affecting *woven goods*, of wool or cotton; in order to present which fully, I submit the following translation from the tariff as to what can or cannot be admitted.

*Extract from the Swedish tariff relating to the duties levied on cotton and woolen manufactures.*

| Articles. | Duty. |
|---|---|
| *Manufactures of silk.* | |
| Plush ... per pound. | $0 60 |
| Crape ... do ... | 2 60 |
| Gauze ... do ... | 3 14 |
| Brocaded with gold or silver, pure ... do ... | 8 00 |
| Do do imitation ... do ... | 2 60 |
| Velvet ... do ... | 1 60 |
| NOTE.—When silk appears on the face and cotton on the back, the articles are charged *as silk*. | |
| All plain, chequered, striped or variegated, in which there is no figure ... | prohibited. |
| Other sorts not specified ... per pound. | 2 40 |
| Shawls, shawletts, and kerchiefs of gauze, beune de soie, or similar fabrics, figured by printing or pressing, including those with stamped figures on the sides and corners ... per pound. | 2 80 |
| All other sorts, whether plain, single, colored or figured. | prohibited. |
| *Manufactures of part silk, mixed with cotton, wool or other materials.* | |
| Plush ... per pound. | 60 |
| Other sorts ... do ... | 1 00 |
| Shawls and kerchiefs under the value of $4 each ... | forbidden. |
| Shawls and kerchiefs of the value of $4 and over, on each $40 of value ... | 8 00 |
| *Cotton manufactures.* | |
| White and other cloths having *over* 76 *threads* to the inch, and at least 36 inches wide ... per pound. | 40 |
| Corduroy, velveteens, satins, jeans, fustians, and similar fabrics ... per pound. | 26 |
| Dimity ... do ... | 35 |
| Plush felt ... do ... | 6 |
| Blankets ... do ... | 14 |

TABLE—Continued.

| Articles. | Duty. |
|---|---|
| Gauze, book muslin, muslin, and mull muslin, per pound. | $0 40 |
| Quilting and quilts..........................do.... | 40 |
| Bobinetts ....................................do.... | 60 |
| Other kind, such as figured...................do.... | 50 |
| Plain, such as calicoes and shirtings................ | prohibited. |
| NOTE.—Such white cottons as are permitted may be imported as kerchiefs, paying the same duties charged for cotton cloth. | |
| *Dyed cottons.* | |
| NOTE.—The same sorts are admitted at the same duties with those denominated white. | |
| Plain .................................................. | forbidden. |
| Of different colored yarn............................... | do. |
| Blankets..................................per pound. | 14 |
| NOTE.—In addition to those paying the same duty as *white*, all others exceeding the fineness of 80 *threads* to the inch...............................per pound. | 43 |
| All other kinds......................................... | prohibited. |
| Cotton shawls and kerchiefs, figured and printed, being 42 inches square without the fringe......per pound. | 43 |
| Cotton shawls and kerchiefs, plain, of dyed yarn, or printed, less than 42 inches square without the fringe .............................................. | prohibited. |
| *Half-cotton manufactures, mixed with flax or hemp.* | |
| Damask ....................................per pound. | 28 |
| Damask diaper...............................do.... | 20 |
| (Other goods pay the same duty as similar articles of cotton.) | |
| *Woolen manufactures.* | |
| Baize.................................................. | forbidden. |
| Cassimere, white, yellow, and red, not over 36 inches in width..............................per pound. | 60 |
| Flannel, of woolen warp and worsted weft, dyed, of greater breadth than 39 inches.................. | prohibited. |
| All other sorts............................per pound. | 28 |
| Blankets and carpets........................do.... | 20 |

TABLE—Continued.

| Articles. | Duty. |
|---|---|
| Frieze, daffle, and Calmuc cloth, ladies' cloth, half-cloth, corduroy buckskins, and also cassimeres of other colors than those above stated, exceeding 36 inches in width | prohibited. |
| Flag-cloth ........ per pound. | $0 40 |
| Packing or rep. cloth ........ do.... | 2 |
| Other sorts ........ do.... | 20 |
| *Mixed woolen manufactures.* | |
| Flannel | prohibited. |
| Other sorts, less than 42 inches in width.... per pound. | 28 |
| 42 inches and over ........ do.... | 40 |
| NOTE.—Articles submitted for duty consisting of *more than half wool* are classed as woolens. | |
| Shawls and kerchiefs of wool and cotton, under the value of $2 50 each | prohibited. |
| Shawls and kerchiefs of wool and cotton, of and above the value of $2 50 each ........ $40 worth. | 8 00 |
| *Manufactures of hemp and flax.* | |
| Canvass ........ per pound. | 10 |
| Bed-ticking ........ do.... | 18 |
| Sacking ........ do.... | 7 |
| Damask ........ do.... | 80 |
| Diaper and twills ........ do.... | 28 |
| Cambric and batise ........ do.... | 1 46 |
| Book muslin ........ do.... | 75 |
| Linen weighing less than 1½ oz. per square of 2 feet.... | forbidden. |
| All other kinds ........ per pound. | 66 |
| Sail and tent cloth ........ do.... | 5 |
| Other sorts ........ do.... | 40 |
| Kerchiefs ........ do.... | 40 |

By comparing the foregoing extract with the duties on woven goods in the tariff of 1846–'48 inclusive, it will be found that no alterations have been made, except striking out one or two reduced duties at which certain articles were admitted when brought direct from the East Indies.

In all that affects American produce and manufactures, there is no change for the better in the present tariff. The *tobacco* duties still remain the same; *sugar* in general is highly taxed, and the admission of *loaf-sugar* forbidden until 1850; while such of our cotton and woolen manufactures as are allowed at all, are loaded with duties so onerous as to prevent their shipment. *Calicoes* and *shirtings* are expressly *excluded*, while *cambrics* and other articles coming under the denomination of "plain cottons" are admitted only when containing over 76 *threads* or 80 *threads* to the inch, as they are white or colored. This, it will be seen, strikes at once from the list of merchandise for Swedish markets all the *coarser* cotton and woolen manufactures which find a ready sale, or yield any considerable profit.

As I have mentioned that the excessive rates of the old are continued in the present tariff, and yet have often alluded to the absence of the former absurd "valuation tables," the matter seems to require a moment's explanation. The duties of the last tariff were all *based on the valuations mentioned*, and the tables were only retained for the purpose of deception. With estimated values *quadruple* the *real cost* of articles, it was, of course, easy to assert that an actual duty of 100 per cent. was only one-fourth of that amount. The removal of the "valuation tables" merely withdraws from the eye of the reader an obvious absurdity, the effects of which still enter into and control existing duties. The high duty, in short, is continued, while the cause which produced it is insidiously concealed.

The calculations made in despatches Nos. 23, 24, 25, under date of January, 1847, exhibiting duties running to 150 per cent. and over on the actual cost of several cotton manufactures, remain, I regret to say, unchanged by the action of the late Diet, notwithstanding the exertions of the reform party.

It should also be mentioned that the sum of *ten per cent. on the duties*, a considerable tax in itself, is added to the rates of the present tariff for town and navigation dues.

The duties in nearly all cases are paid by *weight;* and where this is not so, a per-centage is levied on the actual cost of the article as established by the invoice.

[From a despatch of the United States chargé d'affaires, 5th September, 1850.]

"I have the honor to inform you that the following changes in the Swedish tariff have been made by a recent order of the King, and have been in force since the first day of the present month:

| Articles imported. | Former duty. | Present duty. |
|---|---|---|
| Hemp, undressed...... | Banco 24 skillings per shippund* | Free. |
| dressed........ | 1.00...do......... do..... | Banco 24 skillings per shippund. |
| New cordage.......... | 36...do...per lispund... | 24...do... per lispund. |
| Sail and tent cloth of flax and hemp.......... | 6...do...per pound... | 4...do... per pound. |
| Flax undressed........ | 1.8...do...per lispund... | 12...do... per lispund. |
| dressed.......... | 2.00...do.......do...... | 24...do.......do. |

*A Swedish pound is about 15 English ounces avoirdupois; 20 of these pounds make a lispund, and 20 lispunds a shippund. A Banco dollar (equal to 40 cents) contains 48 skillings.

"In addition to the above changes, the drawback hitherto granted on exportations of hempen packing and sail-cloth will not be paid after the 31st December of the present year.

"During the recess of the Diet, the King has power to diminish the duties as he shall judge best, but has no power to increase them or to create others.

"The foregoing changes, made at the request of Swedish ship-owners, have exclusively the object to encourage ship-building and the home manufacture of rigging, the greater part of which has been hitherto imported from England. The subject, perhaps, has not much importance for the United States, although a market is certainly afforded for the materials quoted."

[From a despatch of the United States chargé d'affaires, August 23, 1851.]

"Upon rice in the husk, or *paddy*, the duties are ordered to be reduced 16.6 per cent. The duties upon coffee, sugar, arrack, and undressed hides, are severally reduced 33⅓, 25, 12½, and 8½ per cent. Cotton yarn, undyed, 20 per cent., and a few cotton and woolen manufactures heretofore prohibited, are to be admitted under high duties. Many prohibitions, however, are continued, and affect what would seem to be most necessary to the people—as blankets, flannels, and thick cloths, which cannot be, or at least never have been, manufactured in Sweden.

"The new tariff is to go into operation on the first of January next; but the most important changes are to date January 1, 1853. The 24th article, which allows differential duties in favor of transatlantic productions, is repealed; and everything imported direct from America, except the articles above enumerated, will, under the new tariff, be chargeable, in 1853, with duties 15 per cent. higher than at present. The repeal of this clause has been made in compliance with the demands, as heretofore explained, of Holland and England.

"The amount of American tobacco annually imported into Sweden is about 3,800,000 pounds, upon which the government, levying a tax of over 100 per cent., receives revenue equal to one-seventh of the whole customs-revenue of the kingdom. Under the new tariff the amount of duty to be charged will be $35,000 a year greater than under the present tariff; an increase, in all probability, sufficient to affect the sale in this country materially."

[From a despatch of the United States chargé d'affaires, January 1, 1852.]

"The new Swedish tariff goes into operation this day. I have made out and arranged alphabetically the accompanying list of all the articles, the duties upon which are altered from the tariff of 1849.

"Four articles heretofore prohibited, namely, loaf and candy sugar, molasses, and stone china, may now be imported, but under severe restriction. The word 'prohibited' appears, however, in the new tariff no less than twenty-six times, embracing a large variety of articles of silk, cotton, woolen, and linen manufacture; gunpowder and saltpetre; certain kinds of distilled liquors; clothing; and cast, bar, and plate iron.

"The reductions, chiefly for the encouragement of ship-building, are more inconsiderable than was expected; and a variety of new taxations are introduced.

"The sole authority applicable to the tariff during the Diet recess is that of the King, whom the constitution permits only to *lower* the duties.

"The repeal of the differential clause, to take effect January 1, 1853, will amount to an increase of 15 per cent. upon the duty now payable upon American tobacco imported direct."

*Table showing the differences between the Swedish tariffs of* 1849 *and* 1852.

The most important alteration is the repeal of the differential clause, (article 24 of the appendix to the tariff of 1849,) which reduces the duties upon articles exported or imported direct to or from remote countries, as follows:

15 per cent. in favor of that part of North America which lies north of the 25th degree of north latitude.

25 per cent. in favor of countries on the east coast of the American continent, south of said 25th degree of north latitude.

33⅓ per cent. in favor of countries on the other side of Capes Horn and Good Hope.

N. B.—The repeal of this clause will take effect on the first of January, 1853. The column headed 1853, is to show the changes in the new tariff, which take effect at the same moment.

Note.—The values in the United States of the money, weights, and measures in the accompanying table, are as follows:

The *riksdaler* [2⅔ of which compose the Swedish specie dollar, which, by act of Congress, (May 22, 1846,) is equivalent to 106 cents] is equal in value to 39¾ cents. It is divided into 48 skillings, and each skilling into 12 rundstycks.

The *Swedish pound (victualie)* is nearly 15 ounces. 100 Swedish pounds are equal to $93\frac{76}{100}$ avoirdupois.

The *lispund* contains 20 pounds Swedish.

The *shippound* contains 20 lispunds.

The *Stapelstad* pound is equal to ⅘ of the victualie.

The *kanna* (liquid measure) is equal to 2¾ quarts. 100 kanna=69.09 gallons.

The *tunna* (dry measure)=4.157 English bushels.

The *lod* (gold weight) (16=1 mark) =about ½ ounce Troy.

*Imports.*

| Articles. | 1849. | 1852. | 1853. |
|---|---|---|---|
| | *Rdr. sk. rst.* | *Rdr. sk. rst.* | *Rdr. sk. rst.* |
| Arrack ... per kanna | 0 32 0 | 0 32 0 | 0 28 0 |
| Bonnets, frames for, with their bands ... per pound | Not named. | 1 0 0 | ... |
| Boots, those known as sea boots ... per pair | ... do ... | 1 0 0 | ... |
| Brandy, spirits, Dutch gin, Cognac, rum, and arrack, per kanna | 32 0 | 32 0 | 28 0 |
| Breadstuffs. [NOTE.—The regulations of the tariff of 1849, therein designated to extend to the end of 1851, are continued in force to the end of 1854.] | | | |
| Canvass, sail and tent cloth ... per pound | 6 0 | 4 0 | ... |
| Carriages, 2-wheeled ... each | 40 0 0 | 25 0 0 | ... |
| other sorts ... do | 100 0 0 | 66 0 0 | ... |
| Cheese ... per lispund | 1 0 0 | 1 12 0 | ... |
| Cider ... per kanna | 12 0 | 24 0 | ... |
| China, stone, plates ... per pound | Prohibited. | Prohibited. | 6 0 |
| other articles ... do | ... do ... | ... do ... | 8 0 |
| Coffee ... do | 3 4 | 3 4 | 2 8 |
| Color boxes ... do | Free. | 8 0 | ... |
| Copper, latten, and nails for sheathing ships .. per shipp'd. | 8 16 0 | 1 32 0 | ... |
| Cordage, cables, rope ... per lispund. | 36 0 | 24 0 | ... |
| Cotton yarn ... per pound | 5 0 | 4 0 | ... |
| Dye, (Fernamluck,) rasped or ground ... do | Free | 6 | ... |
| Dye-woods in block, or not rasped or ground, of every kind, and plants or parts of plants, unmanufactured, serving for dyes, not otherwise named in the tariff, per 100 riksdalers' worth | ... | 1 0 0 | ... |
| Embroidery, gold and silver ... per lod | 32 0 | 20 0 | ... |
| imitation ... do | 20 0 | 24 0 | ... |
| paper ... per pound | Free. | 5 0 | ... |
| silk and cotton, or other material, mixed, per pound | 4 0 0 | 2 0 0 | ... |
| patterns ... per pound | Free. | 5 0 | ... |
| Files and rasps ... do | 6 0 | 4 0 | ... |
| Flints, not agate ... per 100 | 1 0 0 | *1 0 0 | ... |
| Fruits and berries, green ... per tunna | 2 0 0 | 36 0 | ... |
| dried ... per lispund. | 1 12 0 | 32 0 | ... |
| growing under ground, dried, per lispund | 30 0 | 32 0 | ... |
| Glassware, plaited or with handle-work, not used as packing cases, per pound | Free. | 8 0 | ... |
| Gloves, all kinds ... per pound | 3 0 0 | 2 0 0 | ... |
| Goldleaf, pure ... per quire of 24 to 25 sheets. | 8 0 | †8 0 | ... |
| false ... per bundle of 12 quires. | 5 0 | †8 | ... |
| Gold—massive, dust, or ounce ... per lod | 20 0 | 10 0 | ... |
| Gutta-percha, manufactured into articles ... per pound | 6 | 12 0 | ... |
| not manufactured ... do | 6 | Free. | ... |
| Hair, and horse hair wrought, with or without setting, per pound | Free. | 2 32 0 | ... |
| Head-dresses ... per 100 riksdaler. | 25 0 0 | ‡1 32 0 | ... |
| Hemp, hackled ... per shippound. | 1 0 0 | 24 0 | ... |
| not hackled ... do | 24 0 | Free. | ... |
| Hides and skins, dried and unfit for furriers .. per pound | 2 0 | 2 0 | 1 10 |
| India rubber, manufactured ... do | Free. | 12 0 | ... |
| Ink for writing ... per kanna | Free. | 16 0 | ... |
| Lampblack ... per 100 lbs. | 4 0 0 | 2 0 0 | ... |
| Mats of hemp and other materials not specified .. per lb | Free. | 12 0 | ... |
| Musical boxes ... each | Free. | 1 16 0 | ... |

* Per pound. † Per lod. ‡ Each.

*Imports*—Continued.

| Articles. | 1849. | 1852. | 1853. |
|---|---|---|---|
| | *Rdr. sk. rst.* | *Rdr. sk. rst.* | *Rdr. sk. rst.* |
| Molasses, (forbidden prior to 1850)...per pound.. | Prohibited. | 0 3 0 | ......... |
| Neck handkerchiefs, stiffeners...do..... | Free. | 32 0 | ......... |
| stocks of silk...do..... | Not named. | 3 0 0 | ......... |
| other sorts...do..... | ....do.... | 1 16 0 | ......... |
| of leather...do..... | ....do.... | 24 0 | ......... |
| Rice in husk, paddy...per tunna.. | 1 24 0 | 1 24 0 | 1 12 0 |
| Silverleaf, pure...per quire of 24 or 25 leaves. | 3 2 | *2 8 | ......... |
| false...per bundle of 12 quires. | 2 4 | *3 | ......... |
| Silver—massive, dust, or ounce...per lod... | 14 0 | 10 0 | ......... |
| Staves of oak...per 120... | 24 0 | 4 0 | ......... |
| Steel, cast...per 100 pounds Stapelstad weight. | 2 0 0 | 1 16 0 | ......... |
| Strings of gut...per pound.. | 1 24 0 | 1 0 0 | ......... |
| Sugar, loaf, candy, or in cakes...do..... | Prohibited. | 5 0 | ......... |
| crushed lump, Havana terres, and other similar kinds, per pound... | 5 0 | 5 0 | 4 0 |
| Muscovado, brown, yellow terres ordinary, tetes ordinary, and white powdered, per pound...... | 3 0 | 3 0 | 2 3 |
| Suspenders, silk ...... No reduction for the weight of buckles or rings. ...per lb. .. | 1 0 0 | 24 0 | ......... |
| other kinds ... No reduction for the weight of buckles or rings. ...per dozen pairs. | 2 0 0 | †24 0 | ......... |
| Syrups of all kinds and molasses...per pound.. | ......... | 3 0 | ......... |
| Tapestry-work, half-finished or begun, is to be charged, after January 1, 1852, 20 per cent. additional on the duty upon the canvass on which it is sewed. | | | |
| Thread, gold and silver...per lod... | 20 0 | 8 0 | ......... |
| Do......do......imitation...do..... | 13 4 | 5 0 | ......... |
| Yarn, (cotton yarn)...per pound.. | 5 0 | 4 0 | ......... |
| Webs, silk gauze...do..... | 5 16 0 | 6 0 0 | ......... |
| crape...do..... | 6 24 0 | 6 0 0 | ......... |

*Exports.*

| Articles. | 1849. | 1852. |
|---|---|---|
| | *Rdr. sk. rst.* | *Rdr. sk. rst.* |
| Wood, beams of pine and fir of less thickness than 8 inches..each... | 0 3 0 | 0 6 0 |
| Iron, smelted and hammered, or rolled...per shippound. | 12 0 | 6 0 |

* Per lod. † Per pound.

[From a despatch of the United States chargé d'affaires, April 23, 1852.]

"A decree of the King is published to-day, ordering that potatoes shall be imported into Sweden duty free, from this morning until the 31st of August next.

"The wholesale price of potatoes I find quoted to-day at six rix-banco dollars (about \$2 40) per barrel of 4.2 bushels; and the duty payable heretofore upon such barrel has been 16 skillings banco, (about 13⅓ cents,) a little more than 5½ per cent. ad valorem."

---

## NORWAY.

[From a despatch of the United States chargé d'affaires to Sweden, September 10, 1851.]

"I have to report that a new Norwegian tariff went into operation on the 1st of this month. I hasten to lay before you such of its details as may concern American interests, and I have compiled accordingly, as an appendix to this despatch, a table which will exhibit, in alphabetical order, a comparison of the duties chargeable by both the old and new tariffs upon such articles as are usually imported from the United States.

"Barley, oats, rye, and salt-pork are the only articles upon which the import duties have been favorably changed, and the exportation of salt fish is encouraged by a diminution of the export duty fifty per cent.

"The range of the Norwegian tariff is considerably lower than that of Sweden. It will be found, for instance, by including in the estimate the advantages of the weights of Norway over those of this country, that tobacco blades may be imported into Norway at a rate nearly 33.3 per cent. less than here. There is also an oppressive system of false valuation in practice in the Swedish custom-houses which is unknown in the sister kingdom, where, also, a striking consideration is shown to the poor inhabitants of remote provinces. At Bodö and Tromsö, northern ports of Norway, many articles are admitted at half rates of duty, and at Hammerfest, and ports equally remote, they are duty free. This simple justice to inhabitants of far off provinces is not practised in Sweden; and among the poor peasants of districts no further than Dalecarlia, many necessaries of life, which the country cannot supply to them, must be purchased with all the additional costs of inland transportation, and the coast navigation of the Gulf of Bothnia.

"The value and capacities of the Norwegian money, weights and measures, quoted in the following tariff extracts, are as follows:

"The Norwegian specie dollar, divided into 120 skillings, is equivalent to 106 cents of the United States currency.

"The pound weight is about one-tenth more than that of the United States; or, to be more exact, 100 Norwegian pounds are equal to 110¼ avoirdupois. The lispund contains 16 Norwegian pounds, (about 17.6 English,) and the skeppund, twenty times larger, is equal to about 352 pounds avoirdupois.

"The capacity of the tönde is equal to 3.95 English bushels."

*Table exhibiting the duties chargeable by the old and new tariffs of Norway upon articles usually imported from the United States.*

| Articles. | Tariff for 1851 to 1854. | | Tariff for 1848 to 1851. | |
|---|---|---|---|---|
| | Duty. | Quantity allowed in bond. | Duty. | Quantity allowed in bond. |
| | *Sp. skils.* | | *Sp. skils.* | |
| Cotton | 0 0½ per pound | 4,800 pounds | 0 0½ per pound | 2,400 pounds. |
| Cotton yarn, undyed and not twisted | 6 do | 400 do | 6 do | 200 do |
| twisted | 10 do | 240 do | 10 do | 120 do |
| dyed | 12 do | 200 do | 12 do | 100 do |
| Cotton manufactures— | | | | |
| Blond lace, bobbinet, bone lace, gauze | 1 0 do | | 1 0 do | |
| Cloth, common texture | 16 do | 150 pounds | 16 do | 100 do |
| Sail duck | 2 do | Not named | Not named | Not named. |
| Hosiery, all kinds, undyed | 40 do | 60 pounds | 40 do | 50 pounds. |
| Prints | 40 do | 60 do | 40 do | 50 do |
| Other kinds | 32 do | 75 do | 32 do | 50 do |
| Wadding | 5 do | | 5 do | |
| Mixed cotton and other materials | 32 do | 80 pounds | 32 do | 50 do |
| Grain, not ground— | | | | |
| Buckwheat | 36 per tonde | 150 tondes | 36 per tonde | 50 tondes. |
| Barley | 16 do | 150 do | 30 do | 50 do |
| Barley at the custom-houses of Hammerfest, Vadso, and Vardo | 8 do | 150 do | 15 do | 50 do |
| Pease, breadstuffs | 45 do | 60 do | 45 do | 30 do |
| Oats | 12 do | 200 do | 24 do | 50 do |
| Oats at the custom-houses of Hammerfest, Vadso, and Vardo | 6 do | 200 do | 12 do | 50 do |
| Wheat | 72 do | 35 do | 72 do | 30 do |
| Maize | 72 do | | 72 do | |

| | | | | |
|---|---|---|---|---|
| Malt | 45 ....do | 60 do | 45 ....do | 50 do |
| Rye | 24 ....do | 100 do | 45 ....do | 50 do |
| Rye at the custom-houses of Hammerfest, Vardo, and Vadso. | 12 ....do | 100 do | 22½ ....do | 50 do |
| Grain, ground, or grits of— | | | | |
| Buckwheat | 108 per barrel or 10 lispunds. | 24 do | 108 per barrel or 10 lispunds. | 20 do |
| Barley, whole | 1 0 per barrel or 14 lispunds. | 24 do | 1 0 per barrel or 14 lispunds. | 12 do |
| whole, at Hammerfest, Vardo, and Vadso | 60 ....do | 24 do | 60 ....do | 12 do |
| halves. | 100 per barrel or 11 lispunds. | 24 do | 100 per barrel or 11 lispunds. | 12 do |
| halves, at Hammerfest, Vardo, and Vadso | 50 ....do | 24 do | 50 ....do | 12 do |
| Oats | 108 ....do | 24 do | 108 ....do | 12 do |
| Oats at Bodo and Tromso | 27 ....do | 24 do | 54 ....do | 12 do |
| at Hammerfest, Vardo, and Vadso | Free. | | Free. | |
| Flour or meal— | | | | |
| Buckwheat, bean, and pease flour. | 9 per lispund | 13 skeppund | 9 per lispund | 8 skeppund. |
| Barley meal | 9 ....do | 13 do | 9 ....do | 8 do |
| Barley meal at Hammerfest, Vardo, and Vadso | 1⅞ ....do | 13 do | 1⅞ ....do | 8 do |
| at Bodo and Tronso | 3¾ ....do | 13 do | 3¾ ....do | 8 do |
| Oat meal | 7 ....do | 17 do | 7 ....do | 10 do |
| Oat meal at Hammerfest, Vardo, and Vadso | 1½ ....do | 17 do | 1½ ....do | 10 do |
| at Bodo and Tronso | 3 ....do | 17 do | 3 ....do | 10 do |
| Wheat flour, corn meal, and potato meal | 16 ....do | 12 do | 16 ....do | 8 do |
| Rye flour | 10 ....do | 12 do | 10 ....do | 8 do |
| Rye flour at Bodo and Tronso | 1½ ....do | 12 do | 3 ....do | 8 do |
| at Hammerfest, Vadso, and Vardo | Free. | | Free. ....do | |
| Pork and bacon, smoked | 2 per pound | 1,200 pounds | 2 per pound | 600 pounds. |
| salted | 1 ....do | 2,400 do | 1½ ....do | 600 do |
| fresh | 1 ....do | | 1½ ....do | |
| Rice. | 80 per barrel | 30 barrels | 80 per barrel | 15 barrels. |
| Rice flour | 1½ per pound | 1,600 pounds | 1½ per pound | 800 pounds. |
| Stearine | 4 ....do | | 4 ....do | |
| Stearine candles | 8 ....do | | 8 ....do | |
| Spermaceti | Free. | | Free. | |
| Spermaceti candles | 12 per pound | | 12 per pound | |
| oil | 1½ ....do | 1,600 pounds | 1½ ....do | 800 do |

## TABLE—Continued.

| Articles. | Tariff for 1851 to 1854. | | Tariff for 1848 to 1851. | |
|---|---|---|---|---|
| | Duty. | Quantity allowed in bond. | Duty. | Quantity allowed in bond. |
| Tobacco*— | *Sp. skils.* | | *Sp. skils.* | |
| Stems | 0 5 per pound | 1,000 pounds | 0 5 per pound | 1,000 pounds. |
| Blades | 5 do | 1,000 do | 5 do | 1,000 do |
| Snuff | 14 do | | 14 do | |
| Cigars | 30 do | | 30 do | |
| Smoking, chewing, and all other not enumerated | 10 do | | 10 do | |

* No tare is allowed on the paper in which tobacco is wrapped.

## KINGDOM OF THE TWO SICILIES.

[From a despatch of the United States chargé d'affaires at Naples, July 16, 1851.]

"I have great satisfaction in advising you of the successful termination of the negotiation which I entered into with the Neapolitan government, on the 28th of September last, for the reduction of tonnage duties on American vessels destined for this kingdom, and touching at intermediate ports. By the accompanying note from the Minister of Foreign Affairs, it will be seen that vessels from the United States, making indirect voyages hither, will hereafter be subjected to no higher rates than those coming directly. The extra tonnage of forty grains is thus abolished, and four grains only per ton will in future be charged in *all* cases. One of the principal imperfections of the treaty of 1845 is now removed. The burdensome tax which I have succeeded in removing from our commerce will be of great advantage to merchants of the United States, by enabling them to employ their vessels in profitable trade on their voyages to the Two Sicilies in intermediate ports, instead of expediting them in ballast, or with unsaleable freights.

"To avoid all chance of misconstruction of the agreement submitted for my concurrence in the annexed note from the Minister of Foreign Affairs, a personal interview was had with him, and he declared the following to be their understanding and construction of it, viz: 'That a vessel of the United States may load there, destined for this kingdom, with the privilege of touching at intermediate ports to discharge or take other cargo, without being obliged to pay more tonnage on her arrival here than a Neapolitan vessel, (four grains.) The reduction of 10 per cent. duty on the tariff by the *treaty* was limited to *direct* voyages; by this agreement it will be good for *American produce* and *manufactures* for *indirect* voyages, but not for foreign produce and manufactures.' Of course, these privileges are confined to vessels touching at ports *between* the United States and the Two Sicilies, and do not include those loading at Trieste, and elsewhere, and coming here to fill up.

"The severity of these extra tonnage duties is exemplified in the case of the barque Joshua Mauran, Captain Barton, of Bath, Maine, which loaded a full cargo of tobacco at New Orleans for Leghorn and Naples, and after landing the part for Leghorn, came here to discharge the remaining two hundred and twenty-three hogsheads for the Regia. The forty grains per ton duty on this vessel amounted to D. 284.85. I commenced the negotiation with this case, requesting permission for the consignee to be allowed to deposite the duty subject to the result of my application for the abolition of extra tonnage. That being successful, the excess above D. 30.54, (the product of the four grains duty,) viz: D. 254.31, will be refunded. Another vessel is daily expected from the United States *via* Genoa, upon which more than 300 ducats will be saved by the repeal of this oppressive regulation. It will in fact *relieve every vessel of the United States coming indirectly hither from a tax of* $200 *to* $350.

"Considering that the advantages of the accompanying agreement are almost exclusively on our side, owing to the very limited number of Neapolitan vessels engaged in transatlantic trade, and relying upon your sanction of the negotiation as given in despatch No. 7 and upon the action of the Executive in similar cases under the act of Congress of May 24, 1828, and in concurrence with the advice of the consul, I have given my assent to the convention under certain limitations."

[Extract of a note of the Minister of Foreign Affairs, relative to equalization of direct and indirect voyage duties.]

[Translation.]

NAPLES, *July* 9, 1851.

His Majesty has authorized the undersigned to assent to the following agreement:

"It has been determined of common accord, until otherwise disposed, to be reciprocally notified at least three months in advance, that the commercial vessels of the Kingdom of the Two Sicilies, as well as those of the American Union, destined for the ports of either country, shall not only be able by the terms of the treaty subscribed 1st of December, 1845, to be loaded with the productions of their soil and industry, but also that these vessels thus destined, and being loaded only in part with such productions, in their expedition from the ports of the Two Sicilies, and from those of the United States of America, shall have the power of completing their cargo in the ports of foreign intermediate countries, enjoying, nevertheless, those advantages unreservedly stipulated in the aforesaid treaty subscribed the 1st of December, 1845, between the Kingdom of the Two Sicilies and the United States of America."

[From a despatch of the United States chargé d'affaires, July 29, 1851.]

"It will be seen from the accompanying reply of the Minister of Foreign Affairs to my note, acceding to the convention for the equalization of direct and indirect tonnage duties, that orders have been given for the execution of the same on the part of the Neapolitan government, and the restitution of the excess of the indirect tonnage duty paid by the *Joshua Mauran*, over the four grains direct tonnage. The amount to be refunded is 254 ducats and 31 grains. About the same sum will be repaid under this convention to the consignees of the ship *Niagara*, recently arrived from New Orleans with a cargo of tobacco, part of which was landed at Genoa.

"Reluctant as I was to enter into such a convention without special instructions, I look for my justification to the fact that the advantage obtained is entirely on the side of the United States—that it is one of the objects designated by Mr. Buchanan to the negotiator of the present treaty between the two countries, as desirable to be gained, and that it is strictly in accordance with the commercial policy adopted by the United States from its origin of 'perfect equality and reciprocity,' and with the act of Congress of March, 1815, which provides, 'that former discriminating duties on tonnage and on goods, between those of the United States and of foreign countries, by which a much higher rate was imposed on those of the latter, should be removed on a repeal, by any foreign government, of their discriminating and countervailing duties, detrimental to the United States, and the public declaration thereof by the President on such an event;' and also with the later act of 24th May, 1828. Three most important points have been secured for the benefit of American commerce, viz: 1. The procuring of 10 per cent. reduction on the tariff on American produce and manufactures on *indirect* voyages. 2. Liberty to United States vessels to touch at intermediate ports on their voyages to the ports of this kingdom, without incurring an oppressive tax. 3. The abolition of the forty grains tonnage duty on indirect voyages, and the subjection of direct and indirect voyages to an equal duty of four grains per ton. I hope these valuable concessions will commend the convention to your approbation, and to that of the Executive, and will excuse me for having seized on a *propitious* moment to pledge the Neapolitan government to their confirmation by a formal written agreement."

---

## SARDINIA.

[From a despatch of the United States chargé d'affaires to Sardinia, 13th July, 1850.]

"The grain trade carried on within the Mediterranean waters from time immemorial, has been one of the principal sources of the commercial prosperity of Genoa. Genoese ships have had the protection of differential duties, to the effectual exclusion of vessels under all other flags. These long existing privileges in favor of Sardinian navigation had the effect of preventing the government of this country from entering into treaties of commerce with other nations, until I had the good fortune to get round the difficulty in the treaty of commerce which I had the honor to sign in Genoa, in November, 1838, by the provisions of the separate article of that treaty, which served as a model for similar stipulations with most of the other commercial nations of the world. The progress, however, of free opinions on the subject of commerce, has at length induced this country to abandon the differential protection hitherto afforded to Sardinian vessels, in the corn, oil, and wine trade, to which it was limited, for the first time, by our commercial treaty. On the strength of the enclosed letter from the Secretary of State for Foreign Affairs, it can now be officially announced to the commercial public, that American vessels can engage in the grain carrying trade, as well as in all other kinds of commerce between Genoa and other ports within the Mediterranean and Black seas, on the same footing with Genoese vessels. The separate article of the treaty alluded to, with its reserved rights of retaliation, consequently becomes a dead letter. You will perceive, sir, from the letter of the secretary, that he desires a declaration to that effect from the United States government."

*Note of the Sardinian Secretary for Foreign Affairs to the United States chargé d'affaires.*

[Translation.]

TURIN, *July* 12, 1850.

SIR: The National Parliament has just passed a law, which received the royal sanction on the 6th instant, providing that all differential duties of navigation and of commerce, which had hitherto been levied throughout this kingdom, to the detriment of foreign flags, shall no longer be exacted from any of those nations who may be willing to grant a perfect reciprocity to the Sardinian flag.

By the provisions of this law, the *reserved rights*, which constitute the scope of the separate article of the treaty of November 26, 1838, have ceased to exist. Instructions have accordingly been sent to the authorities of all our ports, in order that this measure may immediately go into full operation, in favor of the American flag. I entertain no doubt but that the American government will, on its own part, hasten to assure that of his Majesty that it looks upon the *reserved right* of exacting similar duties, in all the ports of the Union, from Sardinian vessels, as virtually at an end.

[From a despatch of the United States chargé d' affaires to Sardinia, August 4, 1851.]

"By the new tariff, cotton-wool, which is the chief article of American produce consumed here—unless it be tobacco, the trade in which is still a government monopoly—is among the articles of commerce exempted from duty. The import of cotton last year amounted, I am told, to fifteen millions of francs.

"According to article 6 of the treaty with Switzerland, the right of transit through the territories of the respective contracting parties is secured to the commerce of other nations with either, subject only to such duties as are paid by their own citizens."

---

## PARMA.

*Alterations in the Parma tariff, according to returns made to the British House of Commons, March* 26, 1850.

| Import duties. | New duty. | | | Date of alteration. |
|---|---|---|---|---|
| | *£* | *s.* | *d.* | |
| Rice, not cleaned, per cwt...... | 0 | 0 | 2¼ | September 25, 1848. |
| Brandy, per cwt.............. | | 2 | 5 | October 4, 1848. |
| Bulls and oxen, each.......... | | 1 | 3½ | do. |
| Cows, calves, &c., each........ | | | 8 | do. |
| Salted, pickled and smoked bacon, per cwt.............. | | 1 | 8½ | do. |
| Wheat, per cwt.............. | Free. | | | do. |
| Rye, per cwt................ | do. | | | do. |
| Maize, per cwt.............. | do. | | | do. |

## TURKEY.

### *Tariff between Turkey and Great Britain, October 31, 1850.**

[Translation.]

Whereas the term of the tariff which was to be in force for seven years, beginning from the month of March, 1254, (1839,) and which fixed, according to the current prices of that time, the custom duties to be paid by British subjects upon all commodities, being the produce, growth, or manufacture of the United Kingdom of Great Britain and Ireland and its dependencies, and also of other countries, imported by them into the Ottoman dominions, as well as upon merchandise of every description, being the produce, growth, or manufacture of the Ottoman dominions, purchased by them or by their agents in all parts of the Sultan's dominions, for exportation to their own, or to other countries, has expired; and whereas both the parties have, by virtue of the seventh article of the commercial convention concluded between Great Britain and the Sublime Porte, demanded the renewal of the aforesaid tariff, the Sublime Porte, and his Excellency Sir Stratford Canning, ambassador extraordinary and plenipotentiary from her Britannic Majesty, appointed for this purpose commissioners, have negotiated and concluded the following tariff:

*Articles of importation from 1st January, 1847, to 13th March, 1855.*

| | Aspers. |
|---|---|
| Alum, per cantar | 201 |
| Ambergris, ad valorem. | |
| Anchors, per cantar | 389 |
| Aniseed, per cantar | 130 |
| Bacon, per oke | 36 |
| Bark, ad valorem. | |
| Beds, Malta iron, for two persons, each | 317 |
| for one person, each | 288 |
| for children, each | 173 |
| Beef, salt, per barrel of 1½ or 2 cantars | 864 |
| Beer, in large bottles, per dozen | 115 |
| in small bottles, per dozen | 72 |
| Biscuit, ad valorem. | |
| Blacking, in large bottles, per dozen | 58 |
| in small bottles, per dozen | 43 |
| Borax, refined, ad valorem. | |
| Bottles, empty, for wine, of 300 drachms each, per 1,000 | 1,944 |
| Bricks, per 1,000 | 864 |
| Butter, ad valorem. | |
| Buttons, ad valorem. | |
| Camphor, per oke | 52 |
| Candles, spermaceti, per oke | 79 |
| Carbonate of soda, per cantar | 216 |
| Cardamoms, per oke | 187 |
| Cassia-lignea, per oke | 37½ |

* To continue from 1st January, 1847, until 13th March, 1855.

| | Aspers. |
|---|---|
| Cassia, per oke | 11½ |
| Cascarilla, per oke | 26 |
| Chain cables, iron, per cantar | 317 |
| Chairs, Malta, with straw, per dozen | 122½ |
| with bamboo cane, per dozen | 202 |
| Cheese, ad valorem. | |
| Cinnamon, per oke | 46 |
| Clocks, ad valorem. | |
| Cloves, per oke | 34½ |
| Coals, per cantar | 20 |
| Cochineal, per oke | 223 |
| Codfish, per cantar | 216 |
| Coffee, West India and Brazil, per 100 okes | 1,440 |
| Mocha, per 100 okes | 2,016 |
| Copper, nails and sheets, per oke | 50½ |
| Copperas, per cantar | 101 |
| Cream of tartar, per oke | 21½ |
| Cubebs, per oke | 17 |
| Cummin seed, per oke | 7 |
| Currants, Zante, per oke | 7 |
| Dye-woods—logwood, per cantar | 108 |
| Pernambuco, per cantar | 1,282 |
| Santa Martha, per cantar | 274 |
| Earthenware, ad valorem. | |
| Files, common, per dozen | 16 |
| fine, for gold and silversmiths, per dozen | 43 |
| Flour, American, per barrel of 70 okes | 461 |
| Fowling-pieces, ad valorem. | |
| Gin—Holland, juniper, per gallon of 1,070 drachms | 32 |
| Ginger, black and white, per cantar | 432 |
| Glassware, ad valorem. | |
| Gums—Benjamin, per oke | 57 |
| Gotta, per oke | 144 |
| Gum lac, per oke | 29 |
| Gum copal, per oke | 58 |
| Guns, (cannon,) iron, ad valorem. | |
| Hair, human, ad valorem. | |
| Hams, per oke | 36 |
| Hardware, ad valorem. | |
| Herrings, barrel of 600 to 1,000 | 475 |
| Hides, dry, ox and cow, per oke | 26 |
| Hooks, fish, per 1,000 | 29 |
| Jalap, per oke | 86 |
| Jewelry, ad valorem. | |
| Indigo, Bengal, in chests, per oke | 194½ |
| Madras, per oke | 115 |
| Ipecacuanha, per oke | 70 |
| Iron, bars, squares and round, per cantar | 144 |
| pig, per cantar | 72 |
| sheet, per cantar | 260 |
| nail rods, per cantar | 144 |

| | Aspers. |
|---|---|
| Iron, hoops, per cantar | 173 |
| dishes, per cantar | 238 |
| wire, fine, per cantar | 720 |
| wire, thick, per cantar | 418 |
| smoothing, 12 pair | 230 |
| spades and coal shovels, per dozen | 346 |
| Ivory, elephants' teeth, per oke | 202 |
| fish teeth, per oke | 158 |
| in pieces, per oke | 86 |
| Lead, in pigs, per cantar | 331 |
| shot, per cantar | 375 |
| sheets and tubes, per cantar | 418 |
| white, per cantar | 461 |
| rod, per cantar | 389 |
| Leather, sole, ad valorem. | |
| Litharge, per cantar | 403 |
| Locks, (padlocks,) brass, per 100 | 374½ |
| Maccaroni, Malta, per oke | 8½ |
| Magnesia, per oke | 29 |
| Manufactures of cotton, linen, silk or woolen: | |
| Bed ticking, 27 to 32 inches wide, per yard | 7 |
| Do. do. do., 35 to 52 inches wide, per yard | 10 |
| Bobbinet, tulle, white, 35 to 40 inches wide, per yard | 8½ |
| colored, 35 to 40 inches wide, per yard | 10 |
| figured, 40 to 42 inches wide, per yard | 20 |
| Calicoes or domestics: | |
| Gray, of every width and quality (gray shirtings or madapollams excepted,) per oke | 41 |
| White long cloths, and other plain white calicoes, of every width and quality, (white shirtings and madapollams excepted,) per oke | 46 |
| [The tare of each bale of cotton goods at 10 okes.] | |
| Cambrics, plain white, $\frac{5}{4}$ and $\frac{6}{4}$, 34 to 45 inches wide, 12 yards, per piece | 73½ |
| plain white, $\frac{8}{4}$, 58 to 62 inches wide, 24 yards, per piece | 130 |
| figured stripes and spots, 38 to 44 inches wide, 12 yards, per piece | 66 |
| twilled gray, $\frac{6}{4}$, 40 to 42 inches wide, 24 yards, per piece | 72 |
| white, $\frac{6}{4}$ and $\frac{7}{4}$, 40 to 48 inches wide, 24 yards, per piece | 115 |
| dyed and various colors, $\frac{7}{8}$, $\frac{9}{8}$ and $\frac{6}{4}$, 24 to 44 inches wide, 24 to 28 yards, per piece | 118 |
| dyed, Turkey red, $\frac{7}{8}$, $\frac{9}{8}$ and $\frac{6}{4}$, 24 to 44 inches wide, 24 to 28 yards, per piece | 209 |
| Diaper and huckaback, 25 to 27 inches wide, ad valorem. | |
| Drill cotton (American and English,) gray, white and dyed, tare 10 okes per bale, per oke | 52½ |

| | Aspers. |
|---|---|
| Drill linen, and cotton mixed; also fancy colored cotton, ad valorem. | |
| Drill linen, brown or white, or with colored stripes, 25 to 27 inches wide, per yard | 22 |
| Drill, ravens duck, 25 to 27 inches wide, 36 to 40 yards, per piece | 288 |
| Fustians, satins, white and dyed, 23 to 27 inches wide, per yard | 6 |
| cotton velvet, in various colors, 24 to 26 inches wide, per yard | 10 |
| Turkey red, 24 to 26 inches wide, per yard | 27½ |
| printed red, 24 to 26 inches wide, per yard | 13 |
| velveteens, dyed, 15 to 17 inches wide, per yard | 8½ |
| Handkerchiefs, white cambric, with white or colored borders, 29 to 32 inches square, per dozen | 46 |
| Indian silk (corahs,) piece of 7 handkfs | 274 |
| (pongees) piece of 10 handkerchiefs | 360 |
| printed cotton, orange ground, with red and yellow, 20 to 25 inches square, per dozen | 26 |
| printed cotton, blue ground, 22-32 inches square, per dozen | 44½ |
| Turkey red, 22-29 inches square, per dozen | 58 |
| Lappets, 6-4, 40-42 inches wide, 10 yards, white, and with one or two colors; also, Victoria checks and sprigs; per piece | 47½ |
| Lappets, harness, and seno checks and sprigs, per piece | 86½ |
| shawls, white and col'd, 48-52 in. square, per doz | 106½ |
| 63-64 do do | 173 |
| Linen cloth, (Irish,) ad valorem. | |
| Muslins, book, ordinary quality, 38-39 inches wide, 10 yards, per piece | 29 |
| book, good quality, 43-44 inches wide, 10 yards, per piece | 66 |
| jaconetts, (Mermer,) 7-8 and 6-4, 36-44 inches wide, all qualities, 20 yards, per piece | 82 |
| mulls, (Chappali,) 4-4, 7-8, and 6-4, 30-42 inches wide, 24 yards, per piece | 79 |
| mulls, Nos. 5 and 6, 4-4, 7-8, and 6-4, 32-44 inches wide, 20 yards, per piece | 122½ |
| mulls, No. 26 and upwards, ad valorem. | |
| tangibs, (Surai,) 4-4, 31 inches wide, 17 yards, per piece | 36 |
| tangibs, (Sevaspoor,) 4-4, 7-8, and 6-4, 32-43 inches wide, 20 yards, per piece | 50 |
| tangibs, (Sevaspoor,) 7-4, 48-50 inches wide, 20 yards, per piece | 78 |
| Nankeens, plain, colored, and striped, 24-25 inches wide, per yard | 3 |
| India, (buff,) per piece of 7 yards, or 9 to 10 pikes | 72 |
| Oil cloth, (floor,) per square yard | 58 |
| Parasols and umbrellas, cotton and silk, ad valorem. | |

| | Aspers. |
|---|---|
| Printed cottons, 7-8 calicoes, 1 and 2 colors, 28 yards, per piece | 86½ |
| 3 and 6..do....do......do.... | 118 |
| Printed cottons, 9-8 to 5-4, 1 and 2 colors, 30-45 inches wide, 24 yards, dress and furniture patterns, all qualities, fast and loose colors, per piece | 137 |
| Printed cottons, 9-8 to 5-4, 3 and 6 colors, 30-45 inches wide, 24 yards, dress and furniture patterns, all qualities, fast and loose colors, per piece | 202 |
| Printed muslins, all qualities and widths, fast and loose colors, 24-25 yards, per piece | 122 |
| Quilting, printed, 27-28 inches wide, per yard | 20 |
| Sail cloth, cotton, from Malta, all qualities, per canna | 13 |
| hemp, ad valorem. | |
| Shirtings, and madapollams, of all widths and qualities—tare, 10 okes per bale: | |
| Gray, per oke | 52 |
| White, per oke | 59 |
| Dyed, 32-33 inches wide, 24-25 yards, per piece | 79 |
| 36 inches wide, 38-40 yards, per piece | 137 |
| Shirts, Malta, all sorts, and colored or white, per dozen | 202 |
| Stockings, cotton and thread, per dozen | 187 |
| (half stockings,) per dozen | 86 |
| silk, per dozen | 576 |
| (half stockings,) per dozen | 288 |
| Thread, cotton, sewing, white and gray, per oke | 49 |
| Twist, cotton, gray and white, of all qualities, per oke | 33 |
| dyed, dark blue, sky blue, and red, per oke | 52 |
| Turkey red, per oke | 72 |
| Umbrellas and parasols, cotton and silk, ad valorem. | |
| Zebras, 3½ yards, blue and white stripes, blue and orange stripes, orange all over, and orange striped, damasked, blue ground, large and small pines, and ditto imitations, per piece | 39 |
| Zebras, 3½ yards, Fermaish, and imitation rich patterns, per piece | 55 |
| Woolen and worsted goods: | |
| Blankets, each | 115 |
| Carpeting, ordinary quality, 36 inches wide, per arshin | 27½ |
| fine Brussels, 27 inches wide, per arshin | 56 |
| Cloth, army, broad and narrow, per yard | 34½ |
| broadcloth, ladies' cloth, ad valorem. | |
| pilot, Calmouk, and beaver, per yard | 50 |
| Cassimeres, ad valorem. | |
| Damasks, ad valorem. | |
| Lastings, camlets, princettas, imperial crapes, and other summer coatings, 25 to 31 inches wide, 28 to 30 yds., per piece | 576 |
| Merinos, colored, 23 to 25 inches wide, 28 to 30 yds., per piece | 245 |
| colored, 32 to 35 inches wide, 28 to 30 yds., per piece | 324 |
| colored, 42 to 45 inches wide, 28 to 30 yds., per piece | 426 |
| printed, 19 to 22 inches wide, 28 to 30 yds., per piece | 245 |

| | Aspers. |
|---|---|
| Merinos, printed, 32 to 35 inches wide, 28 to 30 yds., per piece | 453 |
| printed, 42 to 45 inches wide, 28 to 30 yds., per piece | 612 |
| Orleans, for linings, figured, 27 to 29 inches wide, 28 to 30 yards (called fodralik shali,) per piece | 173 |
| Orleans, for lining and garments, plain, figured, shot-striped, checked, or plaided, with silk and without silk, 30 to 45 inches wide, (called fustanlik ve fodralik shali,) 28 to 30 yards, per piece | 338 |
| Orleans, superfine, plain, 48 to 49 inches wide, 28 to 30 yards (called zoff duz feregelick,) per piece | 533 |
| Muskets, ad valorem. | |
| Musk, per metical | 86 |
| Nails, assorted, per cantar | 432 |
| for shoemakers, per cantar | 259 |
| Needles, for sailors, per 1,000 | 460 |
| for sewing, per 50,000 | 691 |
| Nutmegs, per oke | 144 |
| Oil, castor, per oke | 29 |
| linseed, per cantar | 533 |
| olive, from Ionian islands, per cantar | 475 |
| Olibanum, per cantar | 331 |
| Paint, (oil,) prepared and assorted, per barrel of 8 to 11 okes | 108 |
| Pans, frying, per dozen | 245 |
| Paper, writing, ad valorem. | |
| Pepper, per oke | 11½ |
| Pimento, per oke | 17 |
| Pins, assorted, per oke | 65 |
| Pistols, ad valorem. | |
| Pitch, per barrel of 2 and 2½ cantars | 101 |
| Pork, salt, per barrel of 77 and 80 okes | 634 |
| Potatoes, per cantar | 86 |
| Precipitate, per oke | 259 |
| Powder, cannon, ad valorem. | |
| Rhubarb, ad valorem. | |
| Rice, ad valorem. | |
| Rum, per gallon of 1,070 drams | 29 |
| American, per gallon of 1,070 drams | 26 |
| Sal ammoniac, per oke | 16 |
| Saltpetre, refined, per cantar | 576 |
| unrefined, ad valorem. | |
| Sarsaparilla, in the root, per oke | 43 |
| prepared, per oke | 72 |
| Salt, common, per cantar | 216 |
| English salts, per oke | 4 |
| Segars, Havana, per 1,000 | 1,152 |
| Malta, 1st, 2d, and 3d quality, per 1,000 | 130 |
| Soap, fine, per oke | 14 |
| from Ionian islands, per cantar | 403 |
| Spelter or zinc, per oke | 8½ |
| Stock fish, per cantar | 216 |

| | Aspers. |
|---|---|
| Stones from Malta, worked and not worked, 25 to 27 inches (called arshinlick,) per 100 | 648 |
| smaller, 14 to 18 barmacks, 20 to 21 inches, per 100 | 389 |
| 9 to 12 barmacks, 17 to 18 inches, per 100 | 245 |
| Stoves, ad valorem. | |
| Sublimate, per oke | 187 |
| Sugar, refined, in loaf, per cantar | 749 |
| crushed, per cantar | 619 |
| Muscovado, all sorts, per cantar | 461 |
| Tamarind, per oke | 16 |
| Tar, per barrel of 2 to 2½ cantars | 202 |
| Tea, per oke | 86 |
| Thimbles, brass, per gross | 46 |
| Tin plates, per the two boxes | 1,152 |
| Tin, in bars, per cantar | 1,584 |
| Tobacco, negrohead and cavendish, per cantar | 663 |
| Virginia, in leaves, per cantar | 345 |
| Vanilla, per oke | 1,584 |
| Watches, gold, silver, and metal, ad valorem. | |
| gold and silver, with music, ad valorem. | |
| Wine, Marsala, per oke | 7 |
| Port, in bottles, per bottle | 34½ |
| Madeira, per bottle | 29 |
| sherry, per bottle | 29 |
| white, from Ionian islands, per oke | 3½ |
| red ... do ... do | 3 |
| Wood, ebony, per cantar | 288 |
| mahogany, per cantar | 360 |
| lignumvitæ, per cantar | 187 |
| Zinc or spelter, per oke | 8½ |

*Articles of exportation from* 1*st January*, 1847, *to* 13*th March*, 1855.

| Articles. | Internal duty. | Export duty. |
|---|---|---|
| | *Aspers.* | *Aspers.* |
| Aniseed, from Cesaria, per oke | 25 | 8 |
| from Romelia .. do | 20 | 6 |
| Bottargo, ad valorem. | | |
| Boxwood, all sorts, per cantar | 136 | 45 |
| Brandy, called raky, per oke | 34 | 11 |
| Boulamah, (a Turkish sweetmeat,) ad valorem. | | |
| Butter ... do. | | |
| Candles, tallow ... do. | | |
| wax ... do. | | |
| Cheese, all sorts ... do. | | |
| Carubi ... do. | | |

TABLE—Continued.

| Articles. | Internal duty. | Export duty. |
|---|---|---|
| | *Aspers.* | *Aspers.* |
| Coffee, Mocha, per oke | 68 | 22 |
| Copper, pig......do. | 113½ | 38 |
| old......do. | 81 | 27 |
| wrought..do. | 204 | 68 |
| Cotton-wool, from Romelia, Syria and Cyprus, per cantar | 1,860 | 620 |
| from Anatolia, all sorts, per cantar | 2,145 | 715 |
| from Egypt, ad valorem. | | |
| Cummin seed, per oke | 20 | 6½ |
| Drugs: | | |
| Colocynth, per oke | 91 | 30 |
| Salop, from Anatolia, per oke | 136 | 45½ |
| from Romelia, ad valorem. | | |
| Senna, per oke | 45 | 15 |
| Scammony, ad valorem. | | |
| Opium, from Egypt, ad valorem. | | |
| from Anatolia, per oke | 1,270 | 423 |
| Dyes: | | |
| Berries, yellow, from Kaisserieh, per oke | 163 | 54½ |
| from Iskilib........do. | 91 | 30 |
| all sorts, from Romelia,.....do. | 41 | 13½ |
| Galls, all sorts, per cantar | 2,722 | 907 |
| Gull bachar, (red dye,) per oke | 18 | 6 |
| Indigo, from Egypt, ad valorem. | | |
| Madder roots, from Cyprus, Syria and Tripoli, per cantar | 885 | 295 |
| from Anatolia, per cantar | 1,588 | 529 |
| Safflower, from Anotolia, per oke | 136½ | 45 |
| from Romelia, ad valorem. | | |
| Saffron, from Anatolia.........do. | | |
| from Romelia.........do. | | |
| Emery stone, per cantar | 180 | 60 |
| Feathers, ostrich.....ad valorem. | | |
| Fish, dried and salted......do. | | |
| Fruit: | | |
| Figs, dried, ad valorem. | | |
| Carabournu raisins, called sultana, per cantar | 1,179 | 393 |
| Chesme and Yerli raisins, called sultana, per cantar | 907 | 303 |
| Vourla raisins, called sultana, per cantar | 1,066 | 355 |
| Chesme, Vourla Aidin, Yerli, and Mentesche raisins, called resaky, per cantar | 635 | 212 |
| Carabournu raisins, called resaky, per cantar | 726 | 242 |
| Beglerge.....do.......do.........do... | 340 | 113 |

TABLE—Continued.

| Articles. | Internal duty. | Export duty. |
|---|---|---|
| | *Aspers.* | *Aspers.* |
| Currants, called kush usumi......per cantar. | 1,021 | 340 |
| Stanchio red raisins, called resaky....do..... | 386 | 128½ |
| Black raisins......................do..... | 308 | 103 |
| Mandalia and Samos raisins.........do..... | 290 | 97 |
| Grain and pulse: | | |
| Barley, per kilot of Constantinople.......... | 56½ | 19 |
| Beans, ad valorem. | | |
| Indian corn or maize, per kilot of Constantinople.............................. | 63½ | 21 |
| Lentils, ad valorem. | | |
| Oats.......do. | | |
| Peas.......do. | | |
| Rye, per kilot of Constantinople............. | 63½ | 21 |
| Wheat ...do........do.................. | 127 | 42 |
| Gums: | | |
| Ammoniac, ad valorem. | | |
| Arabic, per oke.......................... | 59 | 19½ |
| Incense, picked, best quality, per cantar...... | 1,497 | 499 |
| in powder..............do........ | 748½ | 249½ |
| Mastic, per barrel of 70 okes............... | 18,144 | 6,048 |
| picked............per oke........ | 363 | 121 |
| Myrrh.....................do........... | 36 | 12 |
| Sanderach .................do........... | 46 | 15 |
| Tragacanth, lowest quality...do........... | 32 | 10½ |
| second quality...do........... | 91 | 30 |
| best white......do........... | 173 | 57½ |
| Halva, (sort of sweetmeat,)......ad valorem. | | |
| Hides, dry, ox and buffalo, all sizes..do. | | |
| Honey...........................do. | | |
| Horns, buffalo, per 100 pair................ | 2,359 | 786 |
| ox .........do...................... | 1,180 | 393 |
| stag, per oke........................ | 45 | 15 |
| Kufter, paste of boiled grape-juice, per cantar... | 907 | 302 |
| Leeches, per oke......................... | 216 | 72 |
| Liquorice paste, per cantar ................. | 998 | 333 |
| *Manufactures of cotton, linen, silk, and woolen.* | | |
| Boghassi, white, colored and striped, from Denisli and Hamid, per oke..................... | 163 | 54 |
| Calico, printed, from Cyprus, called boghtcha ve yasdik fusta tschiti, per piece of 4.......... | 145 | 48½ |
| Caps, red, Tunis, called medgidiè fez, the 4..... | 907 | 302 |

TABLE—Continued.

| Articles. | Internal duty. | Export duty. |
|---|---|---|
| | *Aspers.* | *Aspers.* |
| Caps, red, Tunis, large, good and common, called medgidiè fez, the 4 | 1,542 | 514 |
| small, good and common, called medgidiè fez, the 12 | 1,542 | 514 |
| Carpets, Turcoman, each | 680 | 227 |
| from Ushack, per oke | 145 | 48 |
| rugs, called segiadè, ad valorem. | | |
| Cloth, horse-hair, and horse-hair thread, called harrar and cazil, from Romelia and Anatolia, per oke | 50 | 16½ |
| Cotton-yarn, Smyrna, white and dyed, per oke | 109 | 36 |
| called richtè argatch ... do | 45 | 15 |
| from Monastir, ad valorem. | | |
| from Bey Bazar, per oke | 113½ | 38 |
| Felt, white and colored, from Kaisseriè, called ketche, per piece | 91 | 30 |
| from Gaschia, used for horses, called ketche, per piece | 182 | 60 |
| Leather, sole, from Yalova, per piece | 408 | 136 |
| from Kaisseriè and Eguin, called sahtian, per 5 pieces | 590 | 196 |
| morocco, scarlet, from Heraclia and Balukesser, per piece | 163 | 54 |
| black, from Isparta, Konieh-Ushak, and Ismid, per piece | 108 | 36 |
| red, from Tosia, and Ushak, per 6 pieces | 680 | 227 |
| scarlet, from Romelia, per piece | 113½ | 38 |
| black and yellow, from Islimia, Tcherbani, and Carlova, per piece | 77 | 26 |
| from Anatolia, (meschin,) per piece | 68 | 22½ |
| sole, from Aidin ... per piece | 272½ | 90½ |
| from Keredè ... do | 272½ | 90¼ |
| scarlet, from Romelia ... do | 50 | 16½ |
| sole, ox and buffalo, called manda ve pismish kiossele, per piece | 1,043 | 348 |
| from Romelia and Anatolia, called meschin, per piece | 32 | 10½ |
| Mohair-yarn, from Angora, per oke | 272½ | 90 |
| Napkins, silk, called sade Hama fotah, per pair | 408 | 136 |
| embroidered, from Hama ... do | 816½ | 272 |

TABLE—Continued.

| Articles. | Internal duty. | Export duty. |
|---|---|---|
| | *Aspers.* | *Aspers.* |
| Napkins and towels, silk, plain, and wrought in gold, per piece | 1,633 | 544 |
| Sash, from Tunis, called kushak, per piece | 363 | 121 |
| from Karagilar, white and colored, per oke | 154 | 51½ |
| from Tripoli, silk, called hairidin kushagi, per oke | 1,814 | 605 |
| from Hama, silk, called kushagi, per piece | 81½ | 27 |
| Shali, from Angora, of all widths and qualities, called sof, per piece of 32 pikes | 3,175 | 1,058 |
| from Tosia, colored, ad valorem. | | |
| from Tullet, ad valorem. | | |
| Shawls, from Tunis, called halali, per piece | 454 | 151 |
| from Tunis, colored, per piece | 454 | 151 |
| from Karagilar, per piece | 127 | 42 |
| Sofa covers, and velvet cushions, wrought, from Biligik, called sadè balin, per pair | 326½ | 109 |
| Stuff, silk, from Broussa, called kutni and moreh, per piece | 612 | 204 |
| called merzifun beldy, per pair | 208½ | 69½ |
| from Broussa, called beldy, per pair | 154½ | 51½ |
| colored and striped, called hamid boghassi, per oke | 163 | 54 |
| woolen, from Tunis, called shali, or donluk-shal, per piece | 544 | 181 |
| woolen, white, from Tunis, called bayazshali, per piece | 163 | 54 |
| from Monemen, called kerbaz, per piece | 100 | 33 |
| from Cyprus, called yorghan ve sofra yuzi, per piece | 91 | 30 |
| called kibriz takim, per piece | 726 | 242 |
| called duschek ve shilte, per piece | 145 | 48½ |
| called kibriz siledgey, per piece | 91 | 30 |
| from Tokat, called tschit ve elvan boghassi, per piece | 63½ | 21 |
| from Tosia, woolen and yellow, called muhairie, per piece | 181½ | 60 |
| black, woolen, called babas muhairie, per piece | 272½ | 90½ |
| called kerbaz-dagh, per piece | 127 | 42 |
| from Malatia, called kerbaz, per piece | 204 | 68 |
| from Alania, narrow, called kerbaz, per piece | 63½ | 21 |

TABLE—Continued.

| Articles. | Internal duty. | Export duty. |
|---|---|---|
| | *Aspers.* | *Aspers.* |
| Stuff, from Alania, wide, called kerbaz, per piece | 81 | 27 |
| called kerbaz drama, per piece | 172½ | 57½ |
| called kerbaz trebisond, per piece | 227 | 76 |
| linen, called kerbaz riza, per oke | 635 | 211 |
| called kerbassi keten, per oke | 127 | 42 |
| from Barian, Castamuni, and Boghaz, called kerbassi golos, per pike | 9 | 3 |
| called kerbaz ladick, per piece | 45½ | 15 |
| called kerbaz merzifoun, per bale of 1,200 pikes | 7,984 | 2,661 |
| called kerbaz kedous, wide and narrow, per bale of 50 pieces | 3,720 | 1,240 |
| called alagia, from Tireh and Bor, per piece | 72 | 24 |
| called alagia, striped, from Manissia, per bale of 100 pieces | 8,165 | 2,721½ |
| called astar, from Castamuni, per bale of 60 pieces | 4,990 | 1,663 |
| called astar, from Tash Kupru, per piece | 54 | 18 |
| called tschit ve yorghan youzu, from Castamuni, per bale of 60 pieces | 7,257 | 2,419 |
| called ibrahimiè, (silk,) per piece | 499 | 166 |
| called sham kutni, (silk,) do | 590 | 196 |
| called halep kutni, (silk,) do | 408 | 136 |
| called halep alagia, (silk) do | 272 | 90 |
| called bamri, (silk,)......do | 454 | 151 |
| called scham tchitari ve kitani ve alagia, (silk,) per piece | 544 | 181 |
| called sherbab kushak, (silk,) per piece | 318 | 106 |
| called sherbab kushak, (cotton)..do | 181 | 60 |
| called gueive astari..........do | 91 | 30 |
| called amid astar, per oke | 200 | 66 |
| woolen, white and colored, from Romelia, called khrams......per oke | 245 | 81½ |
| Thread, linen, from Anatolia...do | 68 | 22½ |
| from Touva.....do | 181 | 60 |
| from Castamuni, Gueive and Alain, per oke | 91 | 30 |
| from Markola........per oke | 73 | 24 |
| from Kelb and Surmene.do | 122½ | 41 |
| from Karagilar.........do | 155 | 51 |
| from Hamelat.........do | 136 | 45 |

TABLE—Continued.

| Articles. | Internal duty. | Export duty. |
|---|---|---|
| | *Aspers.* | *Aspers.* |
| Towels, from Broussa, called peschtemal, per pair | 127 | 42 |
| embroidered, called kouta, per pair | 336 | 112 |
| from Salonica, called peschtemal, per pair | 181 | 60 |
| from Broussa, called bash peschtemali, per pair | 113½ | 38 |
| Mehleb, a black berry......per oke | 45½ | 15 |
| Needles, large, from Anatolia..do | 109 | 36 |
| Nets, for fishing..............do | 181½ | 60½ |
| Nuts: | | |
| Hazel-nut and filberts, (funduk,) per cantar | 499 | 166 |
| Walnuts, (geviz,) per 100 okes | 522 | 174 |
| Oil, olive, per cantar | 1,633 | 544 |
| Oleaginous seeds: | | |
| Hemp-seed, per kilot of 20 okes | 127 | 42 |
| Linseed.......do.......do | 190½ | 63½ |
| Sesamum-seed..do.......do | 290 | 96½ |
| Orpiment, per oke | 32 | 10½ |
| Otto roses, per metical | 136 | 45 |
| Pekmes, boiled grape juice, ad valorem. | | |
| Sal ammoniac, from Egypt, per oke | 100 | 33 |
| Saltpetre, from Egypt, ad valorem. | | |
| Sapanaire, a root for removing stains, per oke | 18½ | 6 |
| Silks: | | |
| Silk cocoons, and silk pods, (straccia di seta,) ad valorem. | | |
| Silk, Cyprus, per oke | 635 | 211½ |
| Aidin, Payambol, Segala, Mentesche, Scham, Aleppo, and Beyrout, per oke | 835 | 278 |
| Yania, Tricala, Yenischeher, Yenischeher Volo, Amassia, Tcherchamba, Bafra Salonica, and Carafereh, per oke | 1,025 | 342 |
| Adrianople, Demotica, Turnova, Philippopoli, Bazargick, Zara Attik, and Zara Yeni, per oke | 1,107 | 369 |
| Broussa, Mohalitch, Kermasti, Panderma, Aydingick, Erdeck, Capou-Daghi, Demirdesch, Pazar-Kioi, Caramoussal, Kuplu, Bilegick, Serit, Ismid, Bahtschegick, Gueive, and Ada Bazar, (including spun silk by European machinery,) of Broussa, Smyrna, and all other places in Anatolia and Romelia, per oke | 1,406 | 468 |

TABLE—Continued.

| Articles. | Internal duty. | Export duty. |
|---|---|---|
| | *Aspers.* | *Aspers.* |
| Soap, per cantar | 1,596 | 532 |
| Sponge, ad valorem. | | |
| Staves....do. | | |
| Skins: | | |
| Angora goat skins, white and colored, ad val. | | |
| Hare skins, from Anatolia, per 100 skins | 907 | 302 |
| from Romelia.......do | 544 | 181½ |
| Lamb and kid skins, per piece | 13½ | 4½ |
| Sheep and goat do....do | 25 | 8 |
| Tallow, called tschervisch, ad valorem. | | |
| called don-yaghi....do. | | |
| Timber....do. | | |
| Tongues, smoked, and all other dried and smoked meats, ad valorem. | | |
| Tobacco: | | |
| Gubeck Baghtcha, per oke | 94 | 31 |
| Kenevir............do | 72½ | 24 |
| Ermieh............do | 59 | 19½ |
| Ermieh Denk.......do | 54½ | 18 |
| Of Bafra, Samsoun, Cumari, Pursitchian, Basma, and other places, ad valorem. | | |
| Tschivisch, a sort of glue used by shoemakers, per oke | 45½ | 15 |
| Valonea, all qualities, per cantar | 476 | 159 |
| Wax, yellow beeswax, per oke | 173 | 57 |
| Wine, all sorts, of the Ottoman empire, (Cyprus Comandaria excepted,) per oke | 14 | 5 |
| Cyprus Comandaria.......do | 45½ | 15 |
| Wool: | | |
| Sheep's wool of Romelia and Anatolia, per cantar | 1,315 | 438½ |
| of Bagdad, Tripoli, and Africa, per cantar | 930 | 310 |
| Goat's wool, (white,) called finik, per oke | 129 | 43 |

The custom duties, to be taken in conformity with the treaty, on all articles imported by British merchants into the Ottoman dominions, or exported by them from the same, shall be levied at the rates fixed by the present tariff, from the market prices of which articles sixteen per cent. on exports, and twenty per cent. on imports, have been deducted from the value thereof for customs duties and expenses.

With regard to those articles which are not mentioned and inserted in this tariff, as also to those which are inserted, but of which the value, not being therein fixed, is referred to the current prices, they shall be calculated at the current price of the article in question.

For articles of exportation, sixteen per cent. will be deducted from the current price; after which will be levied, upon their value so reduced, nine per cent. of internal duty, and three per cent. of export duty. For articles of importation, twenty per cent. shall be deducted from the current price; after which the import duty of three per cent., as also the additional duty of two per cent., shall be levied in the manner established by the treaty.

If, for want of a proper understanding, disputes should arise between the customers and the merchants, concerning the valuation either of merchandise of a new kind which may be imported, or upon merchandise on which it will be necessary, by the present tariff, to levy the custom duties according to the current prices, in that case the custom duties shall be levied in kind, in conformity with the old system.

The present tariff is to be in force at the custom-house of Constantinople, as well as in all the other custom-houses of the Ottoman empire, from the 25th of Moharem, in the year of the Hegira 1263, which corresponds with the 1st of January, of the Christian era, 1847, until the 1st of March; that is to say, the 13th of March, new style, of the Christian year 1855. And whereas, by the lapse of time, a difference may probably take place in the price of commodities, either party shall have the right to demand the revision and renewal of this tariff six months previous to the expiration of the term above stated, that is to say, in the course of the last six months thereof; but in the event of the six months elapsing, after the term fixed as above, without either party having demanded the renewal of the present tariff, the term thereof shall be thereby extended to the seven following years.

---

## CHINA.

### *Tax on teas.*

[From a despatch of the United States chargé d'affaires *ad interim*, of July 19, 1850.]

"I have the honor to transmit herewith a translation of a petition of the old Hong merchants, which has been acceded to by the local authorities, sanctioning the establishment of tea-warehouses, and levying a tax of two mace (28 cents) per pecul on all teas exported." [According to the regulations in this case adopted, the tax so levied is paid by "the dealers in foreign trade who purchase the teas;" or, as stated by Mr. Parker in his communication of the 19th August, 1850, to the imperial commissioner, "the responsibility is fixed upon the Chinese broker, who, on the day of weighing and delivering the teas, is to pay the same to the warehouse firms; and this he will not fail to include in the price of the teas sold the foreign merchant."]

### *Exportation of grains prohibited.*

[From a despatch of the United States chargé d'affaires *ad interim*, of May 21, 1851.]

"I have recently received two despatches from the imperial commissioner; one prohibiting the exportation of *rice*."

[From the same, June 20, 1851.]

"I have the honor to transmit two communications from the imperial commissioner; one prohibiting the exportation of *wheat* and *rice*."

[From the same, October 27, 1851.

"From the joint communication of the imperial commissioner and the governor of Canton, of the 26th ultimo, a copy of which I have now the honor to transmit, it will be seen that the Chinese government persist in the wish that breadstuffs should not be exported; and, as stated in my despatch to the commissioner upon the subject, under date of 9th September, I have acceded to that wish, subject to the decision of the department; and, by circular of the 20th instant, have addressed the consuls of the United States in China, and called upon them to require the merchants of the United States at their respective ports to desist from the exportation of grains, the produce of China. The export trade in grains from this country is not one of much moment; and in view of all the circumstances of the case, the request of the Chinese may be regarded as reasonable."

---

## MOROCCO.

[From a despatch of the United States consul general to Morocco, September 29, 1848.]

"I have the honor and pleasure of informing you of a radical and favorable change in the tariff regulations of this country. A royal order has been received at this place from the court at Morocco, reducing the duties on all goods imported into this empire from 20 per cent. (the former rates) to 10 per cent. *ad valorem*, excepting upon the articles enumerated below, which are reduced as follows:

"On iron, from $5 (former rate) to $4 per cwt.

"On raw cotton, to $3 per cwt.

"On raw silk, from $1 to 50 cents per lb.

"It is to be hoped that these reductions in the rates of duties upon imported articles will afford an inducement to the merchants of the United States to renew and extend their commercial operations with this country, which are now, I regret to find, almost wholly carried on by the English, French, Spanish, and other nations more contiguous than our own."

[From a despatch of the United States consul general to Morocco, December 8, 1848.]

"In my despatch, No. 5, of the 29th September, I advised you of a radical reduction in the *import* duties of this country. I now have the satisfaction of apprizing you that an order has been received from the Emperor, at the several ports of the empire, reducing the *export* duties on a number of the staple productions of this country, as follows:

"Beeswax, from 160 to 120 ounces* per kintal.

"Hides " 53 to 36 " per kintal.

"Washed wool, from 72 to 54 " per kintal.

"Halocah wool, " 48 to 36 " per kintal."

---

* An ounce, or doce, is equal to about 5½ cents our currency.

[From a despatch of the United States consul general to Morocco, June 1, 1851.]

"I herewith enclose a translation of the tariff of Morocco."

| Articles. | Morocco weight. | English weight. | Okiat. | Dolls. & cents. |
|---|---|---|---|---|
| IMPORTS. | *Quintals.* | *Pounds.* | | |
| Iron, the great quintal | 1 | 168 | 68 | 3 77 |
| Silk, raw, the English pound | ........ | 1 | 8½ | 47 |
| Steel and iron nails | 1 | 119 | 85 | 4 71 |
| On all other articles a duty of 10 per cent. is charged on their valuation, except woolen cloths and cotton manufactured goods, on which a duty of 10 per cent. is taken in goods. | | | | |
| Goods monopolized by the Sultan, viz: Coffee, tea, sugar, cochineal, and brimstone. | | | | |
| Goods admitted without duty, viz: Wheat, barley, oil, raisins, figs, flour, honey, potatoes, and provisions of all kinds. | | | | |
| EXPORTS. | | | | |
| Wax | 1 | 119 | 120 | 6 66 |
| Wool, unwashed, gunpowder included | 1 | 119 | 40 | 2 22 |
| washed ... do | 1 | 119 | 56 | 3 11 |
| Hides | 1 | 119 | 36 | 2 00 |
| Leather, tanned, of all kinds | 1 | 119 | 120 | 6 66 |
| Goat skins | 1 | 100 | 36 | 2 00 |
| Sheep skins | 1 | 100 | 36 | 2 00 |
| Almonds, sweet and bitter | 1 | 119 | 25½ | 1 38 |
| Gum arabic | 1 | 119 | 25½ | 1 38 |
| Gum senegal, and white | 1 | 119 | 37½ | 2 08 |
| Gum sandrack | 1 | 119 | 37½ | 2 08 |
| Cummin | 1 | 112 | 12 | 66 |
| Caraway seed | 1 | 112 | 12 | 66 |
| Fennel | 1 | 112 | 12 | 66 |
| Sesame | 1 | 112 | 12 | 66 |
| Gagul | 1 | 112 | 12 | 66 |
| Walnuts, per seron | ........ | ........ | 32 | 1 77 |
| Olives | 1 | 119 | 16 | 88 |
| Oil | 1 | 119 | 48 | 2 66 |
| Privet | 1 | 100 | 36 | 2 00 |
| Sarguina weed | 1 | 100 | 16 | 88 |
| Canary seed | 1 | 100 | 16 | 88 |
| Linseed | 1 | 100 | 12 | 66 |
| Wild marjoram | 1 | 100 | 12 | 66 |
| Slippers, for every 100 pairs | ........ | ........ | 90 | 5 00 |
| Slippers for Alexandria, for every 100 pairs | ........ | ........ | 75 | 4 16 |
| Dates | 1 | 119 | 36 | 2 00 |
| Acorns, per bale | ........ | ........ | 12 | 66 |
| Fowls, per dozen | ........ | ........ | 20 | 1 11 |
| Eggs, per thousand | ........ | ........ | 44 | 2 44 |
| *Observation.*—Bullocks, sheep, mules, horses, asses, &c., cannot be exported without a special license from the Sultan. | | | | |

NOTE.—The quintal of Mogador, Saffi, and Mazagan is equivalent to 119 English pounds. The quintal of Rabat, Larache, Tangier, and Tetuan, is equivalent to 112 English pounds. The rate of exchange used for the conversion of the Morocco moneys into dollars is at the average rate of 18 okiat per dollar.

## HAYTI.

[From a despatch of the U. S. commercial agent, Cape Haytien, February 13, 1849.]

"I herewith transmit a translation of a law by this government, which went into operation on the 1st instant, regulating the prices of certain foreign goods, and monopolizing, in the name of the government, the products of coffee and cotton. A law more injurious to the trade of this country, as well as that of our own with it, could scarcely have been framed, as it must cause the entire cessation of imports from the United States of the articles on which the prices have been fixed, it being impossible to import them for sale at those prices."

### DECREE.

[January 9, 1849, to take effect February 1, 1849.]

Faustin Soulouque, President of Hayti—

According to the law passed on the 26th of October, 1848, which grants to the executive the right to establish and enjoy for the benefit of the government the monopoly of all or part of the products of the soil, by and with the advice of the Secretary General, the High Judge and the Secretary of State, in council assembled—decrees as follows:

Article 1. The government for the present monopolizes only coffee and cotton.

Art. 2. In each of the open ports of the republic there shall be established by the government a commission of monopoly.

Art. 3. The speculators are instructed to buy from the growers, and to sell exclusively to the government, coffee and cotton, at the prices fixed by the tariff No. 1, annexed to the present decree.

Art. 4. The foreign merchandise of "the first necessity," designated in tariff No. 2, annexed to the present decree, cannot be sold above the prices fixed by the aforesaid tariff.

Art. 5. Every dealer who shall sell his goods above the prices fixed by the tariff No. 2 shall be liable to a fine of twenty per cent. on the price of the article sold, provided that the fine shall not be less than five dollars.

Art. 6. The government will only purchase coffee and cotton in the open ports.

Art. 7. The speculators are instructed to deliver every week the coffee and cotton they may have on hand. These products, in order to be received by the commission of the monopoly, should be clean and merchantable.

Art. 8. The speculators shall declare weekly at the bureau of the monopoly the quantity of coffee and cotton they may have on hand; and the director of said establishment shall indicate by a written order the scales where these products shall be weighed.

Art. 9. The director of the bureau of the monopoly shall make out two bills, the first for the amount of the coffee or cotton sold to the merchant, the second for the proceeds of one dollar per hundred pounds of coffee or cotton, reverting to the State on the sale. The amount of the first bill shall be paid over to the speculator, and that of the second to the director of the monopoly, who will transfer it to the public chest.

Art. 10. The products of the soil, sold by the commission of the monopoly to the merchants, shall be accompanied by a bill showing the quantity sold to and the price paid by the exporter. This bill shall be exhibited to the custom-house at the time of weighing, in order that it may be verified if the quantity declared and submitted to be weighed agrees exactly with that sold by the State.

Art. 11. All products declared at the custom-house for shipment, which shall not be accompanied by the bill of sale of the commission of the monopoly, and all quantities exceeding two per cent. over and above those sold, shall be considered as contraband, and confiscated to the profit of the State.

Art. 12. The division of the coffee and cotton monopolized shall be made by a committee named by the merchants of each locality, and composed of three of their number. This committee, renewable every eight days, shall make known to the commission of the monopoly the different quantities of products required by each shipper. The division of the monopolized products shall be made *pro rata*, and according to the importations of articles of "the first necessity" made by each merchant. A statement of each operation of division shall be made out and recorded.

Art. 13. The commission of the monopoly and the committee of division are authorized to consult the records of the custom-house, in order to be acquainted with everything that may concern their operations.

Art. 14. There shall be formed in the capital a commission composed of nine members: among these there shall be at least three merchants. It shall meet every Tuesday, and in case of urgency can be convoked at any time.

Art. 15. The business of this commission shall be: 1st. To superintend the execution of the present decree throughout the extent of the republic, by means of the commission of the monopoly of each locality. 2d. To denounce to the government the functionaries of such establishments of the monopoly as shall not fulfil their duties. 3d. To acquaint the government with the imperfections and inconveniences susceptible of impeding the progress of the present decree. 4th. To decide on all points relating to the administration of the monopoly.

Art. 16. The directors of the bureaus of the monopoly are instructed to forward every eight days to the central bureau a detailed statement of the operations during the week.

Art. 17. Until the directors and clerks of the several commissions of the monopoly shall have been appointed by the government, the judge of peace, the director of the council of notables, and the government storekeeper of each of the open ports of the republic, shall perform this service. The administrator of finances shall put under their order one or two clerks from his own bureau.

Art. 18. The present decree shall go into effect on the first day of February. In consequence, all those who have coffee and cotton on hand are instructed before said day to have such quantities verified by a committee to be composed of one member of the council of notables, the judge of peace, and the commissary or agent of the police, in order that these products, already in store, shall not come under the law of the monopoly. A statement of this operation shall be made out and forwarded to the Secretary of State. After the day fixed for the operation of the law, no claims will be admitted.

ART. 19. All infractions of the present decree will be prosecuted and punished according to law.

*Tariff No. 1.*

| | | | | | | |
|---|---|---|---|---|---|---|
| The speculators shall pay in the open ports, per 100 lbs. of coffee | | | | | | $25 00 |
| Do. | do. | closed | do. | do. | do. | 24 00 |
| Do. | do. | open | do. | do. | cotton | 26 50 |
| Do. | do. | closed | do. | do. | do. | 25 00 |

The price is fixed for cotton in bales ready for shipment.

| | | | | | |
|---|---|---|---|---|---|
| The government shall pay to the speculators, per 100 lbs. of coffee | | | | | 26 00 |
| Do. | do. | do. | do. | cotton | 27 50 |
| The government shall sell to the merchants, | | | do. | coffee | 27 50 |
| Do. | do. | do. | do. | cotton in bales | 28 50 |

*Tariff No. 2.*

| There shall be sold at wholesale— | | At retail. | |
|---|---|---|---|
| Flour, per barrel | $72 00 | | |
| Mess pork, per barrel | 135 00 | per pound. | $0 81¼ |
| Mess beef, do | 105 00 | ..do. | 64 |
| Mackerel, do | 36 00 | each | 18¾ |
| Herring or alewives, per barrel | 35 00 | ..do | 12½ |
| Codfish, per 100 pounds | 31 00 | per pound. | 40 |
| Good soap, per box of 20 bars | 13 00 | per bar | 75 |
| Brown linen osnaburgs, good quality | 1 00 | per ell | 1 12½ |
| inferior | 80 | ..do. | 87½ |
| White linen osnaburgs | 1 20 | ..do. | 1 37½ |
| Checks, 24 inches wide | 90 | ..do. | 1 00 |
| 28 do | 1 00 | ..do. | 1 12½ |
| 35 do | 1 25 | ..do. | 1 37½ |
| Calicoes or prints, ordinary quality | 1 25 | ..do. | 1 37½ |
| Bleached cotton cloth, 29 inches | 90 | ..do. | 1 00 |
| Blue imitation Romal hdkfs., per doz | 7 00 | per hdkf | 62½ |
| Imitation India or Désiré hdkfs., per doz. | 21 00 | ..do. | 1 87½ |

[From a despatch of the U. S. commercial agent, Cape Haytien, February 23, 1849.]

"I enclose the translation of a second decree by the President of Hayti, in relation to the monopoly law. If the situation of American merchants in this island was bad before, it is now much worse, as the only privilege they possessed under the monopoly was the right vested in them to receive a share of coffee, adequate, as far as the supply would permit, to their wants: this is now taken from them, by allowing the consignees of all vessels, whatever they may import, an equal right. European vessels remain in port from forty to sixty days, while ours rarely have more than fifteen to twenty lay-days. Our only alternative now is, to cease our importations, and await the repeal or modification of the existing laws."

[Translation.]

DECREE.—[*February* 16, 1849.]

FAUSTIN SOULOUQUE, President of Hayti, finding it necessary to modify the decree of the *monopoly*, under date of January 9, 1849, by and with the advice of the Secretary General, the High Judge, and the Secretary of State, in council assembled, decrees as follows:

ARTICLE 1. Is hereby annulled the article 12 of the decree of the 9th of January, before cited.

ART. 2. The division of the monopolized products shall be made by a committee named by the consignee merchants of each locality: this committee may be changed every week; it shall give notice to the commission of the monopoly, of the different quantities of products wanted by each commercial house. The division of the monopolized products shall be made between the consignees of vessels loading, according to the importance of the remittances to be made by them, and the urgency of the wants of each. A statement of each operation of division shall be made out.

ART. 3. It is permitted to the consignee at one place to send his vessel under scale duty, or to employ a coaster, in order to take or complete his cargo at any of the other open ports of the republic. His right to the monopolized products at the place to which he may go to complete his loading, shall be established by a certificate from the commission of the monopoly at the port where he resides; it being understood that this privilege cannot be exercised until the wants of the consignee merchants of the place to which he may go shall first have been satisfied, and there should exist there an excess of products. In consequence, the committee of division, as well as the commission of the monopoly, shall see that there shall not be delivered to any one more products than he actually requires or may be entitled to.

ART. 4. The merchant who may receive from the committee of division an order for a portion of the monopolized products, shall take immediate delivery, and pay for them; any delay will be considered as a renunciation of right to his share, and the part apportioned to him may be given to others in want.

[From a despatch of the U. S. commercial agent at Cape Haytien, June 18, 1849.]

"I have to communicate a reduction of one-half of the duties on certain articles of American provisions, (the selling-prices of which are fixed by the law of the monopoly) viz:

| | Reduced duty. |
|---|---|
| Codfish, per 100 pounds | $0 21 |
| Flour, per barrel | 1 00 |
| Pork, per barrel | 1 00 |
| Mackerel, per barrel | 25 |
| Herrings or alewives, per barrel | 25 |

[From a despatch of the U. S. commercial agent at Cape Haytien, August 6, 1849.]

"I forward, enclosed, a copy of the new modification of the Haytien law of the monopoly, by which it will be perceived that the prices of the monopolized staples have been increased, while those of the taxed foreign articles remain the same."

*Modification of the law of the monopoly of the republic of Hayti.—(June 22, 1849.)*

[Translation.]

By virtue of the law of October 26, 1848, which grants to the government the right of establishing and exercising the monopoly of all or part of the products of the soil, by and with the advice of the Secretary General, the Grand Judge, and the Secretary of State, in council assembled, Faustin Soulouque, President, decrees as follows:

Art. 1. The government monopolizes coffee and cotton.

Art. 2. In each of the open ports of the republic there shall be established an administration of monopoly, and a commission for the repartition of the products monopolized. The commission shall be named by the consignee merchants of each locality, and should consist of three members at least, renewable every eight days. In such places where neither directors nor clerks have been especially appointed, the duties shall be performed by the judge of the peace, the director of the council of notables, and the government storekeeper of the locality.

Art. 3. The speculators are required to purchase from the growers, and to sell exclusively to the government, their coffee and cotton, at the prices fixed by the tariff No. 1, annexed to the present decree.

Art. 4. The foreign merchandise specified in tariff No. 2, annexed to the present decree, cannot be sold above the prices fixed by the aforesaid tariff.

Art. 5. The government will only purchase the monopolized products in the open ports: these products, in order to be received by the administration of the monopoly, should be clean and merchantable.

Art. 6. In the morning of Monday of each week, the speculators of the open ports shall declare to the bureau of the monopoly the monopolized products which they may have on hand. The same day, the administration of the monopoly shall make known to the committee of division the quantity of products ready for division. The committee shall immediately establish the rights of each merchant to share, who will be required, the same day or the day following, to put at the disposition of the monopoly the quantity of bags requisite to contain the portion of coffee assigned him. The expenses of filling the bags, and cost of transportation to and weighing at the bureau of the monopoly, shall be paid by the merchants.

Art. 7. In the open ports, the monopolized products bought by the speculators shall on each Tuesday of the week be conveyed directly from their depots to the scales of the bureau of the monopoly, there to be weighed, and kept until the day of their shipment. The same formalities shall be observed, at all times, with the products arriving from the interior or coastwise.

Art. 8. The speculators of the closed ports, or of the towns or villages of the interior, are required to deliver, every fifteen days at least, to the administration of the monopoly, the coffee and cotton of their depots: all retention of these products beyond the delay fixed, shall cause their confiscation, unless the delay be occasioned by unforeseen circumstances, legally justified.

Art. 9. The division of the monopolized products shall be made among the merchants (consignees) of the place, pro rata, and according to the remittances they have to make against goods arriving directly from foreign countries to their address. Such merchants as shall not furnish their bags, according to the terms of article six of this decree, shall not be allowed to participate in the division.

Art. 10. All disputes arising at the repartitions shall be settled by the administration of the monopoly: should it be necessary, however, appeal may be made to the Secretary of State.

Art. 11. The administration of the monopoly, and the committee of repartition, are authorized to obtain from the custom-house such documents as they may deem necessary to establish the rights of the merchants to share in the division of the monopolized products.

Art. 12. The relative position or rights of each merchant having been established according to article 9th, the administration of the monopoly shall proceed to weighing the products allowed to each, and these products shall not be taken away but for the purpose of being conveyed to the scales of the custom-house for immediate shipment.

Art. 13. Every merchant is required to mark his bags; and immediately after weighing his products, to pay the amount of his bill to the administration of the monopoly, who will furnish a quittance and receipt of depot.

Art. 14. The administration of the monopoly shall pay to the speculators the amount of the products delivered by them, and the same day shall deposite in the public treasury the duties reverting to the State on the sale of said products.

Art. 15. The products of the soil, sold by the administration of the monopoly to the importers, shall be accompanied with a bill bearing the number of the bags or bales sold, their weight and the sum paid by the exporter, which bill shall be exhibited at the custom-house at the time of shipment, in order that it may be proved if the quantity declared for shipment corresponds exactly with that sold by the government.

Art. 16. The director of the bureau of the monopoly is required to assist at the shipment of the monopolized products. The bills and depot receipts which accompany them shall be delivered to the director of the custom-house, who shall enregister them, and pass them over immediately to the administration of the finances.

ART. 17. All products presented at the custom-house for shipment, which shall not be accompanied by the bill of sale of the administration of the monopoly, and receipt of depot, and all quantities exceeding two per centum of the quantities sold, shall be considered as contraband, and confiscated for the benefit of the State.

ART. 18. The consignee merchant of one place is allowed to send his vessel under scale duty to any other port or ports of the republic, either to load or complete her loading, under supervision of the bureau of the monopoly. His right to purchase the monopolized products at the place where he may go to load his vessel, shall be established by an order delivered to him by the administration of the monopoly and committee of repartition of the port he leaves.

ART. 19. The orders for the loading of a vessel in one or more ports of the republic shall be discharged by the monopoly and the custom-house, according to the delivery and shipment of the products; and the custom-house of the port which aquits the said order, is required to forward it immediately to the administration of the finances.

ART. 20. No preference shall be made between the merchants of one port and those of another, where they may go to load their vessels, than that existing in consequence of the importance of their respective importations.

ART. 21. In the case that there should be no demand at an open port for monopolized products on the part of the merchants of the locality, the speculators, owners of these products, shall be allowed to ship them to any other open port that they may deem advisable. These products, on their shipment, should be accompanied by a certificate of the administration of the monopoly, descriptive of their nature, the number of bags or bales, and their weights.

ART. 22. Every wholesale and retail dealer, and every consignee merchant, who shall act contrary to the law, and to the decree of the monopoly, shall lose the right to his patent, and cannot again recover it. If the offender is employed by the State, or an agent of the government, he shall be deprived of his office, and be prosecuted according to law.

ART. 23. All merchandise or produce confiscated for contravention to the dispositions of the monopoly shall be sold: two-thirds of the net proceeds shall be paid into the public treasury, and the other third paid to whoever shall give information to cause or facilitate the seizure.

ART. 24. Regarding the seizure of monopolized products, the affair shall be decided in the shortest delay by the administration of the monopoly, assisted by the administrator of the finances and the district attorney.

ART. 25. All merchandise sold above the prices fixed by tariff No. 2 shall be confiscated, and the seller amenable to a penalty of not less than five dollars, nor more than the value of the goods confiscated. The confiscation and penalty shall be pronounced by the tribunal of peace.

ART. 26. There shall be established in the capital a commission, composed of nine members, whose duties shall consist of: 1st. To superintend the execution of the present decree throughout the extent of the republic, by means of the administrations of monopoly of each locality. 2d. To denounce to the government the officers of such establishments of the monopoly as shall not perform their duties. 3d. To make known to the government the imperfections and inconveniences likely to impede the operation of the present decree. 4th. To prepare to the government such modifications as may appear needed in the present decree, and in the annexed tariffs. 5th. To give information on all points relating to the administration of the monopoly. The commission should meet at least once a week.

ART. 27. In twenty-four hours after the publication of the present decree, all coffee and cotton actually in the warehouses shall be verified by the administration of the monopoly, at the requisition of the consignee merchants owning them, under pain of confiscation, according to the terms of article twenty-two of the present decree.

ART. 28. The present decree abrogates those of the 9th of January and 16th of February, 1849, and all preceding dispositions on the monopoly.

*Tariff No.* 1.

The speculators shall pay—

| | |
|---|---|
| per 100 lbs. of coffee | $25 00 |
| per 100 lbs. of cotton, baled | 26 50 |

The government shall pay to the speculators—

| | |
|---|---|
| per 100 lbs. of coffee from the interior | 27 00 |
| per 100 lbs. of coffee coastwise | 28 00 |
| per 100 lbs. of cotton, baled, from the interior | 28 50 |
| per 100 lbs. of cotton, baled, coastwise | 29 50 |

The government shall sell to the consignee merchants—

| | |
|---|---|
| per 100 lbs. of coffee | 29 00 |
| per 100 lbs. of cotton, baled | 30 00 |

*Tariff No.* 2.

| At wholesale. | | At retail. | |
|---|---|---|---|
| Wheat flour, per barrel | $72 00 | | |
| Mess pork, do | 135 00 | per pound | $0 81¼ |
| Mess beef, do | 105 00 | ..do | 64 |
| Mackerel, do | 36 00 | each | 18¾ |
| Herrings, do | 35 00 | ..do | 12½ |
| Codfish, per 100 pounds | 31 00 | per pound | 40 |
| Good soap, per box of 20 bars | 13 00 | per bar | 75 |
| Brown linen osnaburgs, good quality, per ell | 1 00 | per ell | 1 12½ |
| Brown linen osnaburgs, inferior, per ell | 80 | ..do | 87½ |
| White do good quality, do | 1 20 | ..do | 1 37½ |
| Checks, of 24 inches (French) width, do | 90 | ..do | 1 00 |

*Tariff*—Continued.

| At wholesale. | | At retail. |
|---|---|---|
| Checks, of 28 inches (French) width, per ell | $1 00 | per ell....$1 12½ |
| Checks, of 35 inches (French) width, per ell | 1 25 | ..do....... 1 37½ |
| Prints or calicoes, of ordinary quality, per ell | 1 25 | ..do....... 1 37½ |
| Cotton cloth, bleached, (called madapolams,) 29 inches | 90 | ..do....... 1 00 |
| Cotton cloth, bleached, (called madapolams,) 24 inches | 68 | ..do....... 75 |
| Blue Romal handkerchiefs, per dozen.. | 7 00 | per hdkf... 62½ |

[From a despatch of the U. S. commercial agent at Cape Haytien, December 9, 1849.]

"Further to paralyze commerce the government published, on the 1st of December, in the capital, additional export duties of $50 per 1,000 lbs. on coffee, and of $7 per 1,000 lbs. on logwood. This law arrived in Aux Cayes on December 4, and came into force on the 5th."

[From a despatch of the U. S commercial agent at Cape Haytien, December 20, 1849.]

* * * "Since the 1st of October full duties have been exacted on the five articles of American provisions noticed in my despatch No. 22, as having been allowed entry at half duties up to that time.

"This government has recently given orders to charge the additional ten per centum heretofore exacted only on American vessels and their cargoes, on all goods known to be American, whether arriving under our flag or that of any other nation."

[From a despatch of the U. S. commercial agent at Aux Cayes, December 31, 1849.]

"There is one subject to which I beg for a moment to draw your attention; that is, the sudden changes in the laws affecting commercial interests. Within the last six months we have had the closing of the ports of Aquire, St. Mare, Miragoane, Port de Paix, and l'Ansed Hainault. 2. An additional duty of $5 per cent. on coffee and $7 per cent. on logwood; and, lastly, we have had those modifications in the monopoly law, a copy of which I enclose for your inspection.* Almost all these measures were enforced on the day of their publication; merchants only being apprized of the intentions of the government by a vague rumor. With such hasty legislation the most careful and discreet are entrapped, and thus all calculation defeated and frequently heavy losses entailed."

* See decree of 16th December, 1849, *sub*.

[From a despatch of U. S. commercial agent at Port au Prince, January 14, 1850.]

"Since the date of my communication of the 8th ult. there have been various changes in the laws of Hayti affecting commerce. And the great injuries done by these laws, and the frequent modification of them, are more severely felt by American merchants than by those of any other nation.

"The laws before the first of January required certain goods, considered of the first necessity, sold at fixed and very low prices, with the promise of coffee in return, also at a very low and fixed price.

"Through the month of December coffee came in freely, and but little complaint was made by American merchants in this city. But others suffered by the smaller ports being at the time shut against their claims for coffee for merchandise sold in them immediately before their being closed.

"On the first of this month another law* went partially into operation, requiring that all merchandise arriving, included under the monopoly tariff, should be sold on the government wharf or in its stores, under a joint commission of officers appointed by this government and the consignees or owners of the merchandise. Only one cargo and part of two others, principally belonging to Americans, were sold under this law. There was only time to sell the parts of cargoes above alluded to before (on the 11th inst.) another law* was proclaimed, urged upon this government by European merchants, relieving coffee from the law of monopoly, and fixing a low tariff on various kinds of merchandise conforming to the accompanying printed law,* which, in my judgment, is much more injurious to American commerce than either of the preceding ones.

"If this law continues to prevail, all exportations to this island from the United States must cease; for the fixed prices are so low, that ruinous consequences must result to the owners of merchandise thus sold.

"It will be seen by the tariff* enclosed that American goods, and those to these people of the first necessity, are more generally tariffed, and at lower rates, than the merchandise of any other nation.

"I am persuaded that petitions and remonstrances will reach the Department of State from numerous American merchants engaged in the trade of the island, setting forth the injuries that they have already sustained and are sustaining from these suddenly changing and partial and oppressive laws.

"While the citizens of France are scarcely affected, in their importations to Hayti, the Americans here import, and our merchants at home export, scarcely any article that is free.

"I must, consequently, join in opinion with the American merchants that some interference on the part of our government with these people would result favorably to American interests.

"There is another law, which it is well to have generally known, of much interest to American ship-owners whose vessels are in this trade,

---

* See translation with despatch of United States commercial agent at Cape Haytien, January 15, 1850, *sub*.

which fixes the 10 per cent. reciprocity duty on all American merchandise brought in vessels of any nation whatever. This is an advantage to our ship-owners, as one or two vessels, under foreign flags, are running as packets from the United States to this island, and also from the adjacent islands, bringing American goods, the old law giving these foreign vessels a decided preference of freight over American vessels, in saving to the shippers the 10 per cent. additional duty* required always on all goods brought in American vessels; and as far as I can judge, the law does not sensibly diminish the amount of goods usually brought here from the United States."

[From despatch of the U. S. commercial agent at Cape Haytien, January 15, 1850.]

"I herewith transmit a translation of a decree of the Haytien government, under date of 16th December, which was published here on the 27th of the same month, to take effect on the first instant, monopolizing the greater part of the remaining articles of foreign merchandise, including all such as might be in store. This decree is worded so ambiguously, that while it effectually binds the merchants, it leaves room for the authorities to put whatever construction on it they may think proper.

"The emperor has openly asserted, at Port au Prince, that he owes no responsibility to any nation on earth, and that he should make such laws as he pleased for the government of his country. But, will our government longer permit its citizens to be plundered without taking any notice of their claims on its protection? They send their vessels and property here, subject to the existing laws and regulations, and, without any notice or delay, new laws are made, to go into immediate operation; thereby subjecting them to heavy losses, without their being allowed either time or liberty to take measures for their protection.

"The foreign merchants, generally, throughout the island, have protested against the operation of the late decree; refusing to sell or deliver any more of their goods until they shall have been paid in coffee the amount of sales already effected under the monopoly law, and have charged the English and French consuls at Port au Prince with the prosecution of their interests.

"*January* 16.—I have received a copy of a new decree and tariff, under date of the 10th instant, abolishing the last one of the 16th December, which, as yet, has hardly had time to go into operation. This last decree puts the finishing touch to the miseries of commerce here, as it is utterly impracticable for the merchants to conform to it. I enclose herewith a translation of it."

---

*Removed. See *sub*., June 25, 1850.

[With despatch of the U. S. commercial agent at Cape Haytien, January 15, 1850.]

[Translation.]

*Decree and tariff of* 16*th December*, 1849: *to take effect* 1*st January*, 1850.

Faustin I, by the grace of God, and the constitutional law of the State, Emperor of Hayti, to all present and to come, greeting:

By virtue of the law* of 26th October, 1848, on the monopoly—

Considering that the government, in establishing the monopoly, has had in view the benefit of the people, in procuring for them, at reasonable prices, foreign articles of the first necessity;

Considering that the rules and regulations established, in order to arrive at this result, have been recognised as insufficient, and do not sufficiently guaranty the safety of the interests had in view by the government;

Considering that articles of great use, not being tariffed, are sold at arbitrary prices, not at all in proportion to the fixed prices of coffee and cotton, thus obliging the producer to submit to the decree of the monopoly without receiving any benefit therefrom, or enjoying any of the advantages which are intended to be secured to him by it;

Considering, besides, that experience has shown that the division of the monopolized products, by committees chosen by the merchants, has led to abuses which have been the cause of reclamations, it becomes necessary that the government should interfere, in order to establish a just equilibrium.

With the advice of our council of ministers, we have ordered and decreed as follows:

Article 1. Coffee alone shall be monopolized.

Art. 2. Cotton, before being embarked, shall pass through the bureau of the monopoly, in order that it may be weighed and the duty collected thereon, according to tariff No. 1, annexed to our decree of 22d June.

Art. 3. The articles designated in the tariff annexed to the present decree, cannot be sold above the prices fixed by said tariff.

Art. 4. There shall be established in each of the ports of Port au Prince, Aux Cayes, Cape Haytien, Jacmel, Gonaïves, and Jeremie, warehouses, into which shall be put in depot, after having regularly passed through the custom-house, such articles of merchandise as are designated in the tariff annexed to the present decree.

Art. 5. A commission, named by the government, shall be charged, conjointly with the consignee of said articles of merchandise, to take note of them. They shall be sold for cash by the said commission, who are ordered to make immediate payment of the proceeds of sales to the consignees of the same.

Art. 6. Coffee shall only be divided among importers of articles included in the tariff; which division shall be made pro rata, according to the acquired rights of each.

Art. 7. A commission named by the government alone shall be charged with the division of the monopolized produce.

---

* No copy of this law received at the department.

Art. 8. The government reserves to itself the right of retaining out of the quantity of coffee declared for division, a certain portion, to be disposed of according to the necessities of the moment; such portion shall not, however, exceed one-fifth of the existing quantity.

Art. 9. Every dealer who shall be convicted of having sold his goods above the prices fixed by the monopoly, shall, besides the penalties fixed by our decree of the 30th July, be condemned to an imprisonment of at least ten days.

Art. 10. Every consignee merchant who shall be convicted of contravention of the monopoly law, shall be condemned to pay a fine of one thousand dollars; and for a second offence shall lose his patent.

Art. 11. The present ordinance shall go into operation on the first day of January next following. It annuls such dispositions of our decrees of 22d June and 30th July of the present year as are contrary to it; it shall be printed and published, and our ministers are charged, each in that which concerns him, with its execution.

*Tariff annexed to the ordinance of December* 16, 1849.

| Articles. | Wholesale prices. | Retail. |
|---|---|---|
| Flour | $58 00 per barrel | $62 00 per barrel. |
| Butter | 1 25 per pound | 1 37 per pound. |
| Lard | 75 do | 1 00 do |
| First quality soap | 10 00 per box of 20 bars. | 62 per bar. |
| Second quality soap | 8 00 do | 50 do |
| Tallow candles | 93 per pound | 1 00 per pound. |
| Wrought iron nails | 60 do | 75 do |
| Cut iron nails | 48 do | 62 do |
| Codfish | 29 00 per 100 pounds | 37 do |
| Clear pork | 120 00 per barrel | 75 do |
| Mess pork | 100 00 do | 68 do |
| Prime pork | 82 00 do | 56 do |
| Mess beef | 95 00 do | 60 do |
| White pine scantling | 127 00 per M feet | 127 00 per M feet |
| Do.... boards | 122 00 do | 122 00 do |
| Yellow pine..do | 132 00 do | 132 00 do |
| Do.... scantling | 124 00 do | 124 00 do |
| Carolina cypress shingles | 34 00 per M. | 34 00 do |
| Blue drills or denims | 1 30 per ell | 1 37 per ell. |
| Cotton drills, fine quality | 1 75 do | 2 00 do |
| Olive oil, in baskets | 22 00 per doz. bottles. | 2 25 per bottle |
| Do...in boxes | 9 00 per doz. flasks | 1 00 per flask. |
| White cotton stockings, fine | 31 00 per dozen | 3 00 per pair. |
| Do........do.....common | 20 00 do | 2 00 do |
| Do......hose or socks | 8 00 do | 1 00 do |
| Brabant linen, yellow | 1 00 per ell | 1 12 per ell. |
| Fine sewing cotton | 4 00 per pound | 4 25 per pound |
| Alewives | 33 00 per barrel | 12½ each. |
| Mackerel, No. 3 | 36 00 do | 18¾ do |
| Common prints, wide | 1 25 per ell | 1 37 per ell. |
| Fine quality prints, wide | 1 58 do | 1 75 do |
| Real India handkerchiefs, pieces of eight. | 38 00 per piece | 5 25 per hdkf. |
| Fine imitation India handkerchiefs | 15 25 per dozen | 1 50 do |
| Real Madras handkerchiefs, pieces of eight. | 40 00 per piece | 5 50 do |
| Fine imitation Madras handkerchiefs | 18 00 per dozen | 1 75 do |
| Fine bleached cotton long-cloth | 1 93 per ell | 2 00 per ell. |
| Common..........do | 1 05 do | 1 12 do |
| Fine shirting linen | 3 75 do | 4 00 do |
| Do .....cotton | 1 08 do | 1 37 do |
| Common.......do | 93 do | 1 00 do |
| Fine broadcloth | 30 00 do | 34 00 do |
| Medium ..do | 18 00 do | 22 00 do |
| Common..do | 8 00 do | 12 00 do |
| Men's fine silk hats | 188 00 per dozen | 16 00 each. |
| Men's felt or cotton hats | 110 00 do | 11 00 do |
| Common black bombazine | 2 58 per ell | 2 75 per ell. |
| Imitation morocco skins | 48 00 per dozen | 4 50 each. |
| Common white platillas | 1 33 per ell | 1 50 per ell. |
| Fine white......do | 1 90 do | 2 00 do |
| Unbleached. ....do | 68 do | 75 do |
| Slates for roofing | 58 00 per M. | 58 00 per M. |
| Hoes, 4 inches | 38 00 per dozen | 3 50 each. |
| Hoes, 3 inches | 33 00 do | 3 00 do |
| Round-head axes | 62 00 do | 6 00 do |
| German axes | 76 00 do | 7 00 do |
| Manchettes, horn handles | 22 00 do | 2 25 do |
| Do.... wooden handles | 18 00 do | 1 75 do |

[Translation.]

EMPIRE OF HAYTI.—*Ordinance.* (*January* 10, 1850.)

FAUSTIN I, by the grace of God, and the constitutional law of the State, Emperor of Hayti, to all present and to come, salutes:

With the advice of our council of ministers, we have ordered, and do order, as follows:

ART. 1. Is, and remains, suspended, the execution of the law on the monopoly.

ART. 2. The merchants have the faculty of buying coffee at such prices, and in such quantities, as they may judge proper.

ART. 3. Out of the quantities of coffee purchased by the consignee merchants, there shall be taken for the account of the government one-fifth of the same. This fifth shall be settled for at the market price by the government, who shall not, however, pay more than *fifty dollars* per hundred pounds. The market price shall be fixed by the Commission of Control spoken of hereafter.

ART. 4. Foreign merchandise shall not be sold, either wholesale or retail, above the prices fixed by our tariff annexed to our present decree.

ART. 5. Shall only have the right of purchasing coffee for exportation, those merchants who shall make importations of merchandise by suitably assorted cargoes, to be sold on the market. The importation of specie shall give no right to the purchase of coffee.

ART. 6. The refusal to sell, or the suspension of sales, or the act of selling above the fixed prices, shall forfeit the right to purchase coffee, as well as the right of patent.

ART. 7. Every week, a committee of control, named by the government, shall verify in their warehouses the quantity of coffee purchased during the week by the merchants, and shall take away the one-fifth part coming to the State. This one-fifth, paid at the market price, as ordered by article 3, shall be received in compensation of custom-house duties, chargeable on all coffee exported. A duty of one dollar per hundred pounds shall be paid to, and collected by, the Commission of Control on all coffee shipped.

ART. 8. The coffee coming to the government shall be deposited in the warehouses destined for the purpose, under the supervision of the Committee of Control.

ART. 9. Coffee, before being transported to the custom-house, shall be weighed by the Committee of Control, in order to take from it the one-fifth part, and compare the weight of the balance with its reweight at the time of shipment.

ART. 10. No quantity of coffee shall be permitted to be weighed and shipped from the custom-house, without being accompanied by the certificate of its having been weighed by the Committee of Control; which certificate shall be returned by the custom-house to the Committee of Control, with a note of the reweight attached to it. All surplus found on reweighing at the custom-house shall be seized for the benefit of the State.

*Tariff annexed to ordinance of January* 10, 1850.

| Articles. | Wholesale. | Retail. |
|---|---|---|
| Gray colette, of good quality | $1 00 per ell | $1 12½ per ell. |
| Do ... inferior | 80 do | 87½ do |
| Bleached colette, good quality | 1 20 do | 1 25 do |
| Checks, 24 inches wide | 90 do | 1 00 do |
| 28 ... do | 1 00 do | 1 12½ do |
| 35 ... do | 1 25 do | 1 37½ do |
| Prints, fine quality, narrow | 1 25 do | 1 37½ do |
| Do ... wide | 2 00 do | 2 25 do |
| Bleached madapolam cotton, 29 inches | 90 do | 1 00 do |
| Do ... do ... 24 inches | 68 do | 75 do |
| Blue imitation Romal handkerchiefs | 7 00 per dozen | 62½ each. |
| India handkerchiefs, in pieces of eight | 40 00 per piece | 5 25 per hdkf. |
| Madras handkerchiefs, in pieces of eight | 52 00 do | 7 00 do |
| Imitation India and Madras handkerchiefs. Fine quality | 22 00 per dozen | 2 00 do |
| Imitation India and Madras handkerchiefs. Ordinary | 14 00 do | 1 50 do |
| Fine white cotton stockings for ladies | 31 00 do | 3 00 per pair. |
| Common ... do ... do | 20 00 do | 2 00 do |
| Common quality cotton socks | 8 00 do | 1 00 do |
| Colette of Brabant | 1 25 per ell | 1 37½ per ell. |
| Ordinary cotton drills or denims | 1 30 do | 1 37½ do |
| Fine ... do ... do | 1 75 do | 2 00 do |
| Cotton sewing thread | 4 50 per pound | 4 75 per pound. |
| Fine bleached cotton | 2 00 per ell | 2 25 per ell. |
| Common ... do | 1 25 do | 1 50 do |
| Black bombazine | 2 75 do | 2 87½ do |
| Fine linens, according to quality | 2 00 to $6 per ell. | $2 25 to $6 25 per ell |
| Manchettes, horn handles | 26 00 per dozen | 2 50 each. |
| Do ... wooden handles | 22 00 do | 2 00 do |
| Hoes, 3 and 4 inches | 36 00 do | 3 25 do |
| Round-head axes | 62 00 do | 6 00 do |
| German axes | 76 00 do | |
| White linen platillas, common quality | 1 33 per ell | 1 50 per ell. |
| Do ... fine quality | 1 90 do | 2 00 do |
| White cotton platillas, common quality | 1 00 do | 1 12½ do |
| Gray ... do | 90 do | 1 00 do |
| Imitation morocco skins | 48 00 per dozen | 4 50 each. |
| Men's silk or beaver hats, fine quality | 188 00 do | 16 00 do |
| Men's common hats | 110 00 do | 11 00 do |
| Slates for roofing | 58 00 per 1,000. | |
| Fine cloth | 30 00 per ell | 34 00 per ell. |
| Ordinary cloth | 18 00 do | 22 00 do |
| Common cloth | 8 00 do | 12 00 do |
| First quality soap ... in boxes of 18 and 20 pounds and 20 bars. | 12 00 per box | 12 50 per box. |
| Second quality soap. in boxes of 18 and 20 pounds and 20 bars. | 10 00 do | 10 50 do |
| Codfish | 31 00 per 100 lbs. | 33 00 per 100 lbs |
| Clear pork | 140 00 per barrel | 144 00 per barrel. |
| Mess pork | 125 00 do | 130 00 do |
| Prime pork | 97 00 do | 100 00 do |
| Herrings or alewives | 33 00 do | 35 00 do |
| Mackerel | 36 00 do | 38 00 do |
| Mess beef | 105 00 do | 108 00 do |
| Butter | 1 25 per pound | 1 37½ per pound. |
| White pine scantling | 124 00 per M feet | 132 00 per M feet. |
| Pitch pine ... do | 127 00 do | 135 00 do |
| White pine boards | 122 00 do | 130 00 do |
| Pitch pine ... do | 132 00 do | 140 00 do |
| Carolina cypress shingles | 28 00 per M | 30 00 per M. |
| Tallow candles | 93 per pound | 1 00 per pound. |
| Wrought iron nails | 60 do | 75 do |
| Cut iron nails | 48 do | 62½ do |

*Tariff*—Continued.

| Articles. | Wholesale. | Retail. |
|---|---|---|
| Olive oil, in baskets of 12 bottles | $22 00 per basket.. | $2 25 per bottle. |
| in flasks | 9 00 per dozen .. | 1 00 do |
| Flour, wheat | 58 00 per barrel.. | 64 00 per barrel. |
| Lard. | 75 per pound.. | 1 00 per pound |

And all other articles not tariffed shall be sold at prices in proportion to those of the present tariff.

[From a despatch of the U. S. commercial agent at Cape Haytien, June 25, 1850.]

"In consequence of the claims made by merchants of this city, the Haytien government has ordered the removal of the [ten per cent. additional duty charged on American commerce,] to take effect from the 9th of May last, and the restitution of the amounts paid additional on vessels cleared since that date.

"This act of the Haytiens is worthy of credit, as it shows their disposition to cultivate a better understanding with us, and to yield voluntarily that which we could not rightfully claim without formally recognising their independence."

[From a despatch of the U. S. commercial agent at Port au Prince, November 28, 1850.]

"I transmit herewith a law, just published in the papers here, alluding to the appointment of Haytien consuls or Haytien consular agents in Europe and America, and requiring that all *manifests* not certified by a Haytien consul or Haytien consular agent, or, in default of a Haytien officer at the place of shipment, some public officer of the place, shall submit the vessel to four dollars per ton tonnage dues, in place of the legal sum of one dollar per ton. [The law above mentioned was not received.]

"This law will go into effect in the United States and these islands in two months after legal publication."

[From a despatch of the U. S. commercial agent at Port au Prince, January 20, 1851.]

"I enclose herewith another copy of a law of this government, requiring that all vessels which arrive in any ports of the empire, bringing cargoes, shall have on board a manifest of said cargo, verified by a Haytien consul or agent. And in places of departure where there are no Haytien consuls or agents, then the manifest to be verified by some public officer authorized to receive declarations, certifying at the same time that there was no Haytien consul or agent residing at the place at the time of embarkment. [No copy of the above-mentioned law has been received.]

"All vessels arriving in the Haytien ports of the island after the sixteenth of April next, without the required certificate on the manifest, will submit the captain to a fine of one dollar Spanish per ton of his vessel, in addition to the present tonnage dues.

"The first article of the law relates to goods, &c., saved from wrecks, fixing a duty of five per cent. Spanish on Haytien currency; making the duty on such articles, at the present value of Haytien money, more than fifty per cent., which, with salvage and expenses, will leave perhaps nothing for the owners or underwriters."

[From a despatch of the U. S. commercial agent at Cape Haytien, January 24, 1851.]

"Several edicts have been published to-day concerning commerce, translations of which I shall make and forward later; among them is one requiring all foreign vessels to be provided with manifests certified at their ports of lading by the Haytien consuls, or, in their absence, by some public functionary:* another orders the increase of the patents of foreign importing merchants some twenty per cent." [The last mentioned edict has not been received.]

[Received with despatch of the U. S. commercial agent at Cape Haytien, August 4, 1852.]

[Translation.]

*Law respecting the customs, &c., approved June* 29, 1852.

EMPIRE OF HAYTI.

Faustin I, by the grace of God, and the constitutional law of the State, Emperor of Hayti, to all present and to come, greeting:

By and with the advice of the council of ministers and the legislative body:

Considering that the law of the 24th December, 1850, voted with the view of protecting the fiscal revenues of the custom-houses, has not entirely attained the object proposed, and that it becomes necessary to insure by new dispositions the exact collection of the revenues, by protecting them against all attempts at fraud, have proposed the following law:

Article 1. On the entry at the custom-house of a vessel coming from foreign parts, the consignee will present to the director, in addition to the manifest, the original invoice or invoices of all the merchandise forming the cargo of the said vessel, which shall, like the manifest of the said cargo, be clothed with the certificate of the commercial agent of the empire, should there be one at the port of clearance of the vessel.

Art. 2. The invoice should show the marks, numbers and description of the packages: as regards dry goods, the number of pieces or coupons, their measure and dimensions; for such goods as are bought by weight, the gross and net weight; and for all other goods, the precise designation of the quality and number of the articles contained in the packages, the actual price of which should be noted; and the certificate should make mention of the shipper's declaration, before the commercial agent, of the truth of the invoice.

---

* See *supra*, despatches of January 20, 1851, and November 20, 1850

Art. 3. A copy of the invoice shall at the same time be furnished to the agent: this copy need not contain the prices of each separate article, but only the total amount of the original invoice; and it should agree with it in every particular, as regards the description of the marks, numbers of the packages, their contents, measure, width, quantity, weight, and precise designation of the goods.

Art. 4. All goods coming from a foreign port, where the government maintains an agent, which shall not be accompanied by an invoice certified by the said agent, shall not be admitted to verification at the custom-house, at least until a demand shall have been made to the Minister of Commerce by the consignee of the vessel, or by the claimant of the goods. According to the instructions given by the Minister of Commerce, the intendant of the finances shall order the verification, which shall take place in the presence of a commission which shall be named for the purpose.

Art. 5. The non-production of the certificate of the commercial agent at the port of clearance shall carry with it a fine of *five-times* the amount of the invoice not accompanied by the said certificate, and this fine shall be paid into the public treasury at the same time with the duties chargeable on the cargo.

Art. 6. All declarations recognised as false, in consequence of non-conformity between the invoice duly certified and the contents of the packages, shall carry with them the confiscation of the goods, and a penalty equal to double the amount of the duties.

Art. 7. All goods found over and above the quantities charged in the invoice duly certified, and not exceeding two per centum on the amount of the said invoice, shall be subjected to double duties as regards the excess only.

Art. 8. All goods found *less* in quantity than what is actually charged in the duly certified invoice shall be subjected to double duties.

Art. 9. All goods without invoice and not declared on the manifest, whether charged or not on the bills of lading, and which shall be found on the vessel either at the moment of landing, or in being landed out of custom-house hours, shall be seized and sold for the benefit of the State. Besides the seizure, the proprietor of the goods and the delinquents shall each be subjected to a fine equal to double the duties.

The vessel on board of which the goods shall have been found or the crime committed, shall pay a fine of one thousand dollars if the value of the duties on the seized goods does not exceed fifty Spanish dollars; and if the value of these duties exceed fifty Spanish dollars, the vessel shall be confiscated and sold for the benefit of the State.

Art. 10. All contraventions to the dispositions of the law on the customs, which might carry with them the confiscation of vessels or goods, and condemnation to fines and all other penalties, shall be made known by the intendant of finances or the imperial procureur, or denounced to him by any other person, and shall be judged by the tribunals of peace, or imperial courts, competent to take cognizance of them. The sale of articles seized shall take place by public cries, at the bar of the tribunal which shall have had charge of the case, and in presence of the imperial procureur or his substitute.

Art. 11. Whoever shall give notice of the fraud, or shall facilitate the seizure of goods in contraband, shall be entitled to one-half of the net proceeds of the articles seized.

ART. 12. All custom-house regulations relating to masters of vessels coming from foreign parts shall be copied into small books, in different languages, and one of these books shall, on the arrival of the pilot on board of each vessel, be handed by him to the captain, who shall be required, on presenting himself at the bureau of the port, to sign an acknowledgment of the receipt of said book.

ART. 13. Every consul or commercial agent of the empire established in a foreign port shall receive the following charges for certifying invoices and manifests, viz:

| | | | |
|---|---|---|---|
| For every invoice, from $1 to $100 | Spanish | $0 50 | Spanish. |
| 101 to 500 | do | 1 00 | do. |
| 501 to 1,000 | do | 1 50 | do. |
| 1,001 to 5,000 | do | 2 00 | do. |
| 5,001 to 10,000 | do | 4 00 | do. |
| 10,001 to 20,000 | do | 6 00 | do. |
| 20,001 and upwards | do | 10 00 | do. |
| For every manifest | | 2 00 | do. |

ART. 14. The present law shall be put into execution as follows: in three months for vessels coming from ports on the American continent and the islands of the Archipelago, and in four months for vessels coming from ports in Europe; each to start from the day of its promulgation.

ART. 15. The present law abrogates all dispositions contrary to it. It shall be printed and published, and the ministers are charged with its execution, each in that which concerns him.

Approved June 29, 1852.

---

## MEXICO.

[From a despatch of the United States consul at Laguna, May 7, 1849.]

"On the 4th of April last, an order was issued in Mexico to this State, ordering the eight per cent. export duty on logwood to be taken off, and a devolution to be made of all charged since the month of August last. Notice has also been given that this port will be closed for imports on the first of August next."

### *Extract of a decree of 15th May*, 1849.

[Translation.]

ART. 1. Silver in amalgam, or gold in grains, or in plates or bars, coming from foreign countries, shall be charged no duty on its importation into a port, or its transmission into the interior.

ART. 2. The gold referred to in the preceding article is exempted from the duty of three per cent. for quintage.

15

[From a despatch of the United States consul at Tampico, July 12, 1849.]

"The accompanying decree of the Mexican government will inform you of the reduction of export duty on the precious metals of this republic. This is the only change that has been made in the revenue laws of this country, since the retirement of the American forces, that has a favorable bearing upon our commerce."

*Decree of 28th May*, 1849.

[Translation.]

Art. 1. The precious metals, on their exportation, shall pay the following duties: gold, coined or wrought, two per cent.; silver, coined, three and a half per cent.; pure or refined, wrought into figures, certified as having paid the assay duties, four and a half per cent.

Art. 2. Money or coin will pay a circulation duty, on its introduction into the ports, of two per cent.

*Extract of a decree of November* 24, 1849.

[Translation.]

* * * * * * *

Art. 7. The introduction of fire-arms and swords, lances, &c., is permitted on the payment of a duty of $4 the hundred-weight tare.

Art. 8. The eighteenth article of the tariff is hereby repealed, and the articles specified in it will pay 40 per cent. on the invoice prices, the following excepted, which will continue to pay the duties specified in said tariff:

Spirits of turpentine, (or *aqua ras.*)

Water of bitter almonds, cologne, lavender, cherry, laurel, queen's, and all other kinds, whether compounded, distilled, or spirituous.

White lead, whether dry or in oil.

Brass mortars.

Musk, in grains.

Musk, in bag or pouch.

Tar and pitch, rosin, turpentine.

Alum.

Chrome yellow.

Naples yellow.

Arsenite of copper, or Schecles green, and Schwein-forts green, or German green.

Asphaltum.

Prussian blue.

Cobalt blue.

Blue enamel.

Ultramarine blue.

Varnishes of alcohol and rosin.

Vermillion.

Bitumen, from Judæa, or asphaltum.

Spanish white

Armenian bole

White from lead.
Sulphate of copper.
Lamp-black, animal.
Verdigris.
Carmine.
Glue made of hides.
Isinglass, in pouch.
Colors of all kinds, not specified.
Crucibles, *(en barro refractario.)*
Crucibles of black lead.
Crucibles, (porcelain and biscuit.)
Emery.
Sponge, common.
Sponge, fine.
Campechian extracts, for colors.
Phosphorus.
Gum-lacca.
Crocus-color.
Compounded liquors, such as Rossoli.
Hops.
Dye-woods, in powder or otherwise.
Red lead, or deutoxide of.
Mortars of agate.
Mortars of alabaster and marble.
Mortars of porphyry.
Mortars of porcelain and biscuit.
Mortars of glass.
Ochre.
Blue-stone, *(piedra lipis.)*
Platina, in grains, or the ore of.
Platina, in wire, or sheets of.
Platina, articles of, used in laboratory, other than apparatus.
Prussiate yellow.
Prussiate red.
*Rubio tintorio o granza?*
English red.
*Tornasol*, in cakes.
White vitriol.
Zinc, reduced, *(reducido,)* or in cakes.
Zinc, laminated.

Art. 9. The import duties established by the tariff of 4th of October, 1845, are hereby reduced to 60 per centum, in conformity to the requirements of the decree of May 3, 1848.

Art. 10. The reduction which is made on the duties of importations, does not extend to or embrace those of introduction to the interior, nor the consumption duty, nor that of 1 per cent., nor that of 2 per cent., for damages referred to in the decrees of March 31, 1838, and of February 28, 1843; all of which will be collected as heretofore.

Art. 11. The duties on the precious metals shall be as follows:

Gold, coined or wrought, 2 per cent.
Silver, coined, 3½ per cent.

Silver, wrought, assayed, 4½ per cent.

Silver, pure, wrought into figures, and having a certificate that the assay duties have been paid, 4½ per cent.

Art. 12. The circulation duty on coin is reduced to 2 per cent., to be collected on its entrance into the ports.

* * * * * * *

Art. 18. The tariff of October 4, 1845, for the maritime and frontier custom-houses, shall remain in full force, with the additions and explanations made thereto, unless where changed by the present law.

*Extract of a decree of April* 5, 1851.

[Translation.]

Art. 1. The importation of foreign sugar at the port of Matamoras and the frontier custom-houses of the same State, which was permitted by the decree of April 4, 1849, shall cease.

Art. 2. The cessation above referred to shall take effect from and after the termination of sixty days from the publication of this decree in the capital of the republic.

Art. 3. The permission which was granted by the decree of 22d March last, authorizing the taking into the towns of the States of Tamaulipas and New Leon the foreign groceries which had been brought into the republic in virtue of the decree of 4th April, shall, as regards sugar, only have effect up to the day on which the period stated in the previous article terminates.

[From a despatch of the United States chargé d'affaires, Mexico, June 5, 1851.]

"In future, until the government can adopt fixed general rules for the payment of tonnage duties by foreign and national steam merchantmen, the President has ordered that they pay only on their capacity for freight."

"I have enclosed a copy of the order respecting tonnage, issued by General Arista on the 17th of last month."

[Translation.]

His excellency the President orders: That on all steamers belonging to citizens of the republic, or otherwise, pertaining to the merchant service, there shall be collected tonnage duties only on the capacity which they may measure for carrying merchandise.

This order is to be considered as altogether temporary in its character, and is to be so understood by the captains and persons interested in said vessels, until the government shall determine upon the general and fixed basis on which the measurement of steamers shall be established.

[From despatch of the United States chargé d'affaires, Mexico, July 28, 1851.]

"An act of the congress of Mexico, passed the 22d day of last March, permits, for a term of one year, the introduction of flour into Tampico, from New Orleans, upon the payment of duties required to be paid by the act of the 4th of April, 1849, at Matamoras and the custom-houses on the frontiers of the State of Tamaulipas. These laws are enclosed."

### *Decree of March* 22, 1851.

[Translation.]

ARTICLE 1. The articles whose introduction was allowed by the decree of April 4, 1849, are permitted to be taken to the towns of the Norte, in the State of Tamaulipas, and all the villages of the said State, and also to those of New Leon, during the remainder of the period prescribed by aforesaid decree, or previously to the conclusion of that period, should the government think proper.

ART. 2. During the present year [1851] permission is given for the introduction of flour from New Orleans at the port of Tampico, said flour paying the same import duties and in the same terms as prescribed in the aforementioned decree [of April 4, 1849.]

ART. 3. The government will prescribe the proper orders, so that the Mexican consul residing at New Orleans, alone, shall sign the manifests and bills of lading intended for Tampico, which may be presented for the months which intervene from the publication of this decree to the 31st of October of the present year.

ART. 4. The custom-house of Tampico only has the power to furnish permits to enable the flour referred to in this decree to be taken into the interior, to the towns of the State of Tamaulipas.

### *Decree of April* 4, 1849.

[Translation.]

ARTICLE 1. For the period of three years permission is given for the introduction at the port of Matamoras, and the custom-houses of the frontier of the State of Tamaulipas, of the following articles for the consumption of the towns on the frontier of said State: Flour; sugar, of all classes; rice; seeds, of all kinds, known by the name of necessary; lard; bacon, salted or pressed. All the said articles shall pay, on their importation, the following duties only:

|  |  |  |
|---|---|---|
| Common flour, in barrels of eight arrobas | | $1 00 |
| Fine.....do......do........do | | 1 50 |
| Rice | hundred weight | 75 |
| Sugar | do | 1 00 |
| Coffee | do | 1 10 |
| Bacon (salt) | do | 1 20 |
| Lard | do | 1 20 |

Seeds, of the class above described, 20 per cent. ad valorem.

ART. 2. The introduction of wood and timber for building purposes, subject, however, to registry, as provided by the tariff for ordinary articles, is permitted free of duty at the custom-house at Paso del Norte, in the State of Chihuahua.

Art. 3. The government, previously to granting the privilege contemplated by this decree, will ascertain whether there does actually exist in the frontier towns the scarcity of breadstuffs alleged, and will cause said privilege to cease as soon as the said frontier towns shall have been supplied with the articles required by the country commerce.

Art. 4. One thousand one hundred and twenty-five barrels of flour and one hundred and fifty quintals of rice, introduced at Matamoras in the month of January of this year, are to be considered as embraced in the privilege granted by this law.

[From a despatch of the United States chargé d'affaires, Mexico, July 29, 1851.]

"I enclose copies of a tariff of pilotage and port charges for all the ports of the republic."

[Translation.]

*Extracts of regulations for the collection of pilotage and port duties the ports of the republic.* [*April* 22, 1851.]

PILOT DUES.

Article 1. All merchant vessels, foreign or national, which may arrive from beyond sea, shall pay for pilotage, on their arrival at and departure from the ports of Matamoras, Tampico, and Tabasco, for each foot of draught $2 50. In all other ports open to foreign commerce, $1 75 per foot.

Art. 2. Said vessels shall pay for the boat which conveys the pilot, six dollars in the three ports first mentioned, and three dollars in all others; and should they, in case of bad weather, be required to use more than four oars, one dollar shall be paid for each additional oar.

Art. 3. Vessels of war, whether foreign or national, shall pay the same rates; but only in case that they ask for or receive a pilot on board.

Art. 4. Merchant vessels on coastwise voyages will pay for pilotage, in entering or going out of any port, four dollars, and this only in the case expressed in the previous articles; but foreign vessels, whether propelled by steam or sails, and which, by special favor, sail between the ports of the republic, shall not be thereby exempted from payment of pilotage, as is directed in the first article, unless it shall be so expressed in said privilege, or in a corresponding order.

Art. 5. If, after the pilot shall have anchored a vessel in a safe place, the captain shall desire (previously thereto, permission being obtained) to better his position, and shall have a pilot therefor, he shall pay four dollars. But if the pilot shall have anchored the vessel in an insecure place, or in such manner as that damage might result to other vessels, the pilot shall be compelled to correct her position without any right to further pay for such vessel.

Art. 6. Private steamers, used for towing inside or outside of the bars, shall recover the amount agreed upon by the owners thereof with the captains or consignees of the vessels towed, but the captain of the steamer shall be under obligation to take the pilot whose turn it may be; the captain of the port recovering the pilotage therefor, but not that for the boat.

#### FEES OF THE CAPTAINS OF THE PORTS.

ART. 7. For fees of office, the captains of each of the ports of the republic will charge foreign and national merchantmen with sea letters, $3 50.

National vessels, in coasting trade, $3 50.

National vessels (such as pilot-boats, barges, &c.) of less than thirty tons, $1.

Launches, cutters, &c., more than ten tons, employed in the coasting trade, 50 cents.

Launches, cutters, &c., in the coasting trade, less than ten tons, 25 cents.

ART. 8. The fees referred to in the preceding article shall not be collected of vessels of war, foreign or national, nor of fishing-boats, cutters, &c., in going to and returning from places in the same port.

#### BILLS OF HEALTH.

ART. 9. Captains of the ports, as members of the boards of health, will see that for the certificates issued by said boards, none other than the following fees are exacted:

From foreign and national vessels departing for a foreign port, $4.

National vessels clearing for a port within the republic, $2.

Same vessels for a port in same State, $1.

[Articles 10, 11, 12, and 13, show the disposition to be made of the fees, &c.]

ART. 14. All other fees or duties which heretofore have been improperly exacted by captains of ports, such as anchorage, certificates, signatures, &c., are hereby abolished; and the said captains of the ports, under the severest responsibility, will take care that no fees are collected other than those established by these regulations, or which may be established by law.

[From despatch of United States consul at Matamoras, October 8, 1851.]

"I have received from the commanding general at this place a communication informing me that he has declared Matamoras in a state of siege, and permitting the introduction of all kinds of merchandise under the recently established tariff."

[No copy of this tariff was enclosed with this despatch. Its operation seems to have been temporary, as also that of the following tariff established by the *insurgents* at Camargo.]

### *Rates of duties at Camargo.*

White and brown cotton goods, 30 per cent. ad valorem.

Colored cotton goods, 25 per cent. ad valorem.

Woolens, 40 per cent. ad valorem.
Linens, 25 per cent. ad valorem.
Silks, 45 per cent. ad valorem.
Groceries, 15 per cent. ad valorem.
Medicines, free.
Lumber, free.
Mixed goods pay duty upon the stuff which prevails in the mixture.

[From a despatch of the United States consul at Tampico, January 28, 1852.]

"I have the honor to transmit the decree of the State government of Tamaulipas, of the 22d November, 1851, [29th December, 1851,] imposing an additional 'patent tax' on all foreign commercial houses in this place; also a copy of the regulations, as directed by the general government of Mexico, for the collection of a consumption-duty on foreign effects, which is to take effect here on the 9th February next.

"A decree of the general government, augmenting the export duty on silver coin from 3½ to 6 per cent., is also to take effect on the 9th February next. [No copy received.]

"These decrees will have a most onerous and oppressive bearing upon all foreign trade with this place."

[Translation.—Extract.]

*The Congress of the State of Tamaulipas decrees as follows:* [December 29, 1851.]

Art. 3. From and after the 1st of January, 1852, a direct tax shall be paid by every owner of a commercial house or establishment of art or trade already established, or which may hereafter be established in the State, in accordance with the tariff which accompanies this law. The said tax will be paid in advance at the commencement of each month.

Art. 4. The first alcalde-syndic procurator-fiscal, an individual chosen by the commerce, and another chosen by the working class, will, in their respective towns, designate the class to which properly belong every commercial house or establishment of industry as laid down in said tariff. The classification made by said junta shall be submitted for its revision to the government, with full cognizance; and, well-informed in relation thereto, on previous consultation with the council, may amend or alter said classification, and there shall be no appeal from said decision.

Art. 5. During the month of December of the present year the corporate authorities, in their respective towns, shall open a registry in which shall be entered the names of all persons who may now have a commercial or industrial establishment, or who may intend to open one. As soon as said qualifying junta has made the classification referred to in the foregoing article, the corporate authorities shall issue to the party concerned a document in which shall be stated distinctly and with precision the city or town, street or place, in which it may be located, the class and the sum or amount to be paid, the kind of traffic, name of the owner, and the date of issue of said document, which, signed by the president and secretaries of the aforementioned authorities, shall be delivered to the said party.

Art. 6. Without aforesaid document, and unless the quota assigned by said tariff has been paid, no person shall keep open a commercial or industrial establishment for the sale of articles, either at wholesale or retail, within the State.

Art. 7. The authorities and fiscal agents will be held responsible to the penalties established by the law of 15th of November, 1849, for non-compliance with the preceding articles.

Art. 8. The third article of the law of 21st of April, 1847, and that part which refers to the tax on capital employed in commerce or industry, decree No. 23 of 16th November, 1849, imposing a direct tax on brandy and mezcal, and any other law which may conflict with this decree, are hereby repealed.

Art. 9. All other occupations which are not embraced in the nomenclature adopted in said tariff as mercantile and industrial, will be subject to the payment of the contribution established by above-mentioned of 21st of April, and to the requirements and penalties provided by the present law and the aforesaid of 15th (16th?) November, above referred to.

*Tariff referred to in the third article of preceding law, designating the sums to be collected, from and after the 1st day of January, 1852, from mercantile and industrial establishments.*

TAMPICO.

| | 1st class, monthly, by assignment | 2d class, monthly, by assignment. | 3d class, monthly, by assignment. |
|---|---|---|---|
| Warehouses of every kind of effects | 36 | 24 | 18 |
| Dry-goods stores | 14 | 10 | 6 |
| Stores of groceries and mixed | 14 | 10 | 6 |
| Stores of fancy articles | 14 | 10 | 6 |
| Stores of only liquors—drinking-houses | 6 | 4 | 2 |
| Apothecary shops | 8 | | |
| Tendajos, (it is meant by this term, small shops) | 4 | 3 | 2 |
| Manufactories of brandy and liquors | 8 | | |
| Coffee and billiard-rooms | 6 | 4 | 2 |
| Bakeries | 3 | 1.4 | 0.6 |
| Timber or lumber yards | 6 | 4 | 3 |
| Candle-making shops | 2 | 1 | 0.4 |
| Houses for pawning | 2 | 1 | 0.4 |
| Coppersmitheries | 3 | 2 | |
| Perfumery shops | 2 | 1 | |
| Tinsmitheries | 1 | | |

*Tariff*—Continued.

| | 1st class, monthly, by assignment. | 2d class, monthly, by assignment. | 3d class, monthly, by assignment. |
|---|---|---|---|
| Tailors' shops | 3 | 2 | 1 |
| Carpenters' shops | 3 | 2 | 1 |
| Wheelwright shops } Barbers' shops } Shoemakers' shops } Blacksmiths' shops } Watchmakers' shops } Silversmiths' shops } Painters' shops | 2 | 1 | 0.4 |
| Hatters' shops | 2 | | |
| Soapmakers' establishments | 1 | | |
| Nail factories | 1 | | |
| Taverns | 3 | 2 | 1 |
| For each billiard table | 2 | | |

*Law of 9th of October*, 1851, *imposing a consumption duty on foreign effects.* [*To take effect 9th February*, 1852.]

[Translation.—Extract.]

ARTICLE 1. A consumption duty is hereby established of 8 per centum on all foreign effects which may hereafter be introduced through the maritime or frontier custom-houses into the interior of the republic.

ART. 2. The said duty will be collected at once in the place of consumption; the collection of the same being limited to that part of the cargo which does not proceed to the other points for a market.

* * * * * * *

ART. 8. Four months from the publication of this law at the capital of the republic, the collection of the duty authorized by the first article of this law will commence having effect; and from the moment of said commencement, the 3 and 2 per cent. which the States may have collected in virtue of the laws of the general Congress of 22d December, 1824, and 22d of August, 1829, will cease.

* * * * * * *

ART. 10. Foreign effects which may be carried to the fairs are subject to the operation of this law, and to the payment of the duties authorized by it.

## SAN JUAN DE NICARAGUA, OR GREYTOWN.

[From a despatch of Sir H. L. Bulwer, January 4, 1851.]

"I have received information from her Majesty's acting consul-general in Mosquito, that on the 31st December last the Mosquito government would cease to levy duties at Greytown on vessels or goods belonging to British subjects, American citizens, and the citizens of the States of Nicaragua and Costa Rica."

---

## VENEZUELA.

[From a despatch of the United States consul at La Guayra, May 4, 1849.]

"On the 2d instant, the Congress at Caracas decreed that all goods or merchandise, now paying import duties in conformity with the tariff of 1841, shall pay an *additional duty* of 10 per cent. ad valorem, and all goods free of duty by the same tariff shall pay a duty of 15 per cent. ad valorem, to go into force on importation from the islands on the 1st of June, and from the United States and Europe on the 1st of July next.

"Enclosed, herewith, is a printed copy of the decree, which also includes the law levying export duties, which will go into effect when published."

[Translation.]

### *Decree of May* 2, 1849.

ARTICLE 1. An extraordinary tax is hereby imposed for the term of two years on the effects, and in the manner, herein expressed.

ART. 2. Merchandise and effects, which may be introduced from foreign countries through any custom-house of the republic, shall pay, if subject to duty, a duty of 10 per cent. *ad valorem* in addition to the duty now paid; or fifteen per cent. *ad valorem*, if not subject to duty. Gold and silver, coined or in bars, or united with quicksilver, or in grains, are exempt from preceding duty.

1. The avails of this duty shall be paid in cash, when not exceeding $400; or within the period of thirty days, if exceeding that amount.

2. In the liquidation of this duty, the rules and regulations established for the government of custom-houses will be observed.

3. The duty authorized by this article will begin to be charged, from the 1st of June on the commerce of the Antilles, and from the first of July on the commerce of the United States and Europe.

ART. 3. National produce and manufactures which may, from and after the publication of this law, be exported abroad from any one of the ports of the republic, shall pay a duty of 4 per cent. *ad valorem*.

The following articles are excepted from the above duty:

1. Coffee, cotton, and the products from sugar-cane, which will only pay 3 per cent. *ad valorem*.

2. Gold coin will pay only 1 per cent., and silver coin 2 per cent.

3. All articles the products of live stock are exempted from duty, in conformity with the decree of the 13th of May, 1844.

Art. 4. The collectors of customs shall, on the last days of each month, cause a list to be placed on the doors of their offices; said list to contain a price-current of all productions and manufactures which pay export duty under this decree; the list to be signed and sworn to by two merchants and three landed proprietors of known integrity, who are to be selected for the purpose by said collectors of customs.

* * * * * * *

Art. —. The export duty will be charged according to the valuation made in aforesaid price-current.

[From a despatch of the United States consul at La Guayra, May 12, 1849.]

"In my last letter I enclosed a printed copy of a decree of Congress imposing export duties on the produce of this country, and *additional* import duties on imports; and I herewith enclose 'El Pueblo,' containing the valuation of the different articles of export, upon which valuation the import duties will be collected; also a translation of the same.

It is, however, subject to be altered monthly, according to the rise and fall of the different articles in this port, to which it will only apply, as at other ports in the republic similar valuations will be made, and the duties collected in conformity."

[Translation.]

*List of prices fixed, during the present month, on the fruits and productions exportable from the country, by the commission of planters and merchants, named in virtue of the 4th article of the legislative decree of the 2d instant imposing an export duty, and the 1st article of that issued by the executive on the 3d instant regulating the former.*

| Article | Price |
|---|---|
| Balsam capivi, bottle | $0 25 |
| Rum, barrel of 18 gallons | 4 00 |
| Vegetable oil, bottle | 12 |
| Garlic, 100 strings | 12 00 |
| Cotton, 100 lbs. | 7 00 |
| Indigo, 100 lbs. | 62 00 |
| Starch, 100 lbs. | 3 00 |
| Sugar, refined, 100 lbs. | 7 00 |
| Muscovado, 100 lbs. | 3 00 |
| Cocoa, 110 lbs. | 18 00 |
| Coffee, 100 lbs. | 6 00 |
| Sheep, each | 75 |
| Cebadilla, fanega of 110 lbs. | 3 00 |
| Onions, 100 lbs. | 2 50 |
| Goats, each | 50 |
| Chocolate, 100 lbs. | 37 00 |
| Dividivi, 100 lbs. | 1 00 |
| Lignumvitæ, ton | 8 00 |
| Corn, fanega (about 200 lbs.) | 3 00 |
| Vegetables: beans and peas, fanega | 4 00 |

| | |
|---|---|
| Copper ore, ton | $50 00 |
| Fustic, ton | 8 00 |
| Potatoes, fanega, 110 lbs. | 3 00 |
| Papelon sugar, carga of 64 papelons (from 2½ to 4 lbs. each) | 4 00 |
| Salted fish, 100 lbs. | 2 00 |
| Tanned skins, each | 25 |
| Fresh skins, each | 12½ |
| Margarita straw hats, dozen | 75 |
| Palm hats, dozen | 3 00 |
| Imitation jipijapa hats, dozen | 10 00 |
| Tobacco, Curaseca, 100 lbs. | 7 00 |
| Curanegra, 100 lbs. | 10 00 |
| Vanilla, 100 lbs. | 1,000 00 |
| Zarzaparilla, 100 lbs. | 12 00 |

## NEW GRENADA.

[From a despatch of United States consul at Santa Martha, July 5, 1849.]

"I herewith enclose a translation of the law of 2d June, 1849, by which you will see that the captains of merchant vessels are permitted to lodge the registers of their vessels with the consuls of their respective nations, on condition that said consuls give written receipts and obligations not to return them without an order to that effect from the custom-house, which receipts they must deposite in the custom-house immediately after the visit."

*Law of June* 2, 1849, *additional to that of June* 14, 1847, *relating to imports.*

[Translation.]

ARTICLE 1. The register that is exacted from the captains of merchant vessels on entering the port, according to the 4th article of the law of the 14th June, 1847, relating to imports, &c., may be delivered to the consul of the nation that the said vessel belongs to, provided always that that nation practises the same with regard to New Grenadian vessels; but in this case the captain ought to present to the custom-house, immediately after the visit has been paid, a certificate from the consul, in which he acknowledges the receipt of the register, and promising that it will not be returned to the captain until he can prove by the necessary clearance from the custom-house that the vessel is owing nothing to that office, and that it has been despatched by it.

*Import duty.*

Imports into this country have been subjected to an additional duty of 10 per cent. from 1st January, 1850.

[From a despatch of the U. S. chargé d'affaires to New Grenada, June 24, 1852.]

"I send herewith the translation of a law passed at the recent session of Congress, declaring the navigation of the rivers of the republic free in foreign merchant steamers under their own flag.

"The recent Congress passed a law imposing an additional duty of twenty-five per cent. upon the rates heretofore established on all articles imported into the country from and after the first of September next."

[Translation.—Extract.]

ARTICLE 16. All the manifests which may be presented at the custom-houses after the 1st of September, 1852, shall be charged, in addition to the full amount which the merchandise may be liable to under the tariff and other existing legal enactments, a further sum of twenty-five per cent. This sum shall be kept separate in the settlement, and shall be collected forthwith, admitting in payment thereof bonds of the new floating debt, or, in its defect, cash.

## DECREE OF APRIL 5, 1852.

*Law declaring free the navigation of the rivers of the republic in merchant steam-vessels.*

[Translation.]

The Senate and Chamber of Representatives of New Grenada, assembled in Congress, decree:

ARTICLE 1. From the publication of this law, the navigation of the rivers of the republic in foreign merchant steamers under their own flag is free.

Paragraph.—What is declared in this article does not interfere with privileges conceded by laws or agreements approved by the Congress.

ART. 2. Foreign vessels will be subject to all the charges and obligations to which national vessels are liable, and the crews thereof amenable to the national authorities, to which all foreigners are subject.

ART. 3. The law of April 11, 1850, respecting interior navigation, is reformed in these terms:

ART. 4. The disputes which may arise in consequence of this law, or respecting its proper interpretation, will be judged by the magistrates, and in accordance with the laws of the republic. In no case will any foreigner be able to plead immunity or exemption not recognised or expressly conceded by laws or public treaties; nor will the intervention be admitted of any other authority or functionaries than those legally established within the jurisdiction of the same republic.

---

## BRAZIL.

[From a despatch of the United States consul at Rio Grande, March 6, 1850.]

"I have the honor to transmit herewith a translation of a decree of this government prescribing new regulations for the ports of this province; also a slip cut from the Diario de Rio Grande, published on the 4th current, from which the translation was made.

"Article 3 of the regulations in question is particularly oppressive to vessels of the United States, as the principal part of their cargoes consists of produce which must come to this port for a market; while manufactured goods, which comprise the principal part of the cargo of vessels of other nations, find a market in the interior, and are despatched from the custom-house of San José do Norte from motives of convenience.

"The ship canal connecting this port with San José do Norte is one mile and a half in length, and is only navigable for vessels drawing nine or ten feet of water. American vessels frequenting this port generally draw ten and a half to thirteen feet of water, and have heretofore been permitted to lighten at the entrance of the canal, or at San José do Norte; but, according to the new regulations now in force, after commencing to discharge at San José do Norte, which they are compelled to do in order to pass through the canal, they are not permitted to come here with any part of the cargo unless it is destined for both ports.

"The expense of lighterage between the two ports is excessively heavy; so much so that launch hire to convey an entire cargo from the anchorage at San José do Norte to this port, distant about four miles, would in many cases amount to as much as the interest of the voyage.

"I would recommend, as a partial remedy, that vessels of the United States clearing for this port be provided with a set of manifests for the cargo which may be necessary to discharge at San José do Norte in order to pass through the canal, and another set including the remainder of the cargo for this port."

[Translation.]

*Decree No.* 653, *of the* 24*th of November*, 1849, *creating a custom-house in San José do Norte, in the province of San Pedro, and reorganizing the one in Rio Grande and Porto Alegre.*

By virtue of the authority conferred on the government by article 46 of the law No. 54, of the 23d of October, 1848, I have deemed it proper to order, provisionally, the following:

ARTICLE 1. There shall be a custom-house in the town of San José do Norte, province of San Pedro, independent of the one in the city of Rio Grande.

ART. 2. The custom-house of San José do Norte is charged with the inspection, receipt of duties, and the guard of the port of Rio Grande do Sul, not including that of the interior of the ship canal, which continues to belong to the custom-house of Rio Grande.

ART. 3. Vessels arriving from foreign ports and coastwise, having on board goods of foreign production, bound for the port of San José do Norte, Rio Grande, or Porto Alegre, or generally to the port of Rio Grande do Sul, are required to enter at the custom-house of San José do Norte, presenting the respective manifests, the list of provisions and stores, and make declaration as to the increase or decrease of the cargo, in conformity with article 145, sections 4, 5, and 6, of the regulations of 22d June, 1836, decree of 22d July, 1842, and regulation No. 633 of

28th August, 1849. The vessels referred to will be permitted to discharge in the custom-house of San José, or in that of the city of Rio Grande and Porto Alegre, as may be most convenient for them. Having commenced discharging in one custom-house, they cannot change for another, unless they are provided with particular manifests of the cargo for each custom-house.

Art. 4. The vessels concerning which the preceding article treats, can discharge in the custom-house of Rio Grande if they choose, remaining anchored in San José do Norte, the articles discharged being accompanied by guards of the custom-house of the latter port. Vessels bound for Porto Alegre, or those which choose to go there after entering at San José do Norte, are not permitted to proceed without having the hatches sealed and locked, and two guards of the custom-house of San José do Norte, paid at the expense of the vessel, at the rate of their salary on shore and on board.

Art. 5. Vessels bound for Porto Alegre with foreign goods, will not be permitted to ship all or any part of the cargo on other vessels, to be conveyed to the place of destination, without the proper despatch of reshipment in the custom-house of San José do Norte.

[Article 6 is omitted, as it relates only to coasting vessels.]

Art. 7. No vessel, having entered in the custom-house of San José do Norte, can proceed to Rio Grande do Sul or Porto Alegre without being provided with one set of manifests, with the declarations of increase or decrease of stores and baggage of passengers, properly signed by the respective inspector, and by him forwarded in a sealed letter to the custom-house to which it is bound.

[From a despatch of United States consul at Rio Janeiro, July 7, 1852.]

"I have the honor to enclose herewith a printed copy of a decree of his Majesty the Emperor, reducing the anchorage dues on vessels from foreign ports; and also a translation of the same. The reduction is very large, the rate now fixed being one-third of the sum heretofore exacted. The former sum, 900 reis per ton, is about 48 cents of American money, and the 300 reis about 16 cents, at the present rate of exchange.

"I have examined the other decrees referred to in article 2d, and find that the first refers to deductions upon vessels which bring colonists. The 2d and 3d have particular reference to vessels arriving and departing in ballast, and such as enter in 'franquia,' and to those which merely touch without doing business here, and to those which, making three voyages to the port in one year, have been exempted from any anchorage dues on the third voyage, and to those putting in in distress.

"The former regulations, as I understand, in reference to all such vessels, remain unaltered."

[Translation.]

*Decree No.* 928, *of 5th March,* 1852, *reducing the anchorage dues.*

In view of the regulation of article 28 of the law No. 369, of the 18th September, 1845, I deem it expedient to decree:

Art. 1. From the 1st of July, 1852, forward, the anchorage dues on vessels which may navigate between foreign ports and those of the empire shall be reduced to three hundred reis per ton; and the impost of the same denomination which is now paid by coasting vessels, abolished.

Art. 2. The regulations of the 26th of April, 20th of July, and 15th of November, 1844, are to continue in force in the parts not altered by this decree.

---

## URUGUAY, OR CISPLATINE REPUBLIC.

[From a despatch of the United States consul at Montevideo, April 16, 1849.]

"I had the honor of addressing the department under date of 3d of October, 1848, in relation to an exorbitant impost of *fifteen dollars per barrel* levied on the article of flour. Large parcels of flour remained in the stores of our merchants in this city, entirely *unsaleable* in consequence of that enormous exaction. I am enabled to inform you that I have succeeded in inducing the government to abrogate the obnoxious decree, which, in fact, amounted to a prohibition of this article of our commerce with this country.

"I herewith enclose a recent government decree in lieu of the former."

[Translation.]

### *Decree.—Montevideo, April* 6, 1849.

The government being desirous of reducing the impost of *fifteen dollars per barrel* on flour, which powerful reasons compelled it to establish, has found the means, by making other articles (which, from their nature, are better calculated than flour to bear the impost) contribute to raise the amount, then considered indispensable; consequently decrees:

Art. 1. From the first day of the forthcoming May, all merchandise despatched in the custom-house for consumption, (with the exception of wheat-flour and grain,) shall pay a municipal duty of four per cent., at the same time, and in the same office, when the ordinary duties are paid.

Art. 2. Every barrel of flour, or its equivalent, in any other package than those despatched through the custom-house, shall pay, the day after the promulgation of this decree, *twenty rials*, in the manner and place designated in the anterior article.

Art. 3. Each fanega of wheat, of all classes, shall pay *ten rials.*

Art. 4. The flour and wheat despatched by the custom-house, but still under the inspection of the special commission of this article, subject to the impost of fifteen dollars, shall pay, in order to free itself, *twenty rials per barrel*, and *ten rials per fanega* of wheat, in all the present month.

Art. 5. This payment can be made with notes at sixty days' sight, with two endorsers, to the satisfaction of the special commission of this article.

ART. 6. This impost shall last no longer than necessary to pay the debt incurred on the article of flour, the liquidation of which shall take place immediately.

[From a despatch of the United States consul at Montevideo, May 29, 1852.]

"The government, under dates of the 1st and 2d ultimo, issued decrees abolishing the export duty on horse-hides, dry and salted, and the transit duties upon all merchandise."

[From despatch of the same, of June 3, 1852.]

"On the 2d instant the government abolished the former duty of two rials per hide on ox and cow hides, dry and salted, and decreed the duty to be, in future, three quarters of a rial per hide on exportation, to take effect in fifteen days after the publication of said decree."

---

## PERU.

[From a despatch of the United States consul at Lima, January 12, 1850.]

"I have the honor to enclose a printed copy of a law, just published here in 'El Peruano,' of 26th ultimo, taxing with 90 per cent. duty certain articles now subject, according to tariff, to 40 per cent.; also a literal translation of said law. Its operation will not affect much the trade from the United States, as our vessels do not bring many of the articles newly taxed, and the few they do bring are generally for the supply of a small transit demand for other parts of the coast, which the new law will not interfere with. The whole thing, however, is very illiberal."

### *Law of December* 26, 1849.

[Translation.]

TREASURY DEPARTMENT.

The Congress of the Peruvian republic, considering that article seventy-six of tariff law issued on 30th November, 1840, has not been an indirect means sufficiently efficacious to prevent the introduction of manufactured articles made in foreign ports, similar to those made in the country, with notable detriment to the artisans of Peru, whose industry merits the special protection of Congress, decrees:

ART. 1. The executive, according to its attributions, will alter the seventh paragraph of article seventy-six of tariff,* affixing to manu-

* Article seventy-six, paragraph seven, reads as follows: Foreign merchandise will be subject, on importation, to the following duties:

SEC. 7. Thirty-six per cent. to the State, and four per cent. to the *arbitrios*, (internal debt fund,) will be incurred on boots, carriages of all kinds, caps of all kinds; vermicelli, and all other kinds of pastes made of flour; all kinds of furniture, except chairs, and wood shaped for making them; ready-made clothing, hats, saddlery, shoes.

factured articles, which may be imported from abroad, a specific duty that shall be equivalent to nine-tenths of the selling-price of those made in the country.

Art. 2. (Providing for the formation of a statute agreement among the different bodies of tradesmen, binding themselves not to purchase any smuggled article; penalties, and rewards to informers, concealers, &c.)

*Sanctioned by Congress on 21st December, 1849. Approved by the Executive on 24th December, 1849.*

[From a despatch of the United States chargé d'affaires to Peru, April 18, 1852.]

"The Peruvian government has published new commercial regulations, in compliance with an act of the Congress of the republic, passed on the 13th of October, 1851. They are comprised in twenty-six chapters, and three hundred and ten articles; to take effect in three months after the 21st of March last for products of nations situated on the shores of the Pacific, and in six months for produce of other parts of the world, whether the same be already deposited in the custom-house or shall be imported in future.

"I have the honor to annex a translation of the most important articles.

"The present regulations are most liberal, especially with respect to navigation, as foreign vessels are admitted to participate to a great extent in the coasting trade, and may enter places heretofore prohibited."

[Translation.]

## COMMERCIAL REGULATIONS OF 1852.

### Chapter I.—*Of the ports of entry, minor ports and landings, and of the trade allowed in them.*

Art. 1. The ports of entry are: Arica, Islay, Callao, Huanchaco, San José, and Paita. The minor ports are: Iquique, Ilo, Chala, Pisco, Huacho, Casma, Pacasmayo, and Tumbes.

Art. 2. Foreign or national vessels proceeding from foreign countries can only enter a port of entry.

Art. 3. Vessels of every nation coming from abroad may anchor in Iquique, provided that their cargoes consist solely of the merchandise mentioned in article 172.

Art. 4. Whale ships are the only vessels coming from abroad which may enter at Tumbes, or any other minor port, and they only when loaded with products of the fishery, their provisions, and other effects required for the vessel and consumption of the crew.

Art. 5. Callao and Arica are ports of deposite for an indefinite period; in the other ports of entry the term of deposite shall be only three years.

Art. 6. Merchandise which has not been cleared at the custom-house may be re-shipped in vessels of all nations for abroad, or for any of the ports of entry.

Art. 7. The products of the country, and all merchandise upon which the duties have been paid, may be re-shipped in the ports of entry, minor ports and landings, for the ports of both classes and landings.

Art. 8. Transhipments of merchandise may be made in foreign and national vessels, in every port of entry, either for foreign countries or for another port of entry. It shall also be lawful to tranship from one vessel to another the provisions necessary for its consumption.

Art. 9. The transhipment of products of the country, or foreign, upon which duty has been paid, may be made in the ports of entry, minor ports and landings, by vessels which, under these regulations, are permitted to enter such ports and landings.

Art. 10. Where vessels under any flag leave a part of their cargo in a port of entry, and proceed with the remainder to other port of the same class, they may take on board in the port of entry from which they clear, productions of the country, or merchandise on which duty has been paid, and the goods specified in article 16, although they may have on board said remainder of foreign cargo subject to duty.

Art. 11. Vessels of all nations may go with cargoes the duties on which are paid, or with national produce, from ports of entry to minor ports, or from one minor port to another.

Art. 12. Mejillones, Pisagua, Patillos, Chucumata, Morro de Lama Cocotea, Quilca, Lomas, Nasca, Cancato, Chincha, Cerro-Azul, Ancon, Chancay, Supe, Huarmey, Samarco, Chimbote, Santa, Mal-abrige, Eten, and Sechura, are landings from which national products may be exported, and from which merchandise despatched at the custom-houses of ports of entry may be sent into the interior.

Art. 13. National or foreign vessels sailing from a port of entry with cargoes upon which duty has not been paid, can proceed only to a port of entry or for foreign countries.

Art. 14. It is not allowed to anchor in any of the anchorage grounds of the islands within the republic, without a written license from the government.

Art. 15. Vessels can only load guano for abroad at the islands of Chincha. Those who take it for the agriculture of the country may extract it from Pabellon Pica, or from said islands.

Art. 16. Foreign vessels may proceed to the open landings to load Peruvian produce. To do this they must leave ports of entry or minor ports in ballast, or with produce of the country; and they can also carry Brazil or Campeachy wood, cocoa, leather, copper, bark, (cascarilla,) barilla, tin, silver and gold, in bars or dust, or manufactured or coined. They shall be allowed to touch at such minor ports or landings as their captains may think proper, sailing freely from one to another to complete their cargoes, provided that the said ports and landings be expressly named in the license from the custom-houses.

Art. 17. Vessels, whether national or foreign, may sail from the minor ports or open landings for foreign ports, upon taking a license to that effect from the custom-house of the port of entry from which they last cleared.

Art. 18. Small national vessels may trade directly between Tumbes and the coast of Guayaquil, but can import into Tumbes only free articles and provisions of every kind, paying thereon the corresponding duties.

Art. 19. Only national vessels can carry merchandise that has paid duty and products of the country, from ports of entry or minor ports to the open landings, or from one landing to another. But in case of necessity, permission may be granted to a foreign vessel to carry such merchandise to one or more open landings. The permits in such cases must be issued by the collectors of the principal custom-houses when there is a scarcity of national vessels, and express the names of the landings.

Art. 20. In the same manner, if commerce or trade be interrupted by the want of national vessels to carry products of the country from a landing to a minor port or to another landing, their transportation may be made in foreign vessels upon previous application to the collector's office of a port of entry or minor port.

Art. 21. If a vessel, having on board goods which have not been despatched, should wish, before proceeding abroad, to embark produce of the country at a minor port or landing, it shall be permitted so to do, upon depositing or giving bond at the custom-house, in a port of entry, for a sum equal to the value of the duties payable on the cargo she carries; to be returned, or the bond cancelled, upon presentation of a certificate from the custom-house at which she finally clears, testifying that the goods were still on board at the time of sailing for abroad. If the final clearance take place in the port of entry from which the vessel sailed originally, such certificate is not necessary on proof at the custom-house that she carries abroad the said effects.

## Chapter VIII.

Art. 81. Oil and candles landed from whale ships at Tumbes, and sold to purchase provisions, shall not be subject to duty. The same exemption shall be allowed for those landed in the other ports, provided their value by the tariff does not exceed five hundred dollars.

## Chapter XIII.—*Port and tonnage dues.*

Art. 101. Every national or foreign vessel, measuring two hundred tons and upwards, according to her register, arriving from a foreign country, shall, upon anchoring, pay eight dollars in full of all port dues.

Art. 102. Such vessels shall also pay two reals for every register ton, if they load or unload in the port in which they anchor on arriving from abroad.

Art. 103. Said vessels shall pay tonnage duty, although not arriving from abroad, if they anchor in a port after six months shall have elapsed since the last payment of tonnage duties in a national port.

Art. 104. Vessels of every flag, anchoring in a port of entry, arriving from another port of the same class, or from a minor port, shall pay six dollars in full of all port dues.

Art. 105. National or foreign vessels anchoring in a minor port arriving from a port of entry, or other minor port, shall pay four dollars for port dues.

Art. 106. National vessels of two hundred register tons and under shall not be liable to pay the tonnage and port dues mentioned in the preceding articles.

Art. 107. Vessels sailing from one landing to another, or from a landing to a minor port, shall not be charged port dues.

Art. 108. Where a vessel arriving from abroad has not paid tonnage duties in a port of entry, because of not discharging or taking in cargo, she must pay the same in the next port she anchors in, although not arriving immediately from abroad, as she did not pay them at the first port.

Art. 109. Ships of nations in whose ports Peruvian vessels are charged tonnage duties exceeding those paid by vessels under the national flag, shall pay tonnage and port duties in Peru, equal in amount to those charged by such nations upon Peruvian vessels.

Art. 110. Vessels-of-war, foreign transports, if only laden with provisions, coal, or other stores, and whale ships, which, being laden only with the produce of the fishery, embark provisions, and do not discharge said products beyond the value of five hundred dollars, shall not be charged port or tonnage dues in any port; and in Tumbes, whale ships may land any quantity they deem proper.

Art. 111. Vessels touching at the above-mentioned ports for the sole purpose of refreshment, or taking in water, shall not be liable to said dues; as also those anchoring in distress, although they tranship, discharge, or re-load their cargoes in whole or in part.

Art. 112. The dues specified in this chapter shall be collected by the custom-houses, according to the rules in such cases provided.

### Chapter XXI.

Art. 172. Only the following merchandise can be imported into the port of Iquique, in foreign or national vessels directly from abroad, under article 3, chapter 1:

Flour, biscuit, lentils, beans, peas, wheat, jerked beef, suet, lard, vegetables and roots, salt and fresh meat and live stock, barley, bran, Indian corn, firewood, coal, lumber, empty bags, bagging, fire-brick, iron and copper caldrons, iron tools for mining, machines for preparing saltpetre and distilling water, steel, iron, nails, and tallow.

Art. 174. The produce of the whale fishery, introduced duty free, agreeably to the concessions and conditions of these regulations, may be carried to other ports as nationalized articles, upon complying with the requisitions in article 81.

---

## CHILE.

[From a despatch of the United States minister to Chile, May 23, 1851.]

"I herewith send the government newspaper, or official organ, containing important information in relation to a modification of the tariff laws of Chile."

[Translation.]

TREASURY DEPARTMENT,
*Santiago, May* 8, 1851.

In conformity with the authority conferred upon me by the law of December 26, 1850, I have agreed to and determined on the following [tariff law of May 8, 1851.]

## *Extract of Tariff Law of May* 8, 1851.

[Translation.]

CHAPTER I.—*Concerning ports, great, small, and maritime, open to commerce; interior frontier ports of the Cordillera; coastwise commerce; and guano deposites.*

### GREATER MARITIME PORTS.

ARTICLE 1. In all the greater ports permission is given to all merchant vessels to carry on commerce, as follows:

1st. To import all kinds of merchandise, with the exception of articles the sale of which is monopolized by the government, (which can only be introduced at Valparaiso,) and those articles prohibited by this law; it being expressly understood, that of any one cargo, permission is hereby granted to make partial introductions into one or more of the greater ports.

2d. To export all kinds of merchandise, even though the vessels on which they may be embarked may have on board thereof foreign goods, with the exception of ores of silver, the reduction of which is known and practised on a large scale in the country.

3d. To deposite *en route* all kinds of merchandise intended for consumption or for exportation, with the exception of those articles of a quickly perishable character, and that class of articles monopolized by government, and whose disembarkation is restricted to Valparaiso.

4th. To ship all kinds of merchandise for foreign ports or for other ports of the republic, under the restrictions established in articles 3, 5, and 6, of this chapter.

* * * * * *

### LESSER MARITIME PORTS.

ART. 3. In the lesser ports permission is given to all merchant vessels—

1st. To import from abroad directly, or with destinations for other ports of the republic, all articles which are free of duty, and even to carry on board those articles which pay duty; but these last can in no instance be discharged except in the greater ports.

2d. To export all classes of merchandise, except the ores mentioned in the second clause of article 1; and to take on board articles the product of the country, or foreign ones naturalized, (by payment of the duties,) for the purpose of taking them to some foreign country direct, or to another port or other ports of the republic, as objects of lawful commerce.

* * * * * *

MARITIME PORTS OF ENTRY.

Art. 5. In ports of entry, foreign vessels proceeding from some one of the greater ports of the republic are permitted to import the following articles:

Bricks, for smelting furnaces.
Earths, for do do.
Stone-coal.
Iron.
Lumber.
Ores, of all kinds.
And all other articles which the government may designate.

Art. 6. All merchant vessels, proceeding from either the greater or lesser ports of the republic, may export from the ports authorized by law all kinds of merchandise the product of the country, or which has been nationalized, with the exception of silver not assayed, or in bars; copper, and the ores embraced in the second clause of article 1, either directly to a foreign country or to one or more of the ports of the republic, in route to said foreign country; provided that they have not on board other foreign effects than the following, which they shall not, under any circumstances whatever, land, viz:

Those articles which pay no import duties.
Articles produced in the republic which are free from export duty, or which have paid said export duty.
Oil, sperm and whale.
Horns, (of animals,) loose.
*Barbara salvage*, or *flor de piedra*.
Balsam of Peru or Central America.
Hides, loose, with hair on.
Carts, long narrow, and small carts.
Chains, of iron.
Cacao.
Coffee.
Cascarilla bark.
Cochineal.
Matting, loose.
Gum-elastic, unwrought.
Guano.
Bones and hair of animals.
Rushes *(juncos)* from China, loose.
Dye-woods.
Table salt.
Empty sacks.
Raw silk.
Sulphate of quinine.
Vanilla.
Sarsaparilla, not in combination with other medicine.

And all such other articles as the government may designate.

* * * * *

Art. 10. The intendants of the provinces in which are situated the greater ports from which vessels may clear, being thereof informed by the collectors of said ports, will grant the necessary licenses for said vessels to enable them to load at the ports or coves not open by law, or at the guano deposites.

* * * * *

Art. 16. By coastwise commerce is to be understood that traffic carried on in Chilian vessels from one port to another of the republic, in effects of the country, foreign and naturalized. This privilege for the present is made to extend to foreign steam-vessels, as described in the chapter relating thereto. To other foreign vessels the coastwise trade is permitted in the following articles only, to wit:

Bricks for smelting furnaces.
Earth for do. do.
Stone-coal.
Lumber, and such other articles as the government may designate.

* * * * *

*Guano, deposites of.*

Art. 18. Permission to collect guano on the northern coasts of the republic, on the edge of the Desert of Atacama, and on the adjacent islands and keys, is hereby granted to all merchant vessels; they being subject to the regulations in relation thereto, and having previously obtained license as set forth in article 10.

## Chapter II.

Article 1. The importation which is permitted into Chile, of all kinds of merchandise, without restriction as to where from, will be subject to the rules and penalties which are hereby imposed.

Art. 2. All produce or merchandise from a foreign country shall pay an importation duty of twenty-five per cent. on its valuation.

Art. 3. The following articles are free from duty on their introduction, to wit:

Steel.
Cotton, not cleaned, or with the seed.
Mineral pitch.
Common pitch.
Phials.
Anchors, small and large, of iron.
Foreign animals, alive, or dried specimens, or for breeding and improving their breed.
Ploughs.
Quicksilver.
Whalebone not wrought.
Varnish for vessels.
Bars of copper for bolts for ships.
Barrels and pipes, empty.

Trumpets.
Fire-engines.
Boats and launches.
Tar.
Treenails *(cabillas de madera.)*
Cables of six or more inches in circumference.
Iron chains, the links of which are not less than a half inch English in diameter.
Mahogany.
Cedar.
Ebony.
*Jacaranda.*
Sandal and other woods, for cabinet work.
*Camotes* (sweet potatoes ?)
Charcoal.
*Carci*, unwrought.
Meat, salted in barrels.
Charts and plans, geographic and topographic.
Sheathing paper for ships.
Roman cement.
Cocoanuts from Panama.
Iron stands for casks.
Compasses for binnacles.
Compositions, musical, printed, or in manuscript.
Pearl shell, unwrought.
Crucibles.
Drawings or paintings, with or without frames.
Knees for ships, of timber.
Staves, wrought or otherwise.

Articles for divine worship, when introduced from abroad on account of communities, monasteries, or churches, for whose use they are destined. The only requisite to prevent payment of duties will be the presentation of the original invoice, sworn to by the person who presides over said community, or church, to which they may have been consigned; consideration being had that said effects, in their nature and quality, can be applied only to the use of the altar.

Effects which may hereafter be introduced at our ports on account of diplomatic ministers duly accredited from any foreign power near the government of the republic: *Provided*, That said effects are for their use and consumption, their secretaries or other officers attached to their legations. This favor is not to extend to consuls and vice-consuls. A statement over the signature of said agents that the aforementioned effects are for their use, will be sufficient to allow an exemption of duties to said effects.

* * * * * *

Effects of all kinds which may be imported for or on account of the State, or may be purchased in the storage warehouse for transmission to any other port of the republic, sufficient evidence of which will be the presentation on each and every occasion thereof, by the consignee or agent, of a decree of the supreme government, as authority therefor.

Baggage:—by this word is to be understood the clothes and shoes for individual use, jewels, ordinary domestic utensils, printed books, and provisions, the quantity to be in proportion to the circumstances of the owner; and, in addition thereto, any amount of money. But neither furniture for household use (although it may have been used,) nor entire pieces of goods, are to be considered and taken as baggage, and they will be liable to duty on being landed, although they may not be on the manifest.

Veneerings, *(enchapados.)*

Escobenes, (hawse-holes?)

Pitch-brushes.

Topsail-sheets of chain.

Hand-spikes.

Blubber of whales, not melted, (or tried out.)

Block-tin.

Statues: images or figures of saints are not to be embraced under this term, these last paying duties.

Tow, (coarsest part of hemp and flax and oakum.)

Isinglass lanterns.

Plush for sheathing vessels.

Iron, not wrought.

Iron-hoops.

Cambooses for ships.

Fossils.

Fragments of vessels wrecked in or out of any of the ports of the republic. By a fragment of a vessel is to be understood not only the hull, masts, and apparatus belonging thereto, but likewise the boats, utensils and furniture, the stores of pitch, rosin, rigging, and sails, the guns, muskets, swords, powder, and, in general, everything belonging to the proper navigation of the vessel, and destined to the use of the wrecked vessel; *but* the provisions and groceries which were on board said vessel when wrecked are not to be considered as embraced under the title or word *fragments.*

Exotic fruits of every class.

*Ganchos* (hooks?) of wood, of iron, or of copper.

Geographical globes.

*Guias* (?) of powder for use of the mines.

Thimbles *(guarda-cabos)* of any material.

Tools for artisans.

Agricultural implements.

Tin in sheets.

Pots of iron and other instruments for assays.

Lasts and blocks for shoemakers and hatters.

Implements of trades.

Printing presses and accompaniments.

Instruments for surgery, physics, mathematics, and all other sciences.

Rigging or cordage.

Cloth for sacks, of hemp and cotton, called *tocuyo burdo*, to correspond with the samples of same to be kept in the office of the inspectors.

Junk, *(junquillo,)* unwrought.

Fire-proof bricks.

Common bricks.

Wool of the *vicuña*.

Printed books, not prohibited by law.

Pig iron.

Canvass, from No. 1 to No. 7.

Timber for building, of every class and kind of wood.

Machinery for improvement of agriculture, mining, the arts and sciences; and also single pieces belonging to same that may be introduced before or after the introduction of said machinery.

Mineral productions in crude state.

Models of machines and inventions.

Windlasses for raising anchors.

Blocks and pulleys of all classes.

Hops.

Gold or silver, stamped, or in grain or bullion.

Timber for vessels.

Timber for masts of vessels, less than twenty-two feet in length.

Paper for sheathing vessels.

Paper for printing.

Copper bolts for vessels.

Stones for flour and sugar mills.

Grindstones.

Paving stone of every kind.

Whetstones.

Cannon.

Slate with frames, for schools, and without frames, for covering houses.

Sheet-copper, or composition for vessels' bottoms.

Plants, exotic, or seeds thereof; or cereals of all kinds introduced for seed.

Gold and silver plate, broken up.

Pig lead.

Cannon or gunpowder.

Lithographic presses, and for *talla dulce.*

Oars.

Rosin for ships.

Saltpetre.

Leeches.

Roof-tiles, of clay or crockery, for roofs.

Earths for smelting furnaces.

Printers' ink.

All articles the product of the fisheries carried on in Chilian vessels.

Zinc, in sheets or pigs.

Art. 4. The following articles likewise are excepted, which will pay a duty of two per cent. on their introduction:

Fine quill of gold or silver, (cañutillo.)

Fine epaulettes of gold or silver.

Coral, wrought and unwrought.

Trimmings and laces, fine, of gold and of silver.

Fine gold and silver thread.

Trinkets of gold, silver, and of precious stones, or jewelry in general

Fine spangles of gold and silver.

Fine pearls.

Silverware.

Watches and clocks of gold and silver, of all sizes.

Table service of dishes, plates, &c., and all other utensils manufactured of gold and silver.

Art. 5. The following articles are also exceptions, and an introduction duty of six per cent. will be charged thereon:

Jackasses.

Horses.

Hung-beef.

Dried fruits.

Live stock, whether belonging to cow family or with wool.

Mules.

Art. 6. The following articles are likewise exceptions, and will pay an import duty of thirty per cent:

Trunks.

Shoes and boots of all kinds, with or without soles.

Carriages, complete or in pieces.

Coarse cloths of wool.

Furniture.

Clothing, ready-made, of all kinds, with the exception of stockings.

Hats and bonnets, finished and unfinished, of wool, hair, silk, or cotton.

Art. 7. The following articles are also exceptions, and will pay specific duties, as expressed:

Anisette, $1 25 for each basket of two bottles of the common size.

Cider and malt liquor, $1 the dozen bottles, common size.

Cider and malt liquor, 25 cents per gallon.

Cigars, *(puros,)* 75 cents per pound.

Gin, $2 50 the dozen bottles, common size.

Rappee, (snuff,) 75 cents per pound.

Rum, or any other spirituous liquor, $3 the dozen bottles, common size.

Rum, or any other spirituous liquors of the strength of 22°, $1 per gallon. On spirits of wine, rum, and other spirituous liquors which exceed in strength 22°, for every degree there shall be an increase of one per cent. on the number of gallons in estimating the duty.

Cordials, or liqueurs, $3 the dozen bottles, common size.

Tobacco in powder, 75 cents per pound.

Tea, green or black, 25 cents per pound.

White wine, $1 25 the dozen bottles, common size.

White wine, 37½ cents per gallon.

Red wine or claret, $1 the dozen bottles, common size.

Claret or red wine, 25 cents per gallon.

When the wines and liquors, subject to specific duties, are presented bottled, in bottles or flasks not of the common size, the inspector, whose duty it is to examine them, will establish a regulation by which to reduce the contents to the measure on which the duty is founded, and that regulation shall be stated at the foot of the account.

Although merchandise which pays specific duties may prove to have been damaged, it shall not, in consequence thereof, be entitled to any reduction of duty. Wines which have soured are the only article excepted from the above.

Art. 8. Wheat and flour are also excepted, and will pay duty according to the following scale:

Whenever the value of a fanega of one hundred and fifty pounds of Chilian wheat does not exceed four dollars, foreign wheat of the like quantity shall pay $1 50.

When native wheat is worth from four to five dollars, the fanega of foreign wheat shall pay $1 per fanega.

When native wheat is worth from five to six dollars, the fanega of foreign wheat shall pay 50 cents.

If the current price of native wheat should exceed six dollars the fanega, foreign wheat shall pay no duty.

Whenever Chilian flour is worth not more than four dollars the quintal of 100 pounds, foreign flour shall be charged two dollars per quintal as duty.

When Chilian flour brings from four to five dollars the quintal, foreign flour will pay a duty of one dollar and fifty cents per quintal.

When Chilian flour brings from five to six dollars the quintal, foreign flour shall pay one dollar the quintal.

If Chilian flour should be worth from six to seven dollars, each quintal of foreign flour shall pay a duty of fifty cents.

Whenever native flour shall be worth more than seven dollars the quintal, the importation will be permitted of foreign flour duty free.

In order to a proper calculation of the duty to be charged on foreign wheat and flour, two of the inspectors of customs, over their proper signatures, and at the foot of the account, shall certify the current prices of native flour and wheat, and on such price-current, conformably with the above scale, shall be based the duty on the aforesaid articles introduced at the custom-houses.

Art. 9. The following articles, whose introduction is prohibited, are likewise exceptions:

Obscene paintings, and all other articles of merchandise, which, from their nature, tend to pervert public morals.

Provisions, the putrefaction or bad quality of which renders them dangerous to the health of the community.

Ferocious animals and poisonous reptiles and insects, unless with a special permission of the government.

Art. 10. Patterns or samples of those goods which are subject to the duty of twenty-five per cent., shall pay only a duty of ten per cent., but shall not be entitled to a return of the duty in case of their re-exportation; all other goods will pay the duties on samples, to which they are subject on introduction, without the right to drawback.

Art. 11. Duties which do not exceed one hundred dollars in amount, shall be paid in cash; when exceeding that amount, they will be settled by bond, with a credit of six months, and giving, as security, merchants of known integrity and means, all to the satisfaction of the responsible officers of the customs.

Art. 12. Whenever goods on deposite in warehouse are desired for consumption in the interior, the duties thereon may be paid in the custom-houses of the ports where deposited, or in any other of the principal custom-houses of the republic.

Art. 13. The preceding article is not intended to embrace tobacco, cards, and cigars, of leaf tobacco or in paper, which can only be negotiated for at the office of monopoly in the port of Valparaiso.

Art. 14. The introduction of cards, tobacco in leaf, bunches, or cut, and cigars, in leaf or in paper, is allowed only at the port of Valparaiso, and for, and on account of, the office of articles monopolized by government. Cards with foreign marks thereon, not in common use, are exceptions from the preceding.

Art. 15. Wheat and flour, and, as a general rule, all merchandise which pays specific duties, and which may come from foreign countries, shall only be introduced through the custom-houses of Valparaiso, Talcahuano, Coquimbo, and Caldera.

* * * * * * * *

Art. 18. Foreign merchandise embraced in the following list shall be forthwith despatched from the landing for internal consumption, paying, according to its quality and valuation, the regular import duties; likewise all merchandise free of duty, referred to in third article of this chapter, shall be promptly despatched for internal consumption:

Sugar-paste, made with oil of almonds.
Animals, alive or dried.
Sugar, refuse of.
Sweetmeats.
Molasses.
Table-salt.
Sole-leather.
*Yerba-mate*, (Paraguay tea.)

* * * * * * * *

Art. 22. Consignees or owners of merchandise, two days after receiving notice of the amount of duties owed by them, will satisfy the full amount of said duties in bonds payable in six months thereafter.

* * * * * * * *

Art. 27. The fees for written orders, manifests, transfer, and for the key, (*de llave*,) which are now paid by ship-agents, are hereby abolished.

## Chapter III.—*Concerning the exportation of native products and manufactures, and of foreign merchandise naturalized.*

Article 1. The exportation of money, and of every kind of fruits, and manufactured goods of the country, and of foreign merchandise naturalized by the payment of duties, is permitted.

Art. 2. As an exception to preceding article, the exportation of ores of silver and gold, the reduction of which on a large scale is known and practised in the republic, is prohibited.

Art. 3. The merchandise hereinafter mentioned shall pay on its departure from the republic by land, or by sea, whether in Chilian or foreign vessels, according to the valuation thereof, the export duties designated in the following tariff:

1st. Native guano; on every hundred weight thereof 12½ cents.

2d. Silver, in bars or in amalgam, or broken up plate, shall pay on its valuation, during the first year from the commencement of the enforcement of this law, 5 per cent.; for the second year, 4 per cent.; for the third year, 3 per cent.; for the fourth year, 2 per cent.; for the fifth year, 1 per cent.; and after the termination of said five years the duty shall cease.

3d. Copper in pigs, and ores of copper, shall pay, from the commencement of the enforcement of this law—for the first year a duty of 4 per cent., and 2 per cent. for the second year; at the expiration of which time the duty will cease.

4th. Ore of copper, crude, calcined, or *en eje*, when exported from ports of the republic to foreign countries, shall pay an additional duty of 1½ per cent., for the benefit of the municipal treasury of the department in which said ores had been extracted; the aforesaid duty to be collected at the ports where it is shipped.

* * * * * *

Art. 7. The following articles are exempt from export duties:

1st. All other native and naturalized products.

2d. The products of the fisheries, crude or manufactured in Chile; provided that the said articles have been originally taken in Chilian vessels.

* * * * * *

Art. 9. The exportation of guano from the northern coasts of the republic, and the adjacent islands, may be made in native or foreign vessels, by permission from the intendants of the provinces within whose districts are situated the larger ports, from whence shall have sailed the aforesaid vessels.

Art. 10. This species of license will be only granted on the express condition that the vessel soliciting it shall take its departure from one of the great ports of the republic. The vessel thus licensed shall have the right to take aboard, in addition to the list of things contained in article 6, chap. i, the provisions and tools required in taking aboard a cargo of guano.

Art. 11. In the application for license, the name of the vessel, and also of each one of the points to be touched at in taking in the cargo, as likewise her tonnage measurement, must be stated. Said vessel shall not touch at any other ports, whether small or open to entry.

Art. 12. An indispensable condition also will be, the giving bond before the judge of the custom-house of the port of departure for the duties to be caused by the cargo, and for the penalty to which, in case of fraud, the securities and agents will be amenable.

Art. 13. License having been obtained, no use shall be made of it, nor shall it avail, unless all the formalities are complied with, and the aforesaid bond for duties and penalties has been given.

Art. 14. If the period of four months shall have passed from the sailing of a vessel to load guano, without her return to the port in which the bond prescribed in foregoing article was given; and if the owner, consignees, or securities of such vessel should not be enabled to prove her loss, or that a calamity had prevented her from returning, then the said securities or persons who despatched her shall pay the duties in conformity with the tonnage measurement, without at the same time exonerating them from the fine established for such cases.

ART. 15. Aforesaid vessels are under obligation to take on board a guard, who not only shall be maintained on board thereof, but shall receive, in addition to his board, one dollar per day from the day of sailing of said vessel until her return.

* * * * * *

ART. 17. Cargoes of guano may be exported from the country in the same vessels which bring it, or even transfer it to any other vessel, Chilian or otherwise, within the bay of the great ports in which is the custom-house wherein the bond was given.

ART. 18. The export duties on silver, in bars, and on copper, in pigs or in ore, which said minerals pay in favor of the municipalities, and that arising from guano, shall be paid immediately.

ART. 19. In case that any of the fruits or merchandise of the country, or merchandise naturalized, should be returned to the country after having been exported therefrom, they will be subject at the custom-houses of the republic to import duties, as if they were foreign effects.

ART. 20. Native or naturalized merchandise is exempted from the payment directed in the preceding, whenever, by some unforeseen circumstance, it shall have returned without having touched at any port belonging to a foreign power.

ART. 21. Whenever a vessel, without departing from a port, by shipwreck, fire, or any other unforeseen accident, shall lose the whole or a part of the cargo intended to be exported, export duties shall not be exacted on the value of said merchandise so lost.

* * * * * *

ART. 24. Those parts of these regulations which relate to the ports will be enforced from the promulgation of this decree; but those relating to the introduction and exportation of merchandise will only begin to be enforced after the termination of one hundred and sixty days, counted from the promulgation hereof; and said restriction shall apply, without distinction, to all nations.

---

## SOCIETY ISLANDS.

[From a despatch of the United States commercial agent at Tahiti, May 6, 1850.]

"A law imposing a duty on wines and spirits went into effect here at the time of its promulgation, early in April last."

---

## SANDWICH ISLANDS.

[From a despatch of the U. S. commissioner to the Sandwich Islands, February 4, 1851.]

In my despatch of January 24, I alluded to the fact that the Hawaiian government had levied *tonnage duties* on its own and foreign tonnage since the late treaty was ratified. These duties are twenty cents per ton on all vessels bringing foreign products for sale, and ten cents if coming into the harbor for refreshments or supplies. But if landing more than two passengers, these vessels also are liable to pay twenty cents. This tonnage duty falls mostly on American vessels, for there is very little Hawaiian tonnage. I have as yet made no complaints, for the new imposition of tonnage duties does not violate the *letter* of the treaty, and it may be said, in excuse, that the Hawaiian tariff of duties on imports (excepting on spirituous liquors) is five times lower than ours which bears on their sugar.

It is not impossible that the number of vessels sailing under the Hawaiian flag may be greatly increased by merchants here, and that they may do much of the business with the coast. But whether the number be great or small, our government will, I presume, impose the same tonnage duty upon them which is imposed by the Hawaiian government upon ours.

P. S.—I find by inquiry that my information was erroneous in one respect. The duty on foreign tonnage is not *new*. The new law consists in levying duties on Hawaiian tonnage, so as to make the duty on foreign tonnage conform to the treaty. But was it not the understanding that all tonnage duties were to be abolished? I enclose a copy of the custom-house regulations.

*Abstract of Hawaiian laws and regulations respecting vessels, harbors, and customs.*

Vessels arriving off the port of entry, to make the usual marine signal if they want a pilot.

* * * * * * * *

Masters of whale-ships arriving at any of the ports of entry must, immediately after coming to anchor in the harbor, report the vessels at the custom-house.

The commanding officer of any merchant vessel, immediately after her arrival at any of the legalized ports of entry, shall make known to the collector of customs the business upon which said vessel has come to his port; furnish him with a list of her passengers; and deliver to him, under oath, a full, true, and perfect manifest of the cargo with which said vessel is laden—which manifest shall contain an account of the packages, with their marks, numbers, contents, quantities, and also the name of the importers or consignees. When any such officer shall fail to perform any or all of the acts above mentioned within forty-eight hours after his arrival, he shall be subject to a fine not exceeding $1,000.

Passports must be exhibited to the governor or collector by passengers before landing.

It shall not be lawful for the commanding officer of any Hawaiian or foreign vessels to carry out of this kingdom, as a passenger, any domiciled alien, naturalized foreigner, or native, without previous exhibition to him of a passport from his Majesty's Minister of Foreign Relations.

Before landing baggage, a permit for the same must be obtained from the collector. Masters of vessels allowing baggage to be landed before compliance with the laws, are subject to a fine of $500.

All manifests, entries, and other documents, presented at any custom-house, shall be either in the Hawaiian or English language.

The collector, at his discretion, and at the expense of any vessel, may provide an officer to be present on board such vessel during her discharge, to superintend the disembarkation, and see that no other or greater amount of merchandise be landed than is set forth in the permit.

All goods landed at any of the ports of these islands are subject to a duty of five per cent. ad valorem, except spirituous or fermented liquors.

For conducting any vessel to anchorage off the port of Honolulu, if the pilot be not detained on board, from the necessities of said vessel, longer than twenty-four hours, $10; if detained longer than twenty-four hours, $5 per diem for each subsequent day's detention. In case the pilot does not anchor the vessel, he shall be entitled to $1 for health certificate. Should a vessel thus anchored without the harbor afterwards enter, the anchorage-fees above prescribed shall be remitted, and the usual pilotage only exacted.

The following are the only ports of entry in these islands, viz: for merchantmen and whalers, Honolulu, Lahaina, Hilo, Kealakeakua, Kawaihae, and Waimea, (Kanai;) and in addition thereto, for whalers only, Hanalei, Kanai.

The port charges on merchant vessels are as follows: At Honolulu, when anchoring within the harbor, twenty cents per ton, register; buoys, $2; clearance, $1; pilotage, in and out, $1 per foot each way. When anchoring outside the harbor and landing, transhipping, or taking on board cargo, landing or taking on board more than two passengers, five cents per ton, register; buoys, $2; clearance, $1. At Lahaina, five cents per ton, register; pilotage, $1; health certificate, $1; canal, (if used,) $2; clearance, $1. At Hilo, five cents per ton, register; pilotage, $—; health certificate, $1; clearance, $1. At Kealakeakua and Kawaihae, (Hawaii,) and Waimea, (Kanai,) pilotage at each port, $—; for tonnage dues, health certificate, and clearance, the same as at Hilo.

Merchant vessels touching at the port of Honolulu for refreshments only, and neither lading nor unlading cargo, taking or leaving more than two passengers, shall pay but ten cents per ton register; but if they discharge or take cargo, leave or take more than two passengers, they shall pay twenty cents per ton.

The charges on whaling vessels are as follows: for pilotage, buoys, health certificate, and clearance, the same as on merchant vessels. (Permits $1 each, when required.) At Hanalei, pilotage, $—; health certificate, $1; clearance, $1.

Whale ships are allowed to land goods to the value of $200 free of duty, and $1,000 worth additional, subject to a duty of five per cent. ad valorem, without being liable to pay any tonnage dues; but if they land more than $1,200 worth, (including the $200 free of duty,) they shall be subject to the same charges and liabilities as merchant vessels.

The permits granted to whalers do not include the sale, barter, or disposition of spirituous liquors: any such traffic by them (which is prohibited except at Honolulu and Lahaina) shall be held to constitute them merchantmen, and subject them in all respects to like charges and liabilities.

Any master of a whale ship who shall fail to produce his permit when called for, shall be liable to a fine not less than ten nor more than fifty dollars, to be imposed by the collector.

Before obtaining a clearance, each shipmaster is required to produce to the collector of customs a certificate, under the seal of his consul, that all legal charges or demands in his office against said vessel have been paid, and that he knows of no reason why said vessel should not immediately depart.

To entitle any vessel to clearance, it shall be incumbent on her commanding officer first to furnish the collector of customs with a manifest of cargo intended to be exported in said vessel.

Products of the whale fishery may be transhipped free from any charge of transit duty.

Oil, whalebone, or any other article of merchandise, landed or transhipped without a permit, are liable to seizure and confiscation.

Vessels landing goods upon which the duties have not been paid, are liable to seizure and confiscation.

If any person commit an offence on shore, and the offender escape on board of any vessel, it shall be the duty of the commanding officer of said vessel to surrender the suspected or culprit person to any officer of the police who demands his surrender, on production of a legal warrant.

The harbor-master may direct as to the place of anchorage or moorage of all vessels, hulks, boats, and other craft in the harbor, and has the power to change the place of anchorage or moorage at their expense, as circumstances may require, and any resistance thereto is punishable by fine.

It shall not be lawful for any person on board of a vessel at anchor in the harbor of Honolulu to throw stones or other rubbish overboard, under penalty of $100.

All sailors found ashore at Lahaina after the beating of the drum, or at Honolulu after the ringing of the bell, are subject to apprehension and a fine of $2.

Shipmasters must give notice to the harbor-master of the desertion of any of their sailors within forty-eight hours, under a penalty of $100.

Seamen are not allowed to be discharged at any of the ports of these islands, except those of Lahaina and Honolulu.

It shall not be lawful to discharge seamen at any of the ports of these islands without the written consent of the governor.

Honolulu and Lahaina are the only ports at which native seamen are allowed to be shipped, and at those places with the governor's consent only.

Any vessel taking away a prisoner from the islands shall be subject to a fine of $500. * * * *

Honolulu, *October* 12, 1850.

[From a despatch of the U. S. commissioner to the Sandwich Islands, May 21, 1851.]

"I have received a communication from the Hawaiian Minister of Foreign Relations, informing me officially that the act of the Privy Council of March 1, 1852, has been confirmed by the legislative body, and will be a law, if the government of the United States shall agree to it. The proposed mutual and reciprocal repeal of the duties on Hawaiian sugar, &c., and on American flour, fish, &c., will be very beneficial to these islands; but whether the United States government can agree to it without embarrassment is a question which, I presume, has ere this received your attention, if not decision. I enclose a copy of the 'Polynesian,' containing the act."

An Act providing for reciprocal duties on certain articles with the United States of North America. [March 1, 1852. Approved May 25, 1852.]

*Be it enacted by the King, the Premier, and chiefs of the Hawaiian Islands, in Legislative Council assembled:* Sec. 1. All flour, fish, coal, lumber, staves, and heading, the produce or manufacture of the United States, shall be admitted into this kingdom free of all duty: *Provided*, The government of the United States, will admit the sugar, syrup of sugar, molasses, and coffee, the produce of the Hawaiian Islands, into all the ports of the United States on the same terms.

Sec. 2. The evidence that articles proposed to be admitted into the ports of this kingdom, under the preceding section, are the produce or manufacture of the United States, shall be a certificate to that effect from the Hawaiian consul of the port from which such articles are imported; or in case there shall be no such consul resident in such port, a certificate to that effect from the collector of the port.

Sec. 3. This act shall take effect on the day it is concurred in by the government of the United States, and continue in force until annulled by the government of the Hawaiian Islands, or of the United States: *Provided always*, That previous to any such annulment, the government desiring to make the same shall give twelve months' notice of their intention so to do.

www.ingramcontent.com/pod-product-compliance
Lightning Source LLC
LaVergne TN
LVHW010242110826
845151LV00004B/1371